ALL RUSSIA
IS BURNING!

CATHY A. FRIERSON

ALL RUSSIA
IS BURNING!

A CULTURAL HISTORY OF FIRE AND ARSON
IN LATE IMPERIAL RUSSIA

A Samuel & Althea Stroum Book

University of Washington Press
Seattle and London

This book is published with the assistance of a grant from the Stroum Book Fund, established through the generosity of Samuel and Althea Stroum.

Copyright © 2002 by the University of Washington Press
Printed in the United States of America
Design by Michelle Dunn Marsh

Library of Congress Cataloging-in-Publication Data
Frierson, Cathy A.
   All Russia is burning! : a cultural history of fire and arson in late Imperial Russia / Cathy A. Frierson.
   p. cm.
"A Samuel and Althea Stroum book."
Includes bibliographical references and index.
ISBN 0-295-98208-X (cloth : alk. paper)—ISBN 0-295-98209-8 (pbk. : alk. paper)
1. Arson—Russia—History—19th century. 2. Russia—Social life and customs. I. Title.

HV6638.5R8 F75 2002   2001057005
364.16'4—dc21

The paper used in this publication is acid-free and recycled from 10 percent post-consumer and at least 50 percent pre-consumer waste. It meets the minimum requirements of American National Standard for Information Sciences—Permanence of Paper for Printed Library Materials, ANSI Z39.48-1984.

Permission to incorporate previously published work was generously granted by M. E. Sharpe, Inc., for the article "Of Red Roosters, Revenge, and the Search for Justice: Rural Arson in European Russia in the Late Imperial Era" (in *Reforming Justice in Russia, 1864–1996: Power, Culture, and the Limits of Legal Order*, edited by Peter H. Solomon, Jr., 1997, pp. 107–130); the *Slavonic and East European Review* for the article "'I must always answer to the law...': Rules and Responses at the Reformed Volost' Court" (April 1997, pp. 308–334); and *Canadian Slavonic Papers* for the article "Apocalyptic Visions and Rational Responses: Fire Narratives in Fin-de-Siècle Russia" (Sept.–Dec. 1996, pp. 357–384).

CONTENTS

MAPS

TABLES

Acknowledgments

This book has been eleven years in the making, from the moment of its conceptualization in the Smolensk Regional Archive in December 1989 to my submission of the final version in December 2000. When I read my first fire materials in what was then the USSR, I had access to world news in Moscow primarily via BBC radio. The Berlin Wall had just fallen, and citizens across Eastern Europe were rising up in demonstrations that made the unbroken routines outside my hotel window on October Square especially disheartening. Email was not yet a method of communication. The grocery stores in Moscow were empty most of the time, and I depended on water from the US embassy and Fanta soft drinks as potable fluids for my two-year-old son. In the month of my initial research in the (then) Lenin Library in Moscow and the public library in (then) Leningrad, Andrei Sakharov died, and I joined in his memorialization with thousands of Leningrad citizens. My next research trip found me sitting in front of the television in Moscow as Gorbachev resigned and the USSR dissolved. Before the book was finished, I would pay over a million inflated rubles to stay in a Best Western hotel in Novgorod, then two years later sleep in the lavishly restored Hotel Grand Europe in St. Petersburg as the director of a university partnership. My most beloved Russian friend, Viktor Iakovlovich Frenkel, would die of a stroke at 62, due to the strain he endured as a member of the intelligentsia in the collapsed economy of the post-Soviet transition. In sum, during the eleven years it has taken me to research and write this book, the culture I study has been in constant transition. The transition has brought challenges and opportunities of unanticipated access to archives, which generated an irresistible obligation to travel to Russia frequently, at a rate no historian of Russia a mere decade earlier would have imagined either possible or necessary. In these highly unstable times, I have completed a book of this scope only with considerable help from institutions and individuals.

Among the institutions, the International Research and Exchanges Board (IREX) funded several of my research trips to the USSR and post-Soviet Russia. The Kennan Institute for Advanced Russian Studies and the Davis Center for Russian Studies at Harvard University also supported initial phases of research. Rutgers University, Camden College, provided leave time for me to go to the Soviet Union. The National Council for Eurasian and East European Research funded the early work on arson. The University of New Hampshire provided funds through the Arthur K. Whitcomb Professorship and the College of Liberal Arts. The US Department of State made it possible for me to do archival research in Vologda.

Libraries and their staff members in the United States and Russia provided significant assistance. In Russia, the women who work in the Saltykov-Shchedrin Public Library in St. Petersburg, in the reading room and photocopying office, have been unfailingly pleasant and helpful. It has been an honor to work there. In the United States, Debbie Watson at the University of New Hampshire graciously handled request upon request for materials that miraculously (or so it seemed to me) appeared from Moscow within three weeks on average.

Since 1989, archives in Moscow, St. Petersburg, Smolensk, Novgorod, and Vologda have been fully available to me. Mikhail Naumovich Levitin in Smolensk provided access to the files of the governor's chancellery during a 1989 visit, which yielded the first data I saw on village fires. The staff of the Russian State Historical Archive in St. Petersburg guided me to the rich materials in the files of the Economic Division of the Ministry of Interior. Sergei Mikhailovich Kazantsev secured entry for me to the Firefighting Museum in St. Petersburg in 1995 and permission to use figure 2.1. Iakov Viktorovich Frenkel did the preliminary survey of files in the Novgorod Regional Archive in 1997 to make it possible for me to make a quick and productive trip there that fall. In Vologda, Vladimir Nikolaevich Koshko eased access to the regional archive.

I have also been blessed with generous colleagues among fellow historians and Slavists. Most important has been Stephen J. Pyne, who has been a source of support, bibliographical leads, editorial counsel, and inspiration from the beginning. Eric L. Jones and Johan Goudsblom also were exceptionally responsive in their reading of the early chapters. Participants at the University of Toronto conference on judicial reform in Russia, held in the spring of 1995, provided critical support for my conclusions about arson. Jane Burbank, Jane Costlow, Nina Tumarkin, and Samuel Baron provided public forums enabling me to present the work in its formative phase. Jane Burbank has offered me the best of tough-minded, supportive criticism for two decades. The other historians of Russia whose collegial readings of this work carried it forward include Al Rieber, William Wagner, David Ransel, Adrian Jones, Eve Levin, Nadieszda Kizenko, Daniel Field, Gary Hamburg, and Abbott Gleason. They have not always agreed with me, but they have always been willing to join in constructive debates. Melissa Stockdale has been a treasured colleague and friend throughout, the voice at the other end of the telephone for endless conversations about research and writing and for judicious probing of my rethinking of major historical issues. Scholars of Russian literature were willing to contribute their expertise to a historian who rather blithely harvested fire motifs and references from their disciplinary field. Special thanks to Monika Greenleaf, Ronald LeBlanc, and Julie de Sherbinin for this kindness. I wish to acknowledge the contribution of the late Stephen Baehr to references to Dostoevsky in chapter 2.

Fortune has also smiled on me in my academic home departments. I began this book as a Henry Rutgers Fellow in the congenial history department at Rutgers University. I moved to New Hampshire in search of more snow and woods and found myself in the company of talented colleagues in a history department where prize-winning historians are the norm. I have profited especially from the erudition and editorial savvy of Bill Harris, Jeff Bolster, Jeff Diefendorf, Gregory McMahon, and Lucy Salyer.

Institutions and colleagues shape research and writing. Friends and family shape life that makes those activities possible. Paul Josephson has been building my work spaces for almost a quarter century. Isaac Josephson has provided constant entertainment on soccer fields, basketball courts, and baseball diamonds, while indulging his mother's need to bring him hot chocolate in bed every morning to demonstrate her maternal instincts before disappearing behind the closed door of her study. Peter Greenleaf has been a steadying anchor of a friend, whose profound belief in the value of scholarship has made me feel my work is worthwhile. In New Hampshire, Sarah Way Sherman, Jamie and Peter Calderwood, Alix and Josh Handelsman, and David and Drew Christie have shared their time whenever our family needed them. Heather Robbins, Randy Grace, and Debra and Dennis Straussfogel led me to midnight skating on frozen ponds and hikes through snowy woods. Jane and Neil Wylie ensured that wine, hearth fires, and conversation defined winter evenings, and Ruth Sample kept me running on country roads. On Vinalhaven, Virgina Baron kept me in blueberry pie and good spirits. In Russia, the Frenkel family has often given over their home and hearts to our family of three and has welcomed us individually every time we have passed through for fifteen years.

Even these acknowledgments are incomplete. But they suggest the breadth of relationships that shape this scholar's life. It is true that research and writing are solitary occupations, but we rarely locate the path to the archive door or the understanding of what we find there on our own. Nor do we transform our discoveries into comprehensible prose solely through individual effort while living a full personal life. As I have wound my way to the text that follows, I have traversed a path cleared in part by historians before me, made accessible by the institutions that have paid for my passage, and lined on either side by critics, colleagues, and well-wishers. Traveling a course similar to mine, usually racing ahead, only to retrace his steps to urge me forward, ever pointing ahead to the academic goals he cherishes, sharing a commitment to exchanges with our Russian colleagues and friends, cooking not a few meals and washing mountains of laundry, keeping the wood stoves burning, and all the while cheering my every incremental step closer to publication has been my husband and partner, Paul. In thanks, I dedicate this book to him.

ALL RUSSIA
IS BURNING!

Introduction

In 1865, upon taking his oath as heir to the throne of Russia, the future tsar Alexander III issued an official rescript to the minister of the interior, P. A. Valuev. To mark the momentous occasion and show his concern for the people who would fall under his care, Alexander offered financial assistance to victims of two enduring disasters in rural Russia: famine and fires.[1] Famine has loomed large in studies of late imperial Russia. Starving peasants, government assistance programs, and renewed civic activism through famine relief were major features of the late nineteenth century and have been subjects of historical debate.[2] Rural fires have made spot appearances as well. In histories of "peasant Russia," fires always earn a brief mention as one of the catastrophes that could destroy peasant households' well-being.[3] In the historiography of "peasant movements," especially those of the period 1905–1907, acts of arson by peasants against landowners have been employed to illustrate popular political consciousness.[4] But nowhere in the study of late imperial Russia have fires, in and of themselves, received a level of scholarly scrutiny that would make the young Alexander III's choice immediately comprehensible. Unlike him, historians have not placed the "burned-out village" as centrally in the Russian landscape as the "hungry village."[5]

Rural conflagrations, both accidental and intentionally set, were more constant events in late imperial Russia than was famine, and more resistant to efforts at mitigating their effects on the rural population. Between 1860, when annual fire statistics became a regular feature of the work of the Central Statistical Committee of the Ministry of the Interior, and 1904, on the eve of Russia's first revolution of the twentieth century, fires destroyed almost three billion rubles' worth of property across the empire. Rural fires caused almost 90 percent of these losses and were thus one of the countryside's most consistently damaging experiences. As such, they captured the attention of educated observers, who quickly placed the "fire question" at the center of their effort to evaluate Russia's position in modern Europe. By focusing on rural fires in his first step toward formal governance, Alexander III was very much a man of his time, a time when the conviction was gathering that Russia was in fire's unwavering grip.[6] Fires, in turn, came to signify Russia's imprisonment in premodern rural systems. They were the stigmata of backwardness on the body of European Russia.

In the forty years following Alexander III's rescript, fire and arson in the countryside carried intense symbolic and material meaning as part of Russia's search for a modern identity. When Russia joined the European experience of "high modernism," uncontained fire in the hands of recently emancipated peasants came into view for educated Russians and became an object of the campaign against Russia's developmental delay behind the West.[7] James Scott's recent definition captures the essence of the "high modernist" impulse in countries across the northern and western hemispheres in the nineteenth century: "It is best conceived as a strong . . . version of the self-confidence about scientific and technical progress . . . the mastery of nature (including human nature), and, above all, the rational design of social order commensurate with the scientific understanding of natural laws."[8]

Those in the thrall of high modernist views both rejected stasis and negated history as embodied in tradition. The rejection of the status quo in the context of rural fire in Russia meant a new consciousness of and revulsion against a perpetual feature of villages across European Russia. The negation of tradition led to a narrowed, simplified vision of fire and the peasants who continued to employ it. Russia's rural fire culture came to represent the antithesis of a rational and modern society founded on the conquest of natural forces. Within that vision, peasant women emerged as the most backward and pernicious obstacles to a modern Russia, whereas the proposed solutions were masculine schemata, most fully embodied in the volunteer firefighting movement. By 1904, fire and arson as features of Russia's rural condition had generated literary, governmental, and social responses that illuminated not only fire's place in the late imperial countryside but also Russia's bedeviled combination of persistent poverty, official stinginess in social welfare programs, failure to integrate formal law into rural society, genuine civic potential within local organizations, and misogyny at all levels of discussion.

This study of fire and arson focuses on fire's material reality and its functions within the physical and cultural setting of village communities during the second half of the nineteenth century. It introduces rural settlement fires as a factor in Russia's economic history and a partial explanation for the Russian Empire's challenges in economic development. It explores arson as a manifestation of rural values and as evidence of the challenges to would-be reformers who hoped to bring the "rule of law" to the peasants of European Russia.

The history of fire and arson in rural European Russia is also a history cultural meanings and representations in the late imperial campaign for modernity. As such, it offers further evidence of the disenchantment among educated Russians with "their" peasants and the hardening of their view that peasants were a major obstacle blocking Russia's advent into the company of modern, rational, prosperous, civilized nations.[9]

Finally, this book introduces efforts by the state and civil society to proscribe, prevent, and contain rural fires through legal decrees, provincial fire insurance and village reconstruction programs, and volunteer firefighting associations. These efforts display not only the degree to which many educated Russians shared the young Alexander III's perception of fire as a threat equal to famine in the late imperial countryside but also their contradictory impulses to engage and to coerce the peasantry in the campaign to subdue it.

BY THE END of the nineteenth century, uncontrolled conflagrations had emerged in public opinion as a defining feature of Russia's national distinction. The writer-ethnographer S. V. Maksimov stated the case most dramatically in 1896, when he argued that

> forested and wooden Rus' is even in a special, exceptional position in comparison with other countries: it is like an inextinguishable bonfire which, never going out completely, first weakens, then flames up with such monstrous force that any idea of fighting it vanishes: an entire sea of flames is spread by a whirlwind of fire from one end of our unfortunate land to the other, and destroys without a trace forests, planted fields, villages, settlements, and towns.[10]

Maksimov's statement displays the widely held conclusion that Russia's fire condition set it apart from other countries, that fire raced across it with an invincible, monstrous force, and that, consequently, Russia was an "unfortunate land"—a victim of this overwhelming, elemental power.

The conflation of fires with Russia's exceptional position of vulnerability to elemental nature was consistent with apocalyptic patterns of thinking in fin-de-siècle Russia.[11] Such thinking encouraged the development of a rhetoric of victimization, which in turn invited a combination of futility and fatalism. Many educated Russians, from belletrists to state ministers, adopted this rhetoric in their conceptualization of rural fires as an explanation for Russia's lag behind the West,

taneously ascribing the peasants' helplessness to the peasants' own
t in apocalyptic thinking.
res at the same time engendered a challenge to this cultural stance.
he late 1870s and taking full form by the 1890s, an alternative inter-
...on of the relationship among fire, peasants, educated society, the state, and
Russia's cultural development emerged. This interpretation focused not only, or
even primarily, on fire's "monstrous force" but instead on the village culture, physical structures, and materials that fueled it. Proponents of this view presented
materialist explanations for fire's damaging presence in the Russian countryside
and offered rational solutions for the material factors they identified. Whereas
apocalyptic thinking spawned fatalism and victimization, materialist, rational
approaches generated insistence on a progressive future in which Russia could join
the modern nations of Europe, which were no longer so fully at the mercy of fire
and its damages.

The materialist, progressive approach to the fire crisis challenged the
image of peasants as victims and thus informed the educated public's shifting
attitude toward the peasantry in general. Peasants became paradoxical culprits
in the fire question. The paradox lay in their designation as culprits in both
accidental and arson fires. When the subject was accidental fires, progressive
and conservative critics alike berated the peasantry for their ignorance and lack
of self-help. They bewailed the peasants' traditional fire beliefs and practices,
labeling them irrational and superstitious. They charged the peasants with
carelessness, mishandling of fire, and a universal failure to exercise foresight
and fire precautions. In the place of self-help as Samuel Smiles would have used
the term,[12] critics charged, peasants exhibited only fatalistic expectations of
inevitable victimization at the hands of nature or a punitive Holy Father.

When the question was arson, however, peasants emerged as culprits for
the opposite reason—because they were *too* active in practicing self-help. Here
self-help meant several things. First, it meant people's helping themselves in the
juridical sense of resolving disputes or exacting retribution and compensation
from wrongdoers by practicing arson as a form of *samosud* (self-help or mob justice) outside the formal judicial system. Second, it meant helping themselves to
insurance payments by practicing so-called self-arson (*samopodzhog*), burning
down their own insured structures.

Progressive and conservative critics saw two other forms of peasant agency
exacerbating the fire crisis. First, they identified excessive individualism and self-
interest as a contributing factor in runaway fires, pointing to the peasants' habit of
focusing exclusively on pulling their own goods out of their houses and barns dur-

ing village fires rather than joining in to extinguish the blaze. Second, they found peasants' resistance to village reconstruction plans an infuriating obstacle blocking their vision of a rational, fire-proof countryside in European Russia. The emancipated peasantry, whether through insufficient action or excessive action, thus became indicted agents of destruction who contributed to Russia's backwardness and robbed it of prospects for a fully modern future.

Fire was not an imagined or invented feature of rural daily life, however; its significance for Russia's condition did not rest solely in its symbolic or metaphorical meaning as a measure of Russia's modernity or backwardness. Fires did burn. Fires did consume property, livestock, forests, and people. They were a quantifiable factor in imperial Russia's and the Russian peasantry's economic condition that no historian has yet fully explored.[13]

Furthermore, peasants *were* arsonists who did set fires against their neighbors. They most often aimed their incendiarism not against gentry landowners for the political reasons historians have usually sought in moments of social upheaval, but against their fellow peasants in all years and seasons in order to enforce community norms or to exact individual revenge in personal disputes. This fact requires historians of Russia to reconsider both their approach to arson as an element of rural life and their overall vision of peasants as actors. Arson in rural life was only marginally a product of peasant-gentry relations and thus of social, economic, or political protest. The vast majority of arson cases in European Russia between 1860 and 1904 were peasant-against-peasant arson. Many, perhaps most of these cases fit into none of the templates that Soviet/post-Soviet and Western scholars have designed to explain peasant activism or agency.

As a category or term in the Soviet lexicon, arson was a subset of "peasant movements." In histories and document collections, incidents of arson appear almost exclusively when the targets are gentry property. Working with the original police reports in local archives, one can re-create the process of historical selectivity. In the Novgorod regional archive, for example, among the pages upon pages of handwritten accounts of arson and accidental fires reported by district police officers to their governors every two weeks, blue check marks appear in the margins only beside the peasant-against-gentry arson fires. Readers' records at the front of each file identify the pages from which readers have taken notes or of which they have requested photocopies, as well as the dates of the readers' uses of the file. There is a close correspondence between the blue marks and readers' records dating to the period when Soviet historians were compiling documentary records of the "peasant movement."[14] Only those rural fires that could document and illustrate peasant resistance against gentry "exploiters" made their way into the published record. Thousands of other peasant fires and thousands of peasant-against-peasant arson fires recorded in Novgorod, Smolensk, Vologda, and other regional archives were left unmarked, unpublished, and thus invisible in the Soviet history of rural Russia.

Western scholars have similarly envisioned peasant arson within the template of social or economic resistance, most obviously and vividly in studies of the revolutionary period 1905–1907, the Civil War, and peasant protests against the collectivization campaigns of the Stalin era.[15] Lynne Viola most aptly expressed this view in her study of peasant protest in 1930, in which she explained: "What is clear is that fire, represented as arson, invoked fear and punished peasant turncoats, while serving as the peasant flag of resistance throughout the land."[16] When one puts the previously unmarked and historically unremarked fires back into the landscape of late imperial rural Russia, arson serves to document a form of peasant agency that diverges from categories of class or resistance. It documents, instead, a Hobbseian world of unconstrained envy, rebuke, and retribution in which peasants acted against their fellows, often for most inglorious reasons. Peasant arsonists in these cases were neither victims nor valorous protesters against oppression. They were victimizers themselves who used arson as a form of social control even more blatant and obviously damaging than the practice of religious denunciation that Jeffrey Burds has recently explicated.[17]

Fire also provides evidence of another form of peasant agency—the mastery and use of fire. Fire in the Russian countryside was not always a pernicious phenomenon. On the contrary, it was the peasants' most frequent ally and source of energy in illuminating and heating their homes, fertilizing their fields, processing their crops, aiding the sick, and cooking their food. No day passed in the villages of European Russia without the peasants' manipulation of fire. To understand fully the character of peasant culture and educated responses to it in the late nineteenth century, students of Russia need to see fire in these ways as well. They offer answers to the question of why conflagrations were such a stubborn presence in fin-de-siècle rural Russia. They also explain, in part, why educated Russians, who interacted almost exclusively with contained fire in urban settings, found peasants and uncontained fire across all of European Russia such an alarming combination.

THIS BOOK INTERSECTS with several historiographical traditions. In the field of Russian history, it contributes to the study of the peasantry of European Russia and of the interaction between members of educated Russian society and the peasantry. Within these areas, it offers evidence on the representation of peasants by educated society in public discourse, the structures of rural daily life, concepts of justice and methods of enforcing moral values in village culture, efforts to create a civil society through volunteer firefighting organizations, and the zemstvo (public works council) fire insurance program.[18]

This study also introduces the Russian case in fire history and disaster history. As a contribution to fire history, it has been informed primarily by the work of Stephen J. Pyne and Johan Goudsblom, while drawing on such anthropological, psychoanalytical, and philosophical approaches as those of Bayard, Bachelard, Lévi-Strauss, Frazer, and Eliade.[19] The goals of fire history comprise the display and explication of fire cultures or fire regimes within specific national and regional traditions. Alternatively, as in Goudsblom's case, fire history examines fire's meaning across long historical periods as an agent of the evolution of Western civilization. Fire historians emphasize just how long and how recently fire was at the center of human existence, generating not only society's principal energy but also a complex of practices and belief systems that permeated material and spiritual culture. The history of modernization is also the history of containing fire; this is one reason why aspiring modernists in late-nineteenth-century Russia first recoiled from the elaborate and pervasive fire culture in the villages of European Russia and then moved aggressively to define, contain, and extinguish it.

Disaster history issues from the economic histories of Simon Kuznets and Eric L. Jones, who have identified social disasters, including "settlement fires," as handicaps limiting the ability of communities or entire regions to move into periods of sustained economic development.[20] Village conflagrations were a significant brake on individual households', communities', and European Russia's economic development in the late nineteenth century. They suggest why Russia was left out of the "European miracle" of sustained capital accumulation and economic development. Jones's work indicates that historians of Russia need to recognize rural fires and arson not only as Russia's own fire culture but also as economic disasters with major consequences for peasants and tsars alike.

ONCE THE IMPERIAL bureaucracy and public opinion in Russia discovered rural fire and arson as areas of concern, the proliferation of evidence on their existence and meanings began. District policemen filed biweekly reports with their governors on the incidence and nature of local fires, and those reports were deposited in local archives. The governors forwarded the statistics to be included in massive compilations published by the Ministry of the Interior, and to official provincial newspapers. The latter published details about the cause and scale of individual fires. When V. N. Tenishev crafted his survey of rural conditions in 1897, he included several questions relating to fire practices and to the incidence of arson, generating seventy-five files from ten provinces.[21] The Imperial Russian Geographic Society and the Society of Naturalists, Anthropologists, and Ethnographers published reports by their members on local fire beliefs and practices. As arson cases made their way into the court system, the *Court Herald* and the *Judicial Herald* published transcripts of specific trials, and the Ministry of Justice published statistics on arson as a criminal offense. Peasants who found themselves burned out of their homes by massive fires sent written appeals to the tsar and to ministers of the interior, who filed them in their archives. Zemstvo boards published their fire insurance regulations and village reconstruction plans as well as the financial records of their insurance programs. Activists in the volunteer firefighting movement published memoirs of their experiences; local brigades published reports of their finances and activities; organizers published firefighting manuals; and national organs of the movement published journals. The imperial government itself issued laws, decrees, building and fire codes, and regulations governing zemstvo programs and volunteer firefighting organizations. Writers incorporated rural fires in fictional representations of contemporary Russia, employing fire motifs and fire scenes to capture apocalyptic elements in fin-de-siècle mental structures.

This mass of sources, ranging from literary representations and newspaper articles to statistical tables and ethnographers' reports, offered different avenues—one might say different heuristic approaches—to knowing fire. Their ways of knowing fire have largely shaped the structure of this study, in which each chapter constitutes a different way of knowing fire in late-nineteenth-century rural Russia. Each kind of knowledge emerges from a body of sources and set of questions specific to one facet of European Russia's rural fire culture. And just as each chapter offers a different way of knowing fire, so each chapter offers a different way of knowing peasants. Just as fire had different functions and meanings in the Russian village, so the peasants' relationship to fire varied. In some chapters, peasants appear as the masters and manipulators of fire; in others, they are its victims. Employing a variety of approaches to fire in the Russian countryside makes it possible to see peasants' multiple, sometimes contradictory historical character. No one prevailing template in peasant studies can encompass Russian peasants' relationship to fire and the meaning for Russian history which that relationship engendered. Peasants emerge as both victims and agents, legal plaintiffs and outlaws, defenders and violators of private property, obstructionists and inventors, social protesters and social oppressors, enemies of the gentry and partners with their noble neighbors in the campaign against fire.

Three methodological issues remain. First, the chronological boundaries of the study are 1860 and 1904. It was during the years between those dates that rural fire and arson entered Russian national consciousness as features of national identity and as problems requiring the attention of officials and active citizens. The system for collecting data from the European provinces took shape in 1860, yielding a baseline definition of the scope of the "fire question." Over the next four decades, rural fire and arson assumed their attributed meanings within debates about Russia's economic and social development, meanwhile eliciting official and civic responses in a broad campaign against rural fire. The revolutionary events of 1905–1907 would change both the ascribed meanings and the official responses. This study recaptures the fire culture of the period before the blinding conflagrations of those years.

More important is the choice of 1904 as the endpoint. This study focuses on the meanings of rural fire and arson in the nineteenth century before those meanings were narrowed and transformed by the events of 1905–1907. Some historians may still choose to read this work as a prehistory of peasant rebellions or protest in the twentieth century; they will find much consistency in the geographic distribution and rhetoric of arson when they do.[22] This is not, however, a prehistory of the revolution of 1905–1907 or of peasant protest against grain requisitioning and collectivization campaigns in the Soviet period. It is a study of the meaning of fire in rural Russia within the contours of village culture and of the responses of state officials and civic activists before the tortured history of the twentieth century. It restores to rural fire and arson in late imperial Russia the cultural meanings they held before the social upheavals of 1905–1907 and the subsequent dictates of Soviet historiography erased them from the record.

In these goals, my analysis of arson in rural Russia resembles that of Regina Schulte, who wrote a pioneering study of village arson in Germany at the end of the nineteenth century.[23] Schulte sought to "depoliticize" the study of arson, departing from the tradition of Eric Hobsbawm, George Rudé, Douglas Hay, and David Jones to examine arson as a form of individual protest that illuminates the previously "gray area" of the "tensions within the peasant world itself."[24]

Second, this study focuses on rural rather than urban Russia. Including provincial towns and capital cities in the first study of fire and arson in late imperial Russia would have expanded it beyond the constraints of current academic publishing, as well as beyond my desire or capacity to master the historiography of cities and urban planning. The sources for a study of fire and arson in urban Russia, however, are as extensive as those used here, with major conflagrations such as the great Novgorod fire of 1194 and the burning of Moscow in 1812 joining the St. Petersburg arson fires in 1862 as defining moments in Russia's national self-definition. They present a rich opportunity to any scholar who decides to pursue the urban history of fire and arson in Russia.

Third, sources, scope, and the construction of national identity through fire delineated the geographic frame for this study: European Russia. The statistics on fire collected by the Ministry of the Interior were richest on European Russia. Again, the need to focus on a topic of manageable scope favored restricting research to this region. More importantly, for the question of where rural fire and arson fit in the national narrative of self-definition in post-Emancipation Russia, the territory beyond the Urals did not make its way into educated Russians' vision of "our peasants," "our villages," our "unfortunate land"—in sum, into their imagined community, as Benedict Anderson employed this phrase.[25] It was within the geographic and conceptual boundaries of European Russia that the meaning of rural fire and arson came to explain why Russia was not fully European and that peasants came to be identified as the explanation for Russia's delayed advent into the modern. It was there that the battle against rural futility and for Russia's future ensued.

PART ONE

FROM BENEVOLENT FORCE
TO NATIONAL MISFORTUNE:
FIRE'S CONTESTED MEANINGS
IN RURAL RUSSIA

I

Fire as Gentle Cookery and Paradise: Peasants as Mistresses and Masters of Fire

IT SHINES IN PARADISE. IT BURNS IN HELL. IT IS GENTLENESS AND TOR-
TURE. IT IS COOKERY AND IT IS APOCALYPSE.

—Gaston Bachelard, *The Psychoanalysis of Fire*

In central, European Russia, the day began in a peasant household when the mistress of the house rose in the darkness of early morning, often around four o'clock, to begin the three-hour process of firing up the family stove. To do so, she cleared out ashes from the previous day's burning, and perhaps gently removed a sleeping child who had settled inside to enjoy the stove's waning warmth the night before. Gathering the ashes in a bucket, she might discard them in the yard beyond the cottage door or put them aside to use in healing potions for a sick member of the family. Her fuel for the stove was most likely to be wood, which she might take either from within the house or an outbuilding where it had been left to dry or from a woodpile stacked next to the exterior wall of the house, in the alleyway dividing her *dvor*, or farmyard, from that of her neighbor. In regions where deforestation had made wood an expensive commod-ity, she might use straw, peat, or dried dung. From the inner recesses of the stove, she raked hot coals forward from where they had been covered with ashes to retain their fire for the night. Over the next three hours, she would feed the fire to its maximum heat, tending it, adjusting logs or other fuel, adding new ones, and opening and closing the door to regulate the burning. Because most peasant stoves until the end of the nineteenth century had no chimneys, sparks danced and smoke billowed into the room each time she opened the door (fig. 1.1).

As she began this process, she was not moving in total darkness. Often, the heated room was bathed in the dim but steady glow of the lampada, the oil light left burning before the household icon, diagonally across from the stove. In this way the domestic space of the peasants of European Russia was defined by two points of fire, that of the stove, providing physical warmth and energy, and the lamp, illuminating images of Orthodox faith, the source of sacred inspiration. These flame-centered objects in turn represented the primary frames of peasants' material and spiritual culture.

Fig. 1.1. *Russian stove with mouth and shelf.*

For further illumination, the woman of the house might also have lit a luchina, a tarred splint of wood that hung from the ceiling in a metal fixture or lay across a metal stand (fig. 1.2). If her household was extremely prosperous, she might light a candle or, if it was the end of the nineteenth century, a kerosene lamp.[1] One of these she picked up to carry with her as she went into a cold storage shed or out into the yard to gather fuel and wood chips or bits of straw from the ground. She moved in a silence broken only by the sounds her relatives made in their sleep or gradual awakening as they lay above, beside, or wrapped around the immense stove, or by the stove's own expanding conversation of pops, cracks, hisses, and whispers as fuel ignited, shifted, released final bits of moisture, or collapsed into coals and ashes. She might have spoken aloud, addressing the fire itself or the house spirit, the *domovoi*, believed to live behind the stove.

Through these daily firings, the woman of the household developed an intimacy with fire, a knowledge of its properties, and a partnership with its power to heat her home and drive away the cold of the night. For her, fire was a living entity whose personality and eccentricities she had to master and manipulate in order to meet her primary responsibility of ensuring the comfort of her home. For the other members of the household, the firing of the stove came before dawn, before the cock's crowing, and thus was the primary marker of the day's beginning. As the fire expanded within, it spread its warmth through stones and clay to warm their limbs and ease the transition from dark sleep to morning's light. This contributed to the stove's continuing importance in the daily life and consciousness of the peasantry and to their continued respect for fire.[2]

As the source of warmth, the fire in the stove protected against the harshness of nature. It provided a kind of humming companionship in the dark, quiet cold of winter. It may be hard to imagine just how silent the Russian village of the late nineteenth century was in the depths of a winter night. Even for contemporary educated Russians, the closed-in silence seemed stupefying. Sometime in the mid-1870s, P. A. Ivanov tried to capture its effect in the far north in Arkhangel'sk Province:

> In the very long winter, in the villages it is quiet, as if lifeless, it is cheerless in the full sense of the word, and all around there is a deathly silence on the street, with only the trembling howling of strong gusts of wind: beyond for a great distance, there is a flat snowy shroud and dense forests. The houses look monotonous, sad, orphaned; they are buried in snowdrifts.[3]

In this silent world of the snowy pall and the looming forest, it was so cold in the winter that glass windows shattered. To prevent this from happening, the

Fig. 1.2. *Luchina with basin*

peasants replaced glass panes with wooden shutters for the long winter months, thus exacerbating the sensation of burial.[4] In St. Petersburg and Novgorod Provinces, encasement took the form of wrapping the *izba*, the peasant cottage or house, on the outside in straw, sometimes all the way up to the roof, enclosing the peasants in the dark space inside.[5] Within the closed world of human habitation in the forest, it was the huge stove that made winter survivable and the house cozy. It was the stove that forced the living qualities of fire in pressing silence upon the Russian peasants' consciousness.

The stove as the center of heat and cooking brought fire as a benevolent force into the home. Taking up one-fifth to one-fourth of the living space within the izba, the stove occupied one corner; it was built into the structure and surrounded with sleeping lofts, wooden shelves, cupboards, and frames.[6] It defined the home as the heated living space within one house and within the jumble of barns and sheds crowded inside wooden fences demarcating each household's plot of family land.

Ethnographers and other educated people living in rural locations queried peasants in response to surveys they received from St. Petersburg, which included questions to the peasants about their use and understanding of fire in their lives. Everywhere they found a rich array of practices and beliefs, many of which appeared in geographically distant provinces across the European part of the empire. Historians a century later have legitimately questioned the interpretive filters that informed these observers' analyses of the peasants' responses.[7] When they turned to the question of fire, contemporaneous observers directed their gaze according to their own understanding of social development as an evolutionary process marching toward a secular worldview, passing first through the stages of pre-Christian or pagan belief systems and formal Christianity. Recognizing that predilection, historians can still glean fragments of the material features of village life and peasants' behaviors with fire from the reports submitted by their educated interlocutors.

When explaining who constituted their family to ethnographers and other outsiders in the late nineteenth century, peasants included those who "ate from the same pot" of food cooked over the same fire.[8] They explained that when families divided, they transferred live coals or fire from the extended family's stove to the stove in the new house. Often, women of the family bore the responsibility for carrying this hearth fire from the old home to the new. If the distance was too far to carry fire or coals—for example, in the case of families moving to virgin territory during resettlement—the objects associated with the hearth fire served the function of carrying the fire's spirit. Similarly, the use of stokers, pots, and pans during some wedding ceremonies may have stemmed from their association with the hearth fire.[9] When a child was born into the family, in some areas he or she would be carried to the mouth of the stove, a ritual that ethnographers interpreted as presentation of the new family member to the spirit of the ancestors within.[10] Peasants told outsiders that it was a sin to spit into the fire or onto the stove.[11] In many areas, peasants observed a moment of prayer when the fire was being lit. To quarrel before the stove was believed to bring calamity to the household. In these rituals, the writer-ethnographer S. V. Maksimov argued, fire was a personage of the household, seat of the ancestors, and source of well-being or misery.[12]

Although the interpretation of ancestor worship was certainly inviting to educated Russians who conceptualized social development in evolutionary terms, it diminished the reality of the stove's presence and demands on the peasants who used it. The stove was a constant feature among the inherited, daily practices that James C. Scott has termed the *metis* of rural experience.[13] In the most immediate sense, fire was something the peasants could not do without. Not only in the hours before dawn but throughout the day it was at the center of their daily experience. When the woman of the house lit the fire each morning, it is more likely that she thought of herself as bringing essential warmth to her living relatives than as paying homage to her ancestors. Ethnographers who collected information on the veneration of fire (*pochitanie ognia*) in the late nineteenth century tended to see veneration in and of itself as an irrational vestige of something ancient. This led them to focus on rituals before the stove rather than on management of the fire within it. They were attracted by the unfamiliar rituals that they, as city dwellers, had lost. But they often failed to perceive how critical fire continued to be to peasants, and why peasants might honor it.

The stove was for peasants not primarily or just a repository of ancestral spirits as hearth but the very immediate source of vibrant comfort. This becomes all the more apparent when we consider the physical postures of Russian peasants relative to the stove. They literally embraced it as they lay along its shelves and wrapped themselves around it. Lying thus, they would feel the soothing warmth of the heated clay and hear and feel the gentle sputtering and crackling as wood and coals burned within. Children sometimes slept inside the stove on the hearth stone at the end of the day when the fire had died down. This image of the enormous block of a stove—a humming, crackling presence with a door one opened to gain access to the heat and red glow within and a body of warmth to embrace and press oneself against for comfort—makes it a feminine object.[14] This feminized image of the stove found expression in the peasant saying, "The stove is our very own mother."[15]

The feminine associations of the stove itself and, by extension, of the fire inside it were even more direct in the stove's function as the site of food preparation. Located in the woman's corner, the stove was the center of female daily activities within the izba.[16] As her day progressed, the peasant woman who had fired the stove in the morning would then use it to bake bread, prepare soups and kasha, and cook the various root vegetables that dominated the Russian peasant diet. In the extended family household there were usually many mouths to feed, beginning in the early hours of the morning and continuing until the darkness of nightfall. The stove was a site of endless activity, and women were the exclusive actors. Through this role, women were the agents of transformation from "the raw" to "the cooked" and thereby critical players in the most fundamental civilization of the Russian peasantry.[17] This activity drew women into frequent contact with fire and required them to make use of its transformative powers. The practice of creating bread from flour, yeast, and water through the heat of the stove's flames and coals made mundane magicians of peasant women who came to know fire's properties. Through these daily activities in the peasant household, fire was essential to maintaining both warmth and nutrition for survival. It protected against cold and darkness and was an essential tool in the battle against hunger. Fire enabled the peasants of European Russia to maintain their poise, as it were, in their precarious, marginal existence.

Healing Fire

Within the household and beyond it, peasants also wielded fire as a weapon against disease. Ashes were one of the elements drawn from fire that entered the repertoire of healers in the village, most of whom, by the nineteenth century, were women. Through the traditions of folk medicine, peasant women developed a special relationship with fire that reinforced its reputation as a supernatural, living force in daily life.[18] For the peasantry, illness, like most other disasters, was the devil's visitation.[19] In the battle with this manifestation of the unclean spirit, fire was an agent of purification and thus was conceptualized as a force that contributed to an equilibrium between good and evil.[20] Ethnographers and local observers at the end of the nineteenth century reported numerous medicinal practices that relied on fire. In some instances, healers used fire to fight fire, as it were, using flame, heat, or smoke to treat inflammations of various sorts.

In Orel Province, for example, when a child broke out into a scrofulous rash, a woman carried the child to the stove, ignited a rag from the hearth fire, smothered the flame in lard, and then applied it to the rash, saying, "Fire, fire, take your little fire!"[21] Fire's products took on its curative powers. Steam boiled over healing fire took on its properties.[22] Ashes mixed with water provided a potion used for various ailments, sometimes to be imbibed, sometimes as a lotion. Someone with a fever might carry a hot stoker from the stove out of the house in the hope that the fever would go with it. Godmothers used hot coals in an incantation to protect the newborn from the evil eye.[23] In both Belorussia and Russia, peasants used hearth fire as a cure for infantile diseases. Its smoke was used to fumigate newborns' cradles to ensure good health and sound sleep. Infants would be placed to sleep before the fire or even were inserted on a bread board like a loaf of bread to receive the flame's curative powers. The latter was a treatment for rickets, which peasants called "dog's old age." Being placed inside the stove was the final step in a healing treatment in Kazan Province, where healers first bathed the child in the bathhouse with a puppy, striking the child and the puppy alternately with birch twigs while chanting, "Dog, dog, take the dog's old age away from this child!" They would then smear dough all over the child's face, tie him or her to a bread board, and hold the board inside the stove for a few seconds three times, saying, "Dog's old age, bake in the oven!"[24]

As an element of folk medicine, fire was not always confined to the household or taken from the hearth. The flames of sacramental candles from church services also had special curative or ameliorative powers in folk medicine. They could be used to assist in difficult births or to lessen the pains of violent death throes.[25] Peasants fumigated herpes blisters with smoke from tar-covered, slow-burning torches.[26] They also used fire as a prophylactic, as in Novgorod Province, where healthy members of the community leapt through bonfires during typhus epidemics.[27]

The bathhouse was also a healing center, where fire and the heat it generated were again the source of the anticipated cure. There, women came to give birth, feverish children were brought to sweat, and everyone in the village came to bathe. The comfort of the bathhouse depended on the mastery of fire, which had to be built up and maintained in a small stove long enough to meet the needs of whatever number of people were about to use it. In the case of birthing, this length of time was unpredictable, and women were the only ones permitted to enter. Bringing the baby into the world required that the midwife also be a fire mistress.[28]

Nineteenth-century ethnographers did not attempt to explain the logic behind these cures but rather presented them simply as examples of the peasants' associations with fire. It is clear, however, that they were important in contributing to peasants' sense that fire was a positive element in their daily existence. This array of cures drawing on fire offered peasants a sense of protection against disaster and might have contributed to their sense of controlling their fate. In the cures listed above, one can see a use of fire's properties as either purifying or transformative. It is we, of course, rather than peasant practitioners, who would apply such terms. Even the nineteenth-century ethnographers who recorded these cures did not categorize them as such. It would take Sir James Frazer's studies in the 1930s to bring such interpretive labels to fire practices, labels that later twentieth-century scholars borrowed and elaborated.[29]

However labeled, fire was clearly and explicitly a weapon of purification in the battle against disease. Correspondents to the Tenishev Bureau reported from some regions that peasants burned the clothing of those suffering from illness.[30] Similarly, in the late fall, the old women of the village often gathered all of the worn-out bast shoes of summer while young women gathered the summer's soiled straw bedding. With these they lit enormous bonfires which, they explained to ethnographers, would save them from the evil eye and clean the house for the devil's season of darkness.[31] Ethnographers may have been captivated by the reference to the evil eye, but we can equally appreciate fire's contribution to the health of the village by seeing this as a simple act of getting rid of dirty, smelly items. Similarly, the bonfires captured outsiders' attention, but they were also primarily an efficient, coordinated effort by all the households of the community, who were thus also able to control the fires they set for this purpose.

In a world largely devoid of "scientific" medical care, peasants summoned all possible assistance in their struggle against illness.[32] That struggle most certainly included the Christian Holy Father and various saints through prayer, song, and use of the flames of sacramental candles. Healers reportedly began by addressing the Holy Father or the Trinity.[33] In the incantation against the bite of a rabid dog, the healer might call on both the *tsar'-ogon'* (Tsar Fire) and the Archangel Michael.[34]

A particularly rich ritual in which women employed both fire and prayer as prophylactics against disease appeared in reports from Belorussia. As a precaution against cholera, almost all of the married women and adolescent girls would gather in one house with their spinning wheels. Singing sacred songs, they then tried in one night to spin enough thread to weave a sheet from it. Before sunrise of the next day, they would take this sheet out onto the street or even beyond the village and set fire to it. All of the inhabitants of the village would stand in the sheet's smoke. While the sheet was burning, the peasants threw pieces of horse manure and the roots of a special plant through the smoke. After the ritual, the villagers carried these roots in the palms of their hands as talismans against the disease.[35] The image of women as spinners is a familiar one. Here the gift of their handiwork joined the spirit of the Lord through sacred song and the spirit of fire to protect their families against the disaster of cholera.

Not only women used fire as a prophylactic against disease. If an epidemic threatened the village, the men of the community might make new fire as an element of ritualized protection. Peasants continually battled epidemics threatening livestock, one of the misfortunes almost always listed with conflagration as a disaster for peasant households, and fire served as a weapon at their disposal. New fire, created by the friction between two pieces of wood, was called *zhivoi, dereviannyi,* or *drevesnyi, lesnoi, lekarstvennyi ogon'* (living fire, wood fire, fire of the forest, medicinal fire).[36] It was such fires that peasants used for purification and as a prophylactic against disease among animals and people. Maksimov explained that peasants thought new fires had these special powers precisely because they were taken from the tree through the friction between pieces of wood.[37] In Novgorod Province, living fire was used so frequently as a weapon against disease that the peasants erected a permanent fire-making machine of two wooden poles with an apparatus for creating friction.[38] A. Vasil'ev reported from the Cherepovets District that peasants venerated such new fire because it came from wood and was sacred fire, *sviashchennyi ogon',* sent from heaven. In the villages of Gorki and Baskakovo, women did not fire the stoves on the morning of June 1, the day of the healing saints Cosmas and Demian. Instead, they gathered with the rest of the village for a ritual generation of new fire with two pieces of wood. Once these ignited, the peasants carried the new fire to each household to fire up the stoves.[39] The creation of new fire in this ritual incorporated both the veneration of the Orthodox patron saints of healing and the manipulation of fire as a weapon against illness.[40]

Magical Fire

At various points throughout the year, the Russian village was the scene of rituals in which young girls engaged in acts of divination to discover whom they were fated to marry. Here fire most frequently took the form of the flame of a candle's illumination. Sometimes candles were simply a source of light, as in

Poshekhonia, where girls and boys held candles over ice holes on New Year's Eve in order to find the face of their intended lit up in the water below.[41] In the ritual of "looking in the mirror," candles seem to have done more than illuminate in the literal sense of the word. In this fortune-telling procedure, two tables were set up in the middle of a darkened room with the windows shuttered on the inside or the curtains drawn. On each table, beeswax candles were lit in front of a mirror. A young girl then undressed down to her camisole and sat between the two tables to wait until midnight. At midnight, a shadow was expected to appear in the mirrors. It could take one of three shapes: the face of her future bridegroom, the face of someone who had died, or a coffin signifying her own death. Girls were reported to die from fright during this ritual.[42]

Flame and shadow also played against each other in "burning paper" on New Year's Eve. Having laid a piece of paper on a flat surface near a wall, peasants in Arkhangel'sk Province would set all of its edges on fire at once; the shadows the flames cast against the wall as the paper assumed different shapes were believed to presage events in the following year.[43] Coal from the hearth fire was also used in New Year's Eve fortune-telling in some areas.[44] Through fortune-telling, magical fire made its way into the fabric of daily life as an agent for reaching into the unknown and extracting some sign of what it might hold. Through yet another ritualized experience, fire touched rural existence and gained a firmer hold on the imagination of people who wielded it literally and figuratively against the darkness.

Mircea Eliade's work on the magic of the blacksmith as an alchemist suggests the need to search for reports of this figure's role in the Russian village. As a "master of fire," the blacksmith transformed matter and did so by handling both the flames of transformation and the transforming matter in his hands. This granted him "magico-religious power which could modify the world and which, consequently, did not belong to this world."[45] In 1906, as part of her research project on the veneration of fire in Russia, Vera Kharuzina issued a special request for information on blacksmiths and referred to A. S. Ermolov's report that in Tambov Province, it was believed that lightning did not strike the blacksmith's house. Kharuzina's conjecture was that peasants believed this because of the smith's "close relationship with fire."[46] Ermolov, in turn, was no doubt drawing on the report of A. Zvonkov, who had explained in 1889 that the blacksmith did hold a special position in the Elatomsk District of Tambov Province. His description read as follows:

The blacksmith, standing closer than anyone else to the element of fire, figures in legends as a man who is hateful and invulnerable to the evil spirit. According to one story, he refused to forge a weapon for the devil to use in his battle with God. The devil has countless powers, but he cannot forge, so he turned to the smith; the smith refused and God vowed to the devils never to destroy the soul of the blacksmith. According to other versions, the blacksmith made Ilya's [Elijah's] lightning bolts, and the prophet rewarded him with the same power. It is a sign that lightning and swallows never ignite the smithy. The owl, as "the devil's bird," does not even dare to sit on blacksmiths' houses.[47]

This description suggests that smiths indeed took on the aura of the fire they mastered. Transformation became the blacksmith's special association, just as women drew much of their reputation as healers from their mastery of fire's curative properties.

The Flames of Orthodox Belief

Fire also made its way into the popular imagination through Orthodox ritual and iconography. Throughout the territory inhabited by East Slavs, the flame of Orthodox belief took the form of sacramental candles or a lampada illuminating the icon in peasant houses.[48] Often, the icon that hung in the corner opposite the stove was an image of the Mother of God of the Burning Bush, who was considered the protector of the home against fire, especially against lightning fires. She was a female image at the center of the male realm of the house.[49] The formula for this icon placed the Virgin Mary with Christ child against a four-pointed medallion in which at least two of the points

Fig. 1.3. *Icon depicting the Mother of God of the Burning Bush.*

were flame red (fig. 1.3). The interplay between the flame of Orthodox belief in the form of icon and candle and the beliefs associated with the stove found expression in a peasant saying popular in Viatka Province: "A stove in the house is the same as an altar in church: bread is baked in it."[50] The mirroring between the Orthodox sphere and the female sphere was repeated in the practice of placing a round loaf of freshly baked bread on a table below the icon in the "beautiful corner," an act that brought the transformed, cleansed product of the women's manipulation of fire into the circle of the Orthodox candle's flame of illumination as a symbol of the Eucharist. This cohabitation of matriarchal fire with Orthodox, patriarchal fire within the peasants' domestic space was emblematic of the broader interpenetration of belief systems and attitudes about fire in their spiritual world.

As in other faiths, so in Orthodox belief fire had various meanings—as the flame of faith, the flame of the Holy Spirit, punitive fire, and purifying fire.[51] Fire was obviously very much a part of the Orthodox ritual and had constant resonance for peasants, who placed candles before their icons at home and during church services. There were also rituals that reflected the association of fire with death and rebirth; it was customary to extinguish old fires before Easter and Christmas and to light new fires as a sign of birth and resurrection.[52] The midnight procession of candles around the church at Easter also employed flame as a symbol of resurrection. The architecture of the church itself could be seen as an expression of the flame of faith in the shape of the cupolas that leapt into the sky. As Eugene N. Trubetskoi wrote, "The Russian dome is like a tongue of flame topped by a cross, pointed toward the heavens."[53] That flame also represented, in his vision, the flame of the Holy Spirit reaching into the congregation of believers below. "It is through the flame that heaven descends to earth, enters the church, and becomes the ultimate completion of the church, the consummation in which the hand of God covers everything earthly, in a benediction of the dark blue dome."[54]

This imagery was also apparent in icons, in which the Holy Spirit was often depicted as a flame between heaven and earth or as tongues of flame alighting on the heads of the Apostles.[55] In early Russian texts, the term "inspired"—ogned'khnovenyi—contained the root for fire (ogon') and thus also represented the Holy Spirit as a flame.[56] Celestial fire made its way into Russian iconography in images of the prophet Elijah in which the lightning bolt dominated the frame as his primary symbol.[57] An alternative depiction of the prophet focused on his fiery ascent into heaven in a cloud of fire (fig. 1.4). The cloud of fire was also prominent in the story of the "bright cloud" that accompanied

Fig. 1.4. *Icon depicting the prophet Elijah ascending to heaven in a cloud of fire.*
Fig. 1.5. *Icon depicting the Transfiguration of Christ.* Both from Onasch 1969.

Christ's appearance in the story of the Transfiguration. In icons depicting this scene, Christ was placed against a medallion with multiple points, several of them red, in a symbolic representation of flame not unlike that of the Mother of God of the Burning Bush (fig. 1.5). Iconography thus incorporated the various meanings of fire through the flames of the Holy Spirit, the flames of conflagration in the burning bush, celestial fire as Elijah's lightning bolts, and transforming fire in the Transfiguration.

Fire as a punitive element was also evident in Russian Orthodoxy. Drawing on Freudenthal's study of the perception of fire in German culture, Johan Goudsblom points out that the linkage of fire with suffering, much less eternal damnation, was not natural for peoples of the north. They received this representation of burning punishment from the Christian fathers of the church, who developed their vision of scourges in a southern, Mediterranean, urban environment where fire posed more threat than protection.[58] By the time Grand Prince Vladimir of Kiev made Christianity the official religion of his realm in the tenth century, there was a rich tradition of fire in images of hell and damnation for the new church to draw upon. Indeed, according to Nestor's Chronicle, one of the first tenets received by Vladimir was that all those who refused baptism into the Christian faith would burn forever, and all sinners could expect an

Fig. 1.6. *Fresco depicting hell, painted in the village of Feropontovo, Vologda Province, sixteenth century.*

eternal fiery torment.[59] Icons repeated this imagery in their depiction of the Last Judgment, or Doomsday. Employing symbols similar to those in the Byzantine tradition, early Russian iconographers placed Satan in a hell of fire. They portrayed heretics, blasphemers, adulterers, and other sinners in various stages of immersion in a sea of flames. The path to hell was itself often a river of fire, known as the *ogneplapol'nik*, while the adjective *ogn'nyi* was a synonym for hellish.[60] There could be little doubt about the punitive possibilities of fire in the Christian tradition as incorporated in the imagery of Russian Orthodoxy (fig. 1.6).

Russian peasants in the late nineteenth century seem to have internalized these visions to some extent. N. A. Ivanitskii reported that peasants of Vologda Province perceived hell as a subterranean pit of fiery agony.[61] Throughout Russia, peasants believed that the phosphorous fires that erupted in swamps, bogs, and graveyards were little bits of hellfire bursting through the surface of the earth.[62] The image of hellfire as just damnation emerged during a dramatic case of arson in Orel District, Orel Province, in 1884 when local peasants apprehended two arsonists who had set their village on fire. Some of them pushed the culprits into the flames. When the local official urged them to pull the arsonists out of the fire, the peasants replied, "Let them burn! They're headed down that road anyway!"[63] And from the southwestern regions of the empire, with their mixed populations of Russians, Ukrainians, and Poles, ethnographers reported a legend about the origin of fire which stated that fire was the invention of the fallen angels in hell who intended to use it to torment human beings. Jesus Christ and the Apostle Peter stole fire from hell, however, and Christ then showed human beings how to use it for their purposes.[64] This legend confirms the tendency of peasants to ascribe God's moral intent to fire while also illustrating their understanding of hell as a place where fire could harm souls.

Equally important in this parable is the conceptualization of fire as a gift stolen from those who intended to cause harm and then granted as the Holy Father's and Son's benediction to those who could put it to good use. Here fire assumes a meaning more logical for a northern people than the conceptualization inherited from the urban Byzantine church fathers. It is an echo of sorts of the fire-making rituals and namings from the northern provinces. That fire drawn from wood, from the forest, and used in making new fire was sacred (*sviashchennyi*), and that living fire was also "wood fire, fire from the forest" (*drevesnyi, lesnoi*), suggests that fire from the forest held special meanings for rural inhabitants. This association derived from two sources. The first was the deforestation and slash-and-burn (swidden) agriculture that accompanied the East Slavs' early colonization and was still practiced in areas of the north and west in the nineteenth century. The second was the conceptualization of the Prophet Elijah, whose lightning bolts traversed the heavens, striking trees in the forest and bringing celestial, holy fire to the earth. In forested Russia, fire was not only warming, healing, sacred, or punitive. It was also fertile.

Fertile and Transforming Fire in Farming Russia

In the mid-1880s in the Cherepovets District of Novgorod Province, forest fires raged ceaselessly during the hot summer months. Everywhere peasants set ablaze the litter left on the forest floor by commercial lumber dealers as they cleared the trees. A local observer explained that peasants set these fires in order to fertilize the abandoned soil with ashes to prepare it for a bountiful harvest the following season.[65] These fires suggest the extent to which peasants of the area continued to draw on fire as a fertilizing agent in the late nineteenth century. In Novgorod and other areas in the north that were still heavily wooded, the forest's legacy in agricultural practices was at the heart of understanding fire in the Russian village as late as the beginning of the twentieth century.[66]

Well into the seventeenth century, farming in Muscovy rested primarily on deforestation—on the colonization of forest lands through the slash-and-burn method as peasants moved through the deep woods until ax met ax.[67] To the south and west, as Zack Deal has concluded, settlers moving east into Khar'kov Province in the seventeenth and eighteenth centuries transformed that area from one of "impenetrable forests" to one in which "the forested lands were confined to the elevated banks of rivers and other areas inconvenient to plow," as "agriculturalists were rolling back the steppe frontier with fire."[68] As far back as the writing of the first law code in Kievan Rus', one term for a head of household or prosperous man, *ognishchanin*, began with a root denoting his mastery and possession of fire.[69] Fire had joined the ax in serving peasant colonizers of the forest as they cleared their way for open pasture and open sky. Fire became both an essential agricultural tool and a weapon against the darkness, the damp, and the cold.

In the nineteenth century, peasants continued to use fire in their agricultural practices in a number of ways. Reporting from Smolensk Province, A. N. Engel'gardt described local peasants' use of deforestation as a means of establishing new fields, as well as his own efforts to incorporate what he called forest-grain farming in developing more productive systems of field rotation.[70] Deforestation was an effective method not only because it created open fields but also, and more importantly, because when peasants burned the remaining stumps and forest litter that they did not take for firewood, ash enriched the soil. Maksimov offered a description of this practice based on numerous eyewitness accounts at the end of the century. He explained that in the first year following the burning of the cleared land, it could produce a harvest as rich as forty to sixty seeds for each seed planted, a nearly miraculous yield for the selfish soil of European Russia.[71] Engel'gardt reported similar results from Smolensk. This agricultural practice was especially widespread in the forested north in provinces such as Olonets, Vologda, Perm, and eastern sections of Novgorod.[72] This form of fertilization thus created a complex of fire, trees, and striking fertility that ensured that peasants of the late nineteenth century would hold fire in awe.

In the steppe, too, fire served as a source of fertilization. Writing in the 1840s, J. G. Kohl declared that "the burning of the steppe is the only kind of manuring to which it is ever subjected."[73] In Orenburg Province in the southeastern steppe, the use of broadcast fire was so pervasive that the government passed a law in 1850 establishing May 1 as the last day in the year when burning could take place.[74] In forest and steppe regions alike, fire served historically to ensure survival and to enhance the productivity of the soil for those who farmed it. The male peasants who set these fertilizing fires were seasoned fire managers. They developed systems and traditions for felling trees, clearing stumps, leaving the soil to dry, and then burning the litter to create fertilizing ashes. They learned how to schedule these burnings with an eye to wind and rain patterns to prevent fertilizing fire from becoming voracious conflagration. They set this force loose, perhaps every farming season, and in doing so developed an intimacy with fire's properties in its broadcast form that mirrored their wives' intimacy with contained fire in the family stove.

Peasants used fire not only in preparing the soil for planting but also for processing the grain after it was harvested. In the drying barn, peasants smoked grain before storing it in order to prevent rot. There, men built and tended fires in small stoves to provide heat and smoke in a regulated and controlled way. Fire as a furnace in this wooden structure enabled the peasants to provide a store of food for the period between harvests. Fire was also essential in steaming and drying flax and hemp when peasants prepared them for processing into cloth and rope. Drying took place either in the open air or inside the *izba*, next to the stove or sometimes even on it.

Early Russian agricultural practices, developed in the forest and steppe, thus established close associations for the peasantry between fire and fertility. When those practices included planting, sowing, and processing, fire continued to be an essential tool for survival, a tool peasants manipulated in their symbiotic relationship with this powerful force of nature. These practices were tried and true elements in rural Russians', Belorussians', and Ukrainians' metis. Such uses of fire made their way, in turn, into Christian beliefs held by the peasantry in their vision of the Prophet Elijah and in their celebration of the holiday of St. John the Baptist, or Ivan Kupalo.

Elijah's Fire

During the summer season of agricultural field work in the late nineteenth century, when peasants in the field heard approaching thunder, they dropped their farming implements and ran back to the village as fast as they could to close the windows, doors, and chimneys on their *izbas*. In doing so, they were trying to deny the devil access to their houses, which he might choose as a hiding place from the prophet Elijah. They explained that Elijah was chasing the devil and throwing lightning bolts at him, creating rolling thunder as his chariot careened through the sky. If the devil were able to hide in the house, then Elijah's lightning might ignite the home as it struck the devil.[75]

At first glance, it is not obvious why rural beliefs and rituals such as these associated with lightning and the prophet Elijah should be part of a discussion of the relationship between peasants and fire in imperial Russia. Yet for nineteenth-century ethnographers, folklorists, and respondents to ethnographic surveys, their inclusion was nearly universal. It seems that they recorded these rituals with two issues in mind. The first was that lightning could and did lead to conflagrations. The second was their view that beliefs about the prophet Elijah were Christianized versions of beliefs associated with the ancient Slavic god Perun. They were interested in demonstrating both the evolutionary aspect of those beliefs and the way in which they testified to the persistence of *dvoeverie* (dual belief in pagan and Christian figures) in rural culture. The peasants' reaction to lightning fires, furthermore, provided the opportunity to study their responses to fires utterly beyond their control.

These beliefs and rituals offer evidence, moreover, on the connections peasants made between fire, trees, fertility, and morality. What seems clear in their conceptualization of fire and lightning is that they placed the two in frames either of the cosmic contest between good and evil or of the complex of fertility, forest (trees), and fields. Lightning fires were not the products of their hands; they did not control this power. But they personified it in the prophet Elijah as an agent of God, assigned to him various features that contributed to their well-being, venerated him for the good he could bring, and sought to protect themselves against the chance that Elijah might "misfire" and cause them harm. Elijah, in the rural belief system, was often an agent who tipped the odds in the moral or agricultural favor of peasants.

The figure of the prophet Elijah in folk belief served the function of bringing holy fire, God's fire, to earth. As holy fire, lightning was a force against evil. It was also fertile, for peasants believed that the first lightning and thunder of the spring penetrated the earth, woke her up, and made her fertile.[76] Even such an apparently obvious threat as lightning and the fires associated with it, then, had some positive connotations for the peasantry. Fire in this form was again an element that the peasants wanted to have on their side in their struggle to subsist. It was, by the nineteenth century, a Christianized element that brought God's power to their milieu.

Elijah and his lightning elicited the respect appropriate to a deity. Numerous beliefs and rituals surrounded lightning fires that demonstrated its powers of purification and sanctity for rural inhabitants. In some areas, when a building caught fire because of lightning, it was forbidden to try to extinguish it, for that would have been an act against God. In the Nikolaev District of Samara Province, one observer reported that peasants resettled there from Orel Province did not release livestock from a barn set afire by lightning for the same reason.[77] Similarly, peasants in some areas considered those killed by lightning to be holy. Because the prophet Elijah used his lightning bolts to chase out the "unclean spirit," anything struck by this saintly lightning had been cleansed of the devil and made holy. Those who died in this way were guaranteed eternal life.[78] A. D. Neustupov reported, however, that a woman struck by lightning in Kadnikov District, Vologda Province, was considered to be a sinner, whereas a man thus struck was considered righteous.[79] There were numerous reports that peasants believed that if one did try to extinguish a fire caused by lightning, one could use only milk, water mixed with rye, or eggs.[80] Each of these items, in turn, carried connotations of purity or sanctity. By casting sacred or pure objects into the fire, people may have been trying to reestablish a balance of forces between good and evil.[81] At least one report suggested that peasants also believed that lightning possessed healing properties. In Tambov Province, when a child was born with some kind of deformity, the mother might rush with the newborn into the forest to find a tree struck by lightning and then place the child in the hollow of the tree to be healed.[82]

Clearly, peasants also recognized lightning's hazards, and they strove to prevent Elijah from striking their homes and fields. Elijah's Day came on July 20, the height of summer, the hottest and driest season, when the risk of conflagration from lightning was at its peak.[83] Lightning accounted for a relatively small percentage of village fires,[84] but peasants were careful all the same to mollify Elijah by not working on his day. In some areas, July was perennially a month of lightning fires, as in Novgorod Province in the 1880s and 1890s.[85] On the Friday preceding Elijah's Day, peasants fasted as insurance against his wrath, which could come in the form of thunder, lightning, hail, and famine.[86] During thunderstorms, peasants in Orel Province stood silently to show respect until the storm had passed, preventing even children from crying out. Only after each lightning bolt did the adults speak, imploring the prophet, "Sow, Sow!! Sow Lord Savovich! Oh, Prophet Elijah, saint of God, burn us sinners!"[87] An alternative explanation of lightning fires recorded in the Zaraisk District of Riazan Province took harm out of Elijah's hands. There, a correspondent explained, peasants considered lightning to be the devil's weapon as he struck back against Elijah. In this version, it was the devil who set fire to houses and churches and killed humans and other living creatures.[88]

Celestial fire in the form of lightning thus continued to be a living and awesome force for the nineteenth-century peasantry. For them, it was a projection of a superhuman power that transversed the boundary between heaven and earth and did so in the context of a mortal contest between good and evil. The complex of beliefs and rituals associated with the prophet Elijah suggests that conceptualization of fire in this form was part of both a Christian worldview and one in which fertility was central in a subsistence agricultural economy. The same can be said of the rituals associated with the festival of Ivan Kupalo, or St. John the Baptist.

Ivan Kupalo, or St. John the Baptist

In 1872 in the Kupian District, Khar'kov Province, several young people were brought before the local cantonal court for having set bonfires near the villages on June 23 of the previous year and for having jumped through them. The young people defended themselves by saying that "this has been done forever and is called Kupalo." Even so, they were all placed in jail for twenty-four hours for having violated regulations regarding open fires near the village.[89] This confrontation within the peasant community, provoked by the complaint of a local constable that was then enforced by the peasant judges, suggests the tensions that were developing in the countryside over definitions of fire. What the young people legitimately described as a traditional ritual was suddenly susceptible to definition as a crime. The fires that were part of the Ivan Kupalo festival at the summer solstice were now to be considered not a guarantee of fertility but a risk of conflagration. That the young people were so laconic in their defense, however, points further to the fact that for them, this agrarian festival retained its traditional meanings well into the post-Emancipation era.

Agrarian festivals were a time of celebration and merrymaking. When fire was an element in such festivals, it was both agent and object of that celebration. This natural force, which educated Russians were trying to teach peasants to despise and fear, gained positive and happy associations through festivals of the agrarian cycle. Although fire was a prominent feature of several rural festivals, it was most striking in the festival celebrating St. John the Baptist.

At the summer solstice, the celebration of Ivan Kupalo, or the day of St. John the Baptist, bonfires were the distinctive feature of the festival. This holiday was most prevalent in Ukraine and Belorussia but was still practiced in some areas of central Russia in the nineteenth century and appeared across Europe in very similar forms. The nineteenth-century folklorist A. N. Afanas'ev pointed out that the bonfires were sometimes built directly in the forest, which suggested the association with deforestation in farming.[90] The twentieth-century folklorist V. Ia. Propp, drawing on numerous local reports, located the festival not in the forest but in or near the fields. One report from Minsk Province described the ritual of building an artificial grove of trees around the bonfire by sticking green trees into the ground in a circle around it.[91] Creating bonfires of burning trees, either placed in the forest or surrounded by green trees, was, as Propp recognized, a fertility rite. It reflected the common association of fire with sexuality and fertility. For peasants of imperial Russia, that fertility was the very product of the combination of field, fire, and forest.

Peasants did not simply build Kupalo fires. They also jumped through them. Again, this element in the festival suggests an association with fertility, especially in areas where young people jumped over the fires as couples or where young women leapt over the fires. The psychological association of fire with sexuality seems particularly evident in this ritual. First, the Kupalo bonfires were always new fire, that is, fire created through the friction of rubbing logs or sticks against each other in a symbolic repetition of the sexual act of penetration and friction.[92] Second, the licking flames can also be seen as phallic. Third, the tree itself is a phallic symbol, which one recognizes in rituals of girls dancing around maypoles in Europe or the birch trees of Rusal'naia Week in Russia.[93] The Kupalo fires, made from friction and flaming up between the legs of young people who leapt over them, had the power to impart fertility in a symbolic act of insemination.[94]

Sir James Frazer viewed fire festivals such as that of Ivan Kupalo as being linked with both sun worship and the search for protection against natural calamities such as epidemics, famine, drought, lightning, and hail. The solar theory derives from the coincidence of the festivals with the solstices; the purification theory derives from the practice of leaping over fires or leading animals through the fires as a prophylactic against disease.[95] Though all of these elements undoubtedly made their way into the meaning of the Kupalo festivals, I believe their primary meaning was linked to fertility and that the forms of the festivals were linked to agricultural practices. As Stephen J. Pyne has concluded about fire festivals in Europe, "there can be little doubt that what was enacted ritualistically in the fire festivals was, in the distant past, actually practiced, not merely as a tool of exorcism but also as an instrument of primitive land management and animal husbandry."[96] In the case of the Russian peasantry and the Kupalo festival, fire was an instrument not of primitive land management in the distant past but of land management in the present and recent past.

From our perspective in the twentieth century, we cannot know with any certainty what was primary in the understanding of peasants who took part in the Kupalo festival. It was formally a celebration of St. John the Baptist and thus an element of the Orthodox calendar as much as of the agrarian calendar. In areas where the Ivan Kupalo effigy was not burned but drowned or set afloat in a river or pond, the connection with the baptizing apostle seems most important. In areas where the effigy was burned in bonfires, fertility seems to take first place. For purposes of understanding the meanings fire held for the peasantry of European Russia, however, the fiery elements of the Kupalo festival point again to the peasants' manipulation and celebration of fire as an element that enabled them to better their odds in subsistence farming. In that form, fire was fertile and welcome.

New Habits, New Fires in the Fin-de-Siècle Village

Fire was also welcome as a sign of prosperity in new consumer goods at the end of the century. Four new fire-connected artifacts of Russia's emerging industrial, commercial culture made their way into prosperous peasant households toward the end of the century. Kerosene lamps, samovars used in tea-drinking, cigarettes, and phosphorous matches began to be signs of relative wealth within the village community in the 1880s.[97] Each of these brought new hazards as well as benefits. Kerosene lamps gave peasants brighter illumination than smoldering torches or candles, but they could become explosive fire if handled improperly. Cigarettes joined traditional pipes to expand peasants' smoking pleasure, but their trailing ashes and discarded butts were risky in the straw-filled environment of rural Russia. Samovars joined the stove as a domestic technology, but their warming flames could bring disaster if they tipped over onto the izba's wooden surfaces. Phosphorous matches replaced tinder boxes but became an irresistible temptation for unsupervised child's play. This Janus-like character of consumer innovation in the countryside was recognized by outside observers. For some, consumer innovation was identified as more evidence of the loosening of strictures on peasants in the post-Emancipation era.[98] For others, it illustrated the hazards of modern consumption in peasant hands. The report of one A. I. Satin, made to a Committee on the Needs of Agriculture in Grodno Province in 1902, captured this sentiment: "With the introduction into the peasant milieu of the latest fruits of contemporary civilization, which are rather flammable . . . the flammability of the village increases in a terrible progression. Matches, a samovar, cigarettes, kerosene—these have all become necessities in the village now; these all cause many misfortunes for the village."[99]

There can be little doubt that most peasants saw in these items not risk but status. The household with a bubbling samovar and a glowing kerosene lamp set the standard of fashion and wealth in a village community. For the peasant woman, a match made her morning tasks that much easier; for the peasant man, it was simply a treat to be able to open a box of matches to light up a cigarette anywhere in the village, rather than have to find a source of fire. Fire was assuming new forms, each of which eased daily existence and added enjoyment to village life. As some of the first modern items to make their way into Russia's villages, these quickly entered the peasants' fire repertoire.

Conclusion: Fire Worshipers or Fire Practitioners?

The fire culture of the villages of the Russian Empire was rich in both practical uses and meanings. From the perspective of the comparative history of fire and civilization, this fire culture was like others at a preindustrial stage of development.[100] For peasants living in European Russia, fire was still the primary source of energy for heating, illumination, and cooking. They also used it expertly in their preparation of fields for planting and in processing those fields' products. They relied on fire for a variety of home remedies for disease and as a prophylactic against epidemics. In contrast to images that dominated debates over the "fire question" among educated Russians and that have shaped our own images of the relationship between peasants and fire in imperial Russia, peasants were not only victims of fire but also its masters and mistresses. They were talented fire practitioners. In the main, their mastery of fire seems ahistorical at the end of the nineteenth century; most of their technologies and beliefs were identical to or resonant of those of a century earlier. As it was for most of their forebears, fire was part of the daily round of chores as well as part of the larger cycle of birth, life, and death. Fire's new uses as an aspect of consumer society point to incremental changes that were making their way into the peasants' relationship with fire.

From the peasants' perspective, fire continued to hold its favored position in their symbiotic relationship with it and in their manipulation of its energy to maintain their equilibrium in their perennial dance with the geographic, topographic, and climatic elements that surrounded them. Their multiple uses of fire conformed to Jean-Pierre Bayard's description: "Fire is fertile. Well-managed and mastered, it assures reproduction, provides new energy; it rejuvenates, it generates; in its flames the Phoenix is reborn. This Fire which protects—against danger, against evil—is also a source of purification; it destroys all that is bad, inauspicious."[101] Peasants did manage their fire well much of the time, employing it as a weapon in their continuous struggle to beat the odds against Russia's obstinate climate and soil, against the absence of scientific medical care, and even against those who would disrupt the social balance of the village by either profiting excessively or destroying the subsistence of others.

To late-nineteenth-century educated observers, the peasants' continued veneration of fire seemed not only nonsensical but even pernicious. Presented as evidence of the peasants' position in the residual stages of ancestor worship en route to full-blown formal religion and ultimately to a scientific understanding of natural phenomena, rituals before the stove, in honor of the prophet Elijah, or in celebrations of fertility at the summer solstice all bespoke the backwardness of Russia's peasants. These people saw peasants not as fire practitioners but as fire worshipers, with all the associations with primitive peoples that this phrase implied.

The many associations between peasant women and fire are especially important in this light and in the story that follows. Peasant women had become the very embodiment of the countryside's backwardness in public discussion of "the peasant question" after the Emancipation, and their influence in the village had become "the power of darkness" of Tolstoy's construction.[102] As dark images of emancipated peasants came to replace the avuncular images of enslaved serfs that had spurred sympathetic calls for peasant liberation, peasant women were often at the center of society's disillusionment. It was they whose individualistic greed, ignorant superstitions, and female conspiracies undermined the idyllic village of educated society's imaginings. When peasants became the objects of statistical and sociological studies, peasant women emerged as the agents of the patriarchal family's and community's dissolution. When the question was the peasants' relationship to fire, women quickly took center stage again. In this context, their actual role as fire's mistresses inside the home ensured the prominence of women's position in portraits of peasants as fire worshipers whose primary "pagan" altar was the hearth stove. Magical healing and divination practiced by women only added to the construction of women as irrational fire practitioners. When the focus shifted away from rituals to daily practices, women again assumed negative roles as careless, thoughtless actors whose ignorance made their access to fire dangerous for all of Russia.

When educated Russians suddenly caught sight of village fire in the early 1860s, the conflation of loosened peasants and fire on the loose seized their imagination. Fire's benevolent uses and meanings escaped their vision; instead, the same fire that was so central to rural survival and success took on menacing shapes and meanings. For city dwellers whose own contact with fire was almost exclusively in its contained forms, fire lost the full force of its meaning as Bachelard's "gentleness" and "cookery." Stephen J. Pyne concluded for all Europeans' experience that "as urbanites' personal experience of fire waned, so did their tolerance of its consequences. They knew it only in its domiciled forms, as the servile hearth or the anarchic conflagration. As technology increasingly divorced them further from the former, they experienced only the latter. They saw fire as social horror."[103] In the setting of imperial Russia in the 1860s, not only technology and their limited experience with fire shaped nonpeasants' vision of fire and the peasantry. Equally important were new legal and social realities that made fire a harbinger of apocalypse.

2

Fire as Apocalypse or Pathology: Peasants as Victims or Vectors of Fire

FOR, BEHOLD, THE LORD WILL COME WITH FIRE, AND WITH HIS CHARIOTS
LIKE A WHIRLWIND, TO RENDER HIS ANGER WITH FURY, AND HIS REBUKE
WITH FLAMES OF FIRE.

—Isaiah 66:15

THE FIRST ANGEL SOUNDED, AND THERE FOLLOWED HAIL AND FIRE MIN-
GLED WITH BLOOD, AND THEY WERE CAST UPON THE EARTH: AND THE
THIRD PART OF TREES WAS BURNT UP, AND ALL GREEN GRASS WAS BURNT UP.

—Revelation 8:7

As peasant women throughout European Russia were firing up their stoves on the morning of May 16, 1862, events in the imperial capital, St. Petersburg, began to assume a form that would bring those routines and peasants' fire practices in general under increasingly hostile and threatening scrutiny by Russia's educated society. For on that day, the first of a series of fires broke out in the city. Within two weeks, both St. Petersburg's physical cityscape and educated Russians' mental landscape of their country would be transformed. Fires in the city would draw fire in the countryside into the national imagination within the frame of this disaster, introducing rural fire as a newly discovered, hazardous aspect of post-Emancipation Russia.

Like other elements of rural life that seized the attention and imagination of educated society, village conflagrations were not new phenomena of the post-Emancipation era.[1] But the attention they received was. They captured the public's and the government's attention, especially after the St. Petersburg fires. Before 1862, as the contemporary D. M. Pogodin explained, the general attitude was that "summer has come; the fires have begun,—and here, in Rus', this is all as if in the very order of things. Not only fires, but arson also in Russia, are an ordinary affair."[2] In his analysis of rural fire and arson in Russia, Pogodin pointed out that this resigned attitude toward fires gave way with the outbreak of the St. Petersburg fires. Out of the ashes of these mysterious fires, generally believed to have been the work of arsonists, there grew widespread fear of fire and arson. Pogodin explained: "The savage audacity of the arson fires and a disturbed feeling of some kind of ubiquitous danger now trouble and frighten everyone."[3]

Like the fires of the long hot summer of 1967 in cities across the United States, the St. Petersburg fires of 1862 came to symbolize for privileged Russians a deep threat to the existing order of things, following as they did the sea change of the Emancipation and coinciding with student unrest in university cities and growing problems in Poland. Pogodin's use of the phrase "savage audacity" points to their disruptive effect. Both for those who witnessed the St. Petersburg fires and for those who simply shared the experience by reading about them, fire and arson assumed the character of a real and present danger to personal safety, property, and the fate of the Russian Empire.[4]

The Petersburg fires lasted for two weeks, breaking out in rapid succession in different quarters of the city. The fires that broke out on May 16, 17, 19, and 20 were contained and destroyed only uninhabited outbuildings. But the fire that erupted on May 21 opened a week of large blazes driven by high winds that moved so rapidly that they consumed wooden buildings at the rate of six large establishments with outbuildings every thirty minutes.[5] The city's firefighting resources proved incapable of handling most of the blazes. The *St. Petersburg News* and the *Moscow News* called the fires terrifying (*strashnyi*). Indeed, words seemed to fail writers on the fire crisis throughout the period; *strashnyi* or *strakh* (terror) often appeared five times or more in a one-paragraph report.

The St. Petersburg fires terrified because of their relentless reach into all levels of St. Petersburg society. As the May 24 edition of the *St. Petersburg News* exclaimed, both rich and poor suffered. Day in and day out the fires accelerated, each day seeming to be the climax, only to be exceeded in terror by another. Thus, May 23 seemed to be the worst, with five huge fires breaking out across the city, but five days later an entire district of the city burned to the ground, leaving only "heaps of metal and skeletons of houses."[6] Calls for charitable contributions stated that thousands of families had lost their homes. Even the minister of the interior felt the brush of the fires as wind driven by the heat of their blaze blew through his building, taking with it numerous important documents and papers.[7]

Suddenly, fires became newsworthy. Both the *St. Petersburg News* and the *Moscow News* published reports in May and June 1862 about fires in other regions of the empire that had happened months earlier. Such interest in fire would characterize public opinion for the rest of the nineteenth century, and newspapers offered the most immediate information. Newspapers were key contributors to the emergence of a "fire question" and a national fire narrative, for they were the first to bring fire stories and statistics to an expanding reading public.[8] They kept fires before the eyes of readers often far removed from the actual scene, creating a sense of constant menace to the national well-being and reputation. As Louise McReynolds concluded in her study of the capital newspapers: "Communications technology overcame geographical obstacles and made it possible for the press to foster an identity based on territory rather than ethnicity."[9]

Provincial and capital newspapers published regular columns under the heading "Fires," ensuring that fire became a defining feature of Russia as its scattered population came to envision it through the shared experience of reading. Dostoevsky captured fire's grasp on the public attention in *Crime and Punishment*. When Raskolnikov hungrily tries to find news of his crime in the St. Petersburg newspapers, he finds instead that "a merchant is burned out because of drunkenness—a fire on Peskie—a fire on Petersburg Street—another fire on Petersburg Street—another fire on Petersburg Street."[10]

Fire reports had become so much a part of the national idiom that Chekhov could refer to them as a standard form by 1886. In response to a letter to D. V. Grigorovich, who had praised some of Chekhov's short stories, the latter demurred: "Until now, I have treated my work extremely flippantly, carelessly, with no purpose in mind. . . . I have written my stories the way reporters write their fire reports: mechanically, half-consciously, without any concern for the reader or themselves."[11] The foreign press seems to have picked up this kind of reporting as well. As early as 1865, a Russian living abroad felt compelled to write a letter to the editor of the Russian newspaper *The Voice* to respond to the impression he had gained from the German press that the Russian countryside was in the grip of incessant fires. His published letter was reprinted by the official provincial newspaper of Smolensk.[12] Even beyond Russia's political borders, fire narratives were becoming prominent in the post-Emancipation national identity.

The resulting fire narratives displayed a pervasive sense of disequilibrium among the educated elements in Russian culture, who were conscious of the economic and social upheavals wrought by the emancipation of the serfs in 1861 and frightened by probable further consequences of those upheavals. The St.

Petersburg fires confirmed their fears and gave them a form on which to focus that consumed property with an "audacity" that failed to respect the boundaries of class and privilege that had so recently defined Russia.

The image of arson fires in the capital quickly yielded to that of accidental rural fires as a threat to social and economic well-being. Dostoevsky remarked on this shift at its very inception in his St. Petersburg journal, *Vremia*:

> Fires, having started in St. Petersburg, then moved to various corners of Russia; how many there were in all, we, we must apologize, did not count; maybe there really weren't any more or perhaps only a few more than in previous years, but—when fear strikes, one's eyes widen: now every reported fire makes a stronger impression, and for that reason the number of fires seems very large.[13]

He would incorporate this phenomenon into *Devils* ten years later: in part three, the fire at the end of Lembke's ball strikes fear into the hearts of the revelers. Dostoevsky's narrator explicitly notes the nature of newspaper coverage: "Still, the capital newspapers exaggerated our calamity."[14] The narrator's explanation for why he doesn't linger over the description of the fire scene also indicates how ubiquitous fire reports had become by the early 1870s. "I won't begin to describe the scene of the fire: who in Russia does not know what it is like?"[15]

Dostoevsky's suburban arson fire in *Devils* is not typical of the majority of fire narratives, which were exclusively peasant affairs, as the fires themselves were considered to be.[16] Although the St. Petersburg arson fires had opened the drama of fire in post-Emancipation Russia, neither the city nor arson figured as prominently in the public discourse as did accidental village fires. The shift to the countryside and to accidental conflagrations was not only geographical and topical. It also reflected a definition of Russia that placed peasants and the countryside at the center of Russia's national identity.

Within the first decade after the emancipation of the serfs in Russia in 1861, the conviction was gathering in the Russian press that the apocalypse was upon them. A whirlwind of fire had indeed mixed with blood, and evidence was mounting that trees, homes, and people were perishing as the Lord's vengeance swept across the countryside in continuous waves of all-consuming flame. The most compelling and consistent evidence of fire's overwhelming presence in European Russia appeared in the form of numbers—page after page of fire data published by the Central Statistical Committee of the Ministry of the Interior showing an exponential increase in the number of reported fires. Provincial and capital newspapers also printed these statistics in their regular "Fires" columns. The public thus could read that the number of reported fires grew from 58,262 in the period 1860–1864 to 205,598 in 1880–1884. By 1900–1904, the five-year total had risen to 315,227. Readers also learned how many structures burned and what the total reported losses were. By 1904, the cumulative losses attributed to fires in European Russia had reached almost three billion rubles.[17]

These published numbers spawned a public atmosphere of crisis surrounding fire in Russia. Local police officials, *zemstvo* (local public works council) activists, members of the landed gentry, newspaper reporters, amateur and professional ethnographers, ministers of the interior and their deputies, volunteer firefighters, and Russia's most famous authors engaged in the search for data on rural fires and an explanation of their meaning. They demonstrated their fascination with these conflagrations in a multitude of publications ranging from eyewitness newspaper accounts to governmental reports and literary representations. Together they constructed a national narrative of fire in the countryside, a narrative that opened in 1862 and persisted until the outbreak of the most famous of Russia's rural conflagrations, the arson fires of 1905–1907.

The phrase "national narrative" captures the extent to which writings about rural fires both became part of the search for Russia's national identity in the post-Emancipation era and posited alternative plot lines in defining Russia's present and future. Within the discourse about rural fires, divergent representations and expectations emerged. As they took shape, they reflected a contest between apocalyptic sensibilities and expectations, on one hand, and progressivist, ultimately Enlightenment-informed sensibilities and expectations on the other. Throughout the four decades between the Emancipation and popular revolt, apocalyptic reactions to the fire crisis were evident but fading. By the turn of the century, an alternative interpretation had displaced them. Especially by the 1890s, authors and actors responding to the fire crisis were fundamentally historical, anthropological, and technical in their search for what they considered an "epidemic of fire." Self-conscious scientism gradually came to replace apocalyptic visions. The conviction grew that official and civic energies could combine in rational fire prevention and firefighting programs to head off apocalyptic outcomes. "High modernism," in James Scott's sense of the phrase, surfaced in the resulting campaign against fire.

This shift toward materialist explanations for fire's presence in the countryside and toward activist prescriptions for doing battle with it contradicted the spiritual or supernatural conceptualization of fire as an elemental force whose presence was a visitation against which it was futile to struggle. Materialist and activist approaches to fire challenged the "overwhelming sensation of apocalypse and Endzeit" that David Bethea has so convincingly identified as a prominent feature of late imperial Russian culture.[18] Much of Bethea's analysis of Russian fiction applies to writings about fire. First, there is his basic point that the Apocalypse of John in Revelation long informed Russian cultural structures, with the result that "an apocalyptic 'set' or predisposition to read current historical crisis through the prism of the Johannine structures and figures" was evident not only in fiction but also in other writings of the Russian intelligentsia, with Berdiaev's *The Russian Idea* the most obvious example.[19]

Equally important is Bethea's discussion of the distinction between apocalyptic narratives and secular visions of history, contrasting "the idea of history as divinely inspired human activity with an imminent conclusion from without" and "the idea of history as secular progress with an immanent conclusion here on earth."[20] In Russia's national fire narrative, progressive activists came to reject the notion of divine agency themselves and hoped to eradicate it from peasants' perceptions of fire. In common with enlightened would-be reformers from Peter the Great forward, they embraced "notions of progress" that promoted "the spatial image of futurity, the *put'* (path) that was to become the root metaphor for directing and marshalling the 'historical present.'"[21]

Scientific, materialist explanations for fire within a worldview informed primarily by the notion of a future path would have two profound implications for the understanding of fire in village culture. First, rural conflagrations came not to presage a national apocalypse but to embody a national epidemic, with rural fire the pathology. As such, rural fires joined suicide as an "epidemic" phenomenon characterizing Russian culture thrown off balance, out of order, by the Emancipation and its social and economic transformations.[22] Second, the insistence on a "path" imposed linear concepts of time and the future on the peasants' cyclical fire practices. When the goal became progress, fire as an agent of the peasants' equilibrium fell outside the range of modernist comprehension. Whether as apocalypse or epidemic, however, when rural fire entered the national imagination in 1862, knowing fire came to mean knowing disaster.

Fire Mingled with Blood

As the narrative turned to village fires, the metaphor most readily at hand was that of an apocalyptic visitation upon Holy Rus'. Just as an apocalyptic worldview rested on the ahistorical agency of a nonearthly being who would determine the ending, so the concept of Holy Rus' as it had taken shape in the sixteenth century stood outside of time and was impervious to earthly agency. As Bethea explained: "'Holy Russia', though born of a specific time and place, became something nonhistorical, transcendental."[23] The national fire narrative lent itself to this metaphor because fire's elemental force was so overwhelming in Russia's villages and because eyewitness accounts so often recorded the disabling effect it had on its victims. S. V. Maksimov captured this image most eloquently late in the period when he referred to Russia as "like an inextinguishable bonfire" and as "an unfortunate land," laid waste by a "whirlwind of fire."[24] Maksimov based his images in part upon local newspaper reports, which offered the specific examples needed to generate the broader impression. A report on an August 15 fire in the village of Lyskov that appeared in the September 1878 issue of the *Smolensk Herald* typified this representation: "It was terrible to look at this scene of all-consuming flame. Five or six minutes after the first house began to burn, eight homesteads were already enveloped by flames. . . . A terrible wind spread burning shards a great distance and nothing could contain the horrible blaze. . . . The inhabitants, who were dumbstruck with terror, didn't even try to battle it."[25]

Fire often joined with wind, as in this case; when there were human victims, the image of Isaiah's prophecy of a whirlwind of fire joined the apostle's revelation that fire would mingle with blood. The repetition of the words "terrible" (*strashno*) and "terror" (*strakh*) created a veritable doomsday scene in which the last judgment (*strashnyi sud*) had visited the land.

By the 1870s, readers in Russia had access to a steady stream of gruesome and heartrending vignettes from the village. For "boulevard newspapers," which often used language that "evoked an immediate sensation of shock or titillation" in the style of the *St. Petersburg Sheet*, fire was a most opportune event.[26] In vivid descriptions of the deceased, fire narratives offered forensic parallels to those included in suicide reports.[27] The July 25, 1882, number of the *Novgorod Sheet* demonstrated the possibilities fires held for sensational reporting, which could also tap into familiar Biblical prophecies. This newspaper's readers found the following when they turned to page seven:

> "Borovichi"
> A day or two ago, 12 versts from town, a fire destroyed the village of Antonikha. . . . The fire, which began in the farthest izba, quickly consumed the entire village, because the wind was blowing toward the other end of it . . . .
> On the side near the field there lay a naked, burned up old woman with bared teeth. During the fire, she managed to get the child out, but

then, wanting to rescue her money, she ran into the cellar, from which she had trouble scrambling out. All her clothes burned off, and her arms and legs were burned so badly that it was terrible to look at her; her face was completely burned away, and on her head a tuft of hair stood up; she was moaning and mumbling something, asking if her money box were there—it was amazing that she was still alive! . . .

A three-year-old boy burned alive, because he couldn't unlatch the gate; they found his skeleton with its skull cracked by the heat, from which his brain had burst. The corpse of one old woman, pulled out of the same house where the boy, her grandson, burned, looked like a formless mass of scorched meat, on which it was no longer possible to distinguish either head or legs or arms.[28]

In this account, the reporter implies that the first old woman might have invited her fate by rushing into the burning house to retrieve her money box. The same vignette appeared in a report to the Tenishev Ethnographic Bureau from Novgorod seventeen years later, with the respondent recording dismay over the fact that an old woman had rushed back into her burning house to save seven rubles she had hidden behind the stove.[29] Dostoevsky also placed a foolish eighty-year-old woman in the fire scene in *Devils*. The narrator explains: "She had gone back to the burning house herself, while it was still possible, with the insane idea of dragging out her feather-bed."[30]

In these local doomsday scenes, greedy women were consistent with the negative images of peasant women then prevalent in journalism and belles lettres.[31] They became part of the broader emerging consensus that peasant women in general were the most benighted members of village society, whose ignorance and emotionalism invited the ills that plagued rural life, including fire.

Not only sensational newspapers employed the graphic imagery found in the report from Borovichi. M. E. Saltykov-Shchedrin's fable "A Village Fire" mimicked reporting in the provincial press. As a former vice-governor in Tver and Riazan Provinces, Saltykov-Shchedrin had undoubtedly read many fire reports and may have visited burned-out villages. In contrast to his more famous Aesopian prose, he chose in this case a straightforward repetition of the rural images his readers already knew. First, he described the fire's destructive power and the futility of resisting it: "The village was burnt to the ground. . . . Old Granny Praskovya was burnt, and Petka, Tatiana's little boy. The men and women, seeing the thick smoke, ran in from the fields. . . . But by that time there was nothing left to save."[32]

A passage conveying the search for the young boy's body both rivaled the boulevard press and brought divine agency to judgment: "They turned up the fallen roof and under its smoking ruins found the little boy's body. The uppermost half of the corpse was a formless, charred black mass; the side turned toward the floor was untouched. . . . Tatiana . . . gazed with a fixed stare on the line which divided the untouched from the charred half on Petushka's body and kept whispering softly, 'Oh God, do You see?' "[33]

Tatiana's question to God confirmed the prevalent impression that peasants understood fire exclusively as divine punishment. Direct evidence to confirm that impression came in the form of the peasants' own apocalyptic conceptualization of fire in the petitions they submitted to local officials, the Ministry of the Interior, and the tsar himself when they sought emergency relief following devastating fires.

"God Is High and the Tsar Is Far Away"

Peasant appeals for disaster relief displayed a clever mix of apocalyptic imagery and pragmatism. While the oft-quoted peasant proverb declared that both God and the tsar were far away, these petitions reflected the peasants' recognition that the tsar was much closer to hand and more likely to assist them if they presented themselves as helpless victims of divine acts rather than as responsible in any way for their misfortunes. Such appeals were legion. Between January 1896 and March 1898 alone, the Ministry of the Interior received more than three hundred petitions concerning destructive fires. Every appeal that made its way to the Economic Department of the ministry had passed through local offices, usually that of the governor. Sometimes local officials and agents appealed on the peasants' behalf. Whether from peasant or official hands, documents emphasized peasant helplessness in the face of the overpowering nature of fire. One cannot know from a century's distance how much coaching peasant supplicants received from the educated persons who transmitted their appeals.[34] In any event, it is clear that they manipulated images of fire as an apocalyptic force, of the tsar as benevolent father, and of themselves as helpless children.

Many petitions described the now familiar features of a village fire, stressing its overwhelming, destructive force and the futility of fighting it. In the following appeal, the peasants also enjoyed the advantage of identifying the fire as being "heavenly fire" caused by a lighting bolt:

MOST AUGUST MONARCH YOUR MOST MERCIFUL MAJESTY! On July 17 of last year, 1894, at around 6:00 in the afternoon, our entire village—Nechaeva Gora—because of a lightning bolt, burned to its very foundations with all of our property. . . . Having seen the fire and run toward it, we saw our village already burned, with only coals and cinders from the beams left. . . . After the fire, all we had left was what was on our backs, and the livestock who were in the pasture, but absolutely everything else without exception burned and now we have nothing.

Your most faithful slaves, the peasants of Vologda Province, Sol'vychev District, village of Nechaeva Gora.[35]

The peasants of the village of Dymno in Novgorod District, Novgorod Province, opened their petition in 1896 with similar emphasis on the fire's force and their helplessness before it: "A terrible misfortune has befallen us; that is—a fire which stole all of our immovable property, our movable property, our hay, grain, part of our livestock, and from three families—young children. The most important thing was that as soon as the fire broke out in the village, it started to spread so quickly down the street that we were not able to save anything, despite all of our efforts."[36] And in a petition from peasants in Mezensk District, Arkhangel'sk Province, we find this formulaic description of their condition: "We and our families were left without shelter, clothes, or a crust of bread under the open sky."[37]

It undoubtedly served the peasants' interests to stress their victimization and helplessness in the face of an act of God when they turned to the government for assistance. In order to appeal to the tsar for protection, they also chose to stress his role as father, which meant that they had to stress their own child-like qualities. This calculation was particularly evident in a petition submitted by peasants in Kostroma Province in November 1887.

So what kind of condition are we in? To whom do we run first for help? . . YOU, YOUR MAJESTY, as FATHER, and benefactor, protecting YOUR children, who are loyal to YOU, show assistance to your slaves who have suffered, YOUR NAME will be blessed both by us and our children, whom we are trying to raise with the fear of God, so that they will be true sons of their Fatherland and sincere children under the care of YOUR IMPERIAL MAJESTY.

Loyal servants of YOUR IMPERIAL MAJESTY: The burned-out peasants of Miskovo settlement.[38]

Amateur and professional ethnographers also contributed willy-nilly to the vision of peasants as captives of apocalyptic thinking and their comprehension of fires as an act of divine retribution. The widely reported descriptions of lightning bolts as Elijah's fire served as the most frequent evidence of this reaction.[39] So did the equally widespread descriptions of peasants' refusal to attack lightning fires or their recourse to throwing milk, Easter eggs, or *kvas* (a drink made from fermented black bread) onto the blaze.[40] An eyewitness to such a fire in 1894 explained that when someone suggested that the bystanders should do something before the entire thatched village went up in flames, others responded, "No, no. God will put out whatever lightning sets on fire!"[41] Peasants sometimes circled burning structures, holding icons aloft and praying.[42] This also pointed to their reliance on God's intercession, rather than on their own action, to rescue them from misfortune.

The image of peasants as silent witnesses resigned to the futility of fighting fire was eloquent testimony to their imprisonment in apocalyptic thinking. They found themselves in this position, progressive activists believed, precisely because of their continued reliance on divine agency. One delegate to the

Fig. 2.1. "Pozhar," N. S. Mateev, 1891. *This painting conveys the association of peasant women with fatalism, as the woman faces fire with an icon.*

Grodno Provincial Committee on the Needs of Agriculture in 1903 forcefully expressed these views: "The peasant's ignorance is what encourages the villages' flammability. . . . The adults are just as helpless, happy-go-lucky, and careless as their young children, and all of them together depend on their 'avos,' on their faith in God's kindness, and stubbornly hold onto several harmful superstitions and don't take necessary measures when they should."[43] For those who would fight fire, such futility would have to yield to futurity, and passive resignation before divine retribution would have to give way to foresighted prevention and active resistance to fire once it struck (fig. 2.1).

From Futility to Futurity

As early as the late 1860s, an alternative representation of fire's presence and Russia's path emerged in the public discussion of fire. While some residual Biblical imagery remained, this version of the fire crisis turned away from supernatural agency. It approached fire not as an invincible elemental force raging across timeless Holy Russia but as a product of identifiable and alterable aspects of post-Emancipation village culture. Contributors to this representation used the medical metaphor of the epidemic to describe fire's effects in the countryside. In shifting to this metaphor, they identified fire as a pathology in Russia's body. Such a move required that they not only identify the pathology but also define its manifestations, causes, and the agents of its metastasis.

In 1869, one P. Alabin explained that fires were "one of the greatest, almost ceaseless, scourges" endured by the rural population.[44] Pogodin referred to the "epidemic character" of fires.[45] A correspondent to the *Smolensk Herald* repeated the metaphor in 1882 when he reported, "The epidemic of fires that has seized our Russia has also made itself felt in our little corner."[46] An advocate of fire prevention reminded his readers in 1896 that "fires cause just as much harm as various 'plagues,' 'ulcers' and other such illnesses."[47]

At the meeting of the Committees on the Needs of Agriculture of 1903, discussion of the questions of fire, arson, and fire prevention in the countryside displayed a shared conviction that "burning down almost every ten years, our village is ruined by fire more than by any other adversity."[48] As S. A. Kotov, zemstvo fire agent for Borovich District, Novgorod Province, explained: "Fires, like any other epidemic disease, constitute a most murderous evil which radically undermines the economic well-being of our country; they lead to the ruin of rural inhabitants, they retard the cultural development of our people and impede the improvement of agriculture."[49]

The conceptualization of an epidemic depended on knowledge of fires not just in one's own locality or in one region of the empire but in many places at once. The prominence of rural fires in the press provided that vision of a simultaneous, widespread rash of fires spreading across the surface of Russia's temporal, physical body.

Once educated Russians viewed fire as an epidemic, they moved to explore its etiology in order to prevent its harm. Zemstvo activists were among those who took the lead in examining the crisis on the spot and transmitting their observations through reports on individual fires. The following report, published in 1892 by the Novgorod provincial bureau, exemplified the care these activists took in identifying the physical elements in a typical village fire.

At one o'clock in the afternoon of October 3, 1891, a fire broke out that destroyed 21 peasant homesteads. . . . The fire began in a homestead with a thatched roof, owned by the peasant Ivan Timofeev. . . . Timofeev's house and yard were very close to neighboring houses; on the right, Ignatii Kriuchin's house was only three *arshins* [7 feet] away, and on the left, Vasillii Kopusov's house was only three and a half *sazhens* [10 feet] away. Right next door to Kopusov, under the same roof, stood the house and yard of Ivan Mukhovikov. All of these yards had thatched roofs over them. Given such close quarters, the fire . . . quickly moved to Kopusov's yard and Mukhovikov's yard; after approximately ten minutes, these three yards were burning in one flame. . . . Given the sizable blaze and the wind, burning straw and coals were carried onto hay sheds and stacks of grain that were 60–100 sazhens [130–150 feet] from the burning houses.[50]

The clinical tone of this report emanated not from apocalyptic currents in Russian culture but from their opposites: materialism and scientism. Descriptions of old women burnt beyond recognition as human forms and children reduced to fractured skeletons with their organs oozing out were overwhelming, literally stunning visions of hell on earth. Detailed reports such as this one on the patterns of village fires and the material factors contributing to their destructive power invited a different response. They suggested that, like any other plague, this one, if properly diagnosed and broken down into its active agents, was susceptible to successful treatment.

Such diagnostic reports grew more numerous in the 1890s, when zemstvo fire insurance programs were fully established and volunteer firefighting organizations had become a national phenomenon.[51] Chapters 6 and 8 examine these programs in greater detail. In this discussion of the fire narrative, I am interested in how such forensic rhetoric contributed to the pathologizing of fire, the reports' focus on physical factors in establishing an opportunistic environment in which that pathology could thrive, and their conclusion that peasants' disorder and carelessness facilitated the spread of the pathology's effects in the village.

The Novgorod report quoted above was typical of the progressivists' emphasis on the villages' material culture as the first feature of Russia's exceptional fire culture. Crowded construction, wooden houses, and thatched roofs were the key factors in creating an opportunistic environment for runaway fire. Peasant behaviors within that environment made them fire vectors in the village. In both material culture and behaviors, disorder was the central characteristic of village life that emerged in the articulation of the "fire epidemic." The prescription offered for preventing and extinguishing fires was a scientific, rational approach to fire in the countryside; the agents to execute that approach were to be organized state and civic activists who would in turn mobilize the peasantry.

This marked a conscious departure from, even a rejection of, apocalyptic visions. The inaugural issue of the journal of the United Russian Firefighters' Society in 1894 included the declaration, "Until the peasant . . . is convinced of the need to take precautions against fire, until he ceases to view fire as a visitation from God that one must not go against, until then, fires will dispossess Orthodox Rus'."[52] Five years later, the author of a brochure on how to organize volunteer fire brigades explained, "Man's victory over all that surrounds him depends entirely on the development of his mental powers and abilities. . . . Order in life is a great thing everywhere and in everything, and all the more so in the struggle with such a calamity as fire."[53] These calls for action rejected futility and rested on the conviction that it was necessary to replace the peasants' resignation before divine visitation with a rational understanding of fire and a willingness to engage actively to prevent and fight fire as a material presence in the villages of Russia. As one observer concluded, "Russia is burning and needs rational assistance."[54]

Individuals in educated society were determined to segregate Russia's rational and active elements (civil society) from Russia's irrational and passive elements (the peasantry). When they discussed fires' causes, educated outsiders frequently used the words irrational, thoughtless, careless, and ignorant to describe peasant fire practices. Village fires were not only a threat to the material interests of the empire but also an offense to educated people's image of their country as a civilized and progressive culture.

Writers on the fire question betrayed this sense of offense in their frequent use of the term "our peasants" when discussing the causes of conflagrations in the countryside. Nonpeasants' use of the phrases *u nas* (similar to *chez nous* and *bei uns*) to connote Russia and *nashi krest'iane* (our peasants) to connote Russian peasants was more than simply a convention of the language; educated observers of peasant culture usually employed these phrases with an implicit reference to other cultures and other peasantries that did not exhibit whatever characteristic of Russian peasant culture happened to be under discussion. For example, in his 1869 brochure on fire prevention, P. Alabin began his remarks with the question, "*Itak, otchego u nas, na Rusi, tak chasty sel'skie pozhary? Otvechaem: ot russkikh 'avos,' 'nebos,' i 'kak nibud'* " (And so, why is it that here in Russia rural fires are so frequent? The answer: because of the Russian "maybe," "probably," and "somehow or other").[55] Having presented this lackadaisical attitude as peculiarly Russian, Alabin went on to list the various manifestations of the peasants' carelessness and failure of foresight in handling fire.

Thus, Alabin explained, peasants failed to take any precautions as they used lit torches in the attic, hayloft, and other areas where flammable materials lay about. They carelessly threw ashes out into the yard, where firewood litter and other debris lay, ready to ignite. They failed to maintain their hearth stoves. Worse still, they had taken up the habits of drinking tea and smoking tobacco, both of which involved the handling of fire, and "given the well-known carelessness of our folk [*nashego naroda*]," it was only to be expected that samovars would be in faulty condition and that smoking would take place without any thought to the dangers posed by hot ashes and discarded butts.[56] Once they began, fires spread so rapidly, according to Alabin, because of the "*bezporiadochnaia* [disorderly] *i bezobraznaia* [and ugly, disgraceful, outrageous, scandalous, or shocking] *postroika nashikh selenii* [construction of our villages]."[57] Again he used the term "our" to refer to village construction. Village construction was indeed disorderly and haphazard and had been so for centuries, but in the post-Emancipation era of reform, this feature of rural life was no longer simply an accepted feature of the rural landscape; it was now a disgraceful scandal that outraged those with an alternative vision of Russia. Equally important, this was a material explanation for fire's presence and power in the countryside.

Alabin was typical both in his identification of the causes of fires and in his use of the construction "our peasants," or "our villages." Other observers, pamphleteers, zemstvo statisticians, local police officials, and ethnographers would offer the same list of causes over the next forty years with equal stress on the thoughtlessness and irrationality of Russia's peasants.[58] In 1877, the police inspector for St. Petersburg, P. Zinoviev, argued that Russian villages were help-less against fire because the peasants had "absolutely no comprehension whatso-ever of the fact that there exist means to prevent fire." He titled his brochure "Our Village Fires." And again, the construction "our peasants" made its way into his list as he explained in particular that "our village women" dump hot coals from the hearth stove into the yard right next to flammable materials, a point he reinforced further with a footnote describing other dangerously careless fire practices of "our peasant women."[59]

Peasants also contributed to their depiction as hapless, careless victims when they responded to fire investigations by local police officials. Because of their participation at this level, they were the ultimate sources of the statistics on fires in European Russia that the Central Statistical Committee published through the Ministry of the Interior. Their numbers offered quantitative evi-dence for several possible stories. The reading public seized on two narratives embedded in the numbers: the dramatic increase in the incidence of rural fires and the overwhelming preponderance of peasant carelessness as the identified cause for those fires. The statistics showed a rapid growth in the number of reported fires over the post-Emancipation period. But the issue here is not the increase in numbers; it is the reported causes of those fires. For the years 1870–1909, the three categories of causes labeled "carelessness," "badly main-tained stoves and chimneys," and "other" accounted for 85 percent of all reported fires.[60]

Most readers took these numbers at face value, without pausing to consider that it often served the peasant informants' interest to offer explanations that could be lumped under the general heading of carelessness. Mishandling fire was a finable offense; arson was a criminal one that required exile to Siberia in some form for almost all convicted arsonists.[61] By the end of the nineteenth century, when zemstvo insurance programs were in place, there was also evidence that peasants practiced "self-arson" in order to claim insurance payments, although this was financially advantageous only for the poorest peasants in the village.[62]

When local officials, whether from the police or the zemstvo, showed up after they heard of a village fire, it often suited the peasants' purposes either to say they had no idea at all how the fire had begun (in which case the cause would be listed as "other"), to admit to an accident ("careless handling of fire"), or to describe a faulty stove or chimney ("poorly maintained stoves and chim-neys"). The last explanation, of course, also presented peasants as incompetents who could not take care of the most basic and widespread technology in their daily existence. Furthermore, because the stove was almost exclusively under the women's care, this cause served as another point in the indictment against women's pernicious role in the village. For a reading public increasingly or already convinced that village fires exemplified the backwardness of "their" peasants, peasant obfuscation during fire investigations contributed to a shared discourse of epidemic rural ignorance and passivity. Such explanations also denied or obscured peasant agency, here to the peasants' possible advantage.

The juxtaposition of peasant carelessness with an enlightened, rational approach as a contrast between Russia and the West was explicit in the inaugural issue of the journal of the United Russian Firefighters' Society. There, following his call for peasant precautions and their rational understanding of fire, Isaev predicted: "Now that we, following the example of Western nations, have begun to form volunteer fire departments and have established the United Russian Firefighters' Society, we will make giant steps forward toward decreasing this source of loss and sacrifice in Russia."[63] On the occasion of the tenth anniversary of the society in 1903, D. L. Strukov explained that the very beginnings of fire prevention and firefighting in Russia had come from the West early in the nineteenth century: "Western culture brought us embryos, weak at first, of the organization of volunteer fire associations."[64] Firefighters' periodicals also regularly published information about firefighting systems in Europe and the United States, as well as statistics about the incidence of fires there. Leaders in the fire prevention and firefighting effort thus perceived their work as a contest between Western-style rationalism and a scientific approach to fire, on the one hand, and irrational, unscientific attitudes prevalent in Russia's peasant population, on the other.

Reporting on local firefighting practices joined the reporting on causes to highlight the lack of order and reason in the peasantry's encounters with fire. Educated observers overwhelmingly agreed that the peasants' reactions to conflagrations were inappropriate at best and harmful at worst. From Vologda Province, N. A. Ivanitskii reported in 1890 that in the event of a fire, a menstruating woman was called out to run around the burning house three times in order to prevent the devil from carrying the fire to neighboring houses.[65] In at least two areas of the empire, there were reports that peasants believed that fire followed the person who caused it, so that if someone ran out of a burning structure, fire would follow. To prevent this, the peasants held the escapees of the blaze forcibly in one place.[66] The editor of *The Firefighter* opined that "noise, shouts, disorder, lack of leadership, in a word, total chaos" characterized peasants at the scene of a fire.[67] "Noise, shouting, and crying" were the three features of a village fire in the memory of one A. Vasil'ev, reporting from the Cherepovets District of Novgorod Province in 1899.[68] Alternatively, eyewitnesses reported that peasants froze into utter inaction, "standing before the fire as silent witnesses."[69]

Reports often described acts of desperation as peasants risked their lives to save people or property caught in the blaze. These often included dramatic episodes of mothers running into burning structures to save their children, or men of the village rushing in to rescue the elderly.[70] In some cases, the desperation was natural, but dangerous for the community. For example, the villagers of Ustiuzhna, Novgorod Province, struggling to battle a fire, could not afford to waste time restraining a mother trying to get into her burning home, where her two children perished, so they tied her to a tree, where she watched the immolation. As the reporter explained, "It was a heartrending scene; God save you from witnessing it!"[71]

Reports also described full hysteria, and here women again assumed their wonted position as the most extreme example of the negative phenomenon. One report from Smolensk Province stated that peasants often rushed to the scene of a fire empty-handed, screaming, crying, and wailing before they reached the conflagration.[72] Reports to the Tenishev Bureau and to ethnographic and literary-political journals focused on allegedly hysterical women who cried, shouted, fell to the ground, and pulled out their hair.[73] One observer wrote, "She fell to the ground, began to crawl along the street, to tear her hair out, and then she jumped up and threw herself at the burning house."[74] An account from Vologda Province repeated this imagery when it described the master of a burning house as alternately laughing and crying while his wife crawled on the ground, pulling her hair out. In this scene, bystanders stood passively, watching the fire, oohing and aahing.[75] Peasants also appeared in shock, like the silent witnesses just mentioned, or standing with their hands motionless, having sunk into a condition of half-consciousness. These reactions to fire were the very antithesis of what organizers of fire brigades and contributors to fire prevention policies in the Ministry of Interior and zemstvo bureaus wanted to introduce in rural Russia. They were the very expression of the irrationality of rural Russian culture that belied Russia's full membership in the community of civilized and modern nations.

Chekhov's Subverted Apocalypse

When Anton Chekhov published his enormously influential literary sketch of rural life, "Muzhiki," in 1897, he brought the contest between apocalyptic and progressivist representations of the fire question and the peasants' role in it to the heart of his depiction of life in the fictitious village of Zhukovo. Recent studies of Chekhov recognize his appropriation of Christian imagery.[76] It is no surprise, then, that he made use of village fires and their interest to the public in treating rural themes. In both "A Dreadful Night" (1886) and "Muzhiki" (1897), village fires serve the structural function of climax.[77] In both cases, Chekhov combines biblical imagery with details drawn from his own experience or from contemporary fire reports and established formulas in fire narratives.

The fire scene in "A Dreadful Night (*Rough Drafts*)" seems to be a rough draft indeed for the scene in "Muzhiki." Chekhov is experimenting with descriptive metaphors, focusing on the fire itself as subject and conveying the fire's transformation of the rural landscape into an alternative reality where hellish flames consume the physical residue of earthly life and terrified spirits are caught in fiery clouds rising to heaven.

> The entire scene is covered by a massive, forceful, blinding flame in which, as if in a fog, houses, trees, and churches are disappearing. A bright, almost sunlike light is mixed up with columns of black smoke and dull steam; golden tongues [of fire] slip and, with a greedy crackling, smiling and winking merrily, lick the black skeletons. Clouds of red-gold dust rise rapidly toward the sky [or heaven], and, as if to make the illusion all the greater, through these clouds fly terrified doves.[78]

Julie de Sherbinin has argued that this fire scene "resembles Hell, from the blinding flames and dark smoke to the chaotic sounds."[79] Chekhov is clearly toying with apocalyptic images of fire, going so far as to have one of Mar'ia Sergeevna's servants, "wanting to impress the lady," insincerely proclaim that "God [gospod'] punished them for their sins. . . . That's what this is! Man sins and doesn't think about what he is, but God does, that's the truth."[80] He also sketches the plot for "Muzhiki" in Gavrila, the lackey's, judgment that "the important thing is not to let the fire spread. . . . What's needed is someone who is competent, but can some simple muzhik understand that?"[81]

"Muzhiki" also appears upon first reading to confirm apocalyptic currents in late imperial Russian literature and culture. Savelii Senderovich has interpreted Chekhov's vision of peasant life in Zhukovo as a rural "apocalypse" whose "culmination" is the village fire in the fifth section of the story.[82] Chekhov's intention that the reader approach the fire in apocalyptic terms is explicit. His portrait of rural evil in the forms of promiscuous sexuality, child abuse, drunkenness, verbal abuse, and recrimination invited a narrative climax consistent with the Johannine Revelation.

Chekhov also foreshadows an apocalyptic climax in section four, when Motka and Sasha discuss their grandmother's fate on judgment day. Having fallen prey only too often to her vicious whippings, they relish the prospect of her eternal torment. "They quieted down and lay down to sleep, and Sasha, as she fell asleep, imagined the Last Judgment [*strashnyi sud*]: an enormous stove, something like a potter's fire-pit, burned, and an evil spirit with horns, like a cow's, all black, was driving Grandmother into the fire with a long stick, just as she had herself earlier driven the geese."[83] The familiar adjective *strashnyi* appears again, here simultaneously referring to the last judgment and its fiery form.

Chekhov opens the next section of "Muzhiki" with cries and screams as a group of young peasants spy a fire in their village and shout, "Fire! Fire! . . . We're burning!" Chekhov describes this as a despairing cry, *otchaiannyi krik*, thus setting the tone for the confusion and helplessness the peasants will display.[84] In describing their reactions, Chekhov follows the pattern established by eyewitness accounts. Hysterical women appear at three points in his narrative. First, he places Mar'ia outside her izba, "crying, beating her hands, her teeth chattering, although the fire was far away, at the other end of the village."[85] Then he describes a husband and wife, the latter "lying with her face on the ground, half-conscious and moaning."[86] His third image of women presents a group of older women sitting and wailing, "just as if they were at a funeral."[87]

The male peasants fare no better. Some are dumbstruck: "The muzhiks stood around in a crowd, doing nothing, and looked at the fire. Nobody knew how to get started, nobody knew how to do anything, though meanwhile they were surrounded by stacks of grain, hay, sheds, and heaps of dry twigs."[88] Those who did try to do something failed utterly because they were drunk. "They were all drunk, they stumbled and fell, and all of them had a helpless expression and tears in their eyes."[89]

Chekhov changes the tone with a simple but dramatic "but" (*no*), and he shifts the cultural direction with the phrase "from the direction of the lord's estate [*iz gospodskoi usad'by*]" to announce the arrival of the local volunteer fire brigade. His choice of the adjective *gospodskoi* (the lord's) rather than *pomeshchichei* (the landowner's) reinforces his allusion to the religious fire narrative. The chief figure in this efficient, well-equipped little band is a young student, a member of the gentry. Dressed all in white, he rides on horseback before two carts and a fire engine. He is neither the wrathful Lord nor the prophet Elijah, however; he leads his chariots across the ravine to the benighted village with the goal of rescue, not vengeance.

Senderovich argues that the student's name, "Georges," is Chekhov's allusion to St. George, the dragon slayer.[90] Another critic similarly sees the student as a St. George figure "fighting the snake of ignorance in Russia."[91] For Senderovich, the student is "one exceptional, heroic figure" whose action is "difficult to qualify as anything other than a miracle."[92] This is both a misreading of what the student represents and of the larger meaning of this village fire scene in its time and in our understanding of late imperial Russian culture. "Georges" was a French name that bespoke the student's role as the harbinger of Western reason. He does not put the fire out by himself in an act of individual, saintly, miraculous salvation but through a combination of technology (a fire engine), a division of labor among the five assistants and himself, strong leadership, and a rational plan of attack. He is action incarnate: "And in front of them all was the student, who was red and shouting in a sharp, hoarse voice and in such a tone as though putting out fires was an ordinary affair for him."[93]

Chekhov underscores this scene's function as a representation of the struggle between rational, Western firefighting techniques and benighted rural fatalism when Kiriak, the Zhukovo peasant who most fully embodies darkness in rural Russia, lunges at the student's crew. He is knocked down by one of the crew members and crawls out of the scene on his hands and knees. The student and his assistants make quick work of the fire before the hapless peasants.

Chekhov thus both averts an apocalyptic outcome and subverts the apocalyptic motif in the national fire narrative. By incorporating apocalyptic signs throughout the text, he plays to the reading public's familiarity with this approach to village fires in the post-Emancipation era. But in his own time, the character of Georges would also have seemed a mundane representation of gentry fathers and sons who had been establishing volunteer fire brigades in the countryside for the previous twenty years. Through this character, Chekhov placed his bets on progressive activism and futurity rather than on victimization and futility. Unlike Turgenev's Bazarov a generation earlier, Georges succeeds at his task. His rational activism leads not to a premature death and burial in the countryside but to the rapid extinction of the fires of drunken ignorance and a casual return to the estate on the other side of the ravine from Zhukovo.

Conclusion: Apocalyptic Visions and Rational Responses

Chekhov did not so much help create the national fire narrative as capture and echo it. He was ideally positioned to do so because of his practical experience with each of the narrative traditions that contributed to representations of fire.

In his youth, he came to know Orthodox images intimately.[94] As an adult, he was newspaper journalist, ethnographer, and physician as well as belletrist.[95] He both understood the language of the Apocalypse and used it. He was also one of the people in Russia who took action during a potentially apocalyptic disaster—the famine and cholera epidemic of 1891–1892. He captured the shift in ways of knowing fire from apocalyptic visions to the rational responses that newspapers, statistical reports, zemstvo studies, firefighting and fire prevention manuals, and ethnographic surveys embodied.

It was these modern media that enabled such narratives to contribute to a shared national identity. Newspapers were key contributors, for they were the first to bring fire statistics and stories to an expanding reading public. While newspapers contributed urgency, constancy, and shared national dimensions to fire narratives, the periodic publications of the Central Statistical Committee provided what McReynolds has termed "facticity and objectivity" and I have termed "scientism" as essential elements of authority in public discourse during this period.[96] No matter that peasants were the ultimate source of the information in the vast majority of cases; by the time the statistics appeared under the seal of the Ministry of the Interior, complete with impressive analytical introductory essays and hundreds of pages of tables in neatly defined categories, these publications provided evidence of the most "modern," and so legitimate, kind.

Zemstvo publications shared that legitimacy and added further statistical and technical elements to the national fire narrative. Through detailed reports on individual fires that focused on the material factors in rural conflagrations, they defined the etiology of the fire epidemic. Through monthly financial reports on their fire insurance programs, zemstvo boards also maintained running accounts of property losses that added up to a serious national economic problem.

Ethnographic reports about the fire beliefs and practices of the peasantry added evidence of a Russia threatened by fire. By the turn of the century, ethnography was an honored discipline, and ethnographers enjoyed authority by virtue of their reputed empiricism.[97] Reporting from the village itself, they brought peasants to the reading public, with all the peculiarities that so fascinated that public. With their portrayals of remnants of fire worship and bizarre firefighting rituals, ethnographic reports added to the perception that Russian peasants were still prisoners of apocalyptic thinking, which in turn invited a self-image of inevitable victimization.

All of these media challenged apocalyptic currents in late-nineteenth-century culture in two fundamental ways. First, they challenged the ahistoricism of apocalyptic thinking. They were utterly "this-worldly" in their on-the-spot reporting of specific events in specific locations at specific moments in time. The Russia they recorded was not "Holy Rus'" but earthly, material Russia, defined by such mundane factors as housing materials and village construction patterns. Second, they rejected otherworldly agency and its logical companion, the understanding of fire as an act of God. This led them to reject as well victimization and futility. Like Chekhov's Georges, they believed that action could prevent an apocalyptic ending. Through action, in turn, they and the peasants of European Russia could, like Chekhov's Olga and Sasha, leave ignorant, futile victimization behind, strike out on a new path, and embrace futurity through human agency in the material world.

Anyone who has read "Muzhiki" knows that it served as a clinically written coda of sorts to the multiple-voiced representation of emancipated peasants in late-nineteenth-century Russia. Chekhov populated Zhukovo with by-then-stereotypical evil, divisive, or victimized peasant women; brutish, drunken peasant husbands; and passive shades of ignorance and abuse who had assumed their characteristic features over three decades of literary and journalistic representation. His decision to bring the course of their dreadful lives to a climax through the vehicle of a village conflagration illustrates the degree to which "knowing" peasants and "knowing" fire had conflated by the 1890s into a mutually reinforcing cluster of negative conclusions about life in the emancipated countryside.

This conflation owed its hue in large part to the fact of the Emancipation and the anxieties it engendered in Russia's ordered society. For contemporaries, the fact of emancipation and the peasantry's emergence as a new citizenry, liberated from noble tutelage to manage their own affairs, was at once momentous and disturbing. Emancipation set Russia onto a trajectory of reforming progression toward full membership in the community of Western European nations that had already dissolved bondage en route to a modern citizenry. This was cause for celebration and hope for Russia's future.

But imperial Russian society had long been one of legally determined estates. The Emancipation of 1861 disrupted that order. Peasants emerged literally and figuratively from behind their masters' cloaks to take possession of their own bodies, homes, relationships, and actions. As late as 1902, imperial Russia's most famous geographer would write of the Emancipation's effect on the peasant: "And suddenly everything changed,—he (the peasant) lost his protector, his 'father' (as he himself sometimes called him),—often strict and merciless, but one who thought for him and managed his fate."[98] Peasants gained not only freedom but also property—inalienable property in the shape of their homes and the farmsteads (*dvory*) that surrounded them. They gained a private domain behind whose fences they were now masters and mistresses. While they continued to answer to the communal assembly in matters of taxation, redemption payments, and the periodic distribution of arable land, their homes and families were beyond the reach of the gentry and other educated elements in Russian society for the first time in Russia's imperial experience.[99]

At the center of that private, legally defined and protected domain was fire, and standing most closely beside fire were peasant women. That such an elemental power should be both ubiquitous in rural daily life and frequently manipulated by women was a post-Emancipation "discovery" that compounded worries about an unbound peasantry, especially after fire's audacious performance in St. Petersburg in 1862. Fire itself, fire technologies, and peasants wielding fire became menacing. The "mother" stove assumed the form of a frame that failed to contain fire, threatening to let fire loose across the rural landscape. The traditional smoldering torch became less a poor light and more a fiery brand that, mishandled by peasants, could set Russia's villages aflame. When educated observers responded with first an apocalyptic, then a materialist understanding of fire, they were moving toward grasping rural fire and village fire practitioners in the hope of putting them back within bounds and thus back into order. Knowing fire and peasants in these ways prepared official and civil society to develop a campaign against runaway fire and disorderly peasants.

The question arises, however, whether educated Russians' alarmist responses to fire in the countryside were solely an artifact of post-Emancipation concerns about the place of unbound peasants in a modernizing Russia. Dissolving boundaries had not created fire or arson in rural Russia. Both had a long history. The Emancipation and its anticipated challenges may have informed the epistemology of fire in late-nineteenth-century Russia, but it did not invent rural conflagrations or their consequences. Runaway fires and peasant arson were important and damaging features of late imperial rural Russia. As the peasants themselves described fire: "In bounds—a friend; out of bounds—an enemy."[100] The fires were real. So was their damage, to individual peasants, extended families, villages, regions, and the empire as an economic whole.

3

Fire as Russia's Historical Evil:
Peasants Dispossessed by Fire

IN AN ENORMOUS NUMBER OF CASES, THE INDEBTEDNESS, DISARRAY, AND
GENERAL DETERIORATION OF THE PEASANT ECONOMY HAS ITS BASIS IN FIRES.
—Report of the Riazan Provincial Committee

When Ivan Stoliarov composed a memoir of his peasant childhood in Voronezh Province in the 1890s, he placed a fire at the very genesis of his consciousness. "My first memory is connected with our house burning down. I woke up in the middle of the night because someone was screaming, 'We're burning!' I remember being in my mother's lap as she sat in a wagon that was rumbling into the darkness of night, while behind us was the light of the fire."[1]

After the fire, young Stoliarov's uncle died, and his grandfather decided to set his father up in a separate household.[2] As Stoliarov explained, this was a logical decision because "the fire simplified the household division: everything had burned up except for the large livestock. My father's share consisted of one cow and one horse."[3] While he built a new house, Stoliarov's father put the family in his sister's home. Her window became the boy's observation point: "From there I saw the place where the fire had happened and the fire buckets, always filled with water in case they were needed. . . . One day, some people I didn't know ran up, grabbed these buckets and, shouting, 'The shearing shed is burning!' took them somewhere. I couldn't see the fire from my window, but I could imagine it."[4]

From his earliest conceptualization of the world, this peasant boy of three or four years knew village fires as a fact and as a permanent element of his imagination. Further, his family's experience as a nuclear household dated to the conflagration that simultaneously destroyed the extended family's property and forced his father's independence. The fire shaped not only his grandfather's and father's economic condition but also, temporarily, his aunt's, because she had to house, clothe, and feed her brother's family until his new house was built. Finally, the fire site remained a part of the village landscape, as did water buckets at the ready—a reminder of the Stoliarov family's fate. These few lines in a rather laconic memoir provide evidence of the economic and psychological impact of fires on inhabitants of the Russian countryside.

Seminal for Stoliarov, this series of events was commonplace across European Russia throughout the second half of the nineteenth century. Peasant petitions to the Economic Department of the Ministry of the Interior, reports from local observers to the Tenishev Ethnographic Bureau, statements filed before government commissions, fire insurance records at the local level, and empire-wide statistics confirm that charred remains like those Stoliarov watched from his aunt's window marked the actual, as well as the imagined, landscape of every province during every season in every year from 1860 to 1904. Houses, sheds, animal barns, woodpiles, fences, granaries, bathhouses, threshing floors, harvested grain in the fields, poultry, livestock, and human beings turned to ashes with such consistency that fires should be understood as part of the cycle of rural existence (fig. 3.1).

Appeals for emergency relief submitted to the Ministry of the Interior give us a sense of the desperation fires could elicit. In conjunction with other eyewitness reports, they also provide clues about why runaway fires had so much

Fig. 3.1. *A village homestead in Vologda Province, photographed in May 2000, conveys how easily the similar wooden structures of one hundred years earlier might have been ignited. The metal roof of the building on the right probably explains its survival into the twentieth century.*

power in late imperial Russian villages. Among the hundreds who sent appeals each year, peasants from Simbirsk District, Simbirsk Province, requested assistance in December 1892 after two fires in June and July of that year "destroyed absolutely everything."[5] The governor's office of Kostroma Province submitted an appeal on behalf of the peasants of Buisk District after one village experienced major fires in August 1894 and August 1896, affecting more than eighty households, of which eleven had rebuilt after the first fire only to be completely burned out again in the second.[6] An individual peasant, one Mukhomat'ian Burkhanov, sought relief as a victim of a fire in Syzransk District, Simbirsk Province, on July 5, 1895, that completely destroyed seventy-two households and killed nine people.[7]

Even larger fires were not uncommon. From Miskovo settlement in Kostroma Province came the report of a fire in August 1887 that burned 210 dwellings and 91 barns.[8] Fifteen years earlier, the Pavlovo settlement in Nizhnii Novgorod Province had caught fire and five hundred households had been destroyed.[9] D. Shishlov reported to the Tenishev Ethnographic Bureau in 1899 that huge fires were frequent in Zaraisk District, Riazan Province, and offered six enormous fires in 1897 as examples.[10] Z. Lentovskii reported that village fires began every spring in Krasnosloboda District, Penza Province, and that there were usually seven to fifteen fires and as many as fifty to one hundred houses burned before the summer was over.[11]

Sometimes whole districts experienced the debilitating effects of fire, year in and year out. In Iaren District, Vologda Province, three villages were almost entirely destroyed by fire in the ten years from 1892 to 1902: the village of Chasovskoe lost 40 homesteads; the village of Onezhetskoe, 40; and the village of Palevitskoe, 160.[12] In the village of Piashi in Serdob District, Saratov Province, 180 homesteads burned in one fire in 1901, a fire that consumed not only izbas but also the church, the market, all of the village's grain stores, and other property; losses for this one fire exceeded 150,000 rubles.[13]

Fires could mean swift, total, and long-lasting destruction. As some peasants from Alatyrsk District, Simbirsk Province, put it in their request for emergency assistance two years after a fire in 1891: "We were poor before the fire—we've been destitute ever since."[14] Inventories of property lost to fire included not only the structures burned but everything in them—clothes, shoes, furniture, dishes, grain, and fodder. When fire came to call, it often left nothing behind. It raced through izba and grain barn, through stockyard and alleyway, across hayfield and woodpile, consuming everything in its path, leaving only the very few nonwood, nonstraw, noncloth items in the peasants' inventory: a few spoons, the blade of an ax, ceramic bowls, a samovar, metal tongs, the fragments of a kerosene lamp, the stones of the stove. Peasant sayings captured the merciless greed of fire: "At least a thief leaves your four walls standing. Fire takes everything."[15]

There was universal consensus in every type of evidence available on village fires that they moved with overwhelming speed. Petitions to the Ministry of the Interior for emergency relief almost always mentioned it. From Vologda Province, the peasants of Miapukhino explained: "Because of the hot and windy weather, the fire seized the whole village in flames with such speed that there was no possibility whatsoever not only of putting the fire out but even of saving anything."[16] Peasants from Moscow Province described a fire that destroyed fourteen homesteads in two hours on May 14, 1896: "Because the fire broke out when the weather was dry and there was a strong wind, its destructive action spared nothing."[17]

Reports to the Tenishev Ethnographic Bureau offered similar descriptions. One respondent described a fire he witnessed in May on a very windy day in Orel Province: "The entire village was in flames in under thirty minutes."[18] V. Antipov described a fire in Novgorod Province in 1884 that was caused by a candle dropped in a barn. Within five minutes the entire homestead was ablaze.[19] From Riazan Province, P. Zarin described a fire in June 1888, when a windmill 140 sazhens away from the village caught fire. Within fifteen minutes, the flames had spread 300 sazhens (640 meters), "creating a terrible sea of fire," hopping from house to house.[20]

Reporting to the Astrakhan Provincial Committee on the Needs of Agriculture in 1902, L. K. Peterov said that it was the speed of village fires that made them so terrible, and he recounted his experience in the countryside: "Two hours have not even passed since a fire began and the entire street has been turned to ashes. Everything has perished, and only the smoking gate posts stand, like monuments over the grave of prosperity, wealth, and perhaps even happiness."[21]

Newspaper reports placed the same emphasis on fire's speed and destructive force in the villages of European Russia. Fire activists at the 1902 All-Russian Firefighters' Conference agreed. A delegate from Saratov Province explained that "in the shortest time, in around an hour or an hour and a half, the thatched roofs and wooden buildings that have caught fire are engulfed in flames over a considerable distance, creating around them terrible heat. The fire is carried by the force of the wind from roof to roof, and in the majority of cases, the fire ceases its destruction only when there is nothing left to burn."[22] A

Nizhnii Novgorod delegate stated the consensus view succinctly: "Property acquired over the course of years is destroyed by fire in the matter of an hour, and a relatively prosperous peasant becomes almost destitute."[23]

Runaway fires impoverished not only individual families. They acted across the European region of the empire as a major brake on economic development. This thesis goes beyond the formulaic statement that has appeared in virtually every study of rural or peasant Russia—that fires could bring ruin to peasant households, which is true enough.[24] But prior statements have localized and individualized the impact of accidental or arson fires in the countryside. That impact was rarely, however, an exclusively individual experience with economic consequences limited to one household. In cases when a fire indeed destroyed only one family's property, the community contributed to its recovery through donations of labor, goods, temporary shelter, and food. In cases when fires spread to destroy several families' or an entire community's property, the impact extended across all the households in that community and beyond, to neighboring communities who responded with similar donations and to local and central government agencies that were called upon to provide emergency relief.

Such fires in all regions of European Russia constituted disasters of the type Simon Kuznets, followed by Eric L. Jones, identified decades ago as handicaps limiting the ability of communities or entire regions to move into a period of sustained economic development. Jones argued that "net capital formation was held down in the preindustrial world, not merely by lower incomes and lower savings propensities, but by a weaker capacity to control and recover from social and natural calamity."[25] He included "settlement fires" in his category of social disasters that Western European communities increasingly prevented or controlled and whose reduction contributed to "the European miracle" of capital accumulation and sustained economic development beginning in the 1700s.[26] Only in the 1890s was European Russia to experience a stabilization in the incidence of fires in the countryside and gains in the effort to limit damages once they broke out. Until then, rural fires continued to be "abrupt shocks to the economic system" from which neither individuals nor the larger community had much success in recovering before the next calamity struck.[27]

Reading Numbers to Track the Fiery Thief

Statistics gathered by the Ministry of the Interior beginning in 1860 reveal just how widespread these "shocks to the economic system" were in European Russia. As the data accumulated from decade to decade, they showed an alarm-

Table 3.1: Numbers of Reported Fires in European Russia, 1860–1904

Five-Year Period	Reported Fires	Buildings Burned	Losses in Rubles
1860–1864	58,817	284,507	131,569,510
1865–1869	83,972	375,580	146,520,961
1870–1874	128,839	489,517	223,937,201
1875–1879	169,004	595,008	290,673,014
1880–1884	205,547	660,246	370,316,835
1885–1889	238,668	713,163	355,126,657
1890–1894	241,606	806,729	351,898,990
1895–1899	271,468	735,589	359,030,648
1900–1904	315,227	851,181	487,604,261

Sources: Tsentral'nyi statisticheskii komitet, Ministerstvo Vnutrennikh del 1882, 1889, 1897, 1912.

ing increase in the reported incidence of fires, which would add up to a rise of more than 500 percent by 1904 (table 3.1).

Consistently across these four decades, urban fires (*v gorodakh*) represented only 8 percent of the total. These numbers thus largely describe a rural phenomenon. Beginning in 1860, local officials were responsible for reporting the number of fires in their districts, their causes, and the monetary value of the losses to the provincial governor every two weeks. The governor, in turn, submitted these reports to the Central Statistical Committee in the Ministry of the Interior in St. Petersburg. Peasants were the ultimate sources for these numbers in most cases.

Contemporary observers agreed that these numbers were incomplete for two reasons. First, they captured only those fires that were actually reported to the district policemen or that the policemen detected themselves. Second, peasants often did not report fires because they wanted to avoid fines for carelessness, or imprisonment and exile for malfeasance. An arson fire set within the community against a community member who had violated social norms often enjoyed the community's sanction. Further, district policemen had little hope of knowing what was going on in each and every village within their district. They received their information from communal officials, whose duty it was to report any fire immediately.[28] These statistics, therefore, convey fewer than the actual numbers of fires. Even so, the consistency of reporting and categorization across four decades makes them a valuable source for exploring the patterns of fires from season to season, year to year, and decade to decade, across provinces and regions.

We should also consider the question of how to read the nearly fantastic increase in the number of reported fires of more than 500 percent across four decades. There are reasons to argue that the increase is largely the product of reporting bias. At the same time that obstacles to full information hampered local officials' ability to capture all incidents of fire in their reports, the number of local officials spreading out across the countryside of European Russia was growing. In the wake of the Emancipation, peasants found themselves under more frequent and intrusive scrutiny by state—or zemstvo—appointed officials than they had encountered under serfdom. One observer identified forty officials, ranging from the provincial governor and his agents to zemstvo insurance agents, who had jurisdiction of some sort over the peasantry.[29] A. N. Engel'gardt asserted that the petty officials of the post-Emancipation era penetrated the peasants' world more thoroughly and continuously than had any representative of the pre-Emancipation state (indeed, he viewed their increased presence as a virtual invasion).[30] Before Emancipation, the layout of gentry estates created a physical distance between peasant village and the lord's demesne. Except for estate stewards, Russians of the nonpeasant orders had little reason to cross over the rivers, fields, and ravines that isolated and insulated the peasant world during serfdom. With the bonds of serfdom broken, such insularity was no longer permissible. In this, late imperial Russia followed the lead of Great Britain, whose rural police also began to expand in the 1850s. Engel'gardt identified these police as the shining examples for Russian property owners in Smolensk Province, who hoped that new officials would bring new protection against and control over the emancipated Russian peasantry.[31] Even in the face of peasants' reticence about fires, the sheer multiplication of informants in the countryside surely meant that increasing numbers of fires were registered. The impulses to control fire and to rein in an unbound peasantry were twins in the post-Emancipation, modern consciousness that defined what official and educated Russians perceived when they penetrated the veils that had separated gentry and peasant Russia during serfdom.[32] When they pushed those veils aside, petty officials served as reconnaissance scouts on the lookout for evidence of disorder. Fires that had been of no great interest before Emancipation now had a non-peasant audience.

As fires captured the attention of the government and the public, they were also reported more often because of the heightened awareness following the St. Petersburg fires. Finally, the Ministry of the Interior's mandate to the zemstvos in 1864 to develop fire insurance programs added another layer of people investigating fires in the countryside.[33] Although zemstvo insurance agents were involved in the investigation only of fires that damaged insured structures, they shared their information with police officials collecting statistics for the governor and the Central Statistical Committee. Given the heightened awareness of fires and knowledge on the part of the informants that every fire was now of interest, it may also be that a small fire that consumed only one outbuilding, which might not have been reported before the "epidemic," now made its way into the records.

This combination of institutional developments is the most likely explanation for the dramatic increase in the number of reported fires in the 1870s. Both for European Russia as a whole and for individual provinces, the growth of reported fires peaked in that decade and then leveled off through the turn of the century.

These patterns and the nature of fire reporting suggest caveats in working with the Central Statistical Committee's statistics on fires. First, the increase in the incidence of fires appears to be much larger in the first decade or so than it probably was in reality. Second, and equally important, is that although the rate of increase may have been overstated, the numbers of fires reported to and published by the committee were in fact smaller than the numbers of actual fires. So, on the one hand, the growth in the number of fires in the 1860s and 1870s was slower than the statistics conveyed, but on the other hand, the experience of fire at the village level was even more extensive than the Central Statistical Committee or the public responding to its published information knew. Contrary to contemporaries' concerns, the significance for Russian culture had less to do with the statistical increase in the reported incidence of village fires and more with the experience of fire and its impact on the rural standard of living. For that question, these statistics illuminate the reach and effects of rural conflagrations.[34]

To return to the numbers: although there are reasons to argue that the increase is largely the product of reporting bias, there is consistency in an increase of roughly 30,000 reported fires in European Russia during every five-year period except 1890–1894. As a percentage of the absolute number of fires, of course, a steady increase of 30,000 per five-year period meant a slowing of the rate of increase (30,0000 is a smaller percentage of 205,547 in 1880–1884 than of 58,817 in 1860–1864). It is difficult to know, but worth asking, what the steady increase in the absolute number of reported fires at a rate of 30,000 per five-year period meant for the people who witnessed or were victims of these fires. Whereas historians may be able, from a century's distance, to recognize 30,000 as an absolute increase but a decline as a percentage of the whole, individual observers and victims probably read it as more, rather than fewer, assaults on their security of property, self, and community. The figure of 30,000 may well have provided cause for a rural expectation that every year would bring fires, and more of them. Yet the certainty of fire's return did not lessen its shock when it arrived.

It seems unlikely that rural inhabitants would have taken heart at the slowing in the rate of increase in the number of fires, but they might have been heartened by the diminishing damages of individual fires. If the statistics on structures burned per fire are an approximation of reality, then fires consumed fewer buildings in each decade, dropping from an empire-wide average of 4.8 buildings per fire in 1860–1864 to 2.7 in 1900–1904. The average damages declined from 2.2 rubles per fire to 1.5 rubles per fire. The greater attention paid to rural fires and the increase in the number of people recording them may have influenced these figures as well. Whereas in the 1860s, district officials were likely to learn only of major fires, by the 1870s, both zemstvo insurance agents and district policemen were more likely to hear of a fire that consumed only one outbuilding and to include it in their reports. It may have been the case not that fires were actually growing smaller, but that more of the smaller fires were being recorded.

Even this trend, however, might have added to the local consciousness of and anxiety about fires, because official attention magnified the importance of minor blazes. A charred spot in a field became less ephemeral because it entered an official record as a data point, with the investigative presence of outsiders who examined it, interviewed local residents, and wrote their comments down to send to the district or provincial capital. Just as the phenomenon of rural fires, for educated members of society, had gone from being a largely unremarked feature of pre-Emancipation Russia to becoming evidence of apocalyptic disorder after the St. Petersburg fires of 1862, so minor fires in the countryside became official events and objects of heightened awareness and concern for residents of rural Russia by the 1870s.

Fires' Damage to the Economy

Large and small, fires constituted "abrupt shocks to the economic system" on four levels: those of the empire, the region, the local community, and the household. How large a portion of the imperial economy did losses of 131.6 million rubles (1860–1864) to 487.6 million rubles (1900–1904) represent? Beginning with the most basic point, the Russian economy was predominantly agricultural in the second half of the nineteenth century, while undergoing a state-sponsored industrialization. The agricultural sector did not receive state investment. On the contrary, as Arcadius Kahan explained, "the state . . . viewed the agricultural sector as a source of revenue and tried to transfer resources out of agriculture into the area of overhead capital."[35] The one policy followed consistently throughout the period was that agriculture (the agrarian population and its economic activity) ought to carry the chief burden not only of maintaining the political strength of the state but also of subsidizing the modernization of the Russian economy—the creation and expansion of its overhead capital as well as the process of industrialization.[36] The vigor of both the agricultural and industrial sectors thus rested heavily on the former.

Within the agricultural sector, quoting Kahan again, "together all farm structures constituted about 45 percent of the total capital stock in agriculture, excluding land."[37] This 45 percent of capital stock residing in farm structures was a significant factor in the health of the Russian economy as a whole. It was also what burned in a village fire. On the macroeconomic scale, then, how serious a "shock" were rural fires?

Kahan states that "a crude estimate of the rate of growth of the capital stock in the farm sector, excluding land, would be in the neighborhood of 1 per cent annually."[38] In the year he chose—1890—there were 7,838 million rubles in structures as capital stock in the countryside. A 1 percent growth in that capital stock for 1891 would thus have meant a gain of roughly 78 million rubles in structures. Fire statistics establish that in 1890, roughly 70 million rubles' worth of structures were reported burned in European Russia, of which losses 56 million rubles of capital stock were destroyed in the countryside. In order to achieve 1 percent growth in capital stock in rural structures (78 million rubles' worth), then, rural residents (primarily peasants) first had to overcome the loss of 56 million rubles' worth of structures. To achieve the weak gain of 1 percent, they had to build not just 1 percent but 1.8 percent more structures. Fire thus posed a serious challenge to the growth in capital stock, excluding land, in the agricultural sector. One zemstvo fire inspector calculated in 1902 that the equivalent of one-fifth of the total revenues for the empire went up in flames every year.[39] One may eschew the contemporaneous rhetoric of "epidemic" or "apocalyptic" fires in the countryside. But at a time when programs to improve Russian agriculture "were either in their infancy or grossly inadequate," with the result that "the modern agricultural revolution largely bypassed Russia at a time when other countries were already benefiting from it,"[40] the social disaster of rural fire was a legitimate cause for concern and a part of the explanation for why Russia had been left out of the "European miracle."

The disaster of fire and its damages were distributed unevenly across European Russia, with the worst of the fires in number and size occurring largely and consistently in the agricultural heartland in a band stretching across the entire black-soil region. By the 1890s, 34 of 49 provinces in European Russia reported more than 600 fires per year, 20 reported more than 800, and 10 reported more than 1,000 fires per year. (See maps 3.1–3.4.)

Throughout the 1870s, 1880s, and 1890s, Riazan, Tambov, Voronezh, and Saratov Provinces were at the heart of the fire zone. As early as the 1870s, Viatka Province almost always recorded the greatest number of fires (consistently more than four thousand). It was in a category of its own, for reasons I discuss later. The central and southeastern provinces formed a core, however, sharing many of the same characteristics of climate, population, village construction, and farming and labor practices to create the worst-case scenario for fire. It was there that fire struck most stubbornly and ferociously. These provinces suffered both the greatest numbers of fires and the largest fires in terms of number of structures burned per fire (a structure could be as large as a barn or as small as a shed).

Peasants in Saratov Province and peasants in Olonets or Arkhangel'sk Province experienced fire very differently. Peasants living in the agricultural heartland of European Russia had much more to fear from conflagrations than did peasants of any other region. Not only were fires more likely to strike their homes and communities; they were also more likely to consume large portions of them when they occurred. Tambov Province offers an example of fire's continuous presence in this region. One observer calculated that in Tambov Province, in one 16-year period, only 600 villages of the 3,200 in the province did not have large fires. Three hundred had more than 15 major fires, some had 40 major fires, and others had as many as 100 large conflagrations.[41] Stepping down to the level of one district, Borisogleb, for the years 1879–1900 provides a sense of the experience of one locale. Table 3.2 conveys the yearly and accumulating effects of damaging fires there.

Peasants could anticipate different experiences of fires by season as well. Each year, the spring, summer, and fall months brought the largest number of fires. In 1883, for example, 10 provinces reported 150 or more fires during the winter months; 23 reported 150 or more during the spring; 32 reported 150 or more during the summer; and 37 reported more than 150 fires in the fall. In 1893 the number of provinces reporting 150 fires or more by season was, for the winter, 13; for the spring, 35; for the summer, 42; and for the fall, 37. Similarly, in terms of damage, the devastating fires that burned entire homesteads and even whole villages to the ground were most likely to happen in the spring and sum-

Table 3.2: Annual Fire Data for Borisogleb District, Tambov Province, 1879-1900

Year	No. Fires	Izbas Burned	Other Structures Burned	Losses in Rubles
1879	149	1,042	1,476	56,439
1880	165	1,024	1,647	60,683
1881	177	567	787	28,259
1882	153	1,017	1,741	61,991
1883	142	571	806	30,309
1884	149	544	717	27,296
1885	154	1,259	1,612	64,668
1886	186	704	805	35,446
1887	NO DATA	862	1,299	46,200
1888	NO DATA	1,103	1,112	48,054
1889	NO DATA	1,185	1,658	61,685
1890	231	789	757	47,261
1891	274	940	934	53,717
1892	198	954	650	54,090
1893	155	446	381	20,930
1894	200	748	426	30,573
1895	239	1,313	727	54,452
1896	226	630	635	28,553
1897	258	1,154	991	49,550
1898	216	842	850	36,818
1899	247	507	458	22,317
1900	284	1,166	990	48,737

Source: *Trudy mestnykh komitetov* 1903, 41:128.

mer. In 1883, the range of buildings burned per fire in the winter months across European Russia was 0.8-1.7; in the spring, 1-11; in the summer, 1-11; and in the fall, 1-4.9. In 1893, the range was 0.4-5.9 for the winter; 0.6-8.6 for the spring; 0.8-10.2 for the summer; and 0.6-4.2 for the fall.

Numbers such as these illustrate how fires consumed both residential and farming structures, why district officials and residents alike entered each new year and even certain seasons knowing that fire was sure to pay them a call, and how capital losses detracted from any gains made toward sustained prosperity. Borisogleb District was typical of the region in the large numbers of structures burned per fire and the problem of repeated fires. Moving north and west to Novgorod Province, fires broke out in a less conducive natural environment, but even so, between 1860 and 1902, 85,476 property owners lost 134,888 buildings

Map 3.1 Total reported fires by province,1863

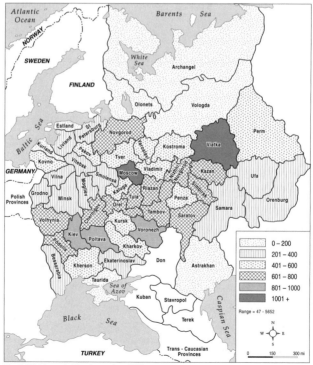

Map 3.2 Total reported fires by province,1873

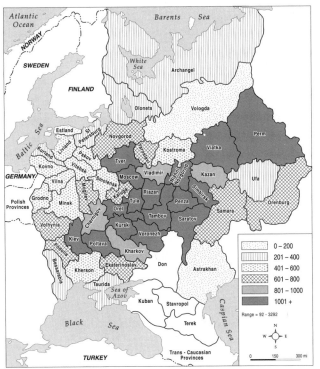

Map 3.3 Total reported fires by province, 1883

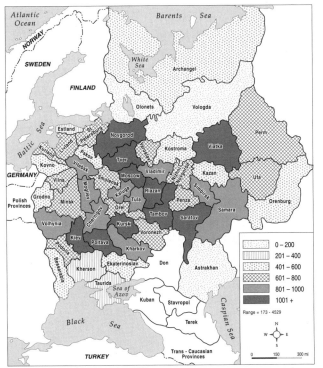

Map 3.4 Total reported fires by province, 1893

77

to fire. Over the period 1866–1902, that added up to 18.1 million rubles in losses reported to the zemstvo fire insurance agents.[42]

Fire-Prone Villages and Pyrogenic Practices

The roots of this devastation lay in both the causes of rural fires and the physical environment in which they occurred. Eric L. Jones's discussion of disasters as shocks to the economic system and his comments about what determines their level of harm are particularly apt in relation to rural fires in Russia:

> The effects are in any case functions of the technological specifica-tions in which they occur and the social and economic systems which play host to them. They are not, in truth, completely exoge-nous acts of God divorced from the choices made by man. For example, the density of human population, their income level and social organization, the crops they grow and the animals they keep all affect the degree of vulnerability to particular shocks and the impact they will have.[43]

Information on the causes of village fires comes from the Central Statistical Committee's publications, zemstvo reports on fire insurance programs, newspa-per articles, eyewitness accounts submitted to the Tenishev Ethnographic Bureau, petitions for emergency relief sent to the Ministry of the Interior, firefighters' publications, the record of the 1902 All-Russian Firefighters' Conference, and materials from the 1902 state-sponsored Committees on the Needs of Agriculture. The limitations of the Central Statistical Committee's numbers apply equally to the information on causes. According to the Central Statistical Committee, the distribution of causes from 1870 to 1904 was that shown in table 3.3. As the editors presenting these figures recognized, the large percentage of fires attributed to "other causes" indicated not only that local officials failed to determine the causes of fires in more than one-third of the cases but also that the accuracy of the other categories was probably open to question as well.

It was extremely difficult for officials to get peasants to provide full infor-mation about a fire's origin if the prospect of a fine or imprisonment loomed. Arson was the most difficult to identify conclusively, for reasons to be discussed in the next chapter. Many educated commentators were convinced that most of the fires that fell under "other causes" were arson fires set by the community or with its sanction. The consistency in the distribution of percentages across four

Table 3.3: Reported Causes of Fires in European Russia, 1870-1909,
as Percentages of All Reported Fires

Years	Lightning	Stoves and Chimneys	Carelessness	Arson	Other
1870–1874	3.3	10.0	33.1	10.6	43.0
1875–1879	3.1	8.6	28.8	12.4	47.1
1880–1884	3.5	10.9	30.6	13.6	41.4
1885–1889	3.2	10.6	35.9	13.2	37.1
1890–1894	3.7	12.5	35.0	12.4	36.4
1895–1899	3.3	14.3	37.6	9.9	34.9
1900–1904	2.7	15.5	36.6	10.3	34.9
1905–1909	2.6	15.3	28.8	14.6	38.7

Source: Tsentral'nyi statisticheskii komitet, Ministerstvo Vnutrennikh del 1912: xl.

decades is striking, however, and that fact alone invites some confidence in the figures. Even in the subsequent five-year period, 1905–1909, when arson fires figured so prominently in peasant rebellions, there was very little shift (table 3.3).

That around 97 percent of reported fires over the entire period were identified as anthropogenic or "other" makes especially pertinent Jones's emphasis on the "technological specifications" and "social and economic systems" in which fires occurred. Technology was implicated most directly in fires attributed to poor stove maintenance and to carelessness.

Domestic Technologies

The peasants' view of fire as friendly when contained but dangerous when it broke free was especially germane to fire in the family stove. Stoves were the most important fire technology in the villages of European Russia. They dominated the physical living space and defined shelter itself. Two and a half to three square meters in size, the stove consisted of two major parts: a wooden frame or cage, and within it, the clay or stone stove itself (see fig. 1.1). Right up to the end of the nineteenth century, many stoves had no proper stovepipe or chimney to release smoke outside the house, and those that did often had wooden chimneys. In some areas, the stove included a stucco peak or cap that released smoke—and sparks—toward the ceiling inside the house. Otherwise, peasants regulated heat and smoke by opening and closing the mouth of the stove. Peasants continued to prefer chimneyless stoves for at least two reasons. First, thatch roofs (which the vast majority of houses had) teemed with insects, and the stove's smoke served as a ready source of fumigation. Second, peasants believed that chimneyless stoves gave off more heat.[44]

A zemstvo statistician, I. P. Belokonskii, had the opportunity to test both propositions during a trip between Orel and Kursk Provinces in the 1890s. Pulling up to a village on a fall afternoon, he saw a cluster of "smoking thatch roofs," sure evidence that in each of them, smoke from the stove was making its way out of the house through the straw above.[45] He asked the local peasant who had picked him up at the train station if there were any houses with chimneys in the village, to which the peasant replied, "None." His "bourgeois mood" plummeting, Belokonskii went to the village elder's house, but one look convinced him that it would be "physically impossible to stay there." The elder's wife suggested that he go over to Daria's house, which she called "the little warm one." Off he went, arriving at Daria's door within moments, and sighing with relief when he saw no smoke inside the house. Daria, it turned out, had come up with her own solution—the mouth of her stove opened not into the izba but into her hay shed. Belokonskii described this as "undoubtedly original progress in housing construction." He conceded, however, that while the izba was smoke-free, it was rather cold, especially on the floor. That was just the half of it.

When he settled down in the evening for his tea before bedtime, the smoke-free room displayed its other disadvantages. First, mice ran freely over the benches and shelves, watching him calmly as he tried to enjoy his tea; again his "bourgeois mood" was destroyed. Second, he noticed the roaches. He asked Daria if there were many roaches in the izba, and she peacefully and with some apparent pride told him, "Sir, we have a flood of roaches."[46] His recollection of this memorable night continued:

> When, having finished my tea, I blew out my candle and lay down to sleep, roaches immediately began to pour down on me like rainfall. I threw myself as if I had been stung off my simple bed, and when I relit the candle, I was dumbfounded by a phenomenon, the likes of which I had never seen: my entire bed looked like a solid, black, moving blot, an incalculable number of roaches continued to rain down. Having pulled hundreds of these vile insects off myself with great effort, I put on my cap as soon as I could and pulled up the collar on my jacket, since the attack on my head did not cease; the walls no less than the ceiling were covered with a solid mass of insects. Moreover, when I looked closer, I saw that in addition to the overwhelming number of cockroaches, there were bedbugs,

lice, and so on, crawling along the walls. There was, of course, no thought of sleep, so I began, frightening the mice, to march from corner to corner, without any end in sight to this pastime, since my pocket watch showed that it was only 8:00 in the evening! Fortunately, my hostess was not asleep, and having heard my steps, came into the "little warm one."

"How can you possibly live in such an izba?" I asked.

"It's even worse in there where we are . . . "

"Where?"

"There, where we're sleeping."

"How can you survive it?"

"God forbid, where we live! . . . We get used to it. The kids scream because of these accursed beasts (she pointed to the insects) until they are about three years old, but then they get used to it. There, listen, the little one's screaming: go in, have a look at what's happening in there."

Having grabbed my candle, I went with my hostess into the other half of the izba, without the "little warm one." When I glanced into the cradle, I simply recoiled: the unfortunate infant was lying in insects as solid as hay, he was covered with roaches, which were crawling in his mouth and his ears, and the helpless little sufferer was trying to beat them away with his little hands.[47]

With images as graphic as this one to illustrate what life without smoke inside a peasant house meant in the absence of pesticides, the revulsion of educated Russians against the peasants' "irrational" preference for chimneyless stoves itself seems irrational. Anyone who has pulled crawling cockroaches off her face during every night spent in the main dormitory of Moscow State University a century after Belokonskii recorded this scene can sympathize with the peasants' preference for warmth and undisturbed sleep over chilly nights in the company of thousands of exoskeletal bedfellows. While this experience was an unprecedented one for Belokonskii, he found as he traveled about the steppe region among villages of former proprietary serfs that they were so similar that it was difficult to distinguish one from another, and he soon lost "the sensation of movement" altogether.[48] Everywhere, chimneyless stoves led to smoking thatch roofs in a monotonous landscape of dust and haze.

Everywhere, equally, this technology was a constant fire hazard. Poor maintenance of the body of the stove could let excessive heat or sparks escape through cracks and ignite the wooden frame. A faulty door enabled shifting logs to fall out or sparks to float up into the wood and thatch interior of the house. A crack in a stovepipe or chimney could bring heat, sparks, or high flames into direct contact with a wooden wall or a wood or thatch roof. The imperial government recognized these hazards, of course, and tried to address them through regulations and threat of punishment. Various building decrees and the Building Code issued in 1857 (amended in 1886 and 1887) called for the elimination of so-called black, or chimneyless, residences "to the extent possible" and for the construction of brick chimneys rising at least one *arshin* (around two meters) above the roof. It also decreed that stoves be built on earth or brick foundations, with bricks separating them from wooden walls.[49] Article 32 of the Fire Code (also issued in 1857; amended in 1876, 1879, 1881, and 1883) stated that heads of households were required to have their stovepipes cleaned at least once a month and to inspect and repair them as necessary every three months.[50] Governors received this and other articles on fire prevention excerpted from the Fire Code as a special circular of the Police Department in 1878.[51] Peasants were also forbidden to light their stoves at night.[52]

"Carelessness" issued from the multiple, repeated uses of fire in everyday life, which offered countless opportunities for lapses in handling fire or watching over it. It combined with technology when peasants mishandled the fire they used for illumination. By far the most common means of lighting houses was the luchina. Candles were a sign of wealth across the period, and kerosene lamps began to appear in only the most prosperous homes in the 1880s and 1890s.[53] Kerosene lamps frequently exploded if they were not filled properly. Within the izba, the luchina seems rarely to have caused fires, because it hung over a bucket or trough of water. But when peasants took a torch or candle into a storage shed or barn, fire often broke out when they were set down on or dropped into straw. For this reason, the Fire Code forbade carrying torches or candles into attics, barns, or storage sheds without some kind of fire-resistant globe ("not made of paper").[54]

In the drying barn, peasants smoked grain before storing it to prevent rot. The dangers of this process were well known and captured in the saying, "The bathhouse won't burn down, but you can't extinguish a drying barn."[55] Fire was also essential in steaming and drying flax and hemp when peasants prepared them for processing into cloth and rope. These activities also fell under building regulations, which decreed that threshing floors and drying barns be built either outside the residential section of villages entirely or at least twenty-five sazhens (around fifty-three meters) from homestead structures.[56] Fire regulations stated that peasants were never to leave these structures unattended when live fires or coals were in use.[57] The imperial government distributed these regulations to governors and local police officials and ordered that they be displayed in posting inns, pubs, and taverns. Failure to comply with them could be a civil or criminal offense.[58]

Samovars and tobacco also provided opportunities for accidents with fire. A typical samovar fire broke out in Sol'vychegod District, Vologda Province, in July 1895 when the peasant Pestich fell asleep after setting up his samovar for a late-night cup of tea. A live coal fell out of the burner as he slept, and it eventually ignited the wood floor and set the whole house ablaze. A passing neighbor saw the fire's glow from the window and banged on the door to arouse Pestich and his family. They all jumped out of the windows and survived.[59] Local observers consistently bemoaned the fact that peasants had careless smoking habits, tapping hot ashes onto straw in the yards and sheds of their homesteads.[60]

Information on the locations in which fires originated reflected fire's multiple uses in daily life. In 1869, for example, of the 414 fires recorded by zemstvo fire agents in Chernigov Province, 143 originated in houses, whereas the rest broke out in outbuildings. From January to June 1870, 81 fires originated in houses, 66 in outbuildings, and 14 in drying barns. The greatest numbers of fires originating in outbuildings, including drying barns, occurred from June through August.[61] In Novgorod Province in 1901, of 1,670 fires reported to zemstvo fire agents, only 17.5 percent originated in houses, whereas 66.7 percent originated in heated farm buildings (threshing barns, bathhouses, drying barns, and so forth), with the balance breaking out in yards, unheated sheds, or mills.[62]

Two groups of the village population were considered especially hazardous around fire "technologies": women and children. Observers castigated peasant women, who were exclusively responsible for tending the stove, for dumping hot coals and ashes directly into the yard outside their door, where straw and wood chips littered the ground.[63] Investigators also found that fires often began because women left flax and hemp on the stove in the izba or another heated structure to dry unattended. Paraskovia Tushchina made her way into the historical record in 1882 when she lit a fire in her bathhouse in Ustiuzh District, Novgorod Province, where she intended to dry recently harvested flax. Having fired up the stove, she left it to get more firewood. In her absence, the bathhouse caught fire, rapidly becoming a charred skeleton. The men of the village had a nasty turn when they tore it down, for under its charred planks they discovered a child's body. Judging by the corpse's size and her granddaughter's absence from the village, grandmother Paraskovia realized that she had unwittingly burned the four-year-old alive.[64]

Farming and Labor Patterns

Children's roles in causing village fires point to "the social and economic systems" that both made accidental fires possible and increased the risk that fires would destroy entire villages. As we have seen, fires were most frequent in the spring, summer, and fall, and the largest fires (as determined by the number of structures burned per fire) also happened during these seasons, the summer months being the worst. These were the seasons of field work in the agricultural heartland, a time when everyone of working age (roughly from ten years old to sixty) spent every daylight hour and many nights in the fields outside the village. Not only from the heartland but from northern provinces as well, fire reports poured into St. Petersburg describing fires set by children playing with matches when they were left unattended during these times (fig. 3.2).[65] From Novgorod District, Novgorod Province, in June 1896, the governor received the report of such a fire, in which child's play burned down sixty-two of the "crowded" sixty-four farmsteads and all of the outbuildings in a village one May afternoon, leading to losses worth more than forty thousand rubles.[66] Not only were all the able adults in the fields during these months, but so were the villages' horses, which meant that they were not at hand to pull wagons with water or any firefighting equipment the peasants might have possessed.[67]

Farming patterns, too, contributed to these planting and harvesting season disasters. Strip farming, the three-field system, and communal land distrib-

Fig. 3.2. *Children in a yard with wood and litter at hand. When such children were left on their own, their idle play became a fire hazard.*

ution scattered crops across a great distance beyond the closely packed village streets. They also drew away family labor units, which might be groups as small as two or as large as ten or more, spread all over the commune's lands. Christine Worobec has calculated, for example, that in the Trubchevskii District of Orel Province, the farthest strips could be as close as three versts (about two miles) or as far as ten *versts* (about six miles) from the village.[68] Word of a fire would have to move through shouted cries from strip to strip. When peasants described themselves in relief petitions as "having seen the fire and run up to it," they literally meant run. How else could they all get back across newly plowed furrows or through fields of mature wheat or over the stubble and stacks of freshly mown hay? And how quickly could they run, when many them were barefoot, and all of the women were struggling against long skirts? A good cross-country runner in modern running shoes on a clean surface could cover three versts in under fourteen minutes and six versts in forty minutes. Strong peasant men in bast shoes or barefoot slogging through uneven fields would take much longer—long enough for a voracious fire to seize most of their village before they got there. Once they arrived, they confronted the challenge of extinguishing enormous blazes. And then the question of missing technology contributed to fire's power, because there was so little firefighting equipment in working order across rural European Russia (a problem to be discussed in chapter 8).

Climatic Factors

Everything came together in the agricultural heartland. Weather conditions ensured that the villages would be veritable tinderboxes. In the central black earth region, heat and drought characterized July and August, when average temperatures hovered around 20 degrees centigrade (68° Fahrenheit) for European Russia as a whole but in Tambov Province could reach 39 degrees centigrade (100° F.), in Kursk, 36 degrees (95° F.), and in Voronezh, 27 degrees (90° F.).[69] It was not unusual for villages to go without rain for weeks. The village of Drobyshev in Orel Province, for example, had no rain for the entire month of July 1891, and the black earth region was in a drought that year from early spring through August. Similar droughts struck in 1880–82, 1890, and 1901.[70] Droughts dried out houses, roofs, fences, sheds, stacked wood and straw, ponds, wells, streams, and riverbeds. The numbers and sizes of the fires reported in 1890 and 1891 in Orel Province were significantly higher than usual (see table 3.4).

The same pattern prevailed in the other provinces in the region. In Riazan Province, the number of buildings burned rose from 5,028 in 1881 to 9,731 in

Table 3.4: Reported Fires and Losses in Orel Province, 1888–1894

Year	Reported Fires	Buildings Burned	Losses in Rubles
1888	1,026	3,917	1,622,807
1889	1,178	3,663	1,697,097
1890	1,291	5,209	2,197,981
1891	1,519	7,078	3,923,597
1892	1,067	3,908	1,938,211
1893	710	2,135	1,017,212
1894	904	2,387	1,201,738

Source: Tsentral'nyi statisticheskii komitet, Ministerstvo Vnutrennikh del 1897: 28.

1882; in Tambov Province, from 5,782 to 9,108; and in Kursk Province, from 3,470 to 6,030.[71] During the next drought, those numbers shot up to 18,626 in 1890 and 19,050 in 1891 in Riazan Province; to 14,315 in 1890 and 14,669 in 1891 in Tambov; and to 6,286 in 1890 and 8,022 in 1891 in Kursk.[72] In Saratov Province, the number of buildings burned in 1890 was 10,509; in 1891 it was 8,656; and the range for the other five years between 1888 and 1894 was 3,608–6,741.[73] Reporting to the Saratov Provincial Committee on the Needs of Agriculture in 1902, the governor, A. P. Engel'gardt, attributed the 1,650 fires and the destruction of more than 50,000 structures in 1901 largely to prolonged drought and high winds and temperatures, but he insisted that these factors only made the fundamental contributors of construction and social patterns worse.[74]

Stephen J. Pyne reminds us that these numbers may seem exceptional in the context of a modernizing country but that they confirmed Russia's continued entrapment in the natural ecological cycles of fire: droughts prepared the fuels and opportunities for fire to feed itself, to clear the landscape, only to leave it ready to renew itself through new growth.[75] Deforestation throughout European Russia in the post-Emancipation period exacerbated the tendency toward droughts and diminished local water sources, making fires more likely and equally disabling the peasants' firefighting prospects. As early as the 1880s, a local surveyor in Saratov Province observed that whole areas had been cleared of trees around local springs. Loss of trees quickened runoff there as surely as it had in colonial New England, with the same results—silted-in rivers and streams, clogged springs, and parched land.[76]

Along with heat and drought, wind also worked with fire and against the peasants of this area. In the summer, prevailing winds came from the southeast, blowing in hot, dry air from the southeastern steppes. Given the relative absence of trees, the winds maintained higher speeds than they did in the forested north.[77] Even in the provinces around Moscow and the upper Volga basin, wind played a cruel trick on the peasants. During the summer farming months, winds were strongest at midday, when all the adults were working in the fields, making it more likely that a small fire started by unattended children would be whipped up into a major firestorm.[78] In the southern steppe, in provinces such as Simbirsk, Samara, and Saratov, whirlwinds often appeared suddenly in summer, when southeast winds were characterized by "remarkably high temperatures."[79] At the end of a dry season, whirlwinds became blinding dust storms, making the steppe in autumn "one solid, immense black spot of inescapable dirt."[80]

These climatic factors contributed to what fire ecologists term a "natural fire danger," to distinguish natural environmental factors from anthropogenic factors such as Jones's social, technological, and economic systems, which in turn contribute—along with lightning strikes—to the "actual fire danger" resulting from "ignition risk."[81] It seems very likely that rural inhabitants of these naturally "hot zones" had some justification for viewing their annual fire seasons as inevitable, unalterable features of their existence, bearable only when conceptualized as "a visitation from God which one must not go against."[82] As Pyne has said of Europe: "It could not remove fire from nature any more than it could extricate itself from fire."[83] Caught in the same relationship, peasants of European Russia received annual reminders of the combined power of heat, wind, drought, and dreaded ignition in the form of lightning, matches, burning tobacco, or the glowing detritus of stoves.

Construction Patterns

If climate, labor, and child-care patterns were partners with fire during the field-work season, the fourth partner, and the one that at first glance seems the most susceptible to change, was the physical environment of the village. Despite some regional variation in building materials and patterns, in all but a handful of provinces of European Russia, villages consisted of wooden buildings topped with straw or wood roofs. Again, Pyne offers perspective from his studies of fire cultures around the world: "those [human settlements] built of wildland materials burned like wildland fires—wooden dwellings flaming like windfall, daub-and-wattle huts torching like brush, thatch roofs flaring like the grasses they are."[84]

By all accounts, thatch roofs were the most pernicious features of the physical environment of rural Russia in terms of flammability. As one peasant saying went, "Fire runs along rooftops."[85] This, too, was a question of technologies as Eric L. Jones employs the term, for the methods and materials of house and roof construction moved the fuels in the environment into an engineered setting. Statistics on the percentages of building materials for roofs and structures in 1882 reveal that in all but a handful of provinces, thatch roofs and wood buildings dominated the villages of European Russia. In Khar'kov, Poltava, Voronezh, Kursk, Podolia, Chernigov, Tula, Orel, Kiev, Kherson, Kovno, Penza, Tambov, Grodno, Vilna, Estland, and Ekaterinoslavl Provinces, more than 90 percent of all structures were roofed in thatch. Only in St. Petersburg, Ufa, Novgorod, Orenburg, Vologda, Viatka, Olonets, Perm, and Arkhangel'sk Provinces were fewer than 50 percent of all roofs thatched; there, wood roofs predominated. As for metal roofs, they constituted more than 1 percent of all roofs in only nine provinces—the highest percentage (10.5 percent) being in Tauride Province, and the next highest (5.03 percent), in Ekaterinoslavl Province.[86] Similar patterns prevailed for the buildings below the roofs. In forty-one of the forty-nine provinces in European Russia, more than 95 percent of all buildings were constructed of wood. Only in Tauride (84.2 percent) and Kherson (63.6 percent) were more than 25 percent of the buildings made of masonry materials.

One student of local fire prevention and fire insurance efforts, I. Gofshtetter, stated in 1902 that the previous thirty years had witnessed a worsening of the thatch roof problem as the deforestation accompanying Russia's population explosion and railroad construction had made wooden roofs prohibitively expensive. Peasants in the forested north, especially, had shifted increasingly to straw as the primary construction material not only for roofs but even, in the areas experiencing the most serious deforestation, for the walls of unheated sheds built right next door to heated residential structures.[87] Novgorod Province offered one example of this trend; there, the proportion of buildings roofed with thatch, which had been only 29.8 percent in 1882, rose to 43 percent in 1884 and 49 percent in 1901.[88] These figures are all the more striking because the Novgorod zemstvo itself spearheaded the effort to develop alternative roofing materials.

The risk of thatched roofs as a fire hazard increased in villages where izbas and outbuildings of one homestead directly abutted the outbuildings and izbas of neighboring homesteads, and where all of these buildings were roofed with straw. Reports throughout the period, right up to those of the district Committees on the Needs of Agriculture, published in 1903, stressed the dangers for fire these villages posed, as well as the difficulties of extinguishing fires once they struck one of these contiguous roofs. In Cherepovets District,

Novgorod Province, for example, a fire broke out in July 1895 that was aided by an abundance of fuel in the form of thatch roofs and by high winds to drive the flames. After consuming one village, the fire literally flew over to a neighboring one, where it burned twenty-four more homesteads.[89]

Even when villages followed prescribed reconstruction plans—to be discussed in chapter 7—fires continued to race through them. A correspondent from Sycheva District to the Smolensk provincial newspaper in 1882 explained: "Even the intervals between buildings, established according to the Building Code's requirements, are no salvation. I have heard, for example, of a fire in a village of the Chernaia Tesovaksaia canton; 10 years ago this village burned to the ground and was rebuilt afterwards with intervals between homesteads according to plan, and now it has burned to the ground again."[90]

Subsequent revisions to the Building Code had brought no significant success twenty years later, judging by the 1903 district committee reports. Changing the village layout simply did not eradicate the hazards inherent in the construction materials themselves. The Bakhmut District committee from Ekaterinoslavl Province described almost all of its villages as "a continuous mass of logs, branches, and straw."[91] Reporting from Syzran District, Simbirsk Province, a zemstvo delegate asserted that "until thatch disappears from the roofs of peasant dwellings, fires will continue their ruinous action in villages."[92] Delegates before the Chernigov provincial committee maintained that one could walk from one end of the village to the other under a continuous thatch roof in northern districts of the province.[93]

P. P. Mikhailov, a zemstvo fire inspector in Nizhnii Novgorod Province, offered a comparison of percentages of buildings with thatch roofs and percentages of buildings burned by district for the period 1868–1896. His statistics demonstrated that the presence of thatch roofs increased the damages caused by fires. Districts with the highest percentages of thatch roofs were also the districts with the largest numbers and percentages of buildings burned in the province. Kniaginin District, for example, where 81.6 percent of the structures had thatch roofs, accounted for 14.3 percent of the buildings burned in the province over the twenty-six-year period. Balakhnin District, where only 40 percent of the structures had thatch roofs, accounted for only 3.2 percent of the buildings burned during those years.[94]

When roofs in European Russia were not thatched, they were almost always made of wood. Less flammable than straw, wood still burned easily, of course, especially during the hot, dry summer months. Wooden roofs also posed a fire hazard during the period in the fall before snow fell to cover them but when threshing and drying barns were heated with fires and when stoves inside the izbas were being fired to maximum heat as the cold weather settled in. Whatever the roof, the fundamental building material for the structures below was likely to be wood. In all but seven provinces, at least 94 percent of the buildings in the villages of Russia were constructed of wood in 1882. Within these wooden and thatch-covered structures lay other flammable materials, most obviously grain, hay, and straw. In the yards and alleyways, to the extent that they existed, there were more piles of straw and hay, along with stacks of fire-

Fig. 3.3. *A street scene in a peasant village in the late nineteenth century features an almost continuous line of wood huts with thatch roofs. Another fire hazard, a woodpile, lies just beyond the cart.*

wood and kindling. It is difficult to imagine a more inviting environment for that unwelcome guest, runaway fire (fig. 3.3).

A. K. Nikitin's statement to the All-Russian Firefighters' Conference in 1902 captured both the Russian problem and its contrast with Europe's advantage:

Every year, with the arrival of the summer period of peasant labor known as the "passion," fires begin in the villages and settlements everywhere in Russia, causing terrible and enormous losses. This phenomenon is so common that it has earned the name of the "fire season," or, as the

Central Statistical Committee of the Ministry of the Interior calls it—"our historical evil," which is unknown to Western Europe, because it is made of stone, while Russia is wooden, or to be more precise—made of wood and straw.[95]

Jones's analysis of the "European miracle" demonstrates that these turn-of-the-century Russian observers were accurate in their conviction that wood and thatch were major handicaps from which Western Europe largely no longer suffered. Jones concluded that construction materials were the key to reducing "settlement fires" across Europe as early as the fifteenth century. "The main cause was rebuilding in non-flammable materials and will probably be found to relate to the advance across the lands of seaboard Europe of a brick frontier, or more precisely of the tile roof frontier that slightly preceded it."[96]

Russia's "historical evil" cruelly worsened when other aspects of rural daily life improved. Not only the appearance of consumer goods such as samovars and matches exacerbated the fire season. The sheer increase in the number of people, a sign of increasing prosperity of its own, also increased fires' capacity to eradicate that prosperity.

Population Growth

There was no doubt among contemporary observers that the dangerous combination of a highly flammable village and multiple uses of fire in that setting had become much more threatening because of population growth among the peasants. A straightforward comparison of the rate of increase in the number of fires and the rate of increase in population shows that the former exceeded the latter but that a relationship existed between increase in population and increase in fires. This relationship in rural Russia was precisely the opposite of that in western Europe's experience. E. L. Jones and L. E. Frost have argued that the ability of European and United States cities to experience rapid population growth while reducing the incidence of fires constituted a "convergence fortunate for the urban capital formation of the nineteenth-century developed world."[97] Rural Russia experienced no such "fortunate convergence." Instead, inhabitants of villages in European Russia found themselves ever more perilously packed into structures that were only marginally transformed from the fuels that would ordinarily feed fire in an uninhabited landscape. In those provinces of European Russia where population was highest, the incidence of reported fires was likely to be high as well.

Map 3.5 Population density in 1897

Map 3.6 Reported fires per population in 1897

In the eyes of contemporaneous observers, increased population exerted pressure on housing. As families grew larger, they required more living space. In this connection, family divisions (*razdely*) also became an element in the fire debate. Although critics of family divisions in the 1870s and 1880s did not emphasize this connection, by the turn of the century it had become prominent in discussions of population growth and the increase in the incidence of fires in the countryside.[98] For when families divided, the new households often built new izbas on the original plot of *usad'ba*, or homestead land, that the family had received as part of the Emancipation settlement, because they did not want to reduce the amount of arable land in their allotment. Worse still, they sometimes built their own collection of outbuildings, even to the extent of constructing separate drying and threshing barns. The result often was that "because 75% of the peasant farmsteads allotted were $1/2$ *desiatina* in size, by now, the crowding of the peasants' buildings has become solid, unbroken construction, roof to roof."[99]

An obvious question concerns the relationship between population density and fires. Data on population density are at hand, but primarily at the provincial level. These are misleading within the context of fire. A glance at map 3.5 for population density in 1897 quickly shows that some of the most fire-prone provinces were not the most densely populated. Mapping the number of fires per one thousand members of the population also challenges the perception of the agricultural heartland as the most hazardous zone (map 3.6). Even Arkhangel'sk Province had more fires per capita than Saratov, Kiev, or Voronezh. How might these discrepancies be explained? The answers lie in population distribution within provinces and construction patterns within villages, as well as in the perspective of the government in St. Petersburg. For the central government, the cumulative losses for European Russia as a whole were more disturbing than the effects on individual communities or provinces. The per capita figures were less worrisome than the total numbers of fires and buildings lost, because the absolute numbers of fires and damages in the agricultural heartland were a larger threat to the imperial economy than were fires in Arkhangel'sk or Novgorod Province.

On the question of population density, the uneven settlement patterns in such peripheral provinces as Perm, Viatka, and Novgorod explain why they could be sparsely populated overall yet suffer some of the greatest numbers of fires. In these regions, settlements clustered in closely packed villages, yielding what New Englanders describe as "thickly settled" areas, whereas much of the province continued to be undisturbed forest or, in the case of Viatka, an industrial forest in the throes of clear-cutting for the lumber market. Viatka Province offers a vivid illustration of how these factors force adjustments to conclusions drawn on the basis of population or population density alone. Villages were concentrated in the southern section of the province, south of the Viatka River. Even individual districts (*uezdy*), density within cantons (*volosti*) varied. One of the most fire-prone districts, Malmyzh, was the most densely populated, but that population was concentrated in one-sixth of the district's area, with the most congested construction and, not least important, the most thorough deforestation. This meant crowded villages in which not wooden but thatch roofs predominated. Finally, Malmyzh District occupied a high elevation exposed to winds.[100] Also in Viatka Province, Orlov District had three distinct population zones, with population density in the north of 27 persons per square verst, in the center, of 40 per square verst, and in the south, of 28 per square verst.[101] Maps from neighboring Vologda province of fire insurance payments show that such variation in fires' intensity and impact, even within individual districts, could be significant (fig. 3.4).

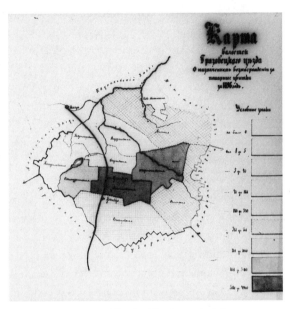

Fig. 3.4. *Map prepared by the Vologda provincial zemstvo insurance program showing the distribution of fire insurance payments village by village in Griazovets District, 1896. Source: GAVO, fond 34, opis' 5, delo 152, l. 2.*

Population growth alone did not determine European Russia's fire culture. The technologies of heating, illumination, construction, and agricultural processing joined with labor and child-care patterns, with the fuel-rich environment, and with fire's companion elements—wind, high temperatures, and drought—to set the terms of human interaction with fire. In Russia's preindustrial rural landscape, where houses were only minimally transformed "wildland materials," fire still had the advantage. Within that complex equation, Russia's considerable human fertility in the late nineteenth century increased fire's opportunities to bring ruin to individuals, families, communities, provinces, and the empire as a whole.

Rendering Assistance and Paying the Costs

Because of the speed and extent of fires, they were often community events, both in the destruction they caused and the community assistance they elicited. Every fire had the potential to spread to the entire community. Even when a fire was contained and only one or two households lost their property, the community paid. Because fire was so insatiable, families often lost everything and were left "without shelter, clothes, or a crust of bread under the open sky."[102] A typical inventory of property lost included clothes, fodder, grain, firewood, dishes, and such furnishings as there were, in addition to the structures themselves.[103] As in the case of Ivan Stoliarov's family, the victims had to secure housing, clothing, and food. Petitions to the Ministry of the Interior often referred to community assistance as the first, albeit inadequate, form of relief. As one particularly eloquent plea cried out after a fire that destroyed 210 homesteads in Kostroma Province in 1887:

> Everyone is shaken by the size of the damages we suffered (400,000 rubles), and that's only obvious, but how are we to endure the loss, to remain without shelter, to lose everything entire families have acquired over many years and to have no hope of regaining our former situation through our own sweat and blood and remaking our family nest without the help of others? . . . To whom can we turn? All those good people nearest to us are giving us what they can, and their name as benefactors will be blessed.[104]

Local support was critical. It was also compulsory, for the imperial government had decreed that peasant communes after the Emancipation in 1861 were responsible for caring for the needy in their midst and for "ensuring that their members did not beg."[105] According to reports to the Tenishev Ethnographic Bureau, local support was a combination of providing temporary shelter, food, and clothing and helping the victims rebuild their homes.[106] Local could mean one's family (as in Stoliarov's case), one's village, or neighboring villages. The period between the fire and recovery could be as short as a few months or as long as ten years, according to various reports. Depending upon the season, a habitable structure could be rebuilt in as little as two months.[107] In the interim, economic hardship diffused, as Vice Governor Frederiks of Nizhnii Novgorod reminded the minister of the interior following a devastating fire in his province: "I should also say that despite the fact that this fire burned down the most prosperous section of the village, . . . the rest of the village and the neighboring villages of Muromsk and Gorokhov Districts will suffer as well from damage to trade and production in the region." Some peasants felt the impact of their neighbors' fire immediately, when the governor asked those in surrounding districts to contribute to a fund for the victims.[108]

For the peasants of Alytyrsk District, Simbirsk Province, it took much longer to get on their feet again after a fire that destroyed their entire village in May 1891. Two and a half years later, entire families were living "in various villages with good people," unable even to put the money together to buy materials to rebuild their homes, because of a series of bad harvests.[109] Peasants from another village in the same district explained that they had been able to rebuild their houses only because they had sold all of their livestock.[110] Several petitioners to the Ministry of the Interior mentioned having sold their animals to buy building materials or grain.

Fire disasters carried their effects beyond the household and community to drain regional, provincial, and national resources as well. Most directly, zemstvo fire insurance programs had to pay premiums to the victims; their experience is discussed more fully in chapter 6. Zemstvos also had little choice but to offer burned-out peasants relief from other obligations, thus diminishing resources for other programs. In 1869, for example, the Sarapul District zemstvo board in Viatka Province granted the burned-out peasants of Laksheva village a waiver of their repayment of grain they had received from the zemstvo grain storehouse and also relieved the commune to which Laksheva belonged of any responsibility for the loan.[111] Peasant appeals to governors and ministers also drained governmental budgets and prompted the publication of case-specific and general decrees on the conditions for grants and loans.[112]

Before the Emancipation in 1861, the state's beneficence was directed primarily toward state and crown peasants. But even to those dependents the tsar did not offer a free hand; instead, he offered interest-free loans of up to 150 rubles in May 1831, to be paid off in ten years.[113] Within six months, the maximum had been raised to 500 rubles, now available to all peasants, still interest free for twelve years. Furthermore, for those with no means to repay, one-time grants of up to 500 rubles to a family or individual were possible.[114] The state also offered free lumber from state lumberyards to fire victims among the state peasants.[115] In 1837, the court had to confront the problem of fire relief for peasants whose homes burned to the ground before they had had a chance to pay off loans they had received for rebuilding after previous fires. After much discussion, the minister of finance recommended that such loans be granted.[116]

These steps in the 1830s prepared the way for the temporary laws introduced in the 1860s as stopgap measures until the anticipated zemstvo mutual insurance programs could be put into effect as a way to replace the serf owners' responsibility and self-interest in rebuilding the burned-out peasant houses on their estates. Chapter 6 describes these temporary laws in greater detail; the relevant issue here is what these transitional measures cost the state. In the period 1862–1865 alone, the state paid out 4.2 million rubles to peasants who had lost property to fires in forty-one provinces, a figure that constituted fully one-fifth of all funds expended on enacting the Emancipation legislation.[117] As the authors of the laws governing these payments explained with evident dismay, fires and state loans for rebuilding after them were eating into the funds set aside to ensure adequate agricultural production after 1861, specifically the planting of fields. As chapter 6 demonstrates, the solution of passing these costs off to the peasants themselves through compulsory mutual insurance programs as of July 1, 1867, proved grossly inadequate. The hundreds of petitions that poured into the Economic Department of the Ministry of the Interior from peasants who were both insured and still destitute after receiving their insurance payments continued to force the government to make unwelcome budgetary choices.

Less easy to quantify in straightforward monetary terms were the hundreds of man hours that governors' chancelleries and central ministerial officials had to devote to considering appeals and deciding upon the levels of grants or loans to issue. Following an enormous fire in the settlement of Pavlovo in Nizhnii Novgorod Province in June 1872, for example, the governor and his assistants corresponded with officials at the Economic Department of the Ministry of the Interior for two and a half years, generating roughly two hundred pages of information, before the Minister of the Interior offered 42,615 rubles in the form of loans and 12,085 rubles as grants to the victims. By the time those figures had been set, the list of officials who had been drawn into the affair—investigating, assessing damages, assisting peasants by drawing up descriptions of their property losses, paying insurance premiums, and distributing relief funds—included the minister of the interior, the minister of finance, bureaucrats in the Economic Department of the Ministry of the Interior, the governor and vice governor, zemstvo fire agents and statisticians, district officials throughout the region, local policemen, and staff members of all the administrative units involved.[118] In this light, Alexander III's rescript in 1865, mandating financial assistance to fire victims, was thus one in a long line of beneficent acts by tsars who had to pay the price for ruling over a rapidly expanding population in a fire-prone empire where building and firefighting technologies were still preindustrial.

Fire's impact extended beyond the obvious damages to structures and movable property. The added misfortune of fires in the autumn was that they often consumed all of the peasants' recently harvested grain. This is why fires in the drying and threshing barns were so crippling. The loss of grain stores in the fall had two delayed consequences. As A. N. Engel'gardt's letters from Smolensk Province in the 1870s and 1880s made clear, the peasants of European Russia annually experienced a calendar of plenty and want—the want arriving like clockwork each spring as their grain stores diminished. In March, April, and May, they typically had to move from pure rye bread to adulterated "chaff bread." When grain ran out entirely, families went from household to household "begging for crusts of bread" in an annual ritual of individual need and community response.[119] Grain stores contained not only the food supply for the year but also the seed grain for the following year's harvest. This, too, the community had to share in order to "top off" what state and zemstvo emergency grain stores doled out. Only a bountiful harvest the following year could pull a family who had lost its harvest to an autumn fire out of its destitution and relieve the community. Finally, when peasant families ran low on grain, they often indebted themselves to their richer neighbors, both peasant and gentry. In exchange for grain, they bartered the one commodity they had left—their labor, which they promised for the next season of planting, harvesting, and processing. A devastating fire could mean the loss not only of property, the material embodiment of prosperity, but also of the freedom to schedule one's own or the family's labor over the next year. When peasants in the fields on a summer's day spied smoke rising from their villages, they raced back to try to save both everything they already possessed and all that they might become. When they arrived to find an "inextinguishable bonfire," hope itself turned to ashes.

Conclusion: An Experience Spectacular and Collective

When they raced back to a burning village, peasants were also drawn by something else—that peculiar mix of dread and excitement attached to disaster. As Stoliarov's memoir illustrates, village fires created indelible memories, shaping the local and national imagination. Their power to do so issued from their qualities as spectacles, complete with a transformation of the daily landscape and stimulation of all the senses, from the taste of smoke in one's mouth to heat against one's flesh and human and animal cries piercing one's ears. Even authors of the most mundane texts found descriptive power in fire scenes. The report of a district police chief in Vitebsk Province included the following: "Simply imagining the terrible scene of a fire when the raging element destroys everything in its path with insatiable greed, this noise, crackling, roaring, licking flames, entire shafts of fire, smoke, water, people shouting, heart-rending cries, horses' neighing, poultry rushing from side to side—simply imagining this terrible scene can be numbing. But actually to experience this disaster—what misfortune!"[120]

Here are the same images of transformation that Chekhov, Saltykov-Shchedrin, and Dostoevsky employed in their more intentionally dramatic contributions to the national imagination. Chekhov went a step further to explore the power of fires to titillate as well as to numb. As Julie de Sherbinin has noted, in "A Dreadful Night" (*Nedrobraia noch'*) Chekhov lingers over Maria Sergeevna's compulsion to view the fire, first from her attic and then on the scene itself. De Sherbinin describes this episode as a "a thrill-seeking excursion" and quotes Chekhov's explanation that "a thirst for powerful sensations gets the upper hand over fear and compassion for the woes of others."[121]

In *Devils*, Dostoevsky also explored fire's fascination and ability to awaken suppressed elements in the human psyche:

> A large conflagration at night always produces an exciting and exhilarating impression; this explains the attraction of fireworks. . . . A real fire is something different: there the horror and a vague feeling of personal danger, added to the thrilling effect of a night fire, produce in the spectator (not, of course, in those whose houses have gone up in flames) a certain shock to the system and as it were a challenge to the destructive instincts. . . . This grim sensation is almost always intoxicating.[122]

And in "Muzhiki," Chekhov's narrator observes that the Zhukovo peasants quickly returned to a heightened holiday mood after Georges and his band extinguished their fire. A correspondent to the Tenishev Ethnographic Bureau from Smolensk Province offered the same observation—that as soon as fires were extinguished, the mood would switch to one of excitement and high-pitched conversation, with peasants talking for days or months about their own experience or role in the fire's drama.[123]

In the end, fires were *de facto* and *de jure* community events. The shared nature of the fire experience is oddly vivid in the Building Code. Having stated that villages had to be rebuilt after fires according to an approved plan and that responsibility for preparing the site for relocated construction rested with the community (the *mir*), the decree continued in Article 496: "And it is the *mir* also that must carry out the cleanup on the former [burned-out] locations and turn them into suitable sites for structures designated by the plan."[124]

After the excitement passed and any corpses had been retrieved and buried, blackened beams, pottery shards, shattered glass, remnants of the stove, and cinders and ashes remained to be gathered or swept up by community members who had thus to revisit the scene and deal with its material consequences. What was a statistic to provincial and central authorities became a palpable, tactile reckoning for victims and their neighbors.

Everything suggests that peasants must have feared and loathed fire for its local consequences as much as the state and progressive activists despised the cumulative consequences that accrued across European Russia in tens of thousands of local blazes. There may indeed have been a congruence of national sentiment in reactions to accidental fires. But not all fires were accidental. Many were intentionally set. Furthermore, peasants often started such fires within their own communities, letting the "red rooster," the flames of arson, free within their own neighborhoods, with all the familiar risks attached. Fire in these cases was equally a community event—often, in fact, an action taken by the community to protect its norms.

Because fire could destroy so much, arson was especially threatening to the economic and social well-being of late imperial Russia. A match or burning cigarette dropped casually but intentionally into a yard full of wood chips and straw, to say nothing of kerosene ignited in a grain barn at night, could bring an entire community to its knees in supplication before the tsar himself. For this reason, generations of lawmakers over the centuries, from the very inception of Rus', had tried to use criminal law as a weapon against arson. As the following two chapters display, however, what lawmakers criminalized, peasants continued to choose as an effective weapon of social control and a language of protest within their own communities, as well as against those they deemed outsiders. When they did so, they returned to their roles as masters, rather than victims, of fire.

PART TWO

LETTING LOOSE
THE RED ROOSTER:
ARSON IN RURAL RUSSIA

Drought struck Penza Province in the summer of 1897, leaving the village of Stepanovka to desiccate in the heat during three weeks without rain. Having watched the sky from dawn to dark for one day too many, searching for any hint of clouds that might bring water to their thirsty crops and shrinking streams, the Stepanovka peasants gathered and came to a decision. They would seek God's assistance by going together, all who were able to walk the six miles, to a spring. There they would lift their voices to the heavens in collective prayer. They waited until the afternoon, when everyone had completed the midday meal, to walk out of their wooden, thatch-covered village along the parched road. Everyone walked away, leaving behind only the smallest children and one mother.

They must have formed a large crowd and a long line of walkers, because the village they left behind included more than one hundred homesteads. Perhaps that is why one woman in the group failed to notice that her next-door neighbor was missing. Perhaps in the excitement and crush of the procession she forgot that she should have looked for her neighbor's face. Or perhaps she was unconcerned because she had already dismissed the shouting match they had had three days earlier. Perhaps she had already forgotten the words her neighbor had hurled in her face: "You just wait! I'll get you with your chicken! I'll remember your chicken with a red rooster!"

Their dispute had been rather small, but it should have suggested that her neighbor was not to be trusted within the community. For the neighbor had stolen a chicken from her yard, then gone to the other end of this large village and sold it to a widow for fifteen kopeks. How could the thief know that her neighbor would chance to walk past the widow's house and recognize her chicken? Or that the widow's recollection would be clear enough to identify the culprit? Confronted with the chicken and the widow's accusation, the thief fought back, ending the quarrel with a promise to set fire to the other woman's property—to release the metaphorical red cock to carry her flames of vengeance.[1] It was no idle threat.

After the hundreds of villagers had filed away, the accused thief began her work. She fired up her stove, gathered hot coals in a basket, swaddled her two young children and went out into her yard. There, she placed the hot coals in the corner closest to the yard of the neighbor from whom she had stolen the chicken. The litter in the yard ignited immediately. She then dragged her two swaddled children over to the chimney of her neighbor's house, where she left them. Did they cry out? We don't know. What we do know is that the fire spread immediately across the street. Within thirty minutes, the entire village was on fire. By the time those who had left to pray for rain had run back at the sight and smell of columns of billowing, black smoke rising over their homes, the fire had died down. Six children, including the arsonist's own, had been burned alive, and 120 homesteads had gone up in flames.[2]

This was rural arson, Russian style, as it was understood at the end of the nineteenth century. The setting, actors, and victims were well-established elements in the mental landscape of educated observers as the century closed. When they spoke of rural arson, this is what they imagined. A village dispute, a mad peasant woman, a threat, a runaway fire, an entire village reduced to embers, and hundreds of peasant victims rendered destitute. From the 1860s through the first decade of the twentieth century, Russian observers comprehended arson in their countryside as a weapon primarily of revenge among members of the peasant population. Furthermore, arson for revenge was reported consistently across the period as an individual and a peculiarly female crime.

This is not rural arson's usual face in the comparative historiography of rural criminality or in the historiography of Russia. Since the publication of Eric Hobsbawm and George Rudé's pioneering study of rural laborers' rebellions in England in the 1830s,[3] arson has been read as a feature of peasants' protest against their "betters"—an example of peasants' agency in their struggle against perceived oppression and exploitation. In the riotous years in England in the 1830s and 1840s, intentional burnings became the most alarming and enduring symbol of upheaval and protest, thus ensuring the immediate linkage of incendiarism with the firing of farmers' and gentry's property and the general description of rebellion as an incendiary activity. Hobsbawm and Rudé's choice of a burning hayrick for the front cover of the 1973 edition of their study, and of a reproduction of a drawing titled "The Home of the Rick-Burner" from *Punch* for its frontispiece, underscored the association between arson and rural protest.[4]

Subsequent studies of rural arson in Russia, Great Britain, and the United States have largely followed their lead. In the historiography of Russia, rural arson long appeared almost exclusively as an element of the "peasant movement," a phrase used to define all forms of peasant protest from the time of the Emancipation in 1861 through the revolutionary upheavals of 1905–1907 and 1917–1921. This portrayal of rural arson conforms to an evolutionary continuum leading to proletarian class-consciousness. Soviet historians searched local archives for reports of arson practiced by peasants against neighboring gentry landowners or merchants, which they included in their compendia of incidents in the "peasant movement."[5] When Soviet and Western historians turned to the history of the peasantry, they located arson as a feature of peasant rebellion, especially during the disturbances of 1905–1907.[6] Teodor Shanin offered a graphic description of the high point of arson in October 1905: "It began in the Saratov *gub.* (province), and somewhat later in the Chernigov *gub.* (province). From these two epicentres it spread like a forest fire in several waves which eventually met, encompassing no less than half of European Russia. . . . Descriptions from Saratov speak of a red night-sky illuminated by the blaze of the burning estates."[7]

Barbara Alpern Engel, in her study of women's patterns of resistance, also restricted her references to arson to peasant-against-gentry arson and mistakenly included such attacks in her list of "unprecedented assaults on landlords' property," along with assaults of equally long standing such as pilfering wood from reserved forests.[8] In a recent monograph on rural crime and justice, the American historian Stephen Frank broke from this pattern in a brief discussion of arson among peasants, confirming my earlier analysis of arson as social control.[9]

For the revolutionary period 1917–1921, even Orlando Figes, who has made an explicit effort to break through the frames of Soviet-style class analysis by exploring relationships among peasants through a "trans-class" analysis, has placed arson within the usual context of peasant-against-gentry actions. Arson appears as part of the narrative about "peasants and squires"; Figes points to the burning of manors in the Volga River region, where, for example, "in Penza Province one-fifth of the manors were burned or destroyed in September and October 1917, alone."[10] Figes moves beyond these conflicts to explore other relationships between peasants and other groups in the revolutionary countryside, and he also notes that the peasants did not display wholesale vengeance even against the "squires." Even so, arson appears within the peasant-squire relationship and willy-nilly confirms its reputation in the historiography of Russia as a means of collective protest against wealthy landowners.

Rural arson after 1917 has likewise been placed within the frame of resistance. Here the category of class begins to pose some difficulties. Historians such as Sheila Fitzpatrick and Lynne Viola, in their studies of peasant resistance in the face of forced collectivization, have turned instead to the frame of peasants as insiders in their communities using arson against outsiders in the form of Soviet officials sent from the center, or in the form of local peasants who joined ranks with the Soviet government as agents of collectivization. Within that frame, Fitzpatrick still employs the language of class analysis offered by the Soviet state itself, identifying peasants who committed acts of violence (of which fourteen hundred in 1929 were arson) as "angry kulaks, or . . . other peasants recruited and directed by kulaks."[11] Although Fitzpatrick acknowledges that there was plain old malice in the Soviet countryside during Stalinism,[12] her interest and emphasis throughout her study are on resistance and protest. Arson appears solely within that frame. Viola is somewhat more cautious in her reading of rural violence during collectivization in 1930 and expands her category of class analysis to include "culture." But, like her Soviet and Western predecessors, she sees arson as a manifestation of resistance and protest—if not always against outsiders who were not part of the peasant culture, then against peasants who had violated peasant culture by allying with the outside forces. "What is clear is that fire, represented as arson, invoked fear and punished peasant turncoats, while serving as the peasant flag of resistance throughout the land."[13]

These scholars share a vision of arson as a collective act, either in the execution of the deed or in the arsonists' communities' tacit acceptance of it. In this interpretation, they conform to the analysis of arson in Great Britain and the United States, which has rested on data originating in the official judicial system. Scholars' reliance on official judicial sources ensured that they would find more incidents whose victims were people who knew how to make use of the judicial system and were confident that it would protect their property interests. David Jones concluded of rural arson in the Victorian countryside that it was "the major form of rural protest until trade unionism took firm hold in the late 1860s and 1870s."[14] The most telling evidence about the class nature of the crimes was the social standing of the arsonist and the victims. "Those attacked represented the whole spectrum of 'upper class' rural society," Jones explained, whereas two-thirds of those brought up on charges of arson "could be broadly described as 'agricultural labourers', the remaining third being chiefly composed of village craftsmen and unemployed labourers."[15] Arsonists were displaying, in the words of E. P. Thompson, the "subpolitical" consciousness characteristic of groups trying to defend "an older moral economy, which taught the immorality of any unfair method of forcing up the price of provisions by profiteering upon the necessities of the people."[16]

In the American South, emancipated slaves acted on the same impulses, according to Albert C. Smith. Arson in "Black-Belt Georgia" during the second half of the nineteenth century, he concluded, should also be understood as "a form of violent protest."[17] Race was also clearly a factor, but it was so tightly bound up with class, as defined by property ownership, that Smith considered the latter the more compelling explanation: "The most frequent and direct form of protest in attacks against private property developed out of class tensions between the propertied and the propertyless, more specifically, in conflicts involving white employers and their black employees."[18] Although the records reveal very few white accused arsonists, Smith recognized their existence as the living models for Faulkner's Abner Snopes in "Barn Burning." As he put it: "If at times blacks resorted to arson against whites as a safer means of protest than personal violence, poor whites, too, may have preferred arson as an outlet for frustrations against their socioeconomic betters."[19] Both John Archer and Stephen Hussey similarly identified rural arson as the handiwork of the unpropertied—the agricultural laborers of industrializing Britain, whose conditions of labor and living conditions, as well as their fundamental sense of human dignity, suffered most severely from the combination of new property laws, wage relations, and poor relief.[20] For all of these scholars, the most telling evidence—drawn largely from court records and newspaper accounts—was the identity of the accused arsonists as propertyless laborers and of the victims as either property owners or wage-paying farmers.

Rural arson in European Russia is equally susceptible to an analysis that sets the stage for peasant revolts in 1905–1907, in 1917–1921, and during the collectivization campaign. Some acts of rural arson were clearly a form of protest against new relationships that emerged between peasants and large property owners after the Emancipation. Their etiology and morphology are virtually indistinguishable from those of the barn burnings in Essex, East Anglia, and Georgia. In these acts, peasants are properly understood as resisters or protesters or even "terrorists." But such acts of arson were relatively infrequent during the second half of the nineteenth century. Arson in rural Russia was much more often a peasant-against-peasant affair. One discovers this immediately upon picking up a local newspaper or beginning to read through the archival files of district policemen's reports on local fires.

Between 1870 and 1909, the Ministry of the Interior received reports of 223,782 arson fires in forty-nine provinces of European Russia (see table 4.1). Yet when Soviet historians compiled their compendia of peasant disturbances, of which arson was only one form, they included only a fraction of this number. For example, P. A. Zaionchkovskii attributed the "crisis of autocracy" in the late 1870s in part to peasant protest. Drawing on his colleagues' compendia, he provided the figure of 328 disturbances between 1875 and 1884, of which 105 fell under the category "land seizures, seizing the harvest, trespassing, wood poaching, etc.," with arson part of the "etc."[21] During these same years, local police officials reported 45,133 incidents of arson. Furthermore, most of them identified the victims as peasants.

These acts of arson suggest that when historians of Russia seek counterparts, they should consider not only Hobsbawm and Rudé but also Regina Schulte. Schulte asks historians to view rural arsonists in upper Bavaria in the period 1848–1910 as farmhands who "acted alone and were often isolated from their peers," and the "acts of arson by day laborers and cottagers directed against their employers" as "individual actions."[22] She also challenges any evolutionary readings of the cases of rural arson she examined, arguing that "the day laborers' hostility toward the large farmers did not lead to any politicization or antipathy toward them. . . . Arson threats remained individual acts."[23] Rather than reading rural arson as part of the history of class struggle in Bavaria, an approach that posits peasants as a group culture, Schulte approaches rural crime, with arson as one example, as a "probe" into the "gray area" of the "tensions inside the peasant world itself."[24] By turning away from peasant revolts to village conflicts, Schulte shifts the scene away from "the old familiar one, the political arena of rulers and 'subjects,' outside the peasant world."[25] Her interest is peasant communities themselves, their networks of relationships, and the tensions and conflicts that surfaced through actions such as arson.

Arson incidents in rural Russia also illuminate the "gray area" of tensions, conflicts, and, most fully, social control within the peasant community itself. Further, arson fires followed such consistent patterns that they can be understood as a language. Sometimes the message they sent was protest. Often it was rebuke. Other times it was pure malice. It was also entrepreneurial, as peasants began to engage in "self-arson" in order to file claims against their compulsory fire insurance. Always, peasant arson was the product of peasant action. Usually, it was so well timed and situated that it displayed the peasants' mastery of fire. In peasant studies, rural arson in European Russia confirms peasant agency, but agency beyond protest or resistance. As subjects of fire history, Russia's rural arsonists displayed their manipulation of fire in their social and community relationships as much as in their relationship with nature, while demonstrating fire's continuing power and appeal in European Russia at the dawning of the twentieth century.

4

The Fiery Brand, Russian Style:
Arson as Protest, Peasants as Incendiaries

GIVEN SUCH A STATE OF AFFAIRS, THE PEASANTS DECIDED THAT THE BEST WAY
TO TAKE VENGEANCE ON HIM WAS TO DESTROY HIS PROPERTY. FIRES THAT BURN
THE GRAIN ON THE SQUIRE CHERTKOV'S ESTATE HAPPEN ALMOST EVERY YEAR.
—Police file, *"Report of the Tambov Provincial Police Chief on the Systematic
Arson Fires on the Estate of the Nobleman Chertkov," 1871*

Arson occupied a prominent place in late imperial rural Russia. Both the Ministry
of Interior statistics and the relative space devoted to arson in public debates
pointed to accidental village fires as the larger threat to the empire, but arson fires
also loomed large in Russia's fire experience and in the public imagination. The
historian of rural arson in Russia may draw on two major bodies of data. First,
published statistics of the Ministry of Justice provide the number of arson cases—
a category of property crime—brought to court, and information about those
convicted, much as similar sources do in Great Britain and the United States.
Second, there is the network of information that eventually made its way to the
Ministry of the Interior on all reported fires in districts. District policemen noted
whether the fires were accidental or due to arson, as well as what burned and,
often, the estate identity of both victim and suspected arsonist. Of these two
sources, Ministry of the Interior statistics enjoy the advantage of being consistent
in their categories and schedule of reporting. Arson fires that appear in the tables
for a given year were reported as having occurred in that year. Ministry of Justice
tables, by contrast, list arson cases filed in that year, of which many were carried
over from the previous year's docket and included events that might have
occurred even earlier. Furthermore, Ministry of Justice statistics for some years
distinguish arson as "arson against inhabited structures" and "other forms of
arson"; for other years they employ the categories "arson against inhabited struc-

tures" and "other forms of property damage of danger to the public," which included other crimes in addition to arson. Neither set of data, of course, captures all the arson fires that happened.

Historians of crime have called the mass of unindicted crimes that never make their way into the public record the "dark figure" in crime statistics. As Eva Osterberg recently explained: "The dark figure can theoretically consist of offenses that were never discovered; offenses that may have been discovered and brought to court but were not registered in the extant judicial sources because, for example, the parties settled their dispute out of court; or behavior that may have been defined as criminal by the law but was not viewed thus by the people, who therefore kept it outside the scope of formal justice."[1]

Because of the nature of arson in general, and because of its social function within peasant communities in European Russia in particular, the dark figure in the official judicial record of rural incendiarism is especially large. Fire statistics, as distinct from crime statistics, may bring the historian of Russia closer to that dark figure, but they certainly fail to capture it entirely. Fire statistics (and the fire reports that lie behind them in local archives) and provincial government newspapers make it possible to see many arson fires that never made it to court. They also offer clues about a range of intentional burnings that, although discovered, might have been kept "outside the scope of formal justice" by peasants' refusal to cooperate with investigations. District police reports tell what burned. Rarely, however, do these laconic reports include the kind of information about the accused arsonists that is available in the Ministry of Justice statistics on cases that actually worked their way through the court system. Historians should neither throw up their hands in despair over the incompleteness of the two sets of numbers nor rush in with overconfident assumptions about what they can tell about arson fires and arsonists. Instead, scholars should look to them for what they suggest about regional and chronological trends and work with the various bits of information one can glean about the arsonists and their targets to decipher the language of rural arson in European Russia.

Local officials supplied data that the Ministry of the Interior worked up into statistics on the number of reported fires determined to be arson and the percentage of the total number of reported fires they represented (table 4.1). These statistics, however inadequate (for the reasons discussed in chapter 3), make one thing clear. Throughout the second half of the nineteenth century and the first decade of the twentieth, arson was a pervasive phenomenon in the empire, and the great majority of arson fires, as of all fires, occurred in the countryside. (Of all the inci-

Table 4.1: Ministry of Interior Statistics on Arson in European Russia, 1870-1910

Five-Year Period	No. Arson Fires	% of All Fires
1870–1874	12,555	10.6
1875–1879	19,213	12.4
1880–1884	25,920	13.6
1885–1889	29,335	13.2
1890–1894	27,396	12.4
1895–1899	24,493	9.9
1900–1904	29,381	10.3
1905–1909	55,489	14.6
Total	223,782	

Source: Tsentral'nyi statisticheskii komitet, Ministerstvo Vnutrennikh del 1912: xl.

dents represented in table 4.1, the total number of reported arson fires in cities and towns was only 18,792.)

Local observers from around the empire were convinced that these numbers reflected only a small percentage of the fires that were actually due to arson. From Grodno Province, where the percentage of fires identified as arson over this period ranged officially between 12.7 percent and 25.4 percent, one delegate to a 1902 local Committee on the Needs of Agriculture argued that "at the very least, no fewer than half of all fires are caused by arson. . . . Some peasant or other, taking his spite out on another peasant, often burns half the village down."[2] A delegate before the Volynia committee went even further, declaring that "the enormous majority of fires result not from chance, but from human evil will. According to private reports that I have received from insurance agents, accidental fires constitute at most 5%–7% percent of all fires, and the rest result from arson."[3] A delegate from Kiev Province presented the same conclusion: "The cause of fires in Russia is primarily arson, and then, carelessness."[4] These spokesmen came from three of the most arson-prone provinces in European Russia, a fact that surely influenced their perception that the "fire question" was really an "arson question."

Ministry of Justice statistics give a sense of arson's relative place in the cases that came before criminal courts. In 1873, for example, 6,728 of 131,023 cases filed in district courts were cases of arson, many of which may have occurred in earlier years but only then made it to court.[5] In 1880 and 1881, the category of arson was folded into the category of "destruction of property," making it difficult to measure its exact weight in all criminal cases. During those two years, 11,914 cases fell into this category, out of a total of 208,866 cases reported,[6] and roughly 87 percent of arson cases originated in rural areas. Across the period, up to the turn of the century, arson cases hovered at around 5 to 6 percent of all criminal cases brought to the court.

Despite the stability of arson's presence in the Russian countryside, there were distinct moments during the half-century when public attention focused on arson more intensely than it did at other times. The two most obvious periods of concern about arson among members of educated society followed the arson fires in St. Petersburg in 1862 and the wave of arson fires in 1905–1907. The rhetoric following each group of fires was strikingly similar, for both times observers construed arson as an indicator of the collapse of social order and of the approaching apocalypse.

The St. Petersburg fires engendered an alarmist consciousness of fire and arson throughout the empire, prompting the entry of a "fire question" onto the national agenda and the emergence of the broad body of publications on fire and arson discussed in the three previous chapters. Forty-five years later, the arson fires that swept through southern Russia and Ukraine as an element in the rural rebellions of 1905–1907 blinded contemporary observers to the evidence on rural arson that the accounts of the previous half-century had provided. Their reactions and language echoed those of the 1860s as they, much like the late-twentieth-century historians who have studied them, perceived these arson fires to be exceptional, even aberrant, in rural culture. Take the conclusions of Minister of Agriculture A. S. Ermolov, for example. "Only in the relatively recent past have fires taken on those threatening proportions and forms that we are now enduring, and that we are fully justified in calling the 'fire epidemic.'"[7] Ermolov went on to say that arson was the chief cause of village fires, adding, mistakenly, that these arson fires had taken on "a completely different and unprecedented character: peasants have begun to burn . . . their own property and to burn out each other."[8] His mistake was in thinking that either of these forms of arson was unprecedented in the village. He was equally mistaken in thinking that the wave of fires, arson or otherwise, from 1905 forward was the first such epidemic.

A look at the *Kursk Provincial News* from 1870 gives a quick sense of how pervasive arson was in the imperial countryside. Beginning in April and extending through September, Kursk entered a veritable arson season, with arson fires breaking out daily in peasant courtyards (fig. 4.1) and on gentry estates alike. On May 8, for example, 25 peasant homesteads burned down in the village of Samodurovka (with losses valued at 4,275 rubles); on May 17 in the village of Mikhel'pol'e, arson took a threshing barn and thresher on a gentry estate (3,000 rubles in losses); 4

Map 4.1 Percentage of reported fires attributed to arson, 1860's

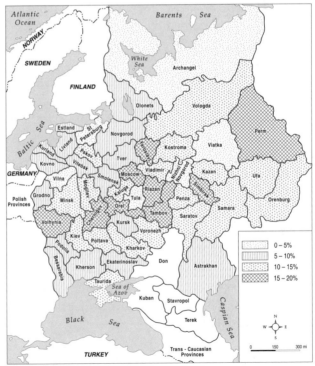

Map 4.2 Percentage of reported fires attributed to arson, 1870's

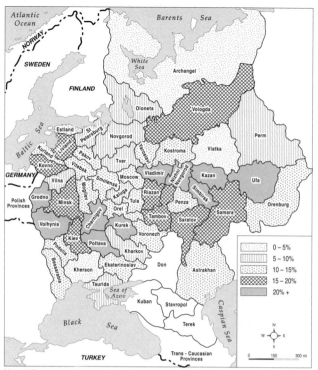

Map 4.3 Percentage of reported fires attributed to arson, 1880's

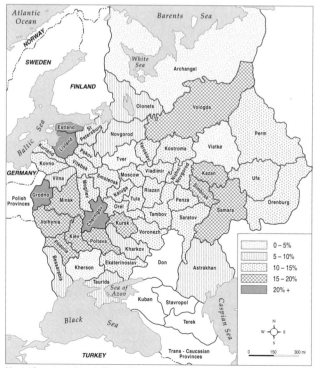

Map 4.4 Percentage of reported fires attributed to arson, 1890's

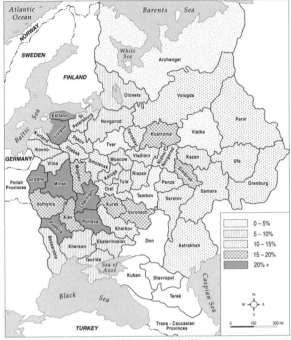

Map 4.5 Percentage of reported fires attributed to arson, 1900 - 1904

peasant houses burned in Shchetinkino on May 23 (1,550 rubles); on July 6 in the village of Khokhlovo, 11 peasant homesteads burned, including grain barns (5,870 rubles); and 16 peasant homesteads went up in flames in the village of Afanas'evskoe on July 13 (3,305 rubles).[9] Mapping arson as a percentage of all reported fires in the provinces of European Russia also shows that Kursk was one of the provinces in which arson accounted for relatively large percentages of all fires over the sixty years discussed here (see maps 4.1–4.5).

These maps reveal that, just as a fire zone stretched across southern Russia, an arson zone also appeared in the southwest during the last two decades of the nineteenth century and the first five years of the twentieth. The 1880s may be considered the worst decade between 1860 and 1904, with nineteen provinces registering more than 15 percent of all fires as proven arson cases, and ten of those registering more than 20 percent. The geographic distribution of arson fires as percentages of reported fires across the provinces of European Russia shifted to a pattern in which, over time, greater numbers of provinces began to register more than 10 percent of all fires as arson, with the largest number of provinces registering more than 20 percent of all reported fires as arson in the decade of the 1880s and the five years of 1900–1904. Together, the data suggest the steady presence of arson across European Russia from the 1870s forward, the general trend in geographic distribution, and the consistency of arson's presence or absence in certain provinces. Ministry of Justice statistics on arson as crime confirm the regional character of arson. In 1876, for example, when the number of arson cases brought to court increased dramatically, making arson the third most frequent crime in European Russia, circuit courts in Nizhnii Novgorod, Tula, and Samara registered very high numbers of arson cases. The Nizhnii Novgorod court registered one

Fig. 4.1. *This late-nineteenth-century photograph conveys the danger a yard could hold should neighborly relations go awry.*

arson case for every 3,425 persons under its jurisdiction, whereas the St. Petersburg circuit court registered only one arson case for every 21,739 persons under its jurisdiction.[10]

Beginning in the 1870s, eight provinces in the southwest (Grodno, Minsk, Volynia, Chernigov, Kiev, Podolia, Poltava, and Kursk), along with Estland and Lifland, had an active arson culture, while in Viatka and Arkhangel'sk, judging solely by percentages, there was virtually no such arson culture. Similarly, Tver, St. Petersburg, Olonets, Vilna, and Tauride Provinces consistently registered fewer than 10 percent of all reported fires as arson. These trends had several implications for contemporary policymakers and rural inhabitants, as well as for the historiography of late imperial Russia a century later.

First, arson contributed greatly to the destruction of property and the financial hardship that accumulated year in and year out, province to province, and constituted one of the factors that frustrated Russia's economic development. Arson also served as evidence of an active peasant fire culture that defied existing imperial laws and obstructed development of the shared, national rule of law to which many progressive, liberal Russians aspired. The constancy of arson also testified to the failures of the police and judicial systems and indicated that rural Russia continued to live outside the law. *Samopodzhog*—self-arson—in the 1880s and 1890s illustrated the peasants' willingness to capitalize on the economic opportunities offered by compulsory fire insurance programs, submitting to one set of laws only to violate others whenever the benefits seemed likely to compensate for the risks attached to fire. Arson in rural Russia served the interests of the peasants who practiced it and introduced proof positive that peasants were active masters as well as victims of fire, which they clearly wielded and manipulated not only in the tasks of their daily life but also in enforcing local norms and enhancing their financial position.

The morphology of arson in rural Russia from 1860 to 1904 challenges scholars to acknowledge the peasants' use against their neighbors of assault on property and, less frequently, on human life as a normal, everyday feature of their community experience. This means that historians of Russia should take a phenomenon largely associated with rebellion and place it squarely in the practice of community control through violence among the peasants themselves. Arson was certainly a feature of rural rebellion in 1905–1907, but class warfare did not give birth to it then, nor had exploitation by gentry and merchant landowners created it in the previous half-century. Individual offenses, disputes, exploitation, and injuries among peasants within their own villages, as well as damages caused to the community by outsiders, brought forth arson as a prominent feature of rural life in Russia. By 1900, it was a well-defined practice that displayed such consistent attributes that it can be understood as a language of community control. The peasantry of European Russia needed no instruction in protest through violence, nor inspiration in the form of radical political ideologies (whether populist or social democratic), in order to wield the fiery brand. In this they were willing and effective experts, having refined their message and techniques through decades of setting fire to structures across their neighbor's fence or down the dusty street.[11]

Arson as Social or Economic Protest

As in other cultures where social historians have studied rural arson, in European Russia it was sometimes a protest against perceived exploitation. Within the discourse about fire and arson among contemporaries, a focus on this type of arson became especially acute after 1907.[12] During the fifty years beforehand, however, such peasant actions against gentry and merchant neighbors were reported as simply one more manifestation of peasants' reprisals—leveled against other peasants, merchants, and gentry landowners alike—for perceived selfishness and unacceptable profiteering. E. P. Thompson's analysis is well taken here, for what peasant arsonists were protesting in these actions were violations of what he termed the "moral economy,"[13] which Russian peasants would have termed "fairness" in a worldview in which cultivation and use of God's gifts to man were the only just sources of ownership. Class analysis does not as easily fit, for peasants were as quick to see wrongdoing in the use of natural resources for profit by other peasants as by gentry or merchant property owners. Natural resources were rightly to be exploited only for subsistence and never to be denied to those who needed them. The most familiar victims to students of rural crime and of arson in particular were gentry and merchants. One natural resource they controlled, which was for peasants most clearly not to be reserved for profit, was the forest.

Peasant against Gentry or Merchant: Forests

Throughout the post-Emancipation period, access to woodlands and forests was a constant source of tensions in the countryside. Under serfdom, peasants had enjoyed restricted access to their lords' forests, the limits of which they often contested through illegal lumbering.[14] After the Emancipation, such poaching became an obsession for educated observers, who invariably pointed to peasant encroachments on forests retained by former serf owners during post-Emancipation land settlements as proof that peasants had no respect for private property or, by extension, the law.[15] No amount of horse or foot patrolling in state or private forests succeeded in deterring the peasants from taking what they needed, believing as they did that "if anyone had a claim on the wood from the forest, it was the man who labored to gather it. Thus, the peasant who chopped and hauled the lumber had the preeminent claim. Neither the state nor the landlord qualified as victims of loss or harm in the peasants' perceptions, because 'God grew the forest for everyone.'"[16] The most authoritative eyewitness reporter on rural culture, A. N. Engel'gardt, quickly came to the conclusion during his tenure in Smolensk Province that it was in his best interest to permit local peasants to continue to gather mushrooms and cut the occasional tree in his forests, rather than poison his relations with them through fruitless struggles against the peasants' evident conviction that such access was a God-given right.[17]

Forest fires were the reprisal that less circumspect owners invited when they pursued peasant poachers. Local reports often ascribed fires in the woodlands to arson caused by peasants' resentment of the gentry for restricting their access to firewood.[18] Peasants also protested the sale of the forest for profit by attacking felled and stacked timber, sometimes after having received payment for cutting and hauling it. Such was a case in the Dorogobuzh District of Smolensk Province when local peasants set fire to 400 sazhens (around 850 meters) of birch in 1887.[19] Similarly, in Sapozhsk District, Riazan Province, over the course of 1901 there were ten major arson fires in the large private forests of one Shuvalov, despite his having doubled his mounted and foot patrols.[20] Laconic fire reports in local newspapers and district police reports to governors often suggested that this kind of arson was the cause of major forest blazes.[21] The relational nature of arson surfaced when gentry or merchant owners were able to name the suspects, as in the case of the merchant Gromov, who, in 1865, lost acres of forest to a fire in Belozersk District, Novgorod Province, and identified the peasants Akimenko, Grigoriev, and Kuzmin as the suspects.[22] In the first three weeks of August 1882 alone, district police officials reported five such fires to the governor of Novgorod Province.[23] Such cases appear time and again in local sources, attesting to arson's use in this way to protest the redefinition and delimitation of forests and wood in the post-Emancipation countryside.[24]

The broader reading public gained an image of these fires from a sketch published in the leading progressive journal of the day, *Notes of the Fatherland*. One of its most popular contributors, G. I. Uspenskii, submitted a long account of fires in the Novgorod forests when he was living in a village nearby.

> The forests burn quietly . . . ; on quiet evenings another tree burns like a candle; birch trees creak and buckle, green leaves burst into flame and curl up, and only occasionally is there a crash, like lightning, and the resinous gas of pine trees scorched by the fire blazes up over the dark forest. . . . While the fire, just as if it were fulfilling some kind of obligation, without hurrying, having cleared a hundred desiatinas of state, or gentry, or peasant forest, and arriving at a clearing where there is nothing to consume, modestly takes up chewing the grass that has been dried up by the heat and hot weather, chews it up, like a modest, mild sheep, bit by bit, blade by blade—
> . . . and, take a look, after a day, after two, another hundred desiatinas will be smoldering in hot coals. At night a burning forest is just like a ballroom or an enormous park illuminated for some ceremonial occasion: everywhere there are fires, stars, fireworks (exploding pines), and among them there are burned over or still burning bushes, just like groups of guests, dancing, crowding around card or food tables.[25]

Uspenskii concluded that these fires arose from disputes between local peasants, gentry, and merchants over access to the forests. He knew the peasant poachers well as a potential customer for the local peasants who stole the wood and sold it at below-market value in their villages. He explained that poaching took place "all winter long, precisely in the corner from which the smoke is now coming."[26]

A correspondent from Cherepovets District, Novgorod Province, to the Tenishev Ethnographic Bureau, A. Vlasov, was able to see such fires, and perhaps fires very nearby those witnessed by Uspenskii, not only as the protest they surely were but also as an expression of the peasants' pragmatic approach to the complex of forest, fire, and farming. He described the mid-1880s in Novgorod Province as a time when "in the hot summers it was unbearable . . . because of the smoke from burning forests; forests were burning in every direction, and this was all the work of arsonists, with the goal of having good spots for planting the next year's crops."[27] Once the forests were clear-cut and abandoned by their owners, the peasants moved in to burn the litter, finishing off the second half of the slash-and-burn process that the forests' owners had unwittingly begun. Vlasov concluded that peasants did not perceive these fires to be arson or a violation of any kind. Nor, perhaps, was protest foremost in their minds. It would have been consistent with peasant attitudes toward land and natural resources to consider the owners' practices doubly sinful—first as a wanton destruction of resources for the sole purpose of profit, and second as total neglect of the clear-cut lands left unattended and uncultivated. Technically, according to the Criminal Code, this was arson, for it was intentional burning of property. The forest fires made their way into the annals of rural arson in European Russia; in the local understanding among farming peasants, they were nothing more than appropriate opportunism. Arson as field preparation was undoubtedly a collective act. It is less certain whether arson against private or state forests was usually individual or collective. The frequency of its appearance, however, and its clustering in Novgorod Province suggest strongly that there was collective sanction at the very least, whether one individual or several actually ignited the blaze.

Peasant against Gentry: Harvested Grain, Barns, Outbuildings

Peasant-against-gentry arson directed at property on the cultivated and inhabited areas of gentry estates displayed none of the ambiguity of peasants' burning litter after clear-cutting in forests. The intention to destroy property was explicit and direct. The evidence comes in the targets, which were the same as those already mentioned for England and the American state of Georgia. When peasants used arson against local landowners, they almost never set fire to the manor house or any other residential structure on the landowner's estate. Instead, they set fire to the source of their resentment: stores of grain harvested by their hands and held by the gentry for sale at a high price when the market was ripe. If not grain stores, then farming equipment and livestock barns were the targets. In one two-week period in 1882 in Smolensk Province, for example, out of thirteen reported fires, four involved gentry property. In the village of Pridishche in Gzhatsk District, a fire of "unknown causes" on a gentry estate burned a full grain storehouse, with losses worth 4,000 rubles. In the village of Lozitskakh in Roslavl District, an arson fire burned a grain merchant's storehouse of grain with losses running to 5,000 rubles. Near the village of Andreikova in Viaz'ma District, a fire of "unknown cause" on a merchant's estate consumed two storehouses containing grain, hay, and farming implements for losses of 6,500 rubles. "Carelessness" on a noble estate on the outskirts of the town of Roslavl led to a fire that consumed 6,000 rubles of property.[28] Though only one of these fires was conclusively identified as an arson fire, "unknown causes" and "carelessness" were often the best that local investigators could come up with, and readers understood that the real cause was probably arson. The local correspondent from Porech'e District reported to the *Smolensk Herald* in October 1882 that there had recently been a series of suspicious fires on gentry estates. The usual targets were full grain barns in the meadows, far from other structures. There was no doubt among the local gentry that these fires resulted from arson and were assaults on their wealth following the harvest.[29] An arson fire in the village of Ostrog, Volynia Province, in 1894 followed this pattern; the livestock barn and other outbuildings on a gentry estate were burned, leading to losses of 15,000 rubles.[30] As police reports reveal, in Novgorod Province, too, when peasants set fire to gentry property they most often chose to burn stacked grain, woodpiles, and storage and livestock barns.[31]

In torching these items in the gentry inventory, peasant arsonists in European Russia were behaving much as their fellow arsonists did across the continent and the ocean. In "incendiary counties" during the Swing revolts, rick-burning was arson's characteristic form.[32] David Jones found in East Anglia that "the targets were usually thatched barns and stacks, threshing machines and furze hedges at some distance from the farmhouse. . . . No personal injury was intended, and with a few exceptions, none was given."[33] Hussey and Swash's survey of arson fires in Essex also identified outlying stacks and isolated barns as targets, whereas "houses were rarely fired."[34] Smith similarly identified such structures as frequent targets of arson attacks in Georgia. "Even more damaging were the frequent and distinctly seasonal attacks on cotton gins, on storehouses and 'cribs' containing food, cotton, and fodder, and on barns and stables."[35]

Such acts of arson often resulted from land disputes between lords and peasants, or from labor disputes between peasant laborers and their gentry bosses.[36] In one such case in 1871 in Nizhnii Novgorod Province, Vasilii District, a peasant torched a neighboring gentrywoman's livestock barn because she had leased land not to him but to another peasant.[37] A case record from 1884 in Smolensk Province explained that a local peasant, Koz'min, was suspected of arson against a notoriously abusive landowner, one Vonlialiarskii, because Koz'min was furious over something that Vonlialiarskii had done to him. Koz'min was so offended that he left the job without receiving his pay.[38]

In Griazovetsk District, Vologda Province, the noble justice of the peace A. S. Poroshin earned the same reprisal from hired hands he shortchanged. In separate incidents in 1887 and 1896, peasants working on his estate in Sviatogor'ia burned four of his hay barns in fields beyond the village.[39] A two-line report of an arson fire on a gentry estate in Krestets District, Novgorod Province, in 1882 explained only that the suspected arsonist was a peasant who had formerly rented from the owner.[40] A "genuine epidemic of arson fires" broke out in Ekaterinoslavl Province in 1901, in response to restrictions on pastures, fines for trespassing, and so on.[41] Peasants consistently set arson fires in nonresidential structures, and most often in structures where grain was being held for the market. These targets symbolized the exploitation they felt and the manifest unfairness of anyone's controlling natural resources for profit. To peasants, arson in this form qualified not as wrongdoing but as justice served upon those who had wronged them.

Peasant against Prospering Peasant: "Our Own Ways"

Wealthy peasants in the village also feared this form of arson. Following Lenin, Soviet historians and many Western historians have consistently referred to such peasants as *kulaks*.[42] This term bears the Leninist disapproval of prosperity in peasant hands, which in another setting might simply signify the peasant's transformation into a "farmer." As Engel'gardt and other observers of rural culture in the nineteenth century recognized, the village community felt some ambivalence toward prosperous peasants; most villagers simultaneously admired and envied them. Outsiders almost universally despised them as strongmen who blocked would-be reformers' access to the community. Of the revolutionary years following 1917, Orlando Figes concluded: "The majority of the richest peasant farmers were respected as well as feared by their poorest farming neighbors."[43]

When scholars employ the term "kulak" to identify wealthy peasants, they implicitly, perhaps unwittingly, endorse actions against them by fellow villagers, because not only Lenin and his followers but also populist and conservative observers of village culture from 1861 forward found these entrepreneurial, individualistic peasants unsettling. Prosperous, economically successful peasants belied both fond visions of egalitarian communes and insistent infantilization of peasants by intransigent paternalists. They had few fans among educated Russians. To use the term kulak already deems them guilty on some level of the corrosive attributes assigned to them by educated Russians, while justifying any move against them. In the discussion of arson, this is especially true, because those arson victims among the peasants who were targeted because of their wealth fit prevailing interpretations about peasant protest against violations of a "moral economy." Ergo, any "kulak" victim was targeted because of his "immoral economy" and was the social and moral equivalent of gentry and merchant victims. If historians eschew the term kulak, they may be able to recognize arson's function within the village community as not only "social justice" but also social control, with coercion and violence as features of that control.

Anticipating that their homesteads would be targets for arson, prosperous peasants preferred to build them smack in the middle of the village rather than on the end of the street or the village periphery. As long as their residences were in close proximity to other homesteads, they could count on their neighbors' fear of a generalized conflagration to counteract their desire to attack peasant wealth.[44] This strategy did not always save them. In the September 1882 report from the *Smolensk Herald* cited earlier, there was also one reported arson fire in Roslavl District directed against peasant houses. In this case four peasant houses valued at 2,400 rubles burned. By contrast, a fire due to "unknown causes" in Sycheva District consumed three peasant houses valued at only 400 rubles. It seems fair to assume that the houses targeted in the arson fire belonged to prosperous peasants.[45] This conclusion is equally valid for two arson fires in Novgorod Province. In the first, one peasant's four full barns burned in Novgorod District on October 10, 1889, with losses of 1,800 to 1,900 rubles reported.[46] The second, in Borovich District on May 9, 1895, burned the peasant Vasilii Lukin's "two-story, 1/2 stucco house," with total reported losses of 3,060 rubles.[47] These reports do not explain who torched the buildings or why they did so. In a third arson case from Krestets District, Novgorod Province, the total losses were relatively small at 300 rubles, but the structures burned included four houses, all owned by one Gregorii Stepanov. Stepanov was at the very least a peasant property owner of some prosperity within his local community.[48]

Sometimes the reasons behind arson against a fellow peasant were clear. In April 1875, the *Court Herald* reported a case in which a woman was convicted largely because of her well-known grudge against the victim, who had refused to let her use his barn to store some of her crops.[49] In Vologda Province in 1891, one Elizaveta Shan'gina, a peasant living in the Sol'vychegodsk District, set fire to a hayrick owned by a neighboring peasant, explaining to fellow villagers that he had charged her too much to dry her grain in his drying barn.[50] In the same year, the peasant Prokopiia Lodygin and his two sons set fire to a neighbor's threshing barn. An eyewitness overheard Luppa Lodygin telling his brother, as they dragged some large beams behind the barn, that "it wouldn't be a bad idea to burn these beams. Maybe they'll even burn up the rich guy's barn." This came after Prokopiia's earlier threat to burn the entire village over a land dispute: "It's time to bring the rich guys down to the poor" (fig. 4.2).[51]

Fig. 4.2. *Case file on the peasants Prokopii, Luppa, and Ivan Lodygin, accused of setting fire to their village in Vologda Province in 1890.*

In 1899, a group of peasants in Poltava Province set fire to hay and buildings belonging to a wealthy peasant who had refused to sell or rent them land or to allow them access to his pond to fish.[52] From Penza Province, A. Lebedev reported an arson fire in Saransk District, a case in which a rich peasant refused a needy peasant's request for a loan of grain from his storehouse in 1898. Shortly after the refusal, the storehouse burned to the ground.[53] This fire, like the torching of four grain storage barns owned by one peasant in Novgorod Province, points to strong beliefs about the immorality of surplus, especially if the owners were susceptible to the accusation of hoarding grain.

Uspenskii encountered this aspect of community morality in Novgorod province. He explained that he and a friend were desultorily hunting one summer afternoon, not really expecting to find any birds to shoot, "because the summer was very dry, no berries ripened, and of course there is no reason for birds to stay in a barren place." As they strolled along, they came upon some peasant-owned forest, which had been largely clear-cut.

And what a sight we beheld: on the large, cleared and smoothly mowed glade there stretched out an enormous haystack of about fifty sazhens length [more than one hundred yards long]; and three sazhens [around twenty feet] from this stack a bonfire of dried twigs and branches was burning; this fire had obviously only just been lit, because the fire was, so far, stirring only in the middle of the bunch of twigs. But what struck us and set us to thinking was that first, there was nobody near the fire, and second, there was a clearly visible path of hay that had been thrown down leading from the fire in toward the stack. . . . And, all around, deathly silence. . . . .

—So what does this mean? I asked my companion, a fellow who is more familiar with the area we were in than I am.

—Oh, that, he said, probably has something to do with "our ways," something to do with "our ways . . ."

He was silent, stared attentively at the fire, looked at the haystack, and the path of hay that had obviously been placed between the fire and the haystack, and then confidently repeated again:

—Yes, undoubtedly, "our ways"![54]

Uspenskii's companion then explained that the hay belonged to the local village elder, who had at one time been an ordinary peasant in the village. As soon as he had assumed the responsibility for collecting taxes and other payments from the peasants in his community, however, he began to gather both money and power in his hands and to use both to squeeze the peasants. Among other things, he was able to buy crops cheaply from peasants who could not otherwise meet their obligations. He would then sell the hay or grain for twice that price and put the difference in his own pocket. His neighbors soon found themselves having to sell him their livestock as well, for want of fodder. From there it was a quick decline to selling themselves as his laborers. Powerless against this profiteer in their own midst, who enjoyed the authority assigned to him as tax collector, the peasants had obviously taken matters in their own hands, having their "own ways" for taking care of such injustices.

Uspenskii went beyond description to contemplate the appeal of such "ways" to the peasants of the area. He zeroed in on their perception that they had no other protection against such exploitation and oppression. He explained that they saw no way to get someone above the elder to intervene and control his appetite and exploitation.

And how could they achieve this in the village, in the forest, where sometimes they don't even know how to articulate their oppressive suffering in words, where they don't know how to write, don't know how to read, don't know from whom to expect protection, where they don't know where to turn to complain, to whom to complain, even how to file a complaint? Yes, and finally, is it even possible to complain somewhere that our neighbor, yes, our elder, our own, has made himself rich? . . . And so in this darkness, in this anguish and need . . . foul ideas begin to ripen.[55]

Without recourse to higher authorities, the peasants used their own methods for accomplishing their goals. In the case of the elder's offensive haystack, Uspenskii and his companion saved it and for the time being spared the elder, whom the peasants intended "to bring 'into line' . . . with the neighbors around him."[56] Uspenskii raised important questions about tensions in the countryside. His concern over the peasants' decision to resort to their own forms of justice and dispute resolution was implicit in the title he gave this sketch: "Their Own Ways." When he settled on "darkness, anguish, and need" among illiterate peasants who had no idea of formal justice or means to seek it by "filing a complaint," he was winding his way toward understanding rural arson as the product of a frustrated sense of injustice and an ignorance about or unwillingness to turn to formal law and justice for protection and recompense.

Unlike landowners and clergy in Britain, especially in Essex,[57] Uspenskii did not describe such actions as irrational or as the work of aberrant individuals. While the arsonists' ideas may have been "foul," they had understandable sources in ignorance about legal recourse ("darkness"), distress over one of their number's violation of moral norms ("anguish"), and economic suffering and disenfranchisement ("need"). Uspenskii recognized arson as social and economic protest. Emancipated peasants responded with arson to new arrangements and possibilities for both large landowners and entrepreneurial peasants to take advantage of new definitions of property, restrictions on natural resources, and administrative positions within the peasant community itself. Unchecked, these new arrangements could further impoverish those who already felt betrayed by the land settlements and payment terms of the Emancipation.

The prominence of peasants among arson victims overall and the specific incidents against identifiably prosperous peasants serve as reminders that most peasants in post-Emancipation Russia were property owners. The template of propertyless agricultural laborers who strike out against property owners who were not of their socioeconomic "class" or legal "estate" does not fit rural Russia. Timothy Mixter, who has examined migrant agricultural laborers in European Russia, acknowledges this from the start, explaining to readers without a knowledge of Russia's post-Emancipation situation that "most migrant labourers were not landless and store buying like classic rural proletarians."[58] Even those without tillable land were still likely to have a house and garden plot, however modest.

Nor does casting all peasants who lived above subsistence level into the category of exploitative "kulaks" work particularly well. In the crucible text for those definitions, Lenin's *The Development of Capitalism in Russia*, his own evidence shows that propertied peasants, who could be defined as living above subsistence level (defined by both the allotment they cultivated, whether purchased or rented, and the livestock they possessed), made up almost 50 percent of the peasantry of European Russia.[59] The massive shift of land out of the hands of the nobility into peasant hands through lease and purchase was another indication of the emergence of an entrepreneurial peasantry. Jeffrey Burds has gone so far as to locate a "mass consumer culture in rural Russia" in the central industrial region around Moscow.[60] A. N. Engel'gardt described villages of such "prospering peasants" near his estate in Smolensk Province in the 1880s.[61] Once the Peasant Land Bank opened in 1883, several villages in his area made large purchases, usually under the pressure of younger people in the community. Engel'gardt also explained that such prospering peasants displayed no hesitation in hiring, then exploiting, their fellow, less fortunate or less energetic peasant neighbors to do wage labor on their new lands.[62] Arson by "peasants" against "peasants" illuminates the tensions in rural communities that issued from these relationships between entrepreneurial and impoverished or apathetic peasants.

Oppression within peasant communities was not new. Steven Hoch concluded about relations among serfs before the Emancipation in Petrovskoe, Tambov Province, that they were the antithesis of mutually supportive or collective. "Insolence, disorderly conduct, quarreling and fighting were common serf behavior. Serfs stole from the estate and from each other. They willingly informed on other serfs to estate authorities. . . . In the end, outweighing the economic exploitation of the landlord was the social oppression of serf over serf."[63] The end of serfdom offered the strong more opportunities to "oppress." In the absence of external agencies to protect these newly propertied "oppressors," arson was a handy weapon of protest against older, now intensified peasant-against-peasant patterns as well as against gentry- or merchant-over-peasant exploitation.

Conclusion: Russian Peasants, Social Rebels

The peasants of European Russia who used arson for these reasons were part of an international fraternity of sorts, a community of frustrated and disenfranchised people who protested the injustice of their situation through incendiarism. Comparative study with emancipated slaves in the American deep south and agricultural laborers during the first half of the nineteenth century in Great Britain highlights the similarities in their motives and methods. One may debate the question of collective versus individual actions, but it seems clear that when individuals torched the property of their "betters," whether gentry landowners, lumber merchants, or prosperous peasants, they enjoyed the tacit support of many members of their community.

In the historiography of rural arson in Russia and the Soviet Union, the continuities in the geographical distribution of arson are striking. As Teodor Shanin and Orlando Figes have both stressed, the lower Volga region was the site of high levels of arson in 1905–1907 and 1917–1921.[64] In the preceding forty years, these areas also displayed a high incidence of arson, although they were not the hottest areas of the empire. That distinction fell to the southwest, which Lynn Viola has identified as the area where arson was the most frequent form of protest by peasants against the collectivization campaigns in the 1930s.[65] This region's historical "arson culture" rose to the surface when peasants found themselves not only disenfranchised and dispossessed but also threatened with social and physical extinction under Stalin.

Although A. S. Ermolov in 1910 and Barbara Alpern Engel in 1994 erred in describing peasant arson as "unprecedented," they were both correct in their perception that the "proportions and forms that we are now enduring," as Ermolov put it, in peasant arson directed at gentry manor houses were a departure from rural arson's traditions in European Russia. When peasants burned gentry homes in 1905–1907, they broke important boundaries. In the geography of class, as Engel nicely describes it, the manor house was at the center of the noble domain, a location that was distant and unapproachable within the gentry estate even for peasants who had worked the gentry's fields or threshed their grain and tended the animals in their barns.[66] To put a burning torch directly onto the noble's front porch was a violation of social space that was the rural counterpart of the lower elements' urban invasion of Nevskii Prospekt during street demonstrations in St. Petersburg, and the comparative counterpart of Abner Snopes's deliberately soiling, then destroying, the Mississippi landowner's Parisian rug in Faulkner's "Barn Burning."

Torching a residential structure was also a violation of the boundaries that had largely defined rural arson in the post-Emancipation era. Peasant arsonists who set fire to gentry homes in the revolutionary period broke away from the moral norms and conventions that had prevailed in the village. In doing so, they introduced a new "fire culture" in twentieth-century rural Russia that has dominated our perception of rural arson ever since. So brightly did the flames of burning manor houses blaze in the contemporary and historiographical imagination that eyewitnesses and historians lost sight of arson's other, more steadfast functions in the imperial countryside. Those other functions help explain not so much why Russia disintegrated into a war between classes in the first decades of the twentieth century as why the rural population was so susceptible to violence and so easily drawn into the murderous experiences of the revolutionary period. Examining arson's Russian face in its several expressions leads into a contentious world where violence against person and property seemed an appropriate and effective way to defend self, family, and community.

5

Arson as Impotent Spite or Potent Practice: Peasants as Vengeful, Covetous, or Wily Actors

VENGEANCE IS LIKE A FIRE. THE MORE IT DEVOURS, THE HUNGRIER IT GETS.

—J. M. Coetzee, *Disgrace,* 1999

ARSON. AUGUST 10, 1895. A PEASANT'S COW-SHED. THE SUSPECTS ARE THE VICTIM'S SISTERS.

—District policeman's report on incidents in Borovich, Novgorod Province.

Fires set by peasant women within their own communities were the most alarming of all fires to educated observers. This is startling in the context of the St. Petersburg arson fires of 1862 and the anxiety about controlling both peasants and fire in the countryside that they generated, and against the backdrop of the historiography of rural arson as protest in Russia and elsewhere. Perhaps the fact that one of Orthodox Russia's first saints was a female arsonist contributed in some way to the ease with which those who wrote about arson combined fire, women, and revenge in their imaginings. Olga, the first Kievan ruler to adopt Christianity in the tenth century, appeared in early chronicles also as the widow who defended Kiev against the assault of rival Derevliane, who sought to exploit dynastic weakness when Olga's husband died. The climax of her incremental strategies was to send pigeons and sparrows into her opponent's wooden town with tiny fiery brands attached to their legs, defeating Derevliane through strategic incendiarism. "There was not a house that was not consumed, and it was impossible to extinguish the flames, because all the houses caught fire at once."[1] It was not for this act that Olga earned sainthood, but she did leave a powerful image of female vengeance in cultural memory to prompt the association of women with fire when arson emerged as a public concern in the 1860s.

As early as 1869, D. M. Pogodin, one of the first authorities on rural arson, declared that "it is the young *baba*, most often a young woman, who has not yet been tempered by every kind of hardship and sorrow, [who is] completely exhausted by the demands of her family and having consequently lost all reason, who takes vengeance; she sets fire to the house of her father-in-law or husband in a fit of meaningless despair and impotent spite."[2] This conviction took hold in the 1860s and held firm for four decades.

Nothing convinced the reading public more fully that peasant women were likely to act out their grievances by practicing arson than the extensive coverage the *Court Herald* gave in July 1867 to the case against Fekla Antonovna Sergeeva, a resident of the village of Zmievka, Riazan Province, who was accused of setting seven fires in her village between August 21 and September 8, 1864. At the time of the fires, Fekla Antonovna was eighteen years old and in a marriage whose unhappiness was common knowledge in the village. Beginning on August 21, fires broke out in various outbuildings belonging to members of her husband's family, whom the fires followed as they moved from household to household. In each case, the fires started in structures where there was no reason to have any fire. Several of the fires had spread. The fire on September 8, for example, consumed eighteen peasant homesteads, including houses and outbuildings. This generalized damage meant that members of the community beyond Sergeeva's in-laws had reason to identify and punish the culprit.

Their decision to accuse Fekla Antonovna was the result of their perception of her family situation. Further, several neighbors testified that they had observed her in the vicinity of the fires when they broke out. During the trial, the defense attorney added another reason for their accusation precisely against Fekla: that she was a woman, that the villagers expected the guilty party of such a crime to be female, and that they had assumed that "she committed arson out of female stupidity and impotent spite."[3] Finally, Fekla Antonovna was an outsider in this community, having only recently been married to a young man in Zmievka. Before that marriage, she had been a stranger. She had remained a stranger for two reasons. First, she was extremely reserved—"rather severe" in her own estimation, "sullen" according to her in-laws. Worse still, having kept entirely to herself while she was with her husband's family, she also took off frequently to return to her mother's home in another village, complaining of leg pain and seeking treatment there. Immediately before the first of the series of arson fires, her father-in-law had gone twice to retrieve her to do her share of the field work during the harvest. She had refused to return the first time and came the second time only when he brought a horse. Witnesses disagreed about the level of force her father-in-law used.

Fekla Antonovna was accused under the Criminal Code articles for intentional burning of a nonresidential structure, attempted arson, and intentional burning of someone else's grain. If found guilty, she would have been subject to deprivation of all rights and exile to Siberia for resettlement. The prosecution's case rested almost entirely on circumstantial evidence and his definition of Fekla Antonovna's motive of vengeance, which in turn rested on the most negative portrayal possible of her position in her husband's family. His witnesses stressed the lack of love on all sides, the harsh demands of the father-in-law for his daughter-in-law's labor, and the weakness of the young husband, who never spoke out to protect his wife. The prosecutor contrasted the prosperity of the young girl's natal home with the poverty and constraint of her marital home. He suggested that it was almost inevitable for a young peasant bride in such bad straits to strike back, especially a bride as sullen and reserved as Fekla Antonovna. "I already said that she is very reserved. With such people, feelings rarely break through, but when they do, they do so strongly."[4] Clearly, the prosecutor was confident that the jurors, in reaching their verdict, would draw associations between women and revenge, arson as their preferred method, and the brutalizing effects of peasant family life.

The defense lawyer took the opposite tack. He downplayed the troubles of Fekla Antonovna's marriage, calling them typical for any peasant household. Their very typicality undermined the presumption that they would provoke resentment in a peasant girl, familiar with conditions of village life, sufficient to prompt her to practice arson for revenge not once but several times. He stressed, further, that her very reserved and undisturbed nature throughout the investigation and trial made it difficult to cast her as one likely to take desperate measures. He recast her visits home as genuine efforts to find medical treatment for a sore on her leg, diagnosed as a "scrofulous ulcer" by the state's doctor after her arrest. The defense lawyer placed most of his weight on bad investigative procedure, calling into question the preliminary interrogation of witnesses, the examination of the fire sites, and the objectivity of the police investigator.

The jury for this trial comprised six peasants, one townsman or petty trader, one merchant's son, two merchants, one bureaucrat, and one colonel. It was not unusual for there to be at least six peasant jurors on such a case, for peasants made up the majority of jurors at circuit courts generally in this period.[5] The jurors offered the following verdicts. When asked to decide, first, whether each fire was the result of arson, they concluded that three fires were arson and four were not. When they were asked to decide if Fekla Antonovna was guilty of setting each of these fires, they concluded that she was not guilty of any of the crimes charged against her. When the jurors' chairman read out their decision, the crowd in the courtroom burst into loud applause. The judge reprimanded the public, saying, "Despite your sincere sympathy, gentlemen, I must stop you; the law forbids any kind of approval or disapproval of the court." He then turned to Fekla Antonovna and told her that she was free, at which point the crowd in the court broke out again into loud and enthusiastic applause.[6]

Fekla Antonovna's case left a vivid image of an otherwise weak woman's possible strength through the manipulation of fire. The *Court Herald* followed the transcript of her trial and its outcome with a report on another, less sympathetic arsonist wife five months later. The December 21, 1867, issue published the transcript of a jury trial against Anna Ivanovna Belonovskaia, a forty-two-year-old peasant woman. In May 1867, Belonovskaia had made it known to her neighbors that she was about to commit a crime shortly before her hay barn went up in smoke, taking her house and the rest of the outbuildings in her homestead with it. Her neighbors took her directly to the cantonal administration office, where she boasted drunkenly that she had started the fire because she hated her husband. The jurors convicted her following testimony from several witnesses who described her as a bad wife and mother and a dissolute troublemaker.[7] Her case confirmed the formulaic explanation that arson in the countryside was the product of *mesti i zloby*, vengeance and spite. In Belonovskaia's case, arson was the product of hatred and drunkenness—the emotional and physical antonyms of reason and law as solutions to family conflict. Her drunken boasts ensured that at least the men in the community would censure her form of vengeance, for it embodied an audacity in the patriarchal village as threatening as the St. Petersburg arson fires' failure to discriminate between rich and poor. The *Nizhnii Novgorod Sheet*'s laconic report of an arson fire in May 1871 stated baldly what incendiary women might do: "The wife of the peasant Zhikov, Ekaterina Ivanovna, is suspected of arson, having intended to burn up her husband."[8]

Mad, bad women also filled police files in Vologda Province. In 1887, forty-three-year-old Pelageia Lytkina set fire to her neighbors' haystacks in mid-July, admitting that she had taken her revenge on them with matches. They described her, in turn, as a menace who consistently threatened the community.[9] An allegedly querulous woman of seventy found herself accused of burning her nephew's rye in October 1890 in the Sol'vychevsk District after the two fought over a piece of family land. During the trial, neighbors agreed that the woman was on bad terms with all of them.[10] A failed love affair could also put the community at risk. Logic does fail in the face of Feodosia Totmanova's decision to set fire to the drying barn on a neighboring gentry estate because a hired hand there refused to marry her after "deceiving her."[11]

The focus on the peasant woman as the emblematic rural arsonist whose "vengeance and spite" lay at the root of malicious burning in the village is all the more striking in light of the generally held view that women were less criminal and less violent than men. As Stephen P. Frank has recently explained, those who studied crime in the post-Emancipation period tended to see women not as criminals but as "passive, religious, maternal and moral models."[12]

Yet even within the sources Frank used to come to this conclusion and the statistical tables he developed on trends in the reporting of female crime by the Ministry of Justice, one finds evidence of interest in peasant women's role in Russia's fire crisis. "Infractions against fire safety rules" and arson appeared as two crimes for which criminal courts convicted women most frequently beginning in the 1830s and continuing up to the reform era of the 1860s.[13] According to Frank's calculations of all women convicted of arson in 1874–1913, 55.5 percent were identified as either "peasant farmers" or "hired rural workers."[14] Ministry of Justice statistics on convictions also pointed to arson as an area in which women had a slightly disproportionate presence. Women represented a higher percentage of convicted arsonists than they did of convicted criminals overall. For example, in 1874, women were 9 percent of all convicted criminals but 14 percent of convicted arsonists. (In the early 1890s and 1902–1904, however, women appeared at proportionally the same rates among arson convicts as they did among all convicted criminals.)[15] When I. Ia. Foinitskii examined female criminality in the 1890s, he identified arson as one of the crimes for which women had a high presence as convicts (13.2 percent of all convicted arsonists were women, as opposed to 9.1 percent of all convicted criminals) and as one of the crimes for which female peasants' share of convictions (14.0 percent) was far higher than female peasants' convictions among all categories of crime (5.7 percent).[16]

Although not entirely consistent, the data suggest that there was some statistical basis for imagining the rural arsonist to be female. However, the number of arson cases ever prosecuted at circuit courts and resulting in convictions made up an extremely small share of all the arson cases reported by policemen to the Ministry of the Interior. In 1895, for example, district policemen reported 5,070 arson fires in the forty-nine provinces of European Russia; the Ministry of Justice reported that 425 arson cases in circuit courts ended in convictions in that year.[17] Sometimes, but rarely, district policemen provided the name and sex of the suspected arsonist, but otherwise public perception of who they were rested on anecdotal evidence.[18]

There are several possible explanations for why the somewhat suggestive but famously incomplete statistics came together with anecdotal reports in newspapers, hearsay, and official reports to generate vivid images of the female peasant arsonist. The first is that observers recognized women's special relationship to fire in the domestic life of the community.[19] Ethnographic reports had made it clear that women controlled fire in its domesticated form in the peasant household. In this context the notion of the peasant woman as maternal keeper of the hearth, as first and foremost a family figure, carried particular resonance. Foinitskii's 1893 article on the woman as criminal conveys what a woman's departure from that benign image might mean in the context of crime; he explains that the interest in woman as criminal was especially compelling because of "the enormous significance the woman holds in our life as our mother, wife, sister or daughter, as the one who gives birth to generations, the protectress of traditions, the first and chief nurturer of man and his best delight."[20] Reports of women using fire to attack the home or even to burn up the patriarch himself made the vision of women as fire mistresses malevolent rather than benevolent. Second, they joined other evidence that peasant women were threatening the stability of rural Russia as the main instigators behind the break-up of extended families into nuclear units.[21]

Third, women's use of fire was attributed to their loss "of all reason." As the expression of "meaningless despair and impotent spite," female arson was the embodiment of irrational fury. Writing almost thirty years after Pogodin, Foinitskii described almost all female criminals as prisoners of their peculiarly female passionate rage. In his view, female crime was distinguished by its labile, impetuous, and violent nature, the product of the woman's imprisonment in "passion" and her arrested psychological development at the stage of male adolescence, which deprived her of the ability to think through or calmly develop an alternative satisfaction for her frustrations. He explained the female peasant's predilection for arson within this frame.[22]

For an educated public in a society enduring the pangs of both emancipation and nascent industrialization and urbanization, the fear of vengeance over serfdom's patriarchal legacy was palpable. Although no evidence has surfaced that any educated commentator envisioned or feared peasant women's letting loose the red rooster against nonpeasants, their willingness to use it against their neighbors, in-laws, or husbands was a warning that patriarchy writ large might be at risk in post-Emancipation Russia. It was much more comforting to label female arson irrational than to contemplate the larger questions of why vengeance might have a place in European Russia. In that light, the chicken-thief arsonist from Penza whose story opened part two was both alarming and comforting. After all, who could doubt the insanity of her unbridled vengeance and her willingness to lay waste to the entirety of her immediate world? In this regard, educated members of Russian society reacted as their counterparts did in Britain, where the impulse was to brand the arson waves of the 1830s and 1840s the handiwork of marginal or aberrant individuals.[23]

Arson was seldom mad, however, within the village community or when peasants moved outside their community to practice it. For example, all of the female arsonists mentioned earlier were taken to court. They were not part of the "dark figure" of rural crime but part of the black-and-white official record. In each case, someone in her community turned the accused arsonist in. This indicates that their suspected actions did not enjoy the immediate community's universal sanction. Much more troubling for those who hoped to protect order through law in the countryside at the time, and illuminating for those of us who hope to decipher village culture, were acts of arson that did enjoy the community's sanction. Such incidents of arson display both the community norms that were enforced through arson and those that served to constrain the use of arson.

Fried Geese and Malice

The files of the Tenishev Ethnographic Bureau provide a particularly vivid account from Orel Province of arson as the imposition of moral norms within the peasant community, as well as of the peasants' recourse to violent self-help when the law failed to protect them. In 1887, in Orel Province, a horse thief, Ivan Tereshin, showed up in the village of Brednikha. When he began to steal from the local peasants, they turned him in to the authorities; he was found guilty and spent time in jail. The community members thus began their struggle with Tereshin by appealing to formal law and the judicial system to protect them. But Tereshin stole from them again, and their reaction was to beat him nearly to death. During the beating he warned them, "You'll remember me, yep, you won't forget me! Van'ka knows how to pay people back!" One night soon thereafter, Ivan and his brother set fire to two houses and made off toward another community. The entire village burned to the ground, but the peasants caught the Tereshin brothers. They beat them, tied them up, and threw them into the flames of a bonfire of the brothers' own property. When a local official urged them to pull the arsonists out of the flame and leave the case to the authorities, the peasants replied, "They're headed down that road anyway."[24]

The Tereshin brothers had violated the community code by stealing within the community, earning reprisals from the local peasants. In vengeance, they then burned the entire village down. But in response, the community members joined together to fight fire with fire, to exact vengeance in the form in which they had received it, even to the point of being willing to burn the arsonists alive. This was not the only report of such punishment.[25] Burning alive arsonists who were caught red-handed was one of the most spectacular forms of *samosud*, or self-help. It conformed to the peasants' usual explanation for preferring self-help to legal procedure: self-help was a more certain way to prevent the arsonist from harming them again. In this instance, the local officials' pleas to leave the arsonists' fate to the authorities and the courts fell on deaf ears. Convinced of the justice of a fiery death as the physical equivalent of moral damnation in hell, the peasants of Brednikha had no inclination to leave this matter to be resolved by the law of the state.

Fighting fire with fire here also reflected the general tendency to adjust the punishment to fit the level of harm done.[26] Because the Tereshin brothers had caused so much evident harm to Brednikha residents, the victims were comfortable imposing the maximum penalties on them: burning their property and consigning them to fire themselves. As they reportedly shouted into the Tereshin brothers' faces after they piled up their belongings in front of them to burn, "You burned our goods, and so let your goods burn!"[27] The same sense of evening the score by forcing the arsonists to experience the loss they had caused inspired some of the villagers' reaction to the death of their poultry and livestock in the fire. Running around their devastated yards, the peasants grabbed the charred carcasses of geese, piglets, and chickens. Shouting, "So it was you who fried this goose! Then you eat it!" they shoved the animals into the arsonists' mouths or swung them against their mouths, faces, and necks. Taking a cue from their elders, the children of the village surrounded the arsonists and cast burned pieces of wood at them.[28] In the end, local officials did arrive and take the Tereshin brothers into custody, saving them from the full force of *samosud*. Instead, they felt the full force of the Criminal Code and were sent to Siberia.

Where should this scene fit in our understanding of rural arson? When the Tereshin brothers practiced it, they were using it as a form of revenge and terror against a community they had already harmed. In this form, arson was pure malice, very much like that of the chicken thief in Penza. It provided an outlet for impulsive violence, ready to hand and effective in punishing

Brednikha's peasants, who lost all of their homes and possessions to the fire. Arson appears in this form in many local reports. Another example comes from Porech'e District, Smolensk Province. Following market day and a church festival on September 8, 1879, the pub opened and a large number of peasants got drunk. Two in particular, Sergei Fedorov and Semen Semenov, got into a brawl, were arrested, and were put in the storeroom of the cantonal administration offices to sober up. They continued to fight there and shouted threats to burn the place down if they were not let out. The village elder and the local policeman paid no attention to them, because they had searched them and taken their matches away. Even so, the storeroom burst into flames fifteen minutes later; the offices burned to the ground, as did the village school attached to them.[29]

A village elder named Matvei Timoshenko and his brother Martyn lost all of their property in 1894 to a similar act of malicious reprisal by one Khomenko. Like the Tereshin brothers in Brednikha, Khomenko had been stealing from people in his own village of Solovev'ka, Radomysl' District, Kiev Province. His neighbors had exercised their power to vote as a legal community (*obshchestvo*) to banish him to Siberia. In return, Khomenko set fire to the Timoshenko brothers' barn.[30]

Not only village officials experienced this form of pressure. In December 1882, the chairman of the Assembly of the Justices of the Peace in Krestets District, Novgorod Province, was the target of an arsonist who set fire to his stacked firewood.[31] In all these cases against officials, the arsonists—the Tereshin brothers, Fedorov and Semenov, and Khomenko—fell into the arms of the law and were subject to exile to Siberia, but they left with the satisfaction of knowing that they had impoverished the communities that had tried to counter their injurious presence.[32] Arson fires of this type were so frequent that the Karsun District zemstvo in Simbirsk Province proposed in 1894 that the zemstvo should pay for the fire insurance on homes of local officials because they were so frequently the targets of arson for revenge.[33]

Arson also served extortionist peasants, who threatened to burn the property of any other peasant who refused to pay them fees. Such was the peasant Golubev, who tyrannized his village generally and, in September 1874, turned to arson as his weapon. On the night of September 8, on the afternoon of September 11, and again on the night of September 12, he set fire to his neighbors' properties, causing ten thousand rubles in losses before they turned him in to the authorities. When the case came to trial, it turned out that Golubev had decided to set fire to one of his victims' houses after he demanded money from her and found the amount she gave him too small.[34] Arson terrorists of this type also appeared in reports of the local Committees on the Needs of Agriculture in

1903.[35] Fire in the hands of these peasants was a threat to the communities they inhabited. Three factors of rural life gave them their power through arson: their intimacy with and willingness to wield fire as a weapon, the flammability of the villages of European Russia and the vulnerability of everyone in those villages to fire, and the justifiably low confidence village residents had in the ability of the law to protect them.

Arsonists in these forms are as infrequently noted in the historiography of rural crime and of arson in Russia as are female arsonists. They do not conform to the notion that rural criminals were agents of social justice. In his study of East Anglia arsonists, John Archer came close to acknowledging that rural arsonists have enjoyed too much idealization in the study of rural crime:

> However, the temptation to hail such men as vanguards of the working class should be resisted. One should just stop awhile and imagine meeting some of these characters in quiet country lanes in the dead of winter. . . . [They] were undoubtedly vindictive and aggressive in the extreme, and were not perhaps the sort of people to engage in conversation, let alone to whom one would wish to extend the apologia of sociology. Some of these men were, in short, brutal and wild men who operated under their own laws, not those of the state or their own communities.[36]

Archer's reference to the laws of the state points to another reason why there has been little room for purely malicious arsonists in our reading of rural culture in the nineteenth century. The failure of the judicial system as a facilitating factor in peasant-against-peasant terror has little place in readings of nineteenth-century formal justice that define the justice system itself as criminal and as a force of cruel oppression against peasants who burn for social justice. Of the latter, George Rudé offered the most explicit example in his *Criminal and Victim*, in which he concluded that the courts in early-nineteenth-century Britain were waging a "class war" against the lower classes, who had been unfairly labeled a "criminal class." He asked, "May the term [class war] be applied more appropriately to the attitudes and measures adopted by the possessing classes, or those in authority, to avert, or to protect themselves against criminal acts on the part of the labourers and poor?"[37] As Joan Neuberger has explained in her study of hooliganism in Russia, Rudé is part of a line of historians and anthropologists extending through Michel Foucault for whom the definition of crime was "at the center of the exercise of power."[38] Their inquiries variously criticized the class motives behind the labeling of deviance, explored the "intentionality, rationality and purpose in criminal acts," or displayed the rich "expressiveness found in popular culture" as clues to popular culture's mores and as evidence of its "self-assertion."[39]

Violence among peasants as an expression of sheer malice, however, exposes a different set of risks for members of the lower estates from the hazards of punitive, class-driven judicial systems (which were a hazard for them). Arson bullies or arson extortionists reveal how a criminal justice system that failed to penetrate popular culture left its weaker or less malicious members open to assault. From the perspective of victims of peasant arson in rural Russia, the problem with the imperial police and judicial systems was not that they were too invasive and punitive but that they were rarely there at all to police and protect against the rural communities' own malevolence.

A recent alternative reading of crime and justice opens the way for placing such unconstrained rural violence in another context, that of Norbert Elias's notion that a feature of "civilized," modern societies was the increasing control of impulsive crime, evident in decreasing rates of crime. Through close comparative analysis of several European cultures, Eric A. Johnson and Eric H. Monkkonen concluded that "the perceived decline in violence over the long term was in fact real and not merely a spurious correlate of a growing interest in prosecuting property crimes in bourgeois society."[40] Beyond that decline in violence, they argued two further theses relevant to rural arson in Russia: that "violence was a common and often tolerated, if not fully accepted, form of dispute settlement in rural areas and villages that dominated premodern society," and that the drop in such rural violence in Europe "was associated with a 'civilizing process' whereby dispute settlement was gradually worked out in court more often than in potentially deadly brawls in taverns and on streetcorners—the growth of the state's power and monopoly over violence helped to retard interpersonal violence."[41] As the twentieth century has only too clearly demonstrated, too much state power invites violence against citizens and increases their defenselessness. But too little state power invites violence of citizens against citizens. Malicious arson in the villages of European Russia reveals that the imperial state heightened peasants' vulnerability through police and judicial neglect as surely as it heightened their material and economic vulnerability through its neglectful economic policy of denying investment to the agricultural sector.

Red Roosters, Outsiders, and Community

The absence of effective "law and order" also left village communities to move against those they considered intruders or outsiders in their midst. Arson was a potential weapon for defining membership in the community. Ministry of Justice statistics suggest that arson was directed against those with whom relations were neither familial nor proximate. They include information on the relationships between convicted criminals and their victims, distinguishing both family and employment relationships from *postoronnie* (outsider, strange, unrelated) relationships. Among arson convicts from 1872 forward, the percentage of relationships identified as "outsider" or unrelated ranged from around 75 percent to almost 90 percent. This does not mean that the arsonists did not know their victims; all the evidence in local police reports suggests the opposite. But in most arson cases, some social or geographical distance existed between culprit and victim, and the greater the distance, the more inviting arson was as a weapon of community control or definition.

Three cases reported from Novgorod Province hinged on the combination of the arson victims' status as outsiders and the community's determination to protect its economic well-being against them. In the first case, a local peasant sold his father's mill to a peasant from another village. The mill had always caused periodic flooding of the village's fields, but so long as a local peasant owned it, the community was willing to tolerate this hardship. As soon as an outsider began to operate the mill, however, and the usual flooding resulted, the local peasants demanded that he close the mill down. When he refused, the community got together and torched it.[42]

A newcomer priest in a second village in Cherepovets District suffered even more vicious incendiary reprisal for failing to submit to his new community's demands. One night when his wife, two children, and their old nurse were inside their new home, every section of its exterior suddenly exploded into flames—the straw roof, the wooden walls, the doorway and windows, the fences—creating an instant, inescapable incinerator that burned them all alive in short order as the village peasants watched. What could have elicited such murderous and popularly sanctioned hatred? The investigation that followed established that the young priest had replaced a familiar, elderly figure. The former priest enjoyed a reputation for generosity. The new priest, by contrast, exacted emoluments that the villagers considered excessive. When they urged him to lower fees, he replied, "No, fellows, it's not up to you to teach me, but me to teach you, and quickly." The peasants' anger and warnings escalated from threats, which he ignored, to setting fire to some of his outbuildings, and finally to burning his entire homestead. Because of the way the house burst into flames on all sides simultaneously, the authorities concluded that the village peasants must have poured kerosene over the house.[43] There can be no doubt about the arsonists' intention in this case to bring utter destruction onto this outsider priest. The community protected the incendiaries; no one was indicted. A new priest arrived. With his predecessor's fate vividly memorialized by the burned-out homestead, he came to terms with the community quickly.

Sometimes an outsider had to do no more than try to make a living to invite an arson attack. The peasant Petrov from Lifland Province discovered this in 1904 when he rented a water mill in Starorusskii District, Novgorod Province. A neighboring peasant who was native to the district, who also ran a mill, decided to eliminate this alien competitor by burning the mill down, leaving Petrov without a livelihood and the mill owner with losses of six hundred rubles.[44] In each of these cases, the victims were outsiders in the sense of entering an established community from another village or region to take up residence and enter into local relationships. There also may have been, within individual districts or cantons, notions of distinct communities that emerged either from diverse ethnic groups within the region or from subcommunities within very large villages. Such notions dividing "us" and "them" may have contributed to the frequency of arson in ethnically complex regions of European Russia.

In his reminiscences of fires in Riazan Province in the late 1840s, D. M. Pogodin recalled that the local people were convinced that the exceptional number of fires in 1847 and 1848 were the handiwork of *nerusskie liudi*, non-Russians, especially along the Astrakhan highway.[45] All of the most arson-prone provinces from the 1870s forward were areas of multiethnic populations. In the southwestern provinces, from Grodno to Podolia to Kursk Province, Poles, Ukrainians, Russians, and Jews made up significant subcultures and communities.[46] Ethnic conflict and "incendiary powders" came together earlier in the century during the "great fire" in Kiev in 1811.[47] In Estland and Lifland, Baltic German gentry lorded over Lithuanian and Estonian peasants in an increasingly volatile atmosphere of competing claims for cultural hegemony.[48] In Simbirsk, Samara, Saratov, and Kazan Provinces, Russian, Chuvash, Mordvinian, Ukrainian, Cheremis, and Tatar peasants lived in neighboring villages that were often physically as well as culturally distinct. This ethnic diversity brought religious diversity as well, with almost 30 percent of the population in Kazan Province and 10 percent in Samara and Simbirsk Provinces being Muslims, according to the 1897 census.[49]

The definition of insiders and outsiders, as well as of acceptable norms of behavior and interaction, took on a more contested nature in such areas, with greater opportunities for perceived injury or violation of morality and greater willingness to use arson as the language of complaint. Unfortunately, neither local police reports nor the Ministry of Interior's fire statistics reveal the ethnic background of either victims or suspected arsonists. The Ministry of Justice's statistics on convicted criminals do identify the nationality of the convicts. For the southwestern regions, they obscure as much as they illuminate, however, because they do not distinguish between Ukrainians and Russians, lumping both under the category of Russians. Throughout the period beginning in the 1870s, the "Orthodox" made up the majority of arson convicts, although that majority shrank steadily from 94 percent in 1873 to 90 percent in 1881, and from 84 percent in 1895 to 79 percent in 1902. By nationality, Russians constituted 72.6 percent of all convicted arsonists in 1873 (there were several convicts of "unknown" nationality), 91 percent in 1881, 81 percent in 1895, and 77 percent in 1902. Among religious groups, the numbers of Catholics, Protestants, Muslims, and Jews among arson convicts grew, while among nationalities, the expanding groups were Poles, Latvians, Jews, and Tatars. By 1902, Catholics comprised 8.6 percent of convicted arsonists, Protestants, 5.4 percent, and Muslims, 3.2 percent.[50] These trends raise questions for which extensive research in local archives, working through the biweekly district policemen's reports and circuit court records, might yield more information. For now, I can say only that published fire statistics and circuit court statistics, however they vary in numbers of arsonists, reinforce one another in pointing to multiethnic areas as fertile grounds for arson.

These areas display not only ethnic diversity but also increasingly crowded living conditions. Several of the arson-prone provinces were distinguished in the 1897 census by their large numbers of "populated locales," outside cities, with more than 500 inhabitants. For the provinces of European Russia, the range for such locations was from 14 communities with 500 or more inhabitants in Estland to 1,833 such communities in Volynia. Orlando Figes noted this factor in the southeastern Volga region in the emergence of "centrifugal social pressures" in the form of economic differentiation in villages that ranged from 500 to 750 peasants.[51] Of the high-arson provinces, those listed in table 5.1 had very large numbers of rural communities with more than 500 residents.

When communities exceeded 500 members, the cohesiveness of the society was at risk, as was any common definition of norms and relationships. In their study of Captain Swing in England, Hobsbawm and Rudé found that "if criminality is any index of the tightness or looseness of social control, [then] the large or open village had more of it."[52] There was more room in such areas for differing appraisals of acceptable levels of wealth, of who was a forbidden target of petty theft, of whose property should be considered within or outside the boundaries of acceptable trespass, and of who was an acceptable partner in an extramarital affair. There was also more room for differing attitudes toward whether arson was justified, and thus a greater possibility that someone in the community would report an incident of arson to the authorities; this would increase the number of reported arson cases. In some of these large communities, informal forms of dispute resolution, which continued to be present in rural communities at least until the 1890s, may have ceased to function.[53] Such organs as family courts, courts of elders, and village assemblies may no longer have seemed viable options in disputes between members of the community who were distant from each other in their residences or in their family memberships. As villages grew larger, even family relationships may have extended beyond the limits of insider status. Arson may have seemed a quick, easy, and certain alternative to the formerly effective informal councils.

Table 5.1: Numbers of Places with 500 Residents or More in Arson-Prone Provinces, 1897

Province	No. Places
Minsk	909
Simbirsk	952
Poltava	1,118
Kursk	1,320
Kazan	1,377
Kiev	1,693
Podolia	1,729
Volynia	1,833

Source: Troinitskii 1905.

The village of Degtianoe in Spassk District, Riazan Province, fits this profile. With two thousand inhabitants, it stretched the concept of "village" or "settlement" to its limits, but that was its official designation. It came to the attention of the local correspondent for the weekly journal *The Firefighter* during the summer of 1894. At midnight on July 26, a barn full of harvested grain caught fire and one hundred stacks of grain burned within thirty minutes. The reaction of the peasants in the neighborhood was telling: "Someone struck the alarm, [and] a small group of peasants ran up, but they remained indifferent spectators before the exploding bonfires of straw. . . . Meanwhile the peasants began to exchange comments that this must have been arson, and even the women, atypically, were not screaming and crying." When he looked into the rumors about arson, the correspondent discovered that there had already been several fires in the village that year, following the previous year's record of twelve major fires, "and almost all of them were arson."[54]

Opportunities for conflict were also higher because of land shortages and the crazy quilts of land allotments in several of these provinces. Judith Pallot and Denis Shaw have explained that as land shortages worsened in the central black-earth provinces, so-called *pestropole*, or mosaic, fields proliferated. "Farmers began to make ad hoc decisions about what to grow, with little regard to the different requirements of crops and land." Kursk was among the provinces where this "totally chaotic" situation was most complete.[55] Land pressures led peasants to depart from traditional planting and harvesting patterns, shifting among changeable combinations of short fallow and long fallow rotations and sometimes abandoning any rotation at all. This agricultural individuation upset collective farming arrangements, cooperative crop scheduling, and what little sense of communal control over the long-term productivity of repartitional lands may have remained by the 1870s and 1880s. Even residents of the village who were deeply embedded in its history and family networks might have become outsiders of sorts when their farming decisions broke with locally prevailing traditions.

Finally, an expanding group of perennial, if temporary, outsiders— migrant agricultural workers—passed through high arson zones on their way to farming regions in the south each spring and summer. The spring hiring market in Tauride Province, according to Timothy Mixter, "attracted as many as 50,000 agricultural workers" looking for temporary employment in the commercial grain fields.[56] Mixter described smaller markets as ranging from five hundred to five thousand workers. These young men and women made their way out of overcrowded provinces such as Kiev and Poltava by foot, steamboat, or crude wooden boat in journeys of several days under difficult conditions. Their destinations lay in Saratov, Samara, Tauride, Ekaterinoslav, and Kherson Provinces. Both en route and once at their temporary employment locations, these migrants moved along the boundaries of local communities. Mixter found evidence that local communities tried to exclude these outsiders. "Those who lived in the vicinity of markets tried to uphold a 'moral economy' which was based on the principle that outsiders should not be allowed to profit from local resources and jobs until all local peasants had been given the opportunity to take care of their subsistence needs."[57] Within the space of the hiring market itself, migrant workers from different regions also displayed intense consciousness of their subgroupings and identities, quickly demarcating themselves from fellow migrant workers "along ethnic and regional lines."

Mixter did not discuss the disruption migrant workers must have caused en route, but it seems likely that both going and coming from their temporary employment, they generated unease and tensions in the insular and defensive communities through which they passed. Opportunities were clearly at hand for conflicts over access to natural resources and food supplies as the often straitened migrants tried to feed themselves during their journey. It is possible that this is one reason why, according to Ministry of Justice statistics, arson fires in Russia, unlike in Britain, tended to be most frequent in the spring and summer months.

Specific incidents, such as those described from Novgorod Province, show that arson was a weapon peasants used against those they considered intruders who might disrupt the local "moral economy." Geographic trends identify regions where villages were large and communities mixed in their ethnic and religious groupings as the most fertile for arson fires as a percentage of all fires. Together these forms of evidence point to arson's function as a form of social control that was not solely determined by economic factors, and certainly not by the question of property ownership. Definition of membership in the community and defense of the community's interests join gender protest and pure malice as motivations for arson distinct from economic protest or the quest for social justice.

Arson's Appeal and Advantages

For each of its functions—protest, dispute resolution, rebuke, social control, or exclusion—arson offered distinct advantages and appeal to the peasants who practiced it. As a weapon of protest, its special qualities have been described most aptly by John Archer, who distinguished the "act of starting the fire—covert and individualistic—from the subsequent reaction that the fire engendered—overt and collective."[58] When arson was covert, it was a relatively safe form of protest, whether that of a disgruntled peasant against a gentry neighbor or of a beleaguered daughter-in-law or wife against patriarchal powers in her household. David Jones emphasized this feature of arson in his description of it as "underground terrorism."[59] For would-be peasant protesters against new restrictions on access to natural resources or the continuing power of the purse enjoyed by post-Emancipation gentry employers, the state's effective resort to legalized violence against peasants at such places as Bezdna in 1861 and Chigirin in 1877 was compelling evidence of the wisdom of avoiding head-on confrontations; they chose anonymous, barely traceable ways of damaging those they considered excessively advantaged.[60] Women may also have feared the power of the male arbiters and judges in their communities, and certainly in their families, and chosen arson as a way of gaining satisfaction, if not release. Christine Worobec found female "hysteria" to have been a common form of protest in the late-nineteenth-century villages of European Russia; female arson was probably a close relative.[61]

Arson as a form of dispute resolution had an alternative in the local courts in the form of either the cantonal court or the justice of the peace through the

1880s. Recent research has demonstrated the growing popularity of the cantonal courts, over which peasant judges presided, as the century drew to a close.[62] Beatrice Brodsky Farnsworth's study of litigious daughters-in-law showed twenty-five years ago that as early as the 1860s, the cantonal court attracted peasant women who wished to resolve just the types of disputes that lay behind Fekla Antonovna's trial or the case of the woman who reportedly burned up her village and her own children over a stolen chicken.[63]

The decision of an injured party, female or male, to take a complaint to the cantonal court required the person to postpone airing his or her grievance and seeking satisfaction and instead hand the issue over to a formal setting in which not only custom but also law entered the process. To go to the cantonal court meant to submit at some level to a procedure driven by the Code of Laws, the physical presence of which in the courtroom, on the court clerk's table, was a constant reminder to plaintiffs that written laws had a role in the outcome of their suits.[64] Arson, by contrast, ensured the arsonist that he or she would enjoy immediate satisfaction and neither have to appeal to texts nor submit to formal procedures to gain it.

Might literacy, and the experience of schooling that produced it, have been a factor when an aggrieved individual decided how to respond? Is it possible that arson held greater appeal in areas where written laws were least within reach because of illiteracy, and that, conversely, higher rates of literacy made the court system more attractive than arson? Ben Eklof's study of peasant schooling makes it clear that one of the hopes of educators was to effect behavioral change as much as to teach reading to their rural pupils. A decrease in crime and an increase in civic engagement were two concrete measures of success. By all accounts, the gains in these areas were modest, at best. "Even after schools had been in the villages for a generation or more, the volumes of reports to the 1911 Zemstvo Congress were full complaints that the schools' influence was virtually negligible, that even the graduate of the primary school soon sank back into the morass of peasant village life."[65]

Given this nearly universal conclusion by contemporaries, the historian does well to be skeptical about any potential effect of schooling and literacy on the practice of rural arson. Yet there is a suggestive geographical congruence between literacy and low arson rates. Six of the seven provinces that consistently identified fewer than 10 percent of all fires as arson fires were also among the provinces of European Russia that, according to the 1897 census, had the highest levels of literacy: St. Petersburg, 55.1 percent; Vilna, 28.8 percent; Tauride, 27.9 percent; Olonets, 25.3 percent; Tver, 24.5 percent; and Arkhangel'sk, 23.3 percent. (The exception was Viatka, with a literacy rate of only 16.0 percent.) In contrast, most of the arson-prone provinces (with the exception of Grodno, where 29 percent of all fires were identified as arson, Estland, with 79.7 percent, and Lifland, with 77.7 percent) fell into the category of the least literate provinces in European Russia: Chernigov, at 18.2 percent literacy; Kiev, at 18.1 percent; Minsk, at 17.8 percent; Volynia, at 17.2 percent; Poltava, at 16.9 percent; Kursk, at 16.3 percent; and Podolia, at 15.5 percent.

It is hazardous to go too far on these numbers, because one cannot even be sure what the relationship was between school attendance and literacy. But if those who were literate had probably completed three or four years of school, then some of the positive responses to zemstvo surveys about the impact of schooling on behavior support the hypothesis that peasants who were literate were more likely to go to court than to burn down someone's barn. Eklof explains that a Perm study from 1901 found that "former schoolchildren were more likely to be elected to positions of authority in the village." Further, the author of the Perm report stated that "the literate is better able to grasp matters under discussion; he conducts himself in exemplary fashion, does not shout without reason, 'understands procedures better,' 'can make better sense of written material,' is 'more articulate' and 'reasonable.'"[66] A massive survey of zemstvo schoolteachers a decade later (and thus beyond the limits of this study) elicited the view from 11 percent of the teachers responding that literate peasants displayed "greater participation in local self-government" and a "higher incidence of election to communal posts."[67]

For peasants who had not gone through the disciplining experience of sitting in school or learning the rules of grammar and the authority of texts, the procedural and textual elements of a day in court, however local, must have seemed at best unfamiliar and at worst alien. In several of the provinces where arson rates were high and literacy rates were low, furthermore, language itself was contested territory, for the languages of plaintiffs, defendants, judges, and written laws may have differed owing to the diversity of ethnic groups in the province. If arson is understood to be a language of its own for expressing individual or community disapproval, responding in petty and major disputes, or protesting perceived exploitation, then the question of literacy is germane to understanding its function as an alternative to dispute resolution through the judicial system and according to written laws.

Jack Goody's reflections on the relationship between literacy and the law in the organization of societies alert scholars to what the spread of writing might have meant in this context. Written law, he argues, creates "a greater distancing between individual language and reference than speech, a greater objectification which increases the analytical potential of the human mind."[68] Writing, and the legal world it creates, also "encourages formalism," and as law moves into the realm of codes and procedures, it becomes the realm of "literate specialists and law is increasingly taken out of the 'amateur' hands of the man in the street."[69] Finally, within a formalized procedure where written evidence comes into play, a literacy-based dispute resolution narrows "the area of dispute and the issues at stake, with important consequences for the notion of relevance."[70] This meant that complaints had to take a form and focus that the court was willing to consider.

The documentary records left behind for cantonal court cases in Novgorod Province demonstrate that going to court involved all of these processes, from the requirement that the complaint be filed in written form through the evolution of the language of peasant complaints, which displayed growing knowledge and linguistic adjustment to both civil laws and procedures at court. Going to the cantonal court required not only "distance" and "formalism" but also patience and tenacity as the process stretched out over months, sometimes years.[71] Arson required none of these attributes, least of all a common understanding of a written language. Furthermore, because of its consistent morphology, it was a language more universally spoken and understood than the articles of the imperial Code of Laws sitting at the cantonal judge's side. It was, indeed, a rather simple language.

Arson as rebuke provided personal satisfaction for the arsonist or the community through its clarity and immediacy. Rebuke by arson was always public, because everyone in the community either witnessed the fire or observed its aftermath as the charred ruins in a courtyard or spot in a neighboring field. In cases of community arson against individuals—like that against the greedy priest in Novgorod Province or the Tereshin brothers in Orel Province—arson as community justice provided intense catharsis and occasion for exultation as the outsiders' real or symbolic self (property) went up in dramatic flames, reducing the offenders before their very eyes. Titillation in Dostoevsky's and Chekhov's sense became positively orgasmic as the community released the red rooster to enforce its values. Both David Jones and Regina Schulte remarked on this aspect of arson's attraction. Jones described the reward of arson as "the glorious prospect of instant revenge" and quoted one convict's explanation that "'it was the most beautifullest blaze I ever saw in my life.'"[72] Schulte stated: "The fire and its dramatic enactment fulfilled a cathartic function."[73] The community's satisfaction extended beyond the few moments required for a building to burn and into the period of watching as the victim labored to rebuild what they had destroyed. In this, arson provided both more immediate recourse than going to court and more prolonged satisfaction than other actions, such as a good beating, public shaming, or smearing manure or tar on someone's fencepost.

Arson as a language of community control displays another feature in the case of the greedy priest, in the peasants' progression from oral complaints to torching an outbuilding to setting fire to a residential structure with human beings inside. Arson was typically relational, part of a longer dispute. Local police reports display evidence that this was so, for the more immediately the report that a fire was due to arson was submitted to the government, the more likely it was that the specific peasant suspects within the community would be named.[74] Contained arson fires were part of a conversation, as it were, between two parties in conflict. Whether gentry or peasant, the victim usually understood the message, as did the community that witnessed the fire or viewed its charred residue. The victim was on notice; undoubtedly, many victims adjusted their behavior to prevent further, more violent and damaging communication. Arson's ubiquitous presence, in fact or in possibility, hovered over the community as everyman's or everywoman's possible form of expression. Schulte concluded that this was equally true in upper Bavaria during the same period: "Arsonists were no folk heroes, but their language was familiar and understood; for ultimately everyone was a potential arsonist and everyone could become a victim."[75]

The familiarity and ubiquitousness of arson's threat provided the otherwise weak individual with power as an incendiary. Historians consider it so frightening a rural phenomenon that it qualifies as a form of "terrorism." Why? Because of the ultimate message that a successful arson attack sent. The specific content of arson's message as rebuke, reprisal, or protest varied according to the relationship whose failure it signaled. But everywhere and always, successful firing delivered the arsonist's message to his or her victim: "I can cause you harm." Arson's power lay in the arsonist's ability to strike when he or she wanted, without fearing the intervention of any community or security force. A blazing hayrick, grain bin, or threshing barn illuminated the property owner's defenselessness against this and possible future attacks. The aggrieved party gained the advantage, both in the instant of the firing and in its smoldering presence in the victim's memory, reducing the previously powerful to a state of public vulnerability.

Despite these advantages, arson was not always perceived by the peasants of European Russia as a legitimate form of protest, dispute resolution, rebuke, or community control. There were certain community constraints on the use of arson. Once a member of the community violated those constraints, he or she became a wrongdoer in the community's eyes, as well as a sinner. In such cases, peasants were more likely to agree that the action warranted reprisal, either through formal justice or through self-help. In evaluating the acceptability of arson as a means to settle a score, peasants imposed norms consistent with those they imposed on all acts of serious wrongdoing.

The Limits on Arson

Local district officials' handwritten reports and the published versions of their biweekly submissions to the provincial governor usually indicate whether arson was an act of peasant against peasant or of peasant against gentry or merchant neighbor, and what burned. In Smolensk, Novgorod, and Kursk Provinces, there are consistent patterns: peasants were the usual arsonists and the usual victims, and the most frequent targets were granaries, barns, and threshing floors.[76] These were often limited fires, injuring the targeted households monetarily but not spreading to injure either the property or person of other community members. Village arson fires thus had much the same profile as peasant-against-gentry fires. For other cultures, historians of arson have argued that outbuildings and hayricks were the preferred targets because of their distance from residential structures; the distance protected the arsonist against detection during the act of setting the blaze. Perhaps this was true on gentry estates, but the nature of village layouts in European Russia offered no such protection to the peasant arsonist striking his peasant neighbor's property. In the Russian context, the choice of targets and the extent of the fires serve as keys for deciphering the language and appeal of arson.

Like other actions that were universally defined as criminal in statutory law but that were susceptible to varying definitions in the peasant milieu, arson varied in its definitions primarily according to three main criteria: the harm it caused to the community, the membership of the victim in the community, and the type of dispute it was being used to settle.[77] The greater identifiable harm arson caused to individuals or to the community, the more likely it was to be declared sinful. Once identified as sinful, it was more likely to be identified as an act requiring a community response.

In that light, an individual act of arson committed against one outbuilding, which consumed only that outbuilding and brought economic loss only to the victim, was considered fully legitimate if the community also acknowledged the legitimacy of the arsonist's grievance. This type of deliberately set fire was least likely to be identified as such in official reports, because the community shielded the arsonist, considering it the arsonist's private retaliation against his or her victim for the perceived offense. As the clearly bewildered correspondent to *The Firefighter* reported from the arson-prone village of Degtianoe in Riazan Province: "There was absolutely no consciousness in their words and stories [about arson fires] of the criminal nature of arson in general or of the damage the fires cause for the entire community."[78] Obviously the arsonist recognized that he or she had destroyed the victim's property—that was the goal of bringing the victim back onto his or her level of economic play—but property damage in and of itself did not constitute a violation of community morality in the villages of European Russia. Arson became punishable wrongdoing when it was simultaneously sinful. And to be sinful, it had to cause debilitating hardship and suffering or take the life of some of God's creatures.

For that reason, the worst kind of arson fire was one that became a runaway conflagration that consumed many homesteads, including residential structures, livestock barns, and grain storage barns.[79] Even if the arsonist had intended to set a limited fire in a single outbuilding, when a fire subsequently spread, he or she was considered guilty of unacceptable, sinful wrongdoing. Despite membership in the community and the intention to commit an act that was implicitly sanctioned by the community, a peasant who was reckless in setting a fire to settle a score was vulnerable to the maximum penalty of death through *samosud* if caught red-handed. "There's no way for him to be excused, because his enemy's innocent neighbor suffered," the peasants of Novoladozhsk District in St. Petersburg Province explained to a correspondent of the Tenishev Ethnographic Bureau.[80]

Intentionally setting fire to a residential structure, setting an arson fire that led to loss of human life or that of livestock or poultry, and burning an icon were all acts that violated community morality and exceeded the use of arson as an acceptable weapon directed toward positive or sanctioned ends. In some areas, it was also considered a sin and thus a crime to set fire to stored grain if doing so deprived the victim of sustenance.

These prohibitions suggest that peasants distinguished between property as shelter and sustenance and property as commodity. These incidents of arson in rural European Russia share the reflection of "an older moral economy, which taught the immorality of any unfair method of forcing up the price of provisions by profiteering upon the necessities of the people."[81] It was not only the practice of forcing up the price of provisions that elicited this form of protest within peasant communities in European Russia, however. Simply withholding assistance when one had provisions to spare, or being visibly better off than one's neighbors, could elicit a warning in the form of contained arson.

It is important to place rural acts of arson within this frame of warnings and rebukes, as statements of individual or community disapprobation or dissatisfaction. Their usual goals were communication and adjustment, not annihilation. Most arsonists were aiming either to get even with the victim or to even the playing field through this particular form of economic leveling. However dramatic and disruptive arson itself may seem because of fire's elemental properties, its function was often to reestablish community equilibrium by countering another disruption in social or economic relationships. By sending a warning against exploitation or profiteering, arsonists set limits on personal gain or wealth within the community. By issuing a public rebuke through the gesture of burning an outbuilding, they put their victim in his or her place, as it were, forcing an equality in community standing rather than tolerating their own diminution through the victim's prior offense. Arsonists in these cases were seeking not to destroy their victims or eliminate them from the community but to maintain the status quo ante within it. When Schulte writes of the "cathartic function" of arson, this is what she has in mind as well. For catharsis provides release, and "afterward, the world was all right again, restored to order, as it were."[82] The murder of the greedy priest in Novgorod Province was unusual; so was the wildly destructive vengeance of the chicken thief in Penza Province. Most acts of arson were limited in their goals, targets, and the amount of damage they caused. This gives grounds for caution in interpreting the uses and meanings of arson in the Russian countryside.

Because of the flammability of villages across European Russia, arson was risky business for those who practiced it. Within their own village, they courted disaster not only for the intended victim but also for themselves and their neighbors if the red rooster they let loose flew too freely. Yet many arson fires did not lead to the devastation of a runaway fire. In Novgorod Province, most arson fires that appear in local police reports were restricted to one owner's outbuildings or stacks of grain and hay. Only after the turn of the century do runaway arson fires appear with great frequency in local district records. Files include reports of three runaway fires in 1901—two in August that burned seventeen and twenty-three peasant homesteads, respectively, and another in October, leading to the destruction of seventy-one peasants' properties and losses valued at 34,395 rubles.[83] As crowding worsened because of expanding population and family divisions, arson became a more dangerous form of reprisal. Up to the turn of the century, however, arson fires remained within the limits of acceptable damage; otherwise arson would not have retained its appeal as an effective form of dispute resolution and social control in the village. The efficacy of arson belied the commonly held view that peasants did not know how to manage fire and were ignorant about fire precautions. It pointed instead to proficient, focused, and eminently satisfying manipulation of fire. This was equally true of another form of arson—the practice of burning one's own insured property for the purpose of receiving payouts from compulsory insurance programs. Unlike other categories of arson in the countryside, which sought to maintain equilibrium, self-arson was enterprising and displayed its practitioners' willingness to take risks to get ahead.

Burning Down the House

In September 1894, a correspondent from Iukhnov District, Smolensk Province, reported an enormous night fire in the village of Ol'khi. Because all of the homesteads in the village were sucked into the blaze, and individual families were trying frantically to pull from the flames whatever they could in the way of property and animals, peasants from neighboring villages pitched in and tried to contain the fire, although there was little hope of salvaging anything of consequence. Once the excitement was over, the Ol'khi peasants and their neighbors began to talk about the cause for the fire. They concluded that it was the result of arson, an intentional fire set by a peasant from Ol'khi who had recently insured his house through a special appraisal at far more than its actual value.[84]

By the late 1870s, self-arson (*samopodzhog*) had become both a phenomenon of village life and a topic of concern in the national discussion of Russia's "fire question." Indeed, by 1882, when N. D. Sergeevskii, a professor of law in St. Petersburg, developed case studies for law students, he wrote of two cases of property owners, one a peasant and one a timber merchant, deliberately burning their own structures in the countryside.[85] Because peasants in European Russia were property owners, and because they were all subject as such to compulsory fire insurance programs, peasant arson in Russia developed yet another face. This one belies both the conceptualization of arson as a social crime and a form of resistance of the propertyless against the propertied and the idea of the arsonist as someone who acted out of irrational vengeance or impotent spite. Self-arson for profit demonstrates, instead, peasant activism for self-enrichment and the manipulation of both property ownership and compliance with compulsory insurance laws to serve individual interests.

Self-arson surfaced after the introduction of compulsory fire insurance programs, which were managed through the local organs of self-governance and public works—the zemstvos—in the thirty-four provinces where they were established in 1864 and by the provincial governor's administration in the fifteen other provinces of European Russia. The following chapter examines this program in detail, but here, in the context of arson, the zemstvo compulsory insurance program is of interest because it was a notable factor in the growth in the number of arson fires in certain provinces. It is likely that it was a major contributor to the higher rates of arson fires as percentages of all fires reported to the Ministry of the Interior in the 1880s. It was a factor, furthermore, that added to the evidence of an active rural fire culture and a re-visioning of the peasants not as victims but as calculating risk takers who were willing and able to turn prescriptive decrees imposed upon them by outside bodies (here, the state through the zemstvo) to their own purposes.

Mutual fire insurance programs appeared as one of the zemstvo's fourteen major responsibilities in the original zemstvo legislation of January 1, 1864. Details of the fire insurance regulations followed in legislation on April 7, 1864.[86] Of the more than eighty articles in the legislation, only a few are relevant to the discussion of self-arson. First, participation in the mutual insurance program was compulsory for all peasants who held property within the boundaries of peasant farmstead settlement (*v cherte krest'ianskoi usadebnoi osedlosti*), leading one observer to conclude that "it would be more accurate to call it peasant fire insurance than zemstvo fire insurance."[87] For all other rural inhabitants, fire insurance through the zemstvo program was voluntary. Each peasant property owner had to submit to a property appraisal and pay into the mutual fire insurance capital fund at the rate assigned by the provincial zemstvo board; this rate was a percentage of the minimum appraised value (*po normal'noi otsenke*) of his property. Peasants and property owners of other legal estates in the countryside could also request a special appraisal (*po osoboi otsenke*) at a higher rate, but each provincial zemstvo board was charged with establishing a maximum appraised value beyond which no insurance premium could go.

Originally, much of the responsibility for executing the insurance program fell on peasant cantonal officials. It was they who were to carry out appraisals, examine damaged buildings after fires and send the reports to the provincial zemstvo board, and make sure that property owners used any insurance payments they received exclusively for repairing or rebuilding the insured structures. It did not take long for peasants in some areas to recognize the opportunity these programs offered them. Some of the best evidence available on how they upended the state's and zemstvo's goals comes from Viatka Province. Despite the statistical insignificance of arson as a cause of reported fires there, the provincial zemstvo board discovered that its own insurance program had encouraged the practice of self-arson in certain parts of the province. Its experience provided a cautionary tale for neighboring provinces not only in their management of fire insurance programs but also for the management of any program that sought to restructure village habits through monetary incentives.

Observing with understandable alarm the enormous increase in the incidence of reported fires in Viatka Province beginning in the late 1860s, and the equally enormous rising deficits in the province's fire insurance capital reserves, the provincial zemstvo board commissioned a comprehensive study of fires' causes, district by district and canton by canton, in 1885. Two districts— Malmyzh and Elabuzh—had the largest number of fires, but within these districts, specific cantons varied in the number of fires. In Malmyzh District, the seven most fire-prone cantons were also the most densely populated and congested. Furthermore, they were in an area that was almost completely deforested, with the result that most peasants had turned to straw roofs. They also sat on an elevated, exposed site, where they were vulnerable to high winds. These factors alone might have explained their higher incidence of destructive fires.[88]

But in Elabuzh District, the statistics on the most fire-prone cantons suggested that arson for profit was the culprit. Closer analysis showed a direct correlation between the incidence of fires, the number of insurance claims, and the level of property valuation for fire insurance purposes. It turned out that in Malmyzh District, each homestead was appraised at 151 rubles, and in Elabuzh District, at 119 rubles. By contrast, homesteads in Viatka District were each valued at 40 rubles, and in Kotel'nichessk District, at 27 rubles. Table 5.2 displays the pattern that emerged.

These figures led the zemstvo bureau to reexamine the process of appraisals and, most importantly, the method of paying the cantonal officials who did them. Formerly, the officials' pay was a percentage of the total value of appraisals they completed. Now, their pay depended upon the number of insured homesteads. Yet as a turn-of-the-century student of this process explained: "But this measure had no effect anytime soon."[89]

The zemstvo study also underscored the fact that among all fires leading to insurance claims, those attributed to arson had risen from 1.1 percent in the 1870s to 13.8 percent in the 1880s.[90] Some villages in Elabuzh and Malmyzh Districts burned repeatedly each summer, with some recording five to ten fires in a season. The peasants in these communities, who came to expect fires as a daily or nightly possibility, kept all of their movable goods loaded onto wagons so that they could drive out of the village with them if necessary. Some even

Table 5.2: Reported Fires and Insurance Claims in Viatka Province, 1886

District	Valuation per Homestead, in Rubles	Homesteads Burned	Claims in Rubles
Malmyzh	151	300	45,500
Elabuzh	119	307	36,500
Viatka	40	31	1,200
Kotelnichessk	27	34	900

Source: Gofshtetter 1902: 92.

approached the zemstvo with the request that property valuations be lowered "so that things will quiet down."[91]

These developments forced the zemstvo board to recognize that local cantonal officials, as members of the community themselves, would quickly facilitate fire insurance payouts through overvaluation, while taking a good cut themselves through their pay. Because these same officials bore the responsibility for reporting fires and assisting in the investigation of their causes, they were in a perfect position to assist peasants who sought to lay their hands on some cash by burning their own property.

The zemstvo's next step was to establish fire insurance agents who were not members of the communities whose property they appraised but were instead salaried employees of the zemstvo board. Property valuations plummeted; the fire agents' reappraisals lowered premiums for the province by almost 1 million rubles. The number of fires also decreased in arson-prone villages. Usadskaia Canton in Malmyzh District, for example, where arson fires had consumed eighty thousand rubles' worth of zemstvo insurance capital in 1877–1888, reported only one fire in the year the fire insurance agent reappraised property there, and reported no fires at all the year after.[92] The number of homesteads burned in Viatka Province started to decline rapidly in 1892. The value of structures burned dropped from 423,000 rubles in 1891 to 128,000 in 1894. The share of reported fires attributed to arson also dropped steadily beginning in 1889, according to Ministry of the Interior statistics, falling from 72 arson fires in 1889 to 37 in 1894.[93] Five years later, the number of arson fires remained at 35, out of 4,922; by 1904, only 23 fires out of 4,971 reported fires were attributed to arson.[94]

The Kazan provincial zemstvo brought even more striking ruin upon itself through its initial system of property appraisals. It found that both the membership of the appraising officials in the local communities and the option of requesting special appraisals at a higher valuation distorted the process. The value of special appraisals for the province nearly doubled between 1880 and 1889, from 13 million rubles to 25 million rubles. The number of fires rose during the same period from 585 to 1,219. Detailed study of the fires' distribution across the province revealed that fires were most frequent where there was the highest percentage of homesteads valued through special appraisals. As I. Gofshtetter concluded: "It became profitable to burn—and people consciously set fire to their own homes, in order to receive double or triple their value, having insured them at the special valuation ahead of time."[95]

Arson for profit created other income possibilities within these Kazan communities. Special carpenters' labor cooperatives formed to meet the need to rebuild. When villages burned several times in a summer, there was money to be made by rebuilding quickly. Cantonal officials began to hire themselves out as framers, only to appraise the resulting izbas at the special rate, then report the fires that resulted, and obstruct investigation into the origins of the fires. Between 1886 and 1891, the number of structures burned in Kazan Province more than doubled, from 3,731 to 9,308. The zemstvo board's insurance capital deficit exceeded the limits of the state's generosity. Having formerly lent the Kazan zemstvo board as much as 600,000 rubles to cover its insurance payments, the state in 1892 refused to cover any further losses.[96] This prompted the board, as in Viatka, to introduce salaried fire insurance agents to carry out appraisals. Within two years, the appraised value of insured structures dropped by more than 3 million rubles, and the number of reported fires in the province dropped from 1,245 in 1890 to 611 in 1892. Reported losses also dropped from 757,000 rubles in 1890 to 692,000 in 1891 and to 264,000 in 1892. The number of homesteads burned dropped from 9,308 to 4,326. Most telling was the decrease in the number of fires that originated in structures insured at the special, higher rate. Before the introduction of fire insurance agents, such fires accounted for 60 percent of all reported fires; after their introduction, such fires accounted for fewer than 30 percent of the total.[97] Ministry of the Interior statistics also show a decline in fires attributed to arson in Kazan Province, from 171 out of 1,085 fires in 1888 to 61 out of 609 in 1894. Five years later, 60 of 607 fires were declared arson fires, and by 1904, the figure had dropped to 51 of 884 reported fires.[98]

The shift to zemstvo fire inspectors and insurance agents who were salaried employees without relationships with the peasants whose property they were appraising was a positive step toward eliminating the incentive for arson-for-profit. As a preventive measure, it sought to limit the number of fires due to *samopodzhog,* and in Viatka and Kazan Provinces, at least, it seems to have had a significant impact. All the same, arson continued to plague the Russian countryside, largely because arsonists remained so often beyond the reach of the law after they set structures, haystacks, and lumber ablaze. The combination of community culture, the nature of arson fires, the weakness of policing in the countryside, and the costs associated with taking a suspected arsonist to court gave rural arsonists a de facto license to burn.

Trying to Outlaw Arson

There was no shortage of laws against arson. From the time of the first law code in Kiev, rulers had considered arson one of the most threatening crimes. From the eleventh century forward, arson called for the severest punishment available, along with murder and horse theft.[99] Early statutes were extremely laconic, so the historian can only infer why arson against houses or threshing barns warranted such severe punishment. P. Besedkin's conclusion that it was the generalized danger that arson brought to the community seems quite plausible. Until the fifteenth century, the punishment for arson remained *potok i razgrablenie,* which many historians have concluded meant some form of exile in combination with confiscation of property.[100]

Exile would eventually appear as a proposed punishment for arson, but only hundreds of years later. In the interim, between the fifteenth century and 1845, the punishment was death, first by burning at the stake and later, in Peter the Great's Navy and Military Codes, by either burning at the stake or by hanging.[101] The impulse to rid society of arsonists through execution was still strong in the legal commissions and projects of the late eighteenth and early nineteenth centuries. The authors of the project of the legislative commission of 1754–1766 continued to call for death by burning for intentional incendiarism. The legislative project of 1813 proposed execution by beheading for intentional incendiarism during an uprising or which was intended to cause an uprising. For other acts of intentional burning that caused either death to individuals or damage to churches, crown properties, public buildings, warehouses, or hospitals, the project called for public shaming and slitting the nostrils of non-noble arsonists, followed by exile to hard labor in the far reaches of the empire for all such arson convicts.[102]

Historically, arson was both a private and a public concern for the law-issuing state, which punished both those who intentionally caused property damage and personal injury and those who intentionally threatened the public order by attacking and damaging public institutions and church and crown properties. This complexity also characterized the Criminal Code of 1845 and its revisions. They constituted the first element in the triad of "codes, courts, and constables" that Goody described as the product of written law and its formalization by a political power.

The law on arson was codified in Articles 1609–1615 of the Criminal Code. For accused arsonists after the Judicial Reform of 1864, courts became either the district or the circuit court before a judge and jury. Constables were the local, district police officials who investigated and reported all fires to the governor and ultimately, via his office, to the Ministry of the Interior. The judicial approach to dealing with arson, however, was universally recognized to be a failure. Everyone who wrote on the subject agreed with A. S. Ermolov's conclusion that "the rural population finds absolutely no real protection whatsoever in the judiciary."[103]

Codes

As Russian law developed, the codes dealing with arson came to include several distinctions in determining the seriousness of the crime and the punishments that each level required. Both intent and actual harm done, as well as the categories of property burned, came to be determining factors. The 1885 edition of the Criminal Code continued to display a hodgepodge of factors and priorities. Besedkin's conclusion that Russian law in general and articles on arson in particular displayed no unifying principles, but rather a collection of responses to individual types of arson or individual incidents, is an apt description of articles 1606–1615 of the Criminal Code.

First, to qualify as arson, the destruction of property by fire had to be intentional—"s umyslom" (Article 1606). Second, most of the space in the code was devoted to defining the seriousness of the crime according to categories of targets or objects of arson. In each of the four categories of punishment, the code identified discrete categories of property. Third, the seriousness of arson also depended in some cases upon the level of harm done, either to human victims of the fire or to provisions for society. Fourth, the Criminal Code paid some attention to the motivation of the arsonist, with the harshness of the punishment also depending in some cases upon the record of the accused, upon whether he or she set the fire at night—an act likely to increase the damage done—and upon whether he or she acted out of the desire for revenge.

Articles 1606–1615 of Part One in the Criminal Code defined the categories of arson and their punishments.[104] Articles 1606–1609 established the first principles for arson against structures; articles 1610–1611 treated attempted or planned arson; article 1612 assigned punishment for setting fire to one's own property to receive insurance money; articles 1613–1614 covered arson against forest or grain; and article 1615 covered arson against any other category of property when the arson was premeditated and driven by the urge for revenge. The three elements of the first article of this section of the Criminal Code were premeditation, destruction of a building, and the presence of people in the building. This article established a baseline for a "first degree arson," carrying a punishment of the deprivation of all rights assigned according to legal status and exile to hard labor for eight to ten years.

Article 1607 defined the most serious forms of arson: those that consumed church or state structures, with the churches and residences of the imperial family listed first; acts of arson that set fires in several places in a city or town at once (as in St. Petersburg in 1862); and setting fire to a gunpowder storehouse or to a hospital with sick people in it. In addition to these categories of targets, one category of culprit elicited the severest punishment available: known recidivist arsonists. The arson laws consistently determined the severity of the crime by, first, the state association of the targeted structures; second, the likelihood that many people would die; and third, the level of malicious intent. Thus, setting fire to state offices, libraries, museums, archives, and jails or setting fire to theaters and other public gathering places when people either were in them or scheduled to be in them was considered the second most serious category of arson. While setting fires in villages and settlements earned the baseline punishment raised by two degrees, doing so in a city in several locations earned punishment raised by three degrees. Starting fires in food storehouses or warehouses of military supplies also called for punishment raised by two degrees, as did arson committed by a gang. A lower level of punishment, the baseline punishment raised by one degree, was called for when the arsonist acted at night.

In each of the remaining articles, a similar concern for the actual or potential harm of the fire determined the severity of punishment. For specific possible targets, such as mines (Article 1608), nonresidential structures and boats (Article 1609), and forests (Article 1613), the punishments increased in severity if the targeted structures were in close proximity to residential structures or shops and warehouses, or if the crime occurred at night. The law also distinguished between arson fully executed and left to burn and an act of arson that was either planned but not carried out (Article 1611) or planned and initiated but aborted by the arsonist who then tried to put the blaze out (Article 1610). Article 1612 assigned different degrees of punishment for arsonists who burned their own property for insurance payments, with the severity depending upon whether neighboring structures belonging to other people burned and upon whether such buildings were inhabited. Finally, Article 1615 was devoted entirely to the category of arson for revenge directed against any kind of property not described in the preceding articles; this crime called for a range of fines or imprisonment for up to eight months.

As these articles reveal, no one principle governed the severity of punishment. Sometimes the object itself determined the seriousness of the crime, while in other cases the degree of harm to human beings was the determining factor. Within the category of the most serious crimes, intentionally burning churches and property of the tsar or the imperial family called for the highest degree of punishment, not because of any harm caused to human life (there was no qualification based on whether these structures were inhabited or not) but because of who owned them, and therefore their symbolic meaning in Orthodox, autocratic Russia. Like the *Russkaia Pravda*, the *Church Statute of Kiev*, and subsequent law codes, the late-nineteenth-century code of law privileged property owned by the church or the state. That privilege applied as well in defining the categories of arson that earned punishment raised by two degrees. There, too, the defining phrase was "places or in general a building in which some part of the government administration or court is located," followed by a list of structures such as state archives, institutes, libraries, and museums. Again, the fact that these structures embodied the state defined the degree of punishment for arsonists who attacked them. Other objects of arson in the code were value neutral in the sense that the articles made no statement about ownership.

The degree of harm or potential harm to human life defined the degree of punishment for burning buildings not defined specifically as churches or the property of the imperial family or the state. Thus, setting fire to a hospital full of sick people equaled burning a church or imperial property in Article 1607. Here, the lawmakers recognized the near certainty of death when someone intentionally set fire to a structure full of incapacitated people. Much the same reasoning was reflected in the inclusion of a gunpowder storehouse in this category of arson, for the resulting explosion would also be very likely to cause extensive destruction and personal injury or death. The same explanation applied to setting fire to several points in a city or settlement at once (Article 1607).

The degree of premeditation entered into the ranking of the severity of the crime and the punishment assigned to it. In descending order of punishment from three degrees above the baseline down to one degree above, the article singled out three types of arsonists: known recidivists, members of gangs (*shaika zlonamerennykh*), and those who set fires at night (Article 1607). The urge for revenge warranted a separate article, Article 1615.

For most of these infractions, the historian of rural arson in Russia can envision a specific fire; this legal code, like all others, reflected deeds that were commonly done and called for proscription. Obviously, laws against arson did not prevent it in the countryside. Part of the reason lies in the disjunction between these approaches to wrongdoing and punishment and popular desires.[105] The emergence of the centrality of property in Russian statutory law resembled that described by Douglas Hay and his colleagues for the eighteenth century in Britain.[106] But equally obviously, personal injury (actual or potential) was as important as property damage in Russian law, so that property analysis alone does not suffice to explain the values of the Criminal Code.

Perhaps more important in explaining the gap that emerged between popular and formal justice were the punishments. The state had moved away from a sentence of equivalency—burning at the stake in exchange for malicious burning—to removing the offending individual from the body of European Russia to its extremities. Furthermore, revenge as a motive was defined as criminal. Together, these two aspects of the Criminal Code illustrated the maturation of Russian law in the opinion of contemporary jurists. As G. Gradovskii explained in defending the court and jury system introduced in 1864 against conservative critics: "In our era, the science of criminal law taught in all universities and juridical institutes, including those in Russia, categorically censures the theory of vengeance and fear for deterrence. In their place, the goal of criminal punishments is the need to protect the state, society, and individuals."[107] Popular justice had not embraced these values in its approach to wrongdoing that violated community norms. Vengeance could be just. Punishment (or arson itself) might have as its goal putting the individual back into his or her proper place within the community, rather than removing him or her from it. Neither the state nor the individual was as important as society. These discrepancies between customary and formal law surfaced in the second critical element in Goody's triad—the courts.

Courts

It seems that Fekla Antonovna's experience before the Riazan Circuit Court in 1867 was typical. Suspects who were indicted for arson were as likely to be acquitted as convicted, especially when there were many peasants on the jury. One delegate reporting to the Minsk Provincial Committee on the Needs of Agriculture in 1902, V. P. Lopott, reported the conviction rates for European Russia for the period 1882–1885. During those years, more than 50 percent of accused arsonists were acquitted. Lopott broke down types of arson cases and found that for cases of arson against inhabited structures, fewer than 50 percent were typically acquitted, whereas for arson of one's own property, more than 70 percent were typically found innocent.[108] In every year during this period, acquittals for arson far exceeded the rate of acquittals for all defendants in all criminal cases, which ranged from 34 percent to 40 percent. A decade earlier, the discrepancy was less consistent; in 1872, 56 percent of all accused arsonists were acquitted, and only 24 percent of all defendants in criminal cases were acquitted. But in 1875, 46 percent of accused arsonists were acquitted, compared with 36 percent of all criminal defendants. E. N. Tarnovskii found that 50 percent of all arson defendants in Russia between 1889 and 1893 were acquitted, compared with 37 percent of the same in France.[109] During these years, the rate of acquittal for all criminal cases in Russia hovered around 32 percent. Throughout the period 1895–1904, 33 percent to 36 percent of all defendants in all criminal cases were acquitted, while arson acquittals ran as high as 56 percent (1903).[110]

At the 1902 All-Russian Firefighters' Conference, E. V. Bogdanovich argued that the main obstacle to conviction before jurors in circuit courts was the severity of required sentences. Because they were so harsh—too harsh in the peasants' eyes—peasant jurors refused to render guilty verdicts, he argued.[111] Participants at the 1902 provincial Committees on the Needs of Agriculture echoed this view.[112] When prosecutors succeeded in securing a guilty verdict, the punishment was likely to be quite harsh. S. M. Porshniakov, an Orel delegate, reported on the basis of Ministry of Justice statistics that 6,833 people had been convicted of arson between 1875 and 1887 in Russia as a whole, and that two-thirds of them were exiled to Siberia.[113]

Getting witnesses to testify in arson cases was also a serious problem.[114] Even when members of the community could easily identify the arsonist, they often chose to remain silent. There were two common reasons for this refusal. The first was that witnesses feared revenge from the arsonist, if acquitted, or from his or her relatives, who might seek vengeance if the arsonist were convicted. Even in cases of arsonists who had harmed or systematically terrorized a community, this fear often prevented peasant witnesses from testifying against them. Because the conviction rate for arsonists hovered around 50 percent, there was an even chance that the arsonist would return to the community.[115] Arsonists and their victims seemed to be fully aware of this, which led to a phenomenon in which arson bullies kept whole villages in fear, extorting from the peasants with the threat of the red rooster.[116] As in the case of the arsonist

Khomenko, who burned down the homestead of the village elder Timoshenko in 1894, the very officials whose duty it was to report and investigate arson fires did so knowing that they put themselves and their families at risk. As the correspondent to *The Firefighter* who described this fire concluded: "It is understandable why village elders fulfill their duties so poorly, especially if they have to deal with people like Khomenko."[117]

Peasants had little confidence in the state's ability to protect them from such arsonists, or from their relatives in the event that the court convicted the arsonists themselves. There was little reason to turn to the law or its agents when it did so little to protect them. Furthermore, there was little reason to serve the law by participating in legal proceedings at court when the costs for doing so could be so high. Peasants were not interested in serving the abstract principles of justice embodied in legal procedure; they were interested in the stability and safety of their individual communities and households. They were intimate with arson fires; they knew how little evidence an arsonist left behind and how difficult it could be to build a formal case.

The second reason for peasants' refusal to identify arsonists was that in cases in which the arson fire remained within the norms of acceptable reprisal in the community, his or her fellow villagers, and even the victims themselves, were unlikely to seek legal redress. The community at large had nothing to gain from formal procedure and much to lose if they were called as witnesses. They may also have condoned the arsonist's action, especially if the arson fire had been limited to an uninhabited structure or other form of property without any personal injury or death.

In the case of Fekla Antonovna, the jurors chose not to convict her, although there was much compelling circumstantial evidence. It is possible only to infer why. Two aspects of the court trial probably contributed to the acquittal. The first is that many may have sympathized with her difficulty as a young bride in an unwelcoming family or with her suffering because of the ulcer on her leg. If their sympathy were adequate, then they might have considered the use of arson a valid form of reprisal. Second, and perhaps more important, is the possibility that the jurors considered the sentences awaiting her too severe.

This was the most important divergence between community responses to arson in the countryside and the dictates of the criminal code. In all cases involving any but the most minor forms of property damage, the sentences in the criminal code called for removing convicted arsonists from their community and dispatching them to "the most distant locations of Siberia." Peasants were willing to make use of this measure, but only in the most serious of cases, and most often when the arsonist was not a member of the community or was an "arson bully."

For most arson cases, however, which entailed burning an outbuilding or some harvested grain or lumber as a way of settling a score or warning the property owner that he or she had stepped outside the limits of community norms, peasants sought mainly to reestablish equilibrium in the community, not to banish the offender. Arson was a language they spoke and understood. When the fires that resulted stayed within bounds, when parties outside the dispute suffered no harm, or even when, by the late nineteenth century, peasant property owners practiced self-arson (*samopodzhog*) without causing damage to any other person or anyone else's property, the rest of the community stood aside. Peasants were not interested in protecting property as sacred, as it was viewed in the criminal code.

Fekla Antonovna's case, reports on rural practices of arson, reports about similar outcomes in cases where peasant jurors acquitted peasant arsonists, and Articles 1606–1615 of the criminal code evince differing definitions of community. For the state, anyone who willfully destroyed property using fire relinquished membership in the community of European Russia for at least a number of years. This was especially true if the property he or she destroyed belonged to one of the pillars of state authority: the church and the crown. Within village communities, there was toleration of certain forms of arson, defying the sanctity of property as the principle defining wrongdoing. Identifiable, actual harm to individuals or to the community had to occur because of arson for the community to mobilize to exact compensation or retribution against the arsonist, either through *samosud* or through resort to the judicial system.

Constables

The foregoing were the larger reasons for the failure of codes and courts to contain arson in European Russia. The final element of that failure was the weakness of policing in the countryside, or what Goody referred to as the constables. David Jones has explored the expansion of local police forces as an expression of a state's desire to penetrate and break up or eliminate groups engaged in newly defined illegal activities. Of their presence in the British countryside after 1856, he wrote that "the new police soon established themselves as an 'improving' force: they brought to the local court cases of assault that had once hardly deserved the term 'criminal'; they set about controlling boisterous recreations; and they broke up gangs of underemployed youths and poachers."[118]

A. N. Engel'gardt's letter to *Notes of the Fatherland* in 1880 finds him making similar observations about the newly established *uriadniki*, or local police.

From Smolensk Province, he reported that the news heartened gentry landowners in his region,

> especially those tearful ladies who were sitting in their boring estates, who were eternally afraid of robbers, arsonists, thieves, about which we have heard nothing in our backwoods. The ladies thought that the new officials would ride around their estates on horseback and keep an eye on everything, in the manner of St. Petersburg policemen, or, even better, the famous London constables.[119]

Engel'gardt explained that these new policemen penetrated village life more than the entire complex of officials that had existed before Emancipation, who had largely kept to the main roads. "But now it is not like that: this one darts about everywhere; he knows that he is more likely to find disorder in an isolated village and take a fine. . . . Furthermore, he is a useful man for those landowners who constantly have quarrels with the peasants about wood poaching, trespassing, failure to do work."[120]

Clearly, the imperial state hoped to bring more law and order to the countryside through these new officials, who, among other charges, were to enforce fire safety regulations. In Engel'gardt's area, at least, this was one of their most despised functions from the perspective of the peasants, who did everything they could to evade the demands of the state that they have night watchmen on duty every night, fire signals on their houses, posted lists of their firefighting equipment, prescribed intervals between all village buildings, and so on, only to find themselves relentlessly pursued by the *uriadniki*, who demanded fines on the spot for any infraction. Equally clearly, however, there were not enough police to do the policing, nor were those who were at work able to break through the wall of collective silence on arson when the community had no interest in reporting or pursuing suspicious fires. As P. A. Zaionchkovskii and George Yaney have each explained, there was fewer than one *uriadnik* for every twenty-five hundred people between the institution of the local police on August 1, 1878, and 1903, when the Ministry of the Interior set that ratio as the new minimum. The average for European Russia was eleven *uriadniks* for each district, which proved to be hopelessly inadequate, given their many tasks, which included, among other charges, "to maintain public peace and to investigate the appearance of any kind of actions and rumors against the government, legal powers and public order or the assault on social morality and property rights."[121] Their duties in enforcing fire regulations and investigating suspicious fires had to compete with their duties to collect taxes, supervise military recruitment, and respond to calls for statistical information of various kinds, while fulfilling their broader responsibility for public order and morality.[122] These impossible burdens worked to arsonists' advantage.

The consensus among educated observers was that few peasant arsonists ever wound up in court, because their victims rarely reported them to the authorities and because police officials were unable to gather enough evidence or witnesses to warrant bringing a suspected arsonist to trial. As P. A. Miller explained in 1903, "in the vast, overwhelming majority of cases, these acts of arson remain unpunished, the guilty parties almost always slip out of the hands of justice."[123] D. M. Bodisko echoed this view before the Chernskii District, Tula Province, local committee, saying that the failure of the investigative branch of the police was the key factor frustrating efforts to uncover arson and bring arsonists to trial. He explained that the investigators always arrived too late at the scene of the fire to find any physical evidence, which was all the more critical given the reluctance or refusal of most peasants to provide any information about the fire or suspected arsonists within their community.[124] Individual reports often confirmed this view when they mentioned that the zemstvo or governor's fire insurance agent showed up two to three days after the fire to investigate its causes and assess its damages.[125] The Kovno District committee of 1902 stated that local police authorities had become so frustrated by their inability to apprehend arsonists that they had virtually decided that it was not worth the effort to try to investigate suspected arson cases at all.[126]

The late autocracy's codes, courts, and constables indicate that the government had the same impulses to protect private property through laws, procedures, and law enforcement that England had demonstrated roughly a century earlier. But it would be wrong to transpose the conclusion from British historiography that these impulses in Russia rested on concern exclusively for the upper orders of society. The authors of the Judicial Reform of 1864, which established circuit courts with trial by jury for criminal cases, and of the *uriadnik* decree of 1878, which attempted to bring more policemen to the countryside, were not blind to the needs of the peasant population, and especially its propertied elements, for protection from the depredations of horse thieves, arsonists, and other criminals who threatened rural prosperity. But the government did not rush into the countryside to assert its official presence. So hesitant was the autocratic government to impose on the emancipated countryside any agents of control who were of gentry background that it left rural society without a significant police force of nonpeasant background for sixteen years (from 1861 to 1878), and only in 1889 reasserted noble supervision in a major institution, the land captain.[127] The same squeamishness about replicating gentry-serf relations after the Emancipation informed the decision to hand over the vast majority of peasant disputes to the exclusively peasant organ of justice, the cantonal court. These self-imposed restraints reflect the fine intentions of the reforming bureaucrats of Alexander II's rule. But the countryside was a rough culture indeed, as it had been under serfdom and continued to be up to the revolutionary events of the twentieth century. The absence of effective law and order through codes, courts, and constables left peasant proprietors as defenseless as their gentry neighbors. It encouraged would-be arsonists to act on their desire for immediate satisfaction of their frustrations, perceptions of injustice, petty grievances, envy, and greed and, in the case of sanctioned wrongdoers, on their desire for the pleasure of one last malicious action against their accusers or jailers on their way out of the community.

Conclusion: Arson's Meanings in Rural Russia

The decade of the 1880s was European Russia's worst in terms of arson fires as a percentage of all fires; in absolute numbers, the incidence of reported arson cases in 1885–1889 was matched again only in 1900–1904 and was surpassed in a significant way only in the revolutionary years 1905–1909. The high percentages during the 1880s may be attributed to at least three factors, each of which may be more compelling as an explanation for specific forms of arson. First, for arson as a form of social protest, deteriorating economic conditions no doubt contributed to tensions both within peasant communities and between peasants and neighboring gentry. As Arcadius Kahan and Stephen Wheatcroft have each explained, this was a decade of droughts, crop failures, and famines.[128] Kahan's regional analysis of both famine relief and natural calamities leading to grain shortages identified the "arson zone" as the area where many provinces suffered most severely during these years, including central, southern, and eastern Ukraine, the middle and lower Volga, and the northern Caucasus regions.[129] Wheatcroft also described declining purchasing power for peasants who faced worsening hardships as they tried to buy grain for their own consumption and as fodder for their livestock.

Second, self-arson for insurance fraud had its heyday during these years. Peasants figured out how to make the system work for them, no doubt drawing encouragement from every successful self-arsonist who got away with fraud. As the examples of Kazan and Viatka Provinces demonstrate, zemstvo boards only slowly recognized the patterns of arson fires and insurance claims, undertook studies, and then moved to limit opportunities for abuse. As more and more

Table 5.3: Rates of Arson as Percentages of Fires Reported to the Ministry of the Interior in Twelve Provinces of European Russia, 1888–1909

Province	1888–1894	1895–1899	1900–1904
Astrakhan	10.0	7.4	10.9
Grodno	22.5	25.4	25.4
Iaroslavl	10.3	13.6	14.7
Khar'kov	10.2	8.5	13.0
Kherson	4.8	3.5	6.9
Kiev	16.7	16.2	18.2
Lifland	20.9	28.8	30.8
Minsk	17.7	18.7	24.5
Mogilev	10.9	13.7	16.2
Podolia	19.6	16.6	20.7
Poltava	19.9	17.3	20.1
Riazan	9.9	10.4	11.8

Source: Tsentral'nyi statisticheskii komitet, Ministerstvo Vnutrennikh del 1897: 66-75, 1912: 128-152.

zemstvos followed their lead by introducing non-native fire inspection and insurance agents, opportunities for and the incidence of arson fraud began to decline in the 1890s.

Third, for all arson fires, one may argue that reporting generated the higher percentages of the 1880s, owing to the introduction of the *uriadniki* (local police) in 1878. Despite their inadequate numbers and overwhelming tasks, they undoubtedly stumbled across more fires and increased the number that made their way into biweekly reports to the governor. Certainly the dramatic increase in the number of provinces with higher arson percentages reported in the 1870s was due in part to changes in the reporting itself, making that decade, rather than the 1860s, the more appropriate baseline decade. The higher percentages of arson fires in the 1880s may be due to each of these factors, to all of them, or to still other factors in rural European Russia. In any event, historians should avoid what Stephen Wheatcroft has referred to as "extreme reductionism" in identifying any one cause of arson, especially purely economic causes, with an eye to seeing arson primarily as a form of protest.[130]

The incidence of arson as a percentage of fires reported to the Ministry of the Interior declined between 1888 and 1904 in thirty-seven provinces of European Russia. Only in twelve provinces did arson increase—most strikingly in Lifland Province, where arson fires constituted 20.9 percent of all reported fires on average between 1888 and 1894, 28.8 percent in 1895–1899, and 30.8 percent in 1900–1904. The other eleven of these twelve provinces showed increases of various sizes, as the table 5.3 reveals.

A glance at map 5.1 shows that eight of the twelve provinces were clustered in the area of the empire that had been an arson zone since the 1870s. It was there that an arson culture was most tenacious. Of the so-called Great Russian provinces of the empire, north of Ukraine and east of the Baltic provinces, only Riazan and Iaroslavl Provinces registered increasing rates, with neither breaking the 15 percent mark. One could reasonably argue that the Russian arson problem was shrinking in significance at the beginning of the twentieth century.

Even so, roughly 10 percent of all reported fires were conclusively established to have been caused by arson. Ministry of the Interior statistics do not segregate losses according to causes, but if 10 percent of the total reported losses were due to arson fires, then arson's economic cost to the empire could be pegged at 36 million rubles in 1895–1899 and 49 million rubles in 1900–1904.[131] Perhaps more important for our understanding of rural Russia and the challenges it posed to the forces of order or progress at the turn of the century, 27,396 individuals in 1890–1894, together with 24,493 in 1895–1899 and 29,381 in 1900–1904, chose

Map 5.1 Provinces where % of fires attributed to arson increased 1888 - 1904

arson as their method for registering protest, settling a dispute, sending a warning, or procuring cash. They often did so with the tacit or active support of their community. And neither agents of order, in the form of the local police, cantonal courts, and jurors in circuit courts, nor agents of progress, in the form of zemstvo agents, seemed to be able to constrain them.

The costs to European Russia and to the Russian Empire of unconstrained arson assume major importance within a comparative discussion of the reduction of unconstrained rural violence and economic development. The state's failure to penetrate the countryside in ways that would have protected peasant victims of arson left the majority population defenseless against coercion and property-terror as weapons of community control, agents of envy, and strategies for self-enrichment through insurance fraud. While less dramatic, perhaps, than blazing gentry property, and of less interest to previous social historians, village arson fires were more continual and more corrosive in undermining the local sense of security, as well as in shortening the range of peasants' economic visions. Contemporaries recognized this. It is for this reason that arson and fires in general were a more central concern of the Economic Department of the Ministry of the Interior than they were for the Ministry of Justice.

In a comparative study of long-range economic development in the United States and Russia, the economic historian Colin White argued that "risk reduction is a necessary precondition" for economic advance.[132] Following Eric L. Jones, he recognized that fires as one of Russia's perennial risks and economic shocks, along with violence in various other forms, "led to . . . a risk environment which discouraged investment in all kinds of capital."[133] The roots of Russia's less dynamic economic development can be explained in large part by the fact that "there can be little doubt that Russian society was more 'shocked' than American—more frequently, more severely, more extensively and more inopportunely."[134] The failure of the police and judicial systems made arson, as one such shock to the economic system, possible. The peasant arsonist, however, was the active agent delivering the shocks.

For educated observers at the time, the peasant arsonist joined the kulak as an active agent and peasant individualist in village culture who went about his or her business beyond the reach of the restraining or guiding hand of tutelary, educated Russia. This conclusion fed educated Russia's frustration over not only the "fire question" but also the broader "peasant question," which placed blame for Russia's failure to become modern, in either the economic or the judicial sense, as much on the peasantry as on the autocracy. Peasant arsonists did not qualify as victims of Russia's backwardness, which in the context of fire had been defined primarily as backwardness in material culture and as ignorance and passivity. On the contrary, peasant arsonists loomed ever larger in the educated imagination as culprits and causes of backwardness, as is evident in statements made before the 1902 All-Russian Firefighters' Conference and the Committees on the Needs of Agriculture that "at the very least, half of all fires are caused by arson," and "the enormous majority of fires result not from chance, but from human evil will."[135]

Defining peasant arsonists as evil invited action against them, not only as outlaws but also as agents of darkness and the unclean. This characterization dovetailed nicely with the image of the kulak that had emerged in the post-Emancipation era and implied that whenever peasants became active, rather than passive, they inevitably turned from being victims of their circumstances to victimizing others.[136] This conclusion about peasants and their village culture within the context of the "fire question" was another step toward the demonization and liquidation of peasant strongmen that would ultimately inform Bolshevik politics during the Civil War and collectivization campaigns.

This interpretation should not blind historians to the fact that arsonists were victimizers and that their assaults against property did damage the lives of other peasants and the community at large. Many of the terms employed here to explain the rhetoric of arson are terms that normally carry positive connotations: equilibrium, morality, goals, purposes, community constraints, and so forth. They conform to the valorization of activism among the lower orders that is embedded in E. P. Thompson's and subsequent historians' studies of popular political consciousness. In my case, however, explication is not meant to be valorization. The words of one peasant victim of a neighboring arsonist from 1904 sum up nicely both the possible forces at play in arson and the impact its frequent practice had on individuals and the community. Having explained to a correspondent for the journal *The Firefighter's Cause* that his house had already burned down six times, a peasant went on to describe a case of arson committed by the wife of one Ivan Grubar', a horse thief who landed in jail. Needing cash to hire a lawyer, she decided to burn some of her property for insurance money. To avoid suspicion, she started the fire on his, her neighbor's, property. The victim continued:

The policeman came, he put together a case, the investigator then had to bring us to court three times. . . . They acquitted the woman [*baba*], because no one saw her setting the fire, nobody was right there, on the spot. But still, it's true—it was her hands that did it; look, the whole village will tell you! So that's why I say this: Why build a good house, when no matter what, you can't protect it from an evil person? It's like this. You're living well, you've got what you need, but that doesn't suit somebody, he's eaten up with envy, so he'll do you a favor— Live like everybody else! And you didn't even have a clue, you went to sleep a rich guy, and you wake up destitute. . . . Everything happens![137]

Such was arson's impact on the village and its inhabitants. First, it was often an agent of fraud, greed, or envy. It served to keep peasants within the limits of community prosperity—to ensure that no one lived differently from or better than anyone else in the village. Second, because of arson's nature, its practitioners often eluded the state, leaving the peasants they targeted without protection. Third, because of their freedom to burn, arsonists were able to blunt their neighbors' desires to invest in their property or their future. In these ways, peasant arsonists robbed their peasant neighbors not only of their prosperity but also of their hope for prosperity. Arsonists thus tipped the balance, as victimizers, in favor of futility for their victims, and against futurity. It was this aspect of rural arson that inspired the most aggressive response from those educated members of Russian society who were determined to build a better future for Russia through civic activism. They would do so through fire prevention and firefighting programs in the countryside.

PART THREE

MOBILIZING TO MAKE
RUSSIA MODERN:
INSURING, PLANNING,
VOLUNTEERING

The failure of the imperial government to diminish the fires of rural Russia was self-evident to virtually all observers by the 1880s. Neither codes nor courts nor constables were displaying much success in preventing accidental and intentional fires in the countryside. As educated members of society moved into a period of "small deeds" activism and Alexander III emerged as a reactionary ruler, rural fire as Russia's "historical evil" became an arena for both service to the nation and criticisms of an ossified, overbureaucratized autocracy.

Three programs embodied civilian efforts to control rural fire in order to build Russia's future: the zemstvo insurance program, zemstvo village planning and reconstruction projects, and volunteer firefighting societies and brigades. To insure for the future, to plan and to reconstruct, to volunteer to fight against fire—each of these responses to the fire crisis was both activist and suffused with a modern, progressive orientation toward the future. Each of these strategies embodied a campaign against one aspect of rural life or peasants' attitudes as they had emerged in the representation and diagnosis of rural fires. The insurance program sought to replace futility before fire with prudent apprehension of the future and preparation for it. Village reconstruction projects sought to eradicate the "disorderly and shocking" layout of Russia's rural settlements. Volunteer firefighting brigades sought to impose rational, efficient order on the "hysteria and total chaos" that observers depicted as characteristic of peasants' firefighting habits. Prudence, planning, and efficient order. These were the values fire activists hoped to bring to the village through their campaign against fire.

The character of the zemstvo was not fully civilian in legislation or in action, but participants in its fire insurance and prevention programs came to display a sense of their separation from the central government and of their proximity to the village "front" in the campaign against fire. In the complicated relationship between zemstvo activists and state officials at the district and provincial levels, there was room for debate about whether the zemstvo was part of the government or belonged to the sphere of private organizations. The fire insurance program contributed, along with programs in public education, health, and agricultural warehousing, to the zemstvos' understanding of themselves as private organizations that were taking over where the government left off and providing critical services to the local population.[1] Imbued with a sense of mission and service, zemstvo fire activists were torn by, on the one hand, their desire to embody local initiative while encouraging the same among peasants and, on the other, their impulse to compel peasants to submit to zemstvo regulations and plans.

Whereas the substance of zemstvo fire insurance programs was defined by imperial law, village reconstruction programs came to be a forum in which zemstvo activists could apply technical expertise and promote progressive visions for the Russian countryside. These visions, in turn, embodied scientific knowledge and aimed to rationalize the disorderly and hazardous villages. The plan came to be the concrete expression of a zemstvo modernist vision. The obstacles to the realization of that vision turned out to be twofold. First, the peasants themselves resisted the restructuring of their physical environment. Second, the government, in the form of the Senate as the supreme legal forum for appeal just below the autocrat himself, refused to allow zemstvos to overrule individual peasants' rights to refuse to relinquish to zemstvo reconstruction plans the specific lands they had acquired through the Emancipation in 1861. By 1900, zemstvo fire programs exhibited the contradictory features of the culture as a whole, in which peasants were both culprits in Russia's backwardness and potential contributors to progress; in which educated activists vacillated between tutelary, coercive impulses and the desire to engage the peasantry in partnership for a more rational future; and in which the central government imposed major responsibilities on educated activists while granting them neither full powers at the local level nor recognition as bona fide experts with the capacity to address challenges that the imperial government had failed to meet.[2]

The volunteer firefighting movement displayed many of the same features, with the exception that it was almost fully a civilian movement. Its gentry leaders saw themselves as service to society incarnate. They eventually became critics of both the imperial government and the zemstvo fire programs. Although they were eager to seek royal patronage and proud to display it at every opportunity once they received it, firefighting activists emerged as some of the government's severest critics by the end of the century, imprecating bureaucrats and ministers for refusing to allocate the resources necessary to rid rural Russia of ubiquitous fire hazards. In Alexander III's and Nicholas II's reactionary reigns, such intense and public criticism of autocratic priorities required self-confidence born not only of social station but also of experience in the countryside organizing fire brigades and fighting fires, which was similar to the confidence-building experiences of zemstvo delegates and employees.

Yet firefighters did not always see themselves as fellow travelers with their zemstvo neighbors; by instinct they were more defensive and reactive than progressive and proactive. By and large, they saw zemstvo visions for preventing fires through reconstruction and village rationalization as futile in the face of rural Russia's poverty and the autocracy's unwillingness to subsidize wholesale rebuilding. They focused instead on putting fires out once they began; their modernist impulses surfaced in their devotion to firefighting technologies and rationalization of firefighting practices in the village itself. Like the zemstvo leaders, however, leaders in the firefighting movement were torn between their impulse to view peasant volunteers as equal partners in the war against fire and their almost reflexive resort to military models, with all the hierarchical traits of authority, rituals, and dress that came with them.

Despite the prominence of gentry in the leading organs of both the zemstvo and the firefighting movements, peasants, too, were innovators and activists in the campaign against fire. The history of efforts to contain fire in the countryside belies both the gentry activists' self-image and historians' tendency to slip into a dichotomous perception of active, educated members of society and passive peasant members of the *narod* (common folk). Peasants also seized the initiative and became technical experts. Some became famous throughout European Russia; others introduced programs in their communities that were touted throughout the empire in zemstvo and firefighting publications. They played a prominent role in fire-prone Viatka Province through their large representation in the zemstvo. The Novgorod provincial zemstvo became the leading light in the fire insurance program, as in many other zemstvo activities, not least because of the contributions of a peasant inventor who developed a fire-resistant roof that met peasants' needs as well as their budgets.[3] Still others attended firefighting and zemstvo conferences, becoming part of the permanent written record of the campaign against fire. Their presence did almost nothing to displace the prevailing notion that peasants were as much culprits as victims in Russia's fire crisis, or that they required the direction of rational, expert, educated leaders to protect them from themselves. But they serve as poignant evidence of potential within the rural community to rise to the challenge of fighting fire through truly local initiative, if only that community had enjoyed the financial support and investment of the central government or had encouraged and nurtured its own most energetic and proactive members.

6

Fire as Insurance Hazard: Peasants as Students of Prudence and Precaution

ALL SORTS OF MEASURES HAVE BEEN INTRODUCED IN OUR REGION TO PRE-VENT MASSIVE FIRES—ADMONISHING MEASURES, ENCOURAGING MEASURES, COERCIVE MEASURES—BUT THE VILLAGE CONTINUES TO BURN ITSELF UP AS BEFORE BY TENS AND HUNDREDS OF HOMESTEADS IN ONE FIRE.

—N. A. Demert, 1902

Imagine that you have just arrived in a village in European Russia on a late spring day in 1880. Your team of three has pulled your carriage down the straight dirt road, which is still muddy from the spring thaws (fig. 6.1). Something of a crowd has gathered, congregating around one house, where you spy a group of men—about ten of them by the looks of it—walking around the side toward the back, counting their steps and poking their fingers into the cracks between the wall's logs or planks. Some of them are looking up into the eaves, while others have veered off to the right, counting their paces as they approach the house next door. One of them is carrying a ledger of some sort and seems to be taking notes in it. As they disappear behind the house, you lean out of your carriage window and ask the closest child to explain.

"It's the fire agent," she says. "They're checking the houses for fire."
An adult steps up and clarifies, "It's for the insurance, you see. We have to do it every year. The tsar and the zemstvo made a law."
"And do fires happen often here?" you ask.
"All the time. The hot weather comes and the fires come with it."
"That's right!" another exclaims. "They've already had the first big one this year over in the next village. Almost burned the whole place down.

Fig. 6.1. *Street scene from the end of the nineteenth century, as local peasants turn to face a visiting photographer.*

When they've finished measuring houses here, they'll head over to see what's left and decide how much insurance to pay out."

"And how did the fire happen?" you continue.

"Lord only knows! Probably some foolish woman tossing hot ashes into the yard," an old man grumbles.

"I heard it was some kids—trying to smoke pipes, they were."

"No, that's not it. It was old man Stepanov. He set it himself. Hoped to get a big payout so he can build a new barn."

The men emerge from the back of the house and crowd their way through the front door—all ten of them pushing into the small space.

"What now?" you ask. "Are they done?"

"Oh, no—they've got to check the stove—see if it's got any cracks in it, how close it is to the wall, and such."

"Seems to take a long time," you opine.

"Yes," the old man answers. "They'll not get to Stepanov's today. By the time they get to his place, there'll be no way for them to know how the fire got started. He'll get away with it for sure."

Such a scene is not only the stuff of twenty-first-century imaginings but also a likely product of the compulsory fire insurance program mandated by the imperial government in 1864 as a method to mitigate the shocks rural fires brought to the Russian economy and social welfare. Throughout villages in the provinces of European Russia where the zemstvo system was introduced to handle public works after the Emancipation, fire insurance became one of the most penetrating features of the government's efforts to transform and regulate peasant behavior as a requirement of rural modernization.

The basic principle governing any insurance program is anticipation. Both the development of an insurance program and participation in it require those involved to anticipate that disaster may strike—is indeed likely to strike—and to prepare for that eventuality by investing in a system that will produce financial assistance when it is needed. This fundamental futurity requires planning and the disciplined diversion of current funds to projected needs. In its modern form, insurance has also rested on the science of mathematics and statistical calculations to predict loss on the basis of recorded and measured experience. The imposition of such a program on the peasants of European Russia by the state through the zemstvo in the thirty-four zemstvo provinces and through the governor's chancellery in the remaining fifteen provinces forced peasants to alter their perception of fire as an act of God and of themselves as futile victims. It denied them their traditional strategy of turning to gentry and peasant neighbors or to local and central officials to rescue them from the ruins of catastrophic fires. As Francois Ewald has concluded, insurance is a vehicle for instruction in the liberal vision of individual responsibility:

Insurance is a moral technology. To calculate a risk is to master time, to discipline the future. . . . To provide for the future does not just mean not living from day to day and arming oneself against ill fortune, but also mathematizing one's commitments. Above all, it means no longer resigning oneself to the decrees of providence and the blows of fate, but instead transforming one's relationships to nature, the world and God so that, even in misfortune, one retains responsibility for one's affairs by possessing the means to repair its effects.[1]

In Britain and the United States, the emergence of insurance as a business generated resistance among religious organizations, who saw in it the loss of faith in God, a departure from the morals of mutual aid among co-religionists, and a willingness to gamble or place a wager on future events.[2] Secular, individual prudence based on calculation seemed to threaten the omniscience of Providence, as the prudential rock of insurance offered an assurance more immediate than providential intervention and assistance. In the Russian setting, the state and its assigned agents in the zemstvo bureaus sought to bring to the peasants prudence based on calculation and anticipation without sacrificing mutuality. Extirpating the peasants' fatalistic conceptions about fire as a "visitation of God" and forcing them to pay for the costs of rural fires were the most obvious and conscious goals of the program. The Russian experience in the zemstvo insurance program thus departs from the model most scholars of insurance have followed, in which participation in an insurance program was a voluntary action to which customers had to be attracted through commercial campaigns. Further, because profit was not the goal of the program, the zemstvo program resembled state-sponsored social insurance programs elsewhere in Europe, absent both state funding and direct state involvement in its operations. Even so, the didactic impulse was present, as was the conviction that Russia's "hapless" peasants needed to abandon their fatalism in favor of prudent adaptation to the prescriptions that the zemstvo bureaus would develop as offshoots of compulsory insurance.

A fire insurance program was necessary after Emancipation because local gentry landlords no longer bore responsibility for assisting the peasantry following disasters, as they had done while serf owners. Furthermore, because peasants became property owners through the Emancipation land settlements, the state was instructing them in the duties of property ownership by requiring them to contribute to a mutual insurance program to mitigate their fire losses. The state's charge to zemstvo boards and governors' offices to introduce and manage a compulsory fire insurance program for the peasant population was an early departure from the "official laissez-faire liberalism" that had informed most aspects of the Emancipation legislation, and a step toward the more interventionist policy that David Macey has identified in the state's approach to the "agrarian problem" from around 1879 forward.[3] From the state's perspective, requiring the zemstvos to run compulsory mutual fire insurance programs for all peasant property owners was a way both to shift the economic costs of fires to the peasants themselves and to place the administrative burdens of running the programs on locally elected public servants rather than on the already beleaguered local state employees. S. Frederick Starr considered the fire insurance programs one of the zemstvos' most progressive features and a sign of the state's solicitude for the peasant population, "providing Russians with a security they had never before enjoyed."[4] Over the first thirty years of its experience, however, the zemstvo fire insurance program was never fully able to provide security for peasants who were victims of accidental fires. Arson for insurance fraud undermined the progressive lessons about discipline and futurity the insurance program might have instilled. Several local zemstvo boards found that the inadequacy of the mutual funds they were able to accumulate through peasant contributions left them perennially in the red (even though in the aggregate, the zemstvo program showed steady gains in reserve capital beginning in the late 1880s) and unable to use surplus funds as they had hoped, in order to strengthen fire prevention programs and reserves of firefighting equipment throughout their provinces. These financial and systemic problems encouraged zemstvo bureaus to turn to village reconstruction as a supplement to insurance programs in mitigating fires' damages to rural Russia. Just as life insurance companies became some of the earliest supporters of prophylactic medicine as a means to prolong their customers' and potential claimants' lives in the United States, so the zemstvo bureaus recognized that it was in their interest to prevent fires and stave off bankrupting claims.[5]

Legal Precedents

The precedent for the zemstvo compulsory mutual fire insurance program for all peasant property owners was a program introduced for state peasants in 1852, following a three-year experiment in St. Petersburg Province. State peasants were those who lived on government properties under the jurisdiction of the Ministry of State Domains and its officials rather than being bound to individual landowners. Statistics gathered on fires and their damages in the 1840s focused the attention of ministry officials on the need both to prevent fires and to reduce the costs to the state of their damages. The number of buildings belonging to state peasants that were reported burned in those years ranged from 10,220 to 32,500.

Before the introduction of the insurance program, the ministry provided assistance to fire victims in the form of cash or wood for rebuilding. When they appeared at the local offices, peasants usually found that they had to wait a long time to receive a pittance of assistance. N. M. Druzhinin found that in 1842, peasants received financial grants that covered only 8 percent of their losses, and in 1848, only 11 percent. At no point before 1852 did assistance cover more than 19 percent of the peasants' losses.[6] Sometimes peasants had to wait as long as two years to receive even this miserly aid.

A decree in 1852 introduced voluntary fire insurance for state peasants; it began to be put into action in 1853. Each household head was to contribute one ruble each year to the mutual fund, but participation was voluntary. The maximum valuation for insurance purposes was set at 133 rubles per structure. On the one hand, the program was successful in that it soon functioned in 34 provinces and covered 2.2 million structures. On the other hand, more than 570,000 state peasants refused to participate. Even more troubling was the fact that insurance payments continued to cover only 28 percent of losses, or less.[7] This left the government in the position of receiving constant appeals for further emergency relief.

In 1858, a new decree on fire insurance on state lands appeared, which made the insurance of peasant houses compulsory, with rates lowered for wooden houses and raised for masonry houses. Insuring barns, sheds, mills, and so forth was voluntary, and all structures in which fire was used (bathhouses and drying and threshing barns, for example) were excluded.[8] The precedent had been set, and reformers in the late 1850s and 1860s could turn to the state peasant insurance program for clues on how to proceed after Emancipation. Between the Emancipation in 1861 and the enactment of the zemstvo insurance program in July 1867, however, the government had to deal with the question of providing assistance to peasants who had no other recourse. Individual decrees addressed specific problems and displayed some of the concerns that would make their way into the design of the zemstvo fire insurance program.

Alexander II issued a decree on government assistance for fire victims within weeks of the Emancipation. On February 7, 1861, in consultation with the ministers of finance and the interior, he ordered the institution of grants-in-aid and loans at a maximum of fifteen thousand rubles per fire. These grants were to follow several procedural steps. Those that would reappear in slightly different form in zemstvo insurance regulations were the requirement for a detailed and as proximate as possible description of the fire; a ceiling of one-third the losses on immovable property and one-tenth the losses on movable property; and ad hoc committees composed of local officials to oversee the distribution of funds and to enforce their exclusive use for rebuilding or replacing property damaged in the fire. The ultimate responsibility for executing this decree lay with the provincial governor.[9]

Nine months later, because of numerous petitions in several provinces requesting assistance to recently emancipated peasants who had suffered from fires in the spring, summer, and fall, a decree addressing their needs was issued on November 1, 1861. The generosity of the treasury had obviously contracted since February, because this decree set the maximum payment to be awarded to any village commune (*sel'skoe obshchestvo*, a legal entity established by the Emancipation) at five hundred rubles per fire, and for any one burned-out homestead, at forty-five rubles. This was described as a temporary measure to remain in place only until a mutual insurance program was set up; any funds peasant victims of fire received before that time were to be treated as loans that they would repay from the mutual insurance funds as soon as reserves accumulated.[10]

The government's anxiety about the costs of fire damages was evident not only in the decision to eliminate any straightforward grants-in-aid in favor of loans, but also in the elaborate procedures for reporting on fires and overseeing the distribution of emergency loans. Responsibility for initially reporting the fire and assessing its damages lay with the cantonal officials, who were to submit their report to a "peace mediator," who could then request up to five hundred rubles in assistance from the Provincial Bureau of Peasant Affairs.[11] He could simultaneously petition for funds above five hundred rubles if losses exceeded that figure. When the time came to distribute the funds, the decree required that the entire village assembly gather, along with twelve "trustworthy" witnesses from neighboring villages, to witness the fire victims' receipt of their cash. Only if the funds to be received by each victim were less than fifteen rubles could the cantonal officials distribute the funds without this public scrutiny. In this, the November 1 decree was an expansion of a brief decree of October 3, 1861, which had called for a minimum of three witnesses to be present when emergency fire payments were issued. Between 1862 and 1865, the government issued 4.2 million rubles to fire victims in thirty-nine provinces of European Russia.[12] In 1867, the government moved again to limit these expenses as it awaited with evident impatience the opening of zemstvos in those provinces where they were legislated but not yet functioning, and their introduction of fire insurance programs, which "should bring to a halt the distribution of fire assistance" by the state.[13]

Zemstvo Legislation

First introduced officially as one of the fourteen major responsibilities of the zemstvo in its founding legislation of January 1, 1864, the zemstvo fire mutual insurance program fell under the new local elective organs' larger obligations to contribute to the "economic benefits and needs of each province and each district."[14] The decree that defined the structure and operations of the program was issued on April 7, 1864. In 1866, emancipated state and crown peasants were added to the program, which required decrees to shift these populations' fire insurance obligations out of the Ministry of State Domains and onto the provincial zemstvo boards in zemstvo provinces.[15] A compulsory mutual insurance program offered the prospect that the state could avoid most of this financial burden by making the victims themselves pay. By the time B. B. Veselovskii surveyed the zemstvo insurance program in 1909, he calculated that the total exposure of the zemstvo program as defined by the total value of properties then insured—some two billion rubles—was roughly equal to the imperial government's budget.[16]

Every provincial zemstvo had to introduce a mutual fire insurance program to collect insurance premiums and to distribute payments to owners whose insured structures were damaged by fire. Not only was every provincial zemstvo obliged to accept this charge; participation in the program was compulsory for all structures, both private and public (e.g., cantonal administrative buildings, school buildings), that were located within the boundaries of peasant settlements. For all other properties in the province, participation in the program was voluntary. This meant that any peasant owner of any immovable structure had to contribute to the mutual fire insurance fund, thus relieving the government, at the very least, of the burden of having to respond to appeals for emergency relief from peasants who had, like the 570,000 state peasants in the 1850s, refused to participate in the then voluntary program.

Within the zemstvo fire insurance program, there were three distinct divisions. Under the compulsory program, in which all property in peasant settlements had to be insured, there were two options. The first was to participate in the program through the "normal" appraisal process, which assigned property values across the board by province, district, or region. The second was by "special appraisal," which permitted a property owner to request a higher individual appraisal and to agree consequently to pay a higher premium for greater protection. The third division of the zemstvo program was the voluntary program. Although it was open to all residents of the province, in practice it became the program of choice almost exclusively for nonpeasant property owners, who used it to insure their shops, factories, and estates. Because my interest is in the complex of peasants and fire in rural Russia and its meanings in Russian culture, my focus here is on the compulsory insurance program alone.

In an apparent effort to reduce the enormous shortfalls in available funds that had occurred in the state peasant program, the zemstvo insurance legislation made the level of contribution a function of anticipated annual fire losses. For the compulsory program, the minimum insured value of structures was set province- or district-wide, with categories of value depending upon construction materials and the building's use. In each province, a maximum value was set beyond which no structure could be insured. The insurance payment was a percentage of the insured value, and it was to be established, according to Article 22, at a level that would guarantee that the sum total of individual contributions would "at least cover the payment of benefits to owners of burned structures and the costs of managing the insurance program."[17] No doubt in order to protect peasants from unexpected expenses, Articles 26 and 27 stated that the level of insurance payments could not be changed between annual assessments, unless the mutual fund completely exhausted its reserves. In the opposite situation, when annual fire damages were less than expected and enough reserves accumulated in the mutual fund to cover damages at a level equal to the average of the previous three years' expenses, the zemstvo could reduce and even eliminate contributions to the fund for the upcoming year (Article 38).[18]

As the previous chapter explained in connection with self-arson, the zemstvo fire insurance legislation initially placed most of the responsibilities for property appraisals, fire reports and investigations, and distribution of insurance payments to fire victims on peasant officials in the cantonal and village administrations. Although Article 44 stated that the provincial zemstvo could hire special fire insurance agents "in those locations where this is deemed necessary," their salaries would have to come from the mutual fund itself. In the early years of the program, most zemstvos barely managed to cover basic expenses, and many, such as those in Viatka and Kazan Provinces, fell into serious arrears, making the decision to divert funds for insurance agents a tough one.

From the start, however, the potential for self-arson was a possibility that the reformers tried to diminish and address in the legislation. First, the maximum payment that could be paid out to a fire victim was two-thirds of the appraised value of the structure, which would blunt the incentive to burn down needed property for the sake of cash for rebuilding or improving it. This stratagem would work, of course, only if the property was not overvalued in the first place. Second, the distribution of the insurance payment was to be held up if self-arson was suspected. And of course no payment was to be issued if self-arson was proven.

Lessons through Insurance: Classifying House and Home

The process of annual property valuation for the insurance program, even in the face of its initial execution almost exclusively by peasant officials, had the potential to make peasants reconceptualize their property, their relationship to fire, and their relationship to their neighbors and external institutions of emergency assistance. The prescribed system for reporting fires and distributing insurance payments also imposed order on the fire experience. Throughout their interactions with the zemstvo insurance program, peasants entered a world of writing, calculation, documentation, witnessing, and testimony. Their residential and farming structures were submitted to evaluation according to their value as well as to their susceptibility to fire and potential hazard for neighboring structures. The language and artifacts of bureaucracy became the experience of every household head, who, in any year, was likely to be a party to those universal features of Russian officialdom: *opisi, otsenki, akty,* and *kvitantsiia* (inventories, appraisals, documents or deeds, and receipts). In the event of a fire, more documents, reports, appraisals, and testimonies followed.

Each year, every household head had to respond to the cantonal officials' question about whether they wanted to pay at the rate set through the minimum valuation for the entire district or province, or whether they wanted to request a special appraisal in order to insure their property at a higher rate. The officials, in turn, had to prepare a list with all property owners' responses to this question, in addition to a master list of all property to be insured through the compulsory program. Working from that list, the officials then carried out the special, individual appraisals. The cantonal elder and the village elder joined with six to twelve "trustworthy" witnesses, of whom no more than half could be from the same village. They inspected the property and recorded its distance from other structures, its physical condition (materials, size, state of repair, etc.), and its purpose. If we pause for a moment to envision this scene, we recognize that it drew peasant homes and farming structures into a taxonomy of sorts, imposing a series of mathematical values and assigning buildings to specific categories. It submitted peasant homes to a series of critical judgments that assigned value and risk in ways the owners might not have otherwise contemplated (fig. 6.2).

As his neighbors, local officials, and outsiders from another village walked around his house, barns, and sheds, entering them to poke into walls or examine the maintenance of the stove, the peasant home owner was taking a lesson in scrutiny of his physical place in the world and his adjustment to the categories the zemstvo and state had defined. The question was not whether his home was cozy or beautiful, whether it was warm, dry, or clean, or whether he was the master of his household. The questions were whether there was a stone foundation; whether the stove was in good repair or showed signs of cracks; how far the stove was positioned from the nearest wooden wall; whether there was a chimney or stovepipe, and if there was, whether it had a metal collar or touched wall or ceiling directly; and of what material the roof was made and how solidly it was constructed, as well as the walls and the substance used to fill in the cracks between logs or planks. Outside, measurements were taken of the length and height of each structure, of the distance of each from all other structures within the owner's yard and from the nearest structures of neighbors. Each of these observations was written down, becoming part of the official record. Then the appraisers gathered to consult and hand the owner their conclusion about the value of his property. Some discussion undoubtedly followed, until agreement was reached. At that point, the officials prepared a written survey document

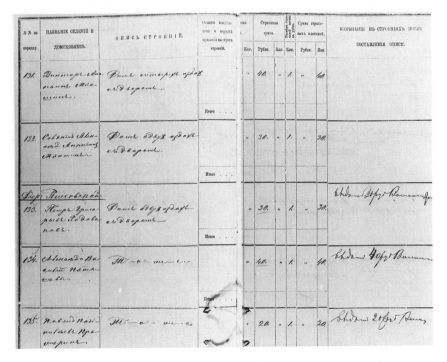

Fig. 6.2. *Register of village properties insured by the Vologda provincial zemstvo in the 1890s. From left to right, the columns list the property number, the name of the village and the home-owner, a description of the building, its appraised value, its insured value, the premium rate, the amount of the insurance payment, and any changes in the building since appraisal. Source: GAVO, fond 34, opis' 5, delo 75, ll. 33–34.*

describing their conclusions and the appraised value of the house, which was signed on the spot by both officials, the trustworthy witnesses, and the property owner. One copy was to be sent to the provincial zemstvo office, a second to the cantonal offices (Articles 45–56).[19]

In order to receive insurance benefits following a fire, the owner had to submit again to a prescribed process based on documentation and appraisal. He or she had to submit a written notice of the fire to the cantonal office within three days of the fire. For the illiterate peasant, this meant finding a neighbor or depending on the cantonal scribe to prepare the document. The cantonal office had only twenty-four hours from the time of receipt of the notice to inspect the remains of the fire. If any portions of the insured structures were left standing, the fire site had to be appraised again by the cantonal and village elders and the six to twelve trustworthy witnesses. Whether the destruction was total or partial, the officials had to prepare a written document answering the following questions: Did the fire start in the insured structure or on someone else's property? Was the fire an accident or was it caused by carelessness or arson? And if the fire had started in the insured structure itself, was there any reason to suspect self-arson? All the written documents related to the fire were then to be sent to the provincial bureau "via the first postal run." The zemstvo was to issue the insurance benefits "without delay," and it was up to the "local village authorities" to ensure that the funds were used exclusively for rebuilding the insured structures (Articles 73–78 and 35).

Anyone who knows anything about the villages of European Russia will immediately recognize the obstacles these prescriptions faced. The most obvious ones were the lack of literacy among the participants and the difficulty of speedy procedures in a world of inefficient transportation along inadequate, often impassible roads. Opportunities for bribery were many. But even more serious was a fact that the authorities did not know (for the Ministry of the Interior's fire statistics had yet to assume their importance in the understanding of fire)— that the spring, summer, and fall months, when every able-bodied worker was in the fields, were also the time of the most frequent fires. It is difficult to imagine how cantonal officials could summon six to twelve witnesses to inspect fires and appraise structures during this time; the officials themselves were peasants who had to sacrifice their own farming time to fulfill these duties.

Neither the peasants nor the zemstvo, however, had any choice but to follow the regulations as they were defined by the state. As observers explained, the results were often sloppy inspections and documentation. But procedures were necessarily followed at a minimum level at least, drawing peasants into the effort to regulate fire's economic costs to the empire. They could no longer appeal to local or central officials for emergency relief solely on the basis of their victimization by fire. First, they had to go through the insurance process, documenting their losses and showing that they were not responsible for the fire; then they had to prove that the insurance they received was inadequate to meet their needs. Further, to forward such an appeal to St. Petersburg, they had to receive the zemstvo's and local state officials' endorsement that each of these statements on their part was true. Willy-nilly, peasants had to define their fire experiences in terms set by the state if they hoped to receive any assistance from the state. Beyond sympathy and charity from local peasant neighbors, peasant victims of fire could turn nowhere for help without submitting to taxonomic definitions of fire and its effects.

From Prescription to Practice

From the perspective of the zemstvo boards and assemblies, the fire insurance program was a pressing obligation that forced them to become familiar with fire conditions in peasant villages. The combination of their charge to concern themselves with local economic conditions and their management of the compulsory fire insurance program meant that fire prevention quickly joined their list of concerns and activities. The zemstvo fire campaign in individual provinces required the same set of decisions that public health campaigns did. The conceptualization of the fire problem as an epidemic was one manifestation of the zemstvos' perception that many of the issues and choices were the same in their discharge of fire insurance duties and public health measures. As in public health, diagnosis of the fire problem preceded and determined the prescribed treatment and investment in a "cure." In public health, zemstvo physicians came to the conclusion that the material conditions of village life were major contributors to disease; this led to public hygiene campaigns to educate peasants about the harmful effects of unvented smoke in houses, filth, and patterns of child care.[20] These campaigns, in turn, rested on a faith in prevention. The analog in the fire campaign was the growing recognition of hazardous construction patterns and fire practices that led several zemstvos to focus on fire prevention through reconstruction, new fire safety regulations, and education.

Fire insurance programs took shape in the thirty-four zemstvo provinces as early as 1866 (in Novgorod and Iaroslavl) and as late as 1876 (in Ufa). Some introduced the compulsory and voluntary programs simultaneously; others delayed the introduction of the voluntary programs because they viewed them as either supplemental or designed primarily for nonpeasant property owners. Setting up a system for addressing village fires and the destruction of peasant property was clearly the first priority and most pressing concern. By 1877, all zemstvo provinces had both a compulsory and a voluntary mutual fire insurance program.[21] The zemstvo boards received no funds from the central government either for the establishment of the administration of fire insurance or for an initial capital reserve fund to meet the needs of fire victims who appealed for assistance before the zemstvo fund grew. In this, the imperial Russian government departed from other European models, especially the French, in which the government moved into social insurance programs by establishing the initial funds from the state treasury and then increasing them through a general tax and contributions from the insured.[22] This made the Russian zemstvo fire insurance program a peculiar amalgam of state origin and exclusively civilian funded operations.

The decisions the zemstvos made about how to structure their insurance programs, the criteria for property appraisals, the setting of rates by risk classification, and the value of premiums had the potential to shape peasant attitudes toward building construction and village layouts. In southern England, by comparison, the emergence of fire insurance companies between 1680 and 1780 and the "discriminatory premiums" they issued "impelled" both new construction and the reconstruction of burned buildings to be done in fire-resistant materials, according to Eric L. Jones's study of these developments.[23] More generally, as Daniel Defert has argued, "insuring a population means classifying it, subdividing it in line with a scale of degrees of risk and an analysis of behaviours, thresholds, marginal categories which are first excluded, then treated as special sub-classes while excluding still more marginal groups, and so on. The method allows an indefinitely generalizable economic treatment of behaviours in terms of their dangerousness."[24]

At first the zemstvos seemed little aware of this potential; instead, they were concerned primarily with figuring out ways to bring in enough payments to cover anticipated losses and to avoid overruns in their budgets because of rural fires. They were guided both by the law's prescription that they set rates at a level equal to anticipated fire damages for the coming year and by their own understandable fear that their overall budgets would be siphoned off by fire costs, just as the imperial budget had been in the previous decade. At the same time, they had to consider the peasants' ability to pay when setting rates, because compulsory insurance payments joined other new monetary obligations that the emancipated peasants were forced to assume for the first time.

Not only did zemstvos have to launch programs with no initial funds from the state. The state also prohibited association among zemstvos beyond the provincial level, which meant that zemstvo men could not consult with one another. They were able to compare and evaluate strategies only when individual zemstvos began to publish reports on their programs. The basic system was prescribed by law. For the compulsory program, the zemstvo in each province established minimum and maximum appraised values for the entire province, or by district or region. It then assigned a percentage of the appraised value as the sum each property owner paid into the mutual fund, the sole prescribed criterion being that the total be adequate to cover anticipated costs. Payments of fire damages could not exceed two-thirds of the appraised value of the structures.

To the extent that generalization is possible, one can say that appraisals were higher for the most fire-resistant buildings (those made of stone or stucco with metal or tile roofs), whereas premiums were highest for the most fire-prone buildings (those made of wood with straw roofs). The decision to appraise stone and stucco buildings with tile or metal roofs more highly seems to have resulted not from the zemstvo's desire to encourage their construction but from its recognition that such buildings were more expensive and would cost more to rebuild. It was in their interest, therefore, to make sure that the owners insured their property at levels that would make any insurance payments they subsequently received adequate for rebuilding, and render the zemstvo, gubernatorial bodies, and central ministries immune to requests for supplemental assistance.

The ways in which provincial boards set the minimum appraisals for different districts or regions within the province reveal their concern over rebuilding costs and zemstvo budgets.[25] In Tambov, Smolensk, and Kostroma Provinces, for example, minimum appraisals were lowest in forested districts where wood for rebuilding was cheapest, and highest in steppe districts or where deforestation was most advanced and wood most expensive. This approach seemed to take the peasants' financial prospects to heart and to be in their interest. Yet the zemstvos also sometimes reduced norms when districts proved to be especially fire prone, as in Samara, Saratov, Tambov, Penza, and Pskov Provinces, "as if to punish them for their flammability," as the zemstvo historian Veselovskii concluded.[26] Early on, village design was rarely a factor, because only a few provincial boards, such as those in Voronezh and Simbirsk, offered higher property appraisals for structures in "well laid-out" homesteads—that is, those that had adequate intervals between buildings.

When they turned to the task of deciding what peasants would have to pay each year to insure their property, the zemstvos required those with the most fire-prone structures to pay the highest percentage of their property's value. It was here that peasants were forced to view their property within the frame of fire safety definitions. Almost everywhere, owners of wooden buildings with straw roofs paid a higher percentage of their property's appraised value than did those who owned more fire-resistant buildings, whether of stucco with metal roofs or of wood with tile roofs or even of wood with wooden roofs. In Ekaterinoslav Province, for example, the differential was significant in the first year of the program, and it increased as the zemstvo evidently became increasingly intolerant of construction that ignored fire safety considerations. In 1866, the owner of a building roofed in metal paid 0.5 percent its appraised value, whereas those with "other" roofing materials paid 1.0 percent, and those with "flammable" roofs paid 1.5 percent. By 1897, the zemstvo had reduced the rate for those with metal roofs to 0.2 percent but required payments on flammable roofs of 1.0–2.0 percent.[27]

Generally, as time passed, provincial boards designed increasingly complex risk classification and premium structures, with more attention to construction materials, regional differences in the frequency and scope of fires, and adherence of villages and individual property owners to the Building Code or zemstvo reconstruction plans. The most fire-prone provinces were the most likely to tinker with their risk classification and premium structures: Saratov Province adjusted rates thirteen times between the 1860s and the first decade of the twentieth century; Viatka did so ten times; and Riazan, Samara, Tula, Tambov, and Simbirsk did so on several occasions each.

Saratov's record of adjustments offers an extreme example of what most zemstvos experienced as they cast about in search of a system that would protect the zemstvo budget, encourage peasants to place fire safety first in their construction and daily habits, and generate enough mutual funds to cover the costs of frequent fires. Initially, the Saratov zemstvo's criteria in 1866 were conformity to the Building Code and construction materials. Premiums were set for individual villages and ranged from 1.5 percent of appraised value for "normal" buildings in villages conforming to the Building Code to 3.0 percent for hazardous buildings in villages that did not conform to the code. Next, the zemstvo shifted to premiums for individual districts, using the frequency of fires in each district as a criterion and increasing the range for premiums from 2.5 percent in the least fire-prone districts to as much as 10 percent for hazardous buildings in fire-prone districts. In each of the years 1873, 1874, 1875, and 1876, the zemstvo tried new systems of risk classification, sometimes for the entire province, sometimes by district, sometimes according to conformity to the Building Code, sometimes according to construction materials or the distance between structures or the average number of buildings burned per fire. By 1883, the structure

Table 6.1: Insurance Rates (in Kopeks per Ruble of Appraised Value) for Compulsory Fire Insurance in Saratov Province, 1903

Village Category	Wooden structures			Brick, Stone, Stucco Structures		
	Straw and Reed Roofs	Wooden Roofs; Straw/Clay Roofs	Metal, Tile, Soil, and Sod Roofs	Straw and Reed Roofs	Wooden Roofs; Straw/Clay Roofs	Metal, Tile, Soil, and Sod Roofs
1.	1.25	1.00	0.50	1.00	0.50	0.25
2.	1.50	1.25	0.75	1.25	0.75	0.50
3.	1.75	1.50	1.00	1.50	1.00	0.75
4.	2.25	2.00	1.50	2.00	1.50	1.00
5.	3.00	2.75	2.00	2.75	2.00	1.50
6.	4.00	3.75	2.75	3.75	2.75	2.00

Source: Veselovskii 1909: 515.

included nine classifications, with variations by village and district, with the result that there were 216 separate rates in the province, ranging from 0.5 percent to 12 percent of appraised value.

Obviously the zemstvo was floundering; equally obviously, the didactic value of the insurance programs for peasant insurers suffered from these repeated changes. How could the average peasant hope to anticipate which criteria would prevail? How could he be sure that any effort he made to bring his homestead into compliance with the Building Code or to encourage his neighbors to join him in doing so would be rewarded, given the zemstvo's shifts from village to province to district categories, as well as the lability of rates in response as much to fiery seasons as to construction?

By 1889, the Saratov zemstvo had simply eliminated compliance with the Building Code as a criterion, because it concluded that there were no villages in the province where the peasants followed its regulations. They offered instead, from 1889 until 1903, varying incentives in the form of reduced rates for fire-resistant construction materials and layouts. The latter became more difficult to achieve as villages swelled in response to population growth and family divisions. The zemstvo acknowledged this by reducing the required interval between buildings from sixty-five feet in 1889 to thirty-nine feet in 1896. Again in 1898, 1900, and 1901, the criteria were changed. Finally, in 1903, the risk classification structure shown in Table 6.1 emerged.

The table offers a visual representation of the categorization of material culture within which peasants had to locate themselves as property owners and legally bound participants in the compulsory mutual fire insurance program. The Saratov system of 1903 was a mature form of the earlier fledgling, and sometimes fleeting, systems of classification to which peasant property owners had to submit. With each new effort to figure out how best to provide coverage while protecting zemstvo budgets, peasant officials who carried out the surveys and appraisals received new forms and orders that they had to explain to their constituents. When zemstvo boards hired fire insurance agents, they received thorough lessons in applying these categories, but they also brought them into the villages under their purview and instructed the peasants on the terms of appraisals and premium rates and rankings.

The emphasis on individual responsibility embodied in the insurance program appeared in two decisions issued by the state's highest legal body, the Ruling or Governing Senate. The first, issued in 1871, stated that zemstvo fire insurance policies could be bequeathed by the original owner to an heir, thus emphasizing that contributions to and any potential gains from purchasing zemstvo fire insurance constituted private property. The second, issued in 1900, rejected the effort of the Penza provincial zemstvo board to force peasant communes to pay arrears on insurance through the system of mutual responsibility, or *krugovaia poruka*. The Senate dismissed the zemstvo's argument that insurance arrears could be treated like any other tax arrears, arguing instead that payments into the insurance program were made by individuals to protect their individual property, and that to try to require all peasants in a community to pay for their fellows' failure to keep up with their insurance payments would undermine the peasants' "conscious relationship to insurance and to its fundamental requirements." Mutual responsibility for arrears, the Senate decision explained, especially contradicted the principles behind the option to insure one's property through a special, higher appraisal in the compulsory program, because "insurance according to a special appraisal depends on the will of the property owner himself."[28]

Successes and Failures in the Insurance System

Over the 1870s and 1880s, the number of properties insured under the compulsory program grew steadily. In the decade between 1882 and 1892, for example, the number grew by 36.5 percent, with the average number for the four-year period 1889–1892 reaching 24.7 million structures. The total value of compulsory insurance premiums in 1892 was 47.2 percent greater than in 1882, thus growing by around 4.7 percent each year.[29] By the late 1880s, most zemstvos had begun to develop some stability in their capital reserves, so that in the aggregate, the zemstvo insurance program was a financial success by the end of the century—if success is measured by the ability of the zemstvo boards to protect themselves from bankruptcy in the face of fire claims. In Novgorod Province, for example, over the thirty-five years from 1866 to 1901, eight districts accumulated a surplus of 1 million rubles, while the remaining three had a cumulative deficit of 449,280 rubles.[30] Often this success rested on the introduction of fire insurance agents as paid employees of the zemstvo boards, with the subsequent specialization of their expertise and their objectivity and distance from the local relationships that had sometimes distorted the insurance process. The Moscow provincial board was the first to hire fire agents in 1869; fifteen other provincial boards had followed suit by 1880.

Until the late 1890s, most zemstvos hired only one agent per district, which limited the scope of their operations primarily to appraisals under the compulsory insurance program. At the turn of the century, their numbers began to grow, as did the number of tasks they performed in the insurance process. By 1901, the Kursk and Tambov provincial zemstvos had each hired the largest number of agents (31), and Olonets, the smallest number (4); the total number was at least 650 agents in the zemstvo provinces. Much as the physicians in the employ of zemstvos began to develop confidence in their ability to recommend public health policies to zemstvo delegates, so fire agents began to view themselves as the local fire experts upon whom the zemstvo should rely in developing fire policies. As early as 1891 in Viatka and Chernigov Provinces, and from the late 1890s in all zemstvo provinces except for Bessarabia, Vologda, Olonets, Poltava, Tauride, and Ufa, fire agents met in provincial conferences to discuss their experiences and to develop strategies to reduce both fires' damages and insurance fraud.[31] For zemstvo apologists, the emergence of zemstvo fire agents as a body of local experts who could voice recommendations to their employers was a laudable phenomenon of local democracy and a legitimate diffusion of power to those who knew best what local conditions were and how to address them. They stressed the need to permit fire agents from different provinces to gather in regional or even empire-wide conventions, a proposal that mimicked the zemstvo liberal leaders' own desire for such national organization and influence.[32]

Some zemstvo boards insisted on a high level of professionalism from their insurance agents. In Vologda Province, for example, the agents' annual reports provided detailed descriptions of their efforts in each district and canton to enlist peasant subscribers to insurance beyond the compulsory minimum, an accounting of the financial aspects of their work, and precise records and analyses on fires involving insured structures in their insurance districts. As early as the 1880s, the Griazovetsk District board fired its insurance agent, one Khudaev, for failing to move quickly enough in appraising losses following fires, which had the effect of delaying relief for the victims.[33]

Despite the apparent success manifested in expanding capital reserves, growing numbers of policyholders, and the emergence of local insurance experts in the form of agents, two serious shortcomings in the insurance experience served as stubborn reminders of the incompleteness of that success. First, the compulsory insurance program failed to relieve the imperial government of significant outlays of relief funds to burned-out peasants. Second, the insurance payments the zemstvo programs issued did not provide adequate relief that could minimize fire's costs to individual households or their larger communities. In other words, the system of requiring peasants to pay for their own fire damages through the compulsory insurance program did not fully reduce the economic "shock" that fire had on individual, community, and national economies.

Certainly the annual outlays of cash to pay fire damages were impressive, though they displayed significant regional variation. In 1890, seventeen zemstvo programs paid out 300,000–500,000 rubles each year; in 1903, fifteen programs paid out 500,000–750,000 rubles per year. Some provincial zemstvo programs, including those in Tver, Tambov, and Riazan Provinces, paid out a million or more rubles each year.[34] Yet behind these numbers there were many peasants with insured property who found themselves seriously short of cash to rebuild their homes and farms after fires.

The first thing to recall is that zemstvo insurance premiums covered no more than two-thirds of the appraised value of the policyholder's property. Second, peasants who wanted to economize opted for the minimum, compulsory program and the limits it set on maximum premiums in the locality, rather than pay extra to receive a higher benefit through a special appraisal. As a zemstvo fire insurance agent in Viatka province explained: "Thanks to the . . . extremely feeble farsightedness of the population, in which the Russian 'whatever' [avos] still plays a very large role, the local population views compulsory insurance in most cases as an unpleasant and undesirable tax on them and therefore try to appraise and insure their structures at as low a level as possible."[35] This meant that many peasants were likely underinsured, especially because the record shows that only the most prosperous rural residents chose to participate in the voluntary program. Thus, although peasant property owners who participated only in the compulsory program contributed to the capital reserves and financial stability of the provincial program, they did not thereby guarantee their own quick financial recovery in the event of a fire.

For the thirty-four zemstvo provinces in the period 1866–1876, the portion of the appraised property value that was covered by insurance was around 64 percent. There were large regional differences, however. In Chernigov, Poltava, and Khar'kov Provinces, insured values were as high as 90 percent of appraised values (Poltava, 1873) and steadily around 74 percent, whereas in Kostroma, Nizhnii Novgorod, and Moscow Provinces, insured values averaged only 44–47 percent of the structures' value.[36]

Underinsurance seems to have been the usual explanation behind the hundreds of appeals for emergency relief that continued to pour into the Economic Department of the Ministry of the Interior. In a catastrophic fire in Pavlovo, Nizhnii Novgorod Province, in 1872, which destroyed 515 houses and all their outbuildings, 317 persons described as engaged in cottage industry suffered 204,860 rubles' worth of losses in movable and immovable property. They received 17,468 rubles through the zemstvo insurance program. Ninety-nine persons listed as "the poorest victims of the fire" suffered 45,525 rubles' worth of losses and received only 4,227 rubles from the zemstvo insurance program.[37] A petition from the "burned-out peasants of Miskovo settlement" in Kostroma Province, dated November 19, 1887, reported that total losses for 205 peasant victims reached 293,914 rubles. The total insurance payments came to only 14,415 rubles. Individual examples from this fire reinforce the conclusion that zemstvo insurance was inadequate. Mikhail Stepanov Ploksin lost 4,200 rubles' worth of property; he had insured 200 rubles' worth but received a payment of only 72 rubles. Aleksandr Porfenov Poslov lost 5,827 rubles in property, of which he had insured only 210 rubles' worth; he received a payment of 173 rubles.[38]

A fire on May 13, 1896, destroyed 62 of 64 homesteads in the village of Bols'shoe i Maloe Perteshno in Novgorod Province, leaving the peasant owners with losses of approximately 40,000 rubles. They received only 3,620 rubles in insurance payments.[39] In 1892, a fire in the village of Bol'shaia in Vologda Province caused losses worth 13,792 rubles. The villagers received only 1,950 rubles in insurance payments toward rebuilding, or roughly 40 rubles per household, whereas each household reported losses of 150–300 rubles. All of the peasant owners had chosen to insure their property at the minimum level for the compulsory program.[40] Petitions also arrived from individuals, such as "the peasant Kozlov" in Smolensk Province, who suffered losses of 1,450 rubles and received only 420 rubles in insurance payments.[41] Province-wide, these disparities took on overwhelming proportions. In Saratov Province, for example, fires destroyed 2 million rubles' worth of property in 1898, of which zemstvo insurance covered only 689,000 rubles.[42] In Viatka Province, reported losses equaled 1.3 million rubles in 1902; insurance provided only 420,000 rubles.[43]

The imperial government acknowledged the economic peril this situation brought to peasant fire victims. In 1899, the tsar approved a law that offered fire victims relief from all government taxes for the tax year following a devastating fire.[44] From the government's perspective, this meant that the imperial treasury might find itself hit twice—first, to supplement emergency funds when zemstvo insurance payments fell short, and second, to forgo tax revenues from the fire victims. In 1901, the zemstvo insurance legislation underwent a further revision that addressed this problem by permitting zemstvos to insure buildings at their full appraised value in both the compulsory and the voluntary programs.

The Tver zemstvo insurance program seems to have avoided additional costs to the government by concentrating on developing its appraisal and rate systems in ways that would maximize coverage for peasant policyholders, at the expense of accumulating large capital reserves. It also made a priority of supporting firefighting activities by giving grants to firefighting brigades and subsidizing the purchase and maintenance of firefighting equipment. From 1875 forward, led by an energetic delegate named P. A. Korsakov, the Tver provincial zemstvo introduced a series of reforms of its fire insurance program toward these ends. The common elements in all of Korsakov's reforms were the rationalization of the process and increasing reliance on fire agents rather than peasant officials at the cantonal or village level. Standard forms and accounting procedures were developed for all aspects of the insurance program, from initial surveys through disbursement of benefits. Conferences of fire agents from the various districts met regularly. Finally, agents worked hard to get peasants to insure their homes not at the minimum, "normal" appraised values and rates but at the "special" appraised values and rates, which would approximate the actual value of the structures and make the benefits following a fire adequate for rebuilding. The average insurance coverage per homestead rose from 68 rubles in 1870 to 251 rubles in 1900. The Tver zemstvo also insured movable property, adding to both the peasants' coverage and the zemstvo's potential exposure. These practices eventually led to an extensive program that was second only to Kursk's in number of clients and value of their policies. By 1903, this meant that insurance payments to fire victims equaled 38 percent of the Tver zemstvo's total budget, far more than the usual proportion elsewhere. In 1900, its reserve capital totaled only 1.3 million rubles—just 1.9 times the annual insurance budget—whereas other zemstvos set as their goal and achieved enormous capital reserves.

Vologda, Khar'kov, and Olonets Provinces offer the most striking examples, with, respectively, 18 times, 14 times, and 9 times their annual budgets in reserves.[45]

Despite the growing capital reserves in most zemstvo insurance programs, as well as the expanding numbers of policyholders and insured structures, no one suggested that the zemstvo fire insurance program on its own could eradicate fire as Russia's "historical evil." Although some observers were willing to applaud the successes the zemstvo program did attain in mitigating the impact of small fires, not even the zemstvo fire activists believed that insurance would accomplish the wholesale cultural transformation that seemed to be necessary to liberate rural Russia from fire's destructive powers. Within the zemstvo system itself, this cognizance encouraged various provincial boards to attempt other approaches to containing fire in the villages of European Russia. These ranged from issuing detailed fire safety and building codes to purchasing firefighting equipment, trying to establish day care for small children during the farming season, issuing village reconstruction plans, and building factories for the production of fire-resistant construction materials.

Beyond Insurance: Zemstvo Fire Programs Extend Their Reach

Legislation governing the zemstvo's activities reflected this expanded vision. A law issued on June 16, 1873, addressed the question of the power of the zemstvos to issue fire prevention regulations that were compulsory for people living under their jurisdiction. It declared that so long as such regulations conformed to existing imperial laws, they were compulsory for all persons living outside of cities, regardless of their occupation, and the local police were responsible for ensuring compliance. Further, this law added a new duty to those assigned to the zemstvo in the founding legislation of 1864: "the preparation of plans for village construction, which comply both with laws governing this sphere and with local fire safety regulations."[46]

A law of May 8, 1879, offered further instructions on zemstvo building regulations for villages. It allowed for diversity of plans for different locales; called for the exclusion of more than fifty articles in the 1857 Building Code, which were to be replaced by regulations addressing the same matters in zemstvo-issued codes; and provided new regulations for dealing with local conditions that precluded strict adherence to the Building Code. This final point would continue to be a source of problems throughout the history of zemstvo village planning. According to the May 8, 1879, law, when obstacles arose that made "precise compliance" with laws governing village construction difficult, deviations from the code could be permitted, so long as village inhabitants received special instructions in the fire prevention measures they had to adopt in the buildings they raised.[47] This law opened the way for numerous disputes that would revolve around individual peasants' objections to proposed plans or around individual peasants' decisions to build as they wished before plans were issued.

In 1890, when zemstvo legislation underwent a full-scale revision, one of the additions to the list of zemstvo responsibilities, distinct from the insurance program (point 6), was point 9, "attention to the prevention and extinguishing of fires and oversight of improved village construction." Article 108 made all zemstvo regulations on fire prevention, firefighting, construction in villages, and storage of highly flammable materials compulsory, so long as they conformed to existing laws.[48] The full meaning of this addition was evident in one of the Senate's many decisions on complaints filed by people who objected to the regulations the zemstvo issued and even more to their enforcement. The Senate explained in 1902 that "the compulsory regulations of zemstvo assemblies have the power of law and are compulsory not only for the local population but also for all officials and institutions."[49]

Imperial laws followed the zemstvos' lead in the campaign against fire. As individual zemstvo assemblies and boards recognized the necessity of trying to prevent and contain fires as a way to protect their own budgets as much as peasants' property and prosperity, the state responded by granting them increasing authority to dictate local conditions as they pertained to fire. Many historians have long interpreted the zemstvo reform of 1890 (often referred to as the zemstvo counterreform) as a move to subordinate the zemstvo to the imperial bureaucracy, by which "the power of the imperial government to control the zemstvo was much increased."[50] But when it came to the problem of fire in the countryside, the state was clearly granting the zemstvo ever-expanding powers to make local laws (under the label of regulations) to which the local population had to submit, under penalty of the law and punishment through the judicial system. Police officers became the zemstvos' agents in enforcing these laws. Fire agents also bore the mantle of imperial authority when they acted in the zemstvo's name to investigate compliance with fire and building codes. The imperial government's long hesitation to permit provincial zemstvos to convene in regional or national congresses to discuss fire programs betrayed continuing anxiety about zemstvo coordination and political mobilization. But within provincial boundaries, the campaign against fire was so crucial to the imperial government that it warranted the expansion, not the contraction, of zemstvo authority.

This reality encouraged provincial zemstvo boards and assemblies to take on the almost utopian challenge of transforming the villages of European Russia from fire-prone to fire-safe communities. The key to that utopia would be rational planning based on mathematical precision and technical expertise, all to be realized through the zemstvos' authority to make their visions compulsory. The zemstvo boards were themselves under the pressure of law to complete village planning and reconstruction. This was not an optional but an obligatory program from 1873 forward; the law stated that district zemstvos were to prepare plans for villages when necessary—"when new villages are being built, when villages are being rebuilt following a devastating fire, and so on."[51] In response to the Penza provincial zemstvo's appeal to be relieved of responsibility for developing a plan for the settlement of Ashevo in Novorzhevsk District, in which it had argued that this settlement included no allotment land and that its population comprised not only peasants but people of various other social estates, the Senate ruled that the legislation had not limited the program either to the peasant population or to land allotted through the Emancipation. Therefore, the zemstvo was required to develop a plan for Ashevo to reduce the hazards of fire, especially in view of its crowded construction.[52] Here, as elsewhere in the zemstvo provinces of European Russia, the responsibility for planning and building a fire-resistant countryside thus rested squarely on the zemstvo organizations, which consequently entered another realm of intervention in the daily existence of the peasantry.

Conclusion

If we return to Francois Ewald's description of the role insurance plays in instilling individual responsibility and attention to the future, we find that it captures beautifully the intention and import of the zemstvo compulsory fire insurance program in late imperial Russia. In the campaign against fire, this modernist impulse informed the zemstvo insurance programs' goal of transforming the relationship between peasants and fire as an element of nature while instilling in them a sense of responsibility for their financial condition, as well as a rejection of futile submission before the powers of the Almighty. Drawing peasants into the practice of insuring against future loss while requiring them to submit to new definitions of house and home through the categories of appraisals and insurance premiums was part of a larger effort to tame nature as runaway fire. Taming nature, in turn, meant disciplining peasants to think about the future and to abandon their *avos*, or fatalistic, approach to their world. When zemstvo boards turned to their expanded vision of transforming villages, they extended the modernist enterprise of planning and action against fire to the constructed environment as well.

7

Fire Contained in the Planned Village: Peasants as Residents in a Disciplined Domestic Order

VILLAGE STREETS MUST BE LAID OUT IN STRAIGHT LINES. TREES SHOULD
BE PLANTED IN ONE ROW NO CLOSER THAN TWO SAZHENS FROM BUILD-
INGS AND AT A DISTANCE OF 1.5 TO 2.0 SAZHENS FROM EACH OTHER.
—Pskov Provincial Zemstvo Compulsory Village Planning Regulations, 1899

New definitions of house and home, as well as mathematization of space in the community, had begun to show up by the 1890s in property disputes among peasants in Novgorod Province. Their facility with the language of fire hazards appears in the records of local courts. In July 1891, for example, the peasant Mikhail Zakharov filed suit against his next-door neighbor, Filip Potanov, for building a house too close to his. As the case made its way through various courts and appeals, Zakharov defined his neighbor's offense as a violation of the prohibition against building structures within less than a prescribed interval between homesteads. Zakharov saw this as an expression of Potanov's willingness to flout the constraints imposed on construction by the Building Code, and he claimed that Potanov's new structures were "dangerous in terms of fire."[1] His original complaint and subsequent testimony also defined the interval between his yard and Potanov's in precise measurements, eliciting from Potanov a response that equally relied on such mathematical precision in his defense. After two full years in the court system, the combined authority of the law, courts, and fire's threat stood with Zakharov. Filip Potanov was forced to destroy his new home and out-buildings and, further, to clear the site entirely of debris.[2]

For Zakharov, the outcome was a vindication and a personal victory; for Potanov, it was a defeat and a humiliation. For zemstvo delegates and other fire activists, Potanov's defeat represented the triumph of law and order over auda-

cious fire and the "disorderly, haphazard, outrageous" villages that had so generously fed it over the previous thirty years.[3] Everything about the villages of
European Russia in the 1870s had attracted zemstvo attention and caused alarm.
The most obvious factors in the fire epidemic were the crowded construction of
homestead against homestead, littered and jumbled yards within each household's fences, the placement within homesteads of buildings in which fire was
used for agricultural processing, and much about the structures themselves:
straw roofs, chimneyless stoves or stoves with pipes that abutted wood or straw,
poor walls, badly constructed or maintained stoves and chimneys, blankets of
straw and wattle wrapped around izbas during the winter months, even candles
before icons. Only when these rural "ills" could be eradicated, the conviction
grew, could runaway fires be prevented or at least restricted in rural Russia. For it
was these physical aspects of rural culture that gave fires their power.

Reconstructing villages, breaking up crowded construction, forcing peasant residences into grids of parallel and perpendicular streets and alleyways,
transforming the materials and methods of building everything from the family
stove to the barn roof would bring the villages of European Russia into line, into
order, on track to a progressive future through the imposition of reason on disorder. In this campaign, legally mandated uniformity and precision, embodied
in detailed plans, offered a panacea for what ailed Russia. And what ailed Russia
in the village curiously resembled what ailed Russia at its center, equally an
object of zemstvo activism: awesome, uncontained, capricious power. Fire
assumed qualities that any late-nineteenth-century Russian reader recognized as
analogous to the tsar's failings. The legal counsel to the Novgorod provincial
zemstvo in 1901, one M. Mysh, expressed the conflation of fire and autocracy as
uncontained threats when he urged the zemstvo to move forward on village
planning, saying that to do otherwise would "leave villages at the mercy of fire's
arbitrary caprice [*proizvol*], which year in and year out destroys the peasant population's property."[4]

When Mysh referred to fire as yet another medium through which
proizvol exercised its destructive will on Russia, he assigned to it a broadly
understood attribute of Russian primitivism. *Proizvol* was the bugaboo of
reform-minded Russians, whether they were calling for a rule-of-law state that
would rein in the tsar's arbitrary powers, for a rule-of-law society that would
curb the arbitrary and venal practices of peasant judges in peasant courts, or for
some protection for peasant women then subject to the arbitrary and drunken
violence of their patriarchal husbands and fathers-in-law. It was a mark of
Russia's distance from the model modernity of the West. Its opposite was the

zemstvo and the values it offered in the battle against primitivism. There can be no doubt that in this campaign, as in their public health and education campaigns, the zemstvos had complete confidence in their enlightening and progressive mission. As a contemporary historian of zemstvo fire measures explained, zemstvo institutions "should play the role of natural transmitters of information . . . into the dark peasant milieu."[5]

The legislation on planning placed the zemstvos squarely between the state and the peasantry, and between the contradictory principles of command and consensus. The state ordered the zemstvos to develop plans for the villages, but they then had to secure the approval of the residents in the village before they could impose the plan. The steps sketched in the 1873 legislation were these: (1) district zemstvos were to develop the plans; (2) they were to present these plans to all of the commune in question and any other individuals who owned land in the village; (3) they had to secure a resolution of assent by the community and responses from any landowners; and (4) they were to send the plans, the resolution, and the responses to the provincial governor for his confirmation.[6] Although the legislation did not specify that communal resolutions regarding village planning had to be unanimous, experience demonstrated that individual property owners, in most cases peasants, could vote against both initial resolutions and final plans and stymie the entire process. Until the plan had gone through the entire procedure and been approved by the governor, it was not binding. This meant that unless an approved plan was already in place, a major fire could prepare the way for village reconstruction. The approval process for that reconstruction could take so long that the burned-out peasants simply built as they pleased and needed to, rather than remain homeless in the name of honoring the planning mission. These realities led to considerable frustration for zemstvo fire activists, who subsequently came to long for the ability to command peasants to follow plans that the zemstvo itself had been commanded to design. The history of the zemstvo village planning program thus illuminates the tensions inherent in this modernist, progressive enterprise when legal values and autocratic impulses clashed in the campaign against fire.

Novgorod's Example

The Novgorod provincial fire regulations illustrate the breadth of the zemstvo fire mission. They serve as one example of the rules zemstvos established across European Russia beginning in the 1870s and continuing through the end of the century.[7] Prepared in 1901, these regulations amended those the Novgorod zemstvo had issued between 1876 and 1879; their juxtaposition enables us to see the adjustments the zemstvo made in response to problems that persisted in the intervening twenty years, as well as its move toward more mathematical precision. The 1901 publication organized the articles of both old and new versions in ten chapters:

I	General Fire Safety Measures
II	The Firefighting System in Villages
III	On Village Planning and the Structure of Streets, Alleys, Squares, and Blocks
IV	Homestead Plot Size, Intervals between Buildings, and Regulations on Building Construction
V	On the Construction of Threshing Barns, Drying Barns, Storehouses, Mills, Manufactories, and Factories
VI	Exceptions to These Regulations
VII	On the Prohibition against Using Untreated Straw and Other Highly Flammable Materials for Roofs, Walls, and Other Sections of Residential and Nonresidential Structures
VIII	On Attaining Written Permission to Construct Buildings and the Supervision of Their Proper Construction
IX	On Moving Homestead Buildings to New Locations
X	On Safety Measures against Fires in Fields and Forests and on Extinguishing Them

In addition to these chapters, the published version of the 1901 project included instructions on the preparation and approval of village reconstruction plans, and it reprinted the articles in the Building Code that remained in effect after 1879.[8]

The regulations in chapter 1, on fire safety precautions and prescriptions, were not fundamentally new; they reiterated similar provisions in the imperial Fire Code. But by incorporating these provisions in their regulations and thereby claiming them for their jurisdiction and that of their hired agents, the zemstvos brought the power of the law closer to rural communities. These general measures applied to four areas: planting trees and building water reservoirs, constructing and maintaining stoves and chimneys, handling fire, and storing highly flammable materials. Every property owner was ordered to plant deciduous trees that would grow to be tall around their courtyards and between buildings. There was no mention of where the peasants might locate or purchase such trees, or of any financial support the zemstvo might provide. While at first glance it would seem that birch seedlings along the forest's edge might have provided a ready supply, the rapid deforestation in Novgorod Province and the increasing commodification of the forest might have made this an unlikely source of free trees. Compliance was evidently a problem in Novgorod Province, as it had been in Smolensk Province, where A. N. Engel'gardt observed in the 1870s that peasants would stick birch branches in the ground for zemstvo agents to see when they came to inspect tree planting, only to let them dry up and die once the inspection was over.[9] Perhaps similar experiences prompted the Novgorod zemstvo to include the prescription that if any trees were destroyed by fire "or any other cause," the property owner had to replace them.

The rules on stove and chimney construction in the 1901 fire regulations displayed the Novgorod zemstvo's insistence on mathematical precision, in contrast to similar regulations of the 1870s. Whereas the 1870s regulations had called for stoves not to be in crowded spaces, those of 1901 stated that both chimneys and stoves had to built at least "6 *vershoks*" (around eight inches) from wooden walls in homes. In threshing and drying barns, stoves had to be at least 12 *vershoks* from wooden walls; chimneys had to be made of fired bricks and extend at least 12 *vershoks* from the roof's peak; and there had to be a metal or brick collar at least 2 vershoks in width at the chimney's point of entry on the ceiling or roof. To the twenty-first-century mind, these prescriptions seem absolutely ordinary. But within the context of villages in Novgorod Province in 1901, they required that peasants use measuring tools in order to satisfy the mathematically minded fire agent when he came to call. A similar faith in precision planning was apparent in the revised regulations on firefighting equipment. The 1901 regulations included a table with the ten items required in each village and the number of each item required for every 10, 20, 40, 60, 80, or 200 households. Whereas the 1870s regulations made purchasing fire hoses and other such equipment voluntary, the 1901 regulations required that villages of more than sixty households acquire them, with grants from the zemstvo to subsidize their purchase.

The impulse toward cultural transformation through detailed redefinition and delimitation of the physical space of the village was most evident in chapters 3 through 9 of the regulations. Planning itself was hardly a new phenomenon in imperial Russia, having been the hallmark of Russia's rulers most famously from Peter the Great in the early eighteenth century forward, but also in the fire safety regulations of Ivan IV (the Terrible) and his successors beginning in the sixteenth century. These planning efforts, however, had been directed at Russia's cities and towns. Only in the 1830s did the imperial government begin to address construction patterns in villages as contributing factors in fires. In 1837, the rural police were instructed to ensure that no new buildings went up in villages except according to plans that specified distances for agricultural buildings that employed fire. Further, they were to try to supervise the planting of trees as fire walls, supervise inspections and maintenance of stoves and chimneys, and prevent the practice of drying hemp and flax within households. Special interest in fire prevention, including village planning, also was directed at state peasants beginning in 1838. Provincial departments over the state peasants were ordered to prepare plans for state peasant villages.[10] After the Emancipation, the zemstvos became the state's partners in its growing ambition to penetrate and reorder rural communities that had remained largely outside the state's purview throughout centuries of serfdom and gentry tutelage. That ambition had been evident in P. D. Kiselev's reforms directed at state peasants beginning in the 1830s; the zemstvos took up the next leg in their thirty-four provinces while governors' administrations assumed this role in the remaining fifteen provinces of European Russia, drawing former proprietary serfs into restructuring as the state peasants had been earlier.[11]

For any student of Russia, "the plan" resonates with images of the overweening statism of the planned economy of the Soviet period, and especially of the Stalinist period. The zemstvos' village planning program invites a teleological analysis linking it with Soviet Five-Year Plans, especially because its wellspring of faith in science and its attachment to geometric, mathematical definitions of living space so closely resemble characteristics of Soviet architectural planning, to say nothing of the imposition of other numerical norms and quotas on peasants from the Civil War forward.[12] The common elements include confidence in rational organization over spontaneous disorder, a conviction that rural culture was both emblem and source of Russia's backwardness, an almost reflexive worldview placing peasants at the bottom of the social hierarchy in Russia, and the concomitant assumption that it was the educated elements' role to define the future and instruct the peasants about their role in that future.[13] But the zemstvo planning program is a problematical example of nascent modernism as the liberal precursor to the horrors of Soviet totalitarian visions, because the zemstvo was itself part of civil society, and its fire programs, part of the civilian campaign against fire. Furthermore, in this case it was not civil society that checked the impulses of the state to subsume individual rights in a modernist campaign, but the state that checked the zemstvo's impulses by defending peasants' individual rights to refuse as property owners to submit to plans.

The zemstvo village planning program illustrates not continuous modernist etatism in Russia but the power that modernist visions held within educated civil society. Fire activists assumed that their mission was to save Russia from the peasantry's enfeebling ignorance and disorder, which threatened to give the *proizvol* of fire free rein in the countryside, something as disastrous as the reign of *proizvol* in the Winter Palace in St. Petersburg. Fire was the enemy zemstvo planners sought to eradicate in the countryside; it was a genuine threat to Russia's prosperity and worthy of the energy they sought to mobilize against it. Because it was not only an elemental power, however, but also one that depended upon peasants' daily decisions and practices about and within their physical environment, the peasants' way of life became the arena for the contest against it.

Standardization and uniformity would characterize the planned village, replacing idiosyncrasy, crowding, and clutter. The goal of the planning regulations in the Novgorod project was a village defined by straight lines, grids of streets and alleyways, homestead plots that fell within a specified range of size, village squares, and regular intervals of minimal width between buildings and homesteads. Of the nineteen articles in chapters 3, 4, and 5 on the village's layout, thirteen prescribed a specific numerical measurement of some sort. Streets were to be straight and even and at least 10 sazhens wide (around 60 feet); alleyways at least 6 *sazhens* in width were to be placed after every eighth homestead; and squares of at least 12 *sazhens'* width were to be built whenever there were at least 80 households in the village. For newly constructed villages, homestead plots were to be at least 12 *sazhens* wide facing the street and 60 *sazhens* deep. Within the boundaries of homesteads that were only 10 *sazhens* wide because of land shortages, buildings could occupy only 4 *sazhens* across the front, and the remaining 6 *sazhens* had to planted as gardens. Neighboring homesteads had to maintain 6 *sazhens* of open space between their buildings; no private buildings could be built within 20 *sazhens* of a church or public grain storehouse; and there had to be at least 50 *sazhens* between neighboring settlements. All outbuildings that housed fire (bathhouses, threshing and drying barns, smithies) had to be at least 30 *sazhens* from the nearest residential or public structures, and they had to be situated at least 6 *sazhens* from each other.[14]

The Novgorod zemstvo changed the procedures for developing plans and securing communal approval for them from the 1870s regulations to the 1901 regulations. The changes suggest some of the challenges that had slowed village reconstruction in the intervening years. According to the 1870s procedures, the district zemstvo was to prepare plans and present them to all property owners in the village. Once village residents and any landowner with land there accepted the plan, it was to be sent to the governor for approval and then returned to the district zemstvo for implementation. Residents were given a month in which to reply to the proposed plan; failure to reply was considered acceptance. If the peasant commune refused to pass a resolution approving the plan, it had to send a written document stating as much to the district zemstvo. There, the finalization of the plan would proceed without the commune's participation in the process. In this case, the failure to send a resolution would be interpreted as acceptance of the plan. New plans were to be implemented in any case after fires.

The 1901 regulations took the peasants' role and consent in the process more seriously. Although the district zemstvo was to initiate the process by proposing to "property owners in crowded villages" that they gather and prepare a unanimous resolution, the peasants were to state in that resolution how they would like their village to be reconstructed in line with the zemstvo building regulations. The zemstvo was then to send a zemstvo delegate or insurance agent to the locale to verify the plan's details and compliance with fire and building regulations. If he found it satisfactory, it was to be sent first to the land captain (an administrative-judicial official introduced in 1889) and then to the governor for confirmation. The planning process clearly moved in 1901 to one in which the "consent of the governed" was more actively invited, perhaps because peasant innovators were central to the development and construction of fire-proof roofs in Novgorod Province in the 1880s and 1890s.[15]

Zemstvo planning prescriptions served, first, as a guide for fire agents, land surveyors, and zemstvo members who were to draw up plans to present to individual communities for approval. They served also as the limits cantonal elders had to enforce any time a peasant wanted to rebuild an old structure or erect a new one. In order to do so, the peasant had to secure written permission from the elder, who, in turn, had to confirm that the structure complied with all fire and construction regulations. The insistence on specified widths and distances, all subject to measurement, introduced another layer of outsider-developed and outsider-enforced mathematization of the physical environment of peasants' daily life, beyond the regulations of their compulsory participation in the mutual fire insurance program. The sketch reproduced as figure 7.1, which was published by the Novgorod zemstvo after the project of 1901 was approved in 1902, illustrates the orderly vision, complete with geometry, that the zemstvo fire programs conveyed.

The restrictions placed on the use of hay, straw, and other flammable materials in construction, embodied in chapter 7 of the Novgorod fire regulations, were new in the 1901 project, reflecting the leading role the Novgorod zemstvos had taken since the 1870s in developing fire-resistant roofing materials, to be dis-

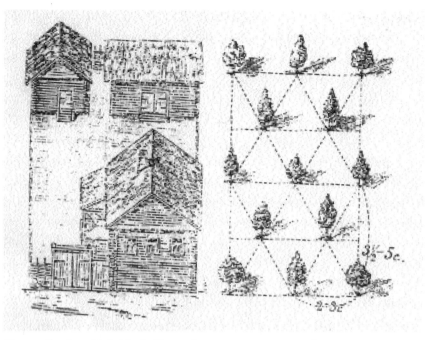

Fig. 7.1. *Sketches published by the Novgorod Province zemstvo as part of its 1901 fire regulations.*
Source: Novgorodskaia gubernskaia zemskaia uprava 1902.

cussed later. Here it is worth noting that the zemstvo members recognized the
necessity of compromise in order to accommodate the realities of village needs
and resources. Although Article 47 of the 1901 regulations forbade the use of
"untreated straw or hay or similar flammable material" for wattle, for wrapping
walls, or in ceilings or fences, it made an exception by allowing wattle and straw
to be used to wrap houses for further insulation in the winter months, as was the
practice in this region. Also, while the regulations forbade the use of untreated
straw for roofs, requiring that the straw at least be mixed with clay, they stated
that an exception would be granted if the local authorities sent a written testimo-
nial that the village had no clay in its area. Such provisions pointed to the poverty
and isolation of the peasants in Novgorod Province, as well as to the zemstvo's
own budgetary limitations. It obviously did not have the financial resources to
purchase clay from another region or to deliver it to villages that needed it.
Although the question of clay seems a minor and deadening detail to privilege
with a place in the historical record, it illustrates the bind that peasants, peasant
officials, and zemstvo bureaus were in when they tried to eradicate the physical
attributes of European Russia's villages that made them so fire-prone.

Beyond Novgorod

Fire safety regulations like Novgorod's were standard zemstvo fare throughout European Russia, and the zemstvos in the northern and eastern provinces were especially active in village planning. Several zemstvos encouraged peasants to move to planned settlements following major fires by providing grants and loans for resettlement. In some cases these expenditures were impressive. The Nizhnii Novgorod provincial zemstvo, for example, gave out 101,715 rubles to 12,805 household heads between 1889 and 1905; the Riazan zemstvo gave out 517,300 rubles between 1877 and 1901.[16]

The Kazan provincial zemstvo had great success in both developing plans and realizing them in village reconstruction. Over thirty years of consistent focus and effort, virtually all the villages in the province adjusted to zemstvo plans. In the 1890s, 28,177 locales conformed to the prescriptions governing intervals and limits on the number of households that could be in one quarter or block. Another 1,213 households decided to separate entirely from their crowded homesteads and set up new, fully planned communities on new lands. When I. Gofshtetter drove through the province to inspect the progress of village planning, he found that almost all of the villages he visited had been divided up into clusters of no more than six homesteads, with most comprising three, four, or five. Builders had followed the prescribed intervals of six to eight sazhens between homesteads and fourteen to sixteen sazhens between blocks or clusters. Gofshtetter also observed that the nature of fires in these villages reflected the benefits of such planning. Although the number of fires did not decrease, their scope did. The average number of structures burned fell steadily from 7.6 in 1890 to 5.3 for the period 1892–1896—approximately the number of structures in the individual blocks of households. The intervals between them thus did contain fires except when the winds were high.[17] For some Kazan zemstvo delegates, this success whetted their appetite for more victory over fire through restructuring the village environment; they called for forcible separation of households from large villages in order to reduce both the number and scope of fires. This the peasants would surely have resisted, but such delegates held a minority position. The zemstvo continued to work with the peasants to improve the situation within existing villages while offering financial support to any households that chose to move to new land.

The story of zemstvo plans for village reconstruction in Perm Province offers the opposite example. The number of buildings burned per fire rose there to as high as twenty-five per fire in 1890 (despite the fact that only around 30 percent of the roofs there were thatched). This record pointed to crowded village construction as the major factor in numerous, large-scale fires. The need for village reconstruction was obvious and acknowledged. Yet right up to the turn of the century, the Perm zemstvo could not get it right. It was among the first of the provincial zemstvos to hand village planning over fully to land surveyors as putative technical experts. At great cost to the zemstvo budget, these surveyors toiled away, some with no results whatsoever. One particularly notorious failure, named Klimov, continued to receive his annual salary of fifteen hundred rubles for eight years, which he seems to have devoted almost exclusively to writing letters of frustration to the zemstvo board, explaining why, in village after village, he had failed to develop a plan or present it to the local peasants for their approval. Everywhere, it seemed, local peasant authorities conspired against him, refusing to convene assemblies, even when he summoned police assistance. It is hard to say whether Klimov was simply incredibly inept in his relations with the peasants or whether the peasants were effectively using this approach to resist the redesign of their communities. But the cost to the zemstvo proved to be high, with no product to show for its expenses.

Perm was also one of the provinces in which would-be reconstruction projects were foiled by the peasants' insistence on their property rights in their homestead land, and therefore by their ability to reject plans that required them to move to other parcels. There was no shortage of plans in Perm Province; some portion of the preparation and approval of new village plans had been completed in more than six thousand villages by 1895. This left some five thousand more without any plans in process. Between poor organization, excessive indulgence of incompetent surveyors, and peasant resistance, the entire planning program in Perm Province remained, in 1902, essentially "a paper affair."[18]

Zemstvo Impulses and State Constraints

In other provinces, whose fire programs fell somewhere between Kazan's success and Perm's failure, enforcement had the potential to generate some interesting contests over authority and rights in rural Russia. Challenges to the zemstvo's authority or to the prescriptions set out in its plans were ultimately tests of the zemstvo's legal authority or the authority of the law itself to define community norms and physical realities. As such, they made their way into the records of the judicial system, from local courts to its highest instance, the Ruling or Governing Senate. Senate decisions revealed state priorities in zemstvo insurance programs: that these programs impress upon individual property owners both their responsibilities and the advantages of participation in the fire insurance program, and that the authority the zemstvos received through their enabling laws enjoy the imperial government's full support. Yet the Senate also defended the principle of private property in land for peasants, who appealed to this principle in refusing to comply with reconstruction plans.

The steps required for developing and approving village plans, as well as the option of granting exceptions, also opened the way for disputes over jurisdiction among zemstvo and provincial authorities. In 1899, the Senate decided on a complaint that had originally been sent to the Moscow governor in 1896. The peasant "T." charged that the district zemstvo had granted another peasant, "Ch.," permission to build a house "right next to his house at a distance of 10 *arshins*" on a piece of land where the approved village plan prohibited any construction. Not only the peasant T. but also the priest "O." had filed a complaint with the zemstvo provincial board before the matter had gone to the governor. In the course of the Senate's discussions and correspondence, it emerged that the structure was a large, two-story, masonry house. That the complaint came from members of the community rather than from a member of the police (as many other such complaints did) suggests that the peasant Ch. did not enjoy the community's affection; perhaps T. envied the wealth that made it possible for Ch. to build such a large masonry house right next door.

The case proved even more tangled when the district zemstvo sent a representative to the village to inspect the situation, with approved plan in hand, and discovered that Ch.'s lot had mistakenly been dedicated to a large alleyway, which should have run through another peasant's land. With that mistake and the provincial zemstvo's general effort to get peasants to build masonry houses, the district zemstvo concluded that it should grant Ch. permission to build his house. In response to T.'s and O.'s complaints, the provincial zemstvo rejected the district zemstvo's reasoning and pointed instead to the violation of planning procedures that their permission constituted. The provincial zemstvo reminded the district board that Ch. could not build until a new plan, with the alleyway in the correct location, had been approved. Exercising his right to appeal, as granted in Article 119 of the 1864 zemstvo legislation, Ch. took his case to the Moscow governor, who refused to address it, which in turn led Ch. to take the case to the Senate.

The Senate confirmed the provincial board's argument that the planning procedures had been violated and rejected Ch.'s appeal. Recognizing, however, that the mistake lay not with Ch. but with the district zemstvo, the Senate advised Ch. to sue the district zemstvo for any financial losses he had incurred.[19] This case illustrates the primacy that procedures assumed in the state's approach to local disputes, even in the face of what seems to have been a logical and legitimate complaint. The Senate and provincial zemstvo's first priority was clearly that the system for developing and approving plans maintain its integrity; second was that the costs of the district zemstvo's mistake not fall on the peasant Ch. The case also illustrates that the peasants involved had a clear idea of the procedures both for planning and for filing complaints with local and central authorities. Finally, it demonstrates the kinds of disputes that could emerge over rule making and breaking, even within the zemstvo organization of a single province.

The Senate demonstrated the same level of commitment to procedures, and peasants demonstrated the same degree of tenacity in filing appeals, in a case that emerged in Vladimir Province in 1897. The peasants of the village of Moshka requested of the provincial zemstvo that all of the structures in their community be appraised according to a special appraisal under the compulsory program. The provincial zemstvo refused this request because the village was crowded and had not been rebuilt according to plan. The peasants then sent their appeal to the Senate, which decided in their favor. The Senate argued that the law governing the fire insurance program stated clearly that all property owners had the right to request a special, higher appraisal, and the "Vladimir provincial zemstvo assembly had no foundation for depriving the property owners of this right," although it could either require these peasants to comply with its fire regulations or demand higher insurance payments from them.[20] Having recognized the didactic potential in insurance, the Vladimir zemstvo had hoped both to protect itself against the high claims that were more likely in an unplanned, crowded village and to force the peasants to rebuild according to plan in the face of their certain impoverishment if they could insure only at the lower, "normal" rate.

This contest over planning visions and peasants' rights surfaced also in the desire of some zemstvos to overrule individual property owners' objections to the zemstvos' proposed plans and their refusal to alter or move their homesteads in conformity with them. According to the Emancipation legislation, the rights to land the peasants' received as homestead land (that is, the land on which their homes, barns, and household gardens sat) was hereditary for those who lived there.[21] The Senate concluded that this was an inviolable right that required any district or provincial zemstvo to receive the unanimous consent of all peasants whose homestead land would be affected by proposed plans and reconstruction. On three occasions, the Viatka zemstvo asked that the Senate permit plans to go forward on the basis of only a two-thirds vote from the affected village. On each occasion, the Senate refused the appeal.[22]

The Nizhnii Novgorod zemstvo similarly found the legislation an obstacle to its planning program, but it took heart from a Senate decision of 1885 stating that although the peasants' right to the hereditary use of their homestead land was inviolable, zemstvos did have the right to proscribe building on that land that violated zemstvo compulsory fire safety and construction regulations.[23] The Senate decision was unequivocal, however, about the restrictions on imposing plans on family-owned homestead land, stating that "the Governing Senate rules that for planning after a fire that requires the exchange of homestead locations, the consent of all the household heads in the village is necessary; without such consent, the commune does not have the right to enact an agreement that would violate the peasants' hereditary use of homestead lands."[24]

In the early 1890s, the Ufa provincial zemstvo grew increasingly frustrated by its inability to plan as it pleased, and it objected to the power the Emancipation legislation gave the peasants. As the journal *The Firefighter* explained by way of background to the Ufa zemstvo's strategy, the Senate's consistent defense of the peasants' hereditary, law-given rights to their homestead land meant that "no authority for any reason whatsoever had the right to remove a peasant's homestead land or to replace it with another plot of land without the property owner's direct consent without breaking the law." The Ufa zemstvo proposed, therefore, to change the law—to request that the Senate amend Article 110 of the legislation governing peasant administration following the Emancipation, which had granted peasants property rights over their homesteads, and that it change the regulations on the zemstvo's authority in village planning to place the approval process exclusively in the hands of the provincial zemstvo, leaving the peasants out of the process entirely.[25] This the Senate did not do, but the Ufa zemstvo's ambitious appeal reveals that, in a spirit almost completely opposite that of the Novgorod zemstvo's 1901 regulations, Ufa, like many other zemstvo boards, hoped to place its authority and plan ahead of the peasants' individual rights, all in the name of a rational defense against fire.

These impulses were also evident in discussions before local sessions of the Committees on the Needs of Agriculture in 1902. The Tambov provincial committee presented as one of its priorities in policy recommendations that the contradiction between Article 110 and the building decrees be eliminated. The Chernigov provincial committee recommended that peasant resettlement out of crowded villages be made compulsory, even in the face of peasants' resistance. The Kursk provincial committee also called explicitly for the authority of the zemstvos to be extended to enable them to move peasants off their homestead land onto their allotment land, "even without the peasants' consent." The

Grodno local and provincial committees exhibited an exceptionally paternalistic, tutelary attitude toward the peasantry in general, which was evident in its recommendations on the fire question. The Belostoko-Sokol'skii district committee argued that peasants should be left out of the discussion and decisions entirely, and that it was essential that no measures be made dependent on their approval. Instead, the committee members called for all measures to be directed and imposed from above. Alone in the discussions of village planning and reconstruction, L. K. Domeiko, a delegate to the Slonimskii district committee, advocated the political advantages of village reconstruction with the aim of breaking up crowded communities, saying that it "would make any revolt, mob attack and solidarity in hostile relations to private landowners and state power less attainable." Domeiko's position was both extreme and exceptional in its explicitly defensive expression, but it suggests the potential conjunction of fear of peasants, fear of fire, faith in planning, and coercive impulses that could surface in the question of village reconstruction.[26]

Fire-Resistant Construction and Peasant Innovation

Despite Kazan's exceptional success, most zemstvos were never able to execute their plans and had to concede that, as one Nizhnii Novgorod zemstvo delegate complained, their lovely plans "remained pictures that had no significance whatsoever and cost a great deal of money."[27] Plans for reconstructed villages did not disappear from the national fire discussion, as the numerous proposals put forward in 1902 by local Committees on the Needs of Agriculture testify. Almost every one of the provincial committees placed village reconstruction through planning and enforcement of the Building Code at the top of their list of policy recommendations on the fire question. Some offered statements by peasant delegates to their committees in support of reconstruction, in order to reinforce the argument that this was a universally recognized necessity.[28] Others provided blueprints for reconstructed villages. But, like the Saratov provincial zemstvo in the late 1880s, some zemstvos retreated from grand visions of eliminating crowding and disorder in village layouts and turned to the more incremental step of changing individual structures, roof by roof and, sometimes, wall by wall. The logic behind such an approach was that in the face of the villages' seemingly intractable crowding, creating clusters of fire-resistant roofs that would slow down or even serve as fire lines in runaway fires would be an achievable goal that could reduce the damages fires caused, even if their incidence remained high. As the governor of Saratov Province, A. P. Engel'gardt, explained to the minister of the interior in a lengthy discussion of the fire question at the turn of the century:

> This all leads to the indubitable conclusion that the sole route out of this situation must be the speediest possible replacement of village construction with fire-resistant buildings or, at the very least, the replacement of thatched roofs with fire-resistant ones, and only through this, and this measure alone, is it possible to protect the village from frequent, total immolation, and its inhabitants from the perennial and extreme losses which fires cause them.[29]

This challenge became all the more daunting at the turn of the century, as rapid deforestation in certain regions drove up the cost of wood for roofing and house construction while also speeding up erosion, the desiccation of ponds, and the absorption of rainfall and streams, thus creating a more fire-prone environment and decreasing the water supply.[30]

It is a telling reflection of the economic limitations that faced the zemstvo fire activists that the options for developing fire-resistant materials came to mean clay—as a material either to mix with straw for roofs, to be mixed with water to make stucco, or to be made into bricks. While all contributors to the discussion of fire-resistant roofing recognized that tile and metal roofs were superior, they recognized equally that tile and metal roofs were beyond the means either of individual peasants or of zemstvos that might hope to subsidize their production and purchase. When the Samara provincial zemstvo issued a compulsory order in 1894 that all straw roofs be replaced with wood, metal, tile, or, at the very least, straw mixed with clay, the majority of the communal officials throughout the province responded that this was simply impossible because of the economic costs involved.[31]

Several zemstvo organizations experimented with fire-resistant building techniques, but Novgorod Province gained the reputation, by the turn of the century, for being the most successful in developing effective and affordable fire-resistant roofing. This success was largely due to an innovation introduced by a peasant by the name of Anton Grigor'evich Adamov in 1895. Before Adamov roofs became the roofing of choice in zemstvo provinces, Kazan and Simbirsk Provinces had experimented with combinations of clay and straw (Kazan) and clay, straw, and manure (Simbirsk). The goal was to encase the straw in a material that would not burn easily, that would be readily at hand for peasants, and that was inexpensive. Although these roofs were somewhat effective, they often cost too much or were susceptible to cracks and rot. One type, the Krasnoufimsk roof, was both complicated to construct (being woven in advance on the ground, then lifted onto the structure) and often too heavy for the building below to sustain it. The Novgorod zemstvo decided against the Krasnoufimsk roof and sent a fire insurance agent to Kursk Province, where the peasants had long built clay and straw roofs. Upon his return, he shared the techniques he had observed with another agent, N. P. Chernov, who developed a method in which roofing straw was first soaked in clay, then layered with further clay spread between each layer of straw.

The peasant Adamov observed the construction of Chernov roofs in his village and came up with a lighter, cheaper, more effective way to construct a clay and straw roof that soon dominated the roofing trade. While Watt's innovation on the steam engine would spur England's industrial development, Adamov roofs had the potential to enable peasants across European Russia to defend themselves against the financial disaster of fire and to begin the critical process of capital accumulation and steady economic growth that was otherwise hobbled by the frequent "shocks" of runaway fires.

Adamov's innovation was to eliminate any packing of clay between layers of straw, which made the roof much lighter. He also cut off any ears of grain that remained in the straw, which had caused problems by continuing to sprout after the roofs were constructed, producing cracks in the clay. Once the clay-soaked sheaves of straw were laid on the roof, Adamov raked through them, then used a shovel to pat down the straw and create a smooth surface, off of which water poured more rapidly than from other clay-straw roofs.[32] The Novgorod zemstvo immediately recognized the advantages of Adamov roofs, which required less clay and straw and which were lighter and more quickly laid. They invited Adamov to train "master roofers," who spread out across the province teaching peasants how to install Adamov roofs. The number of Adamov roofs began to grow rapidly after 1896. Both zemstvo roofers and individual homeowners installed them, as table 7.1 shows.

Although the total of just over fifteen thousand Adamov roofs in a province of roughly ten thousand villages and settlements hardly transformed "wooden and straw Russia," there was much to applaud in Novgorod's experience. First, the relationship between the zemstvo and the peasantry was such that a peasant innovator found a receptive audience for his technique and a sponsor willing to disseminate it under his name. Second, peasants throughout the province recognized Adamov's technique, took the initiative to install Adamov roofs or hire someone else to build one for them, and invested in their choice. After Adamov made his improvement, far more peasants built roofs than

Table 7.1: Numbers of Adamov Roofs Installed in Novgorod Province, 1888-1902

Year	Installed by Homeowners or Independent Roofers	Installed by Zemstvo Masters
1888–1896	1,546	1,783
1896	828	440
1897	2,186	604
1898	1,462	324
1899	1,225	197
1900	1,153	129
1901	1,859	296
1902 (through Oct.)	883	235
Total	11,142	4,007

Source: Novgorodskaia gubernskaia zemskaia uprava 1902: 6.

zemstvo masters, revealing their willingness to follow the lead of a fellow peasant whose influence enjoyed zemstvo support. Third, the zemstvo continued to pay master roofers to demonstrate the roofing technique years after its introduction. However small the numbers were within the context of the total population, the Novgorod Adamov roof program illustrated the potential that lay in successful zemstvo-peasant relations, devoid of compulsory prescription.

Finally, the zemstvo publicized its success, which in turn attracted invitations from other zemstvo boards to Novgorod's Adamov roof masters to come to their provinces and teach the technique. Through 1904, twenty-three provincial zemstvo boards hired Adamov master roofers, some for annual visits.[33] By 1902, Novgorod had set the standard for roof construction as a fire prevention measure, as is evident in numerous references to it in comments before the Committees on the Needs of Agriculture as a model to be emulated.[34] Adamov was not alone among peasants as someone who saw the need for replacing thatched roofs and took the initiative toward finding a solution. In Samara Province, the entire program of roof replacement began in 1866 when peasants from the village of Ekaterinovka in Samara District approached the provincial zemstvo with a proposal that the assembly discuss the feasibility of introducing a compulsory program in fire-resistant roofing in the province.[35]

Did these roofs make a difference? Anecdotal evidence suggests that they did. Reports began to appear of incidents in which fires threatened to consume entire villages, only to be stopped in their tracks by a cluster of clay and straw roofs. Or they in fact burned all the structures in the village except the one or two that had clay and straw roofs. This was proof of the best possible kind, quick evidence for peasant observers of the advantages of fire-resistant roofing. A correspondent from Kursk Province reported to *The Firefighter* that during a fire on August 14, 1894, twenty homesteads with all their outbuildings and stacked grain burned because of a strong wind. Those who were at the fire were amazed, however, that in the middle of the burning houses, one stood untouched. Afterward, there was much talk about the roof on this house—it was of straw with a thick layer of clay. Though it was not an Adamov roof, the clay in its structure had been enough to protect it from the blaze that consumed all the neighboring structures.[36]

Saratov governor A. P. Engel'gardt offered another such example from the village of Idolgi. Engel'gardt explained that despite a series of devastating fires, the peasants of the area had been slow to switch from untreated straw roofs, until one peasant in Idolgi put a clay and straw roof on his house. When a fire broke out in the village shortly thereafter, it quickly destroyed seventy-six homesteads with all of their buildings—but the house with the clay and straw roof did not catch fire, "despite the fact that every structure surrounding it burned." Seeing the virtues of the new roof with their own eyes, "the majority of the peasants then decided to introduce that kind of roof." Remarkably, when the peasants' appeal to the Ministry of the Interior for emergency assistance was granted, the fire victims voted to encourage construction of fire-resistant roofs throughout their canton. By the time of Engel'gardt's report, 824 of the 1,095 homesteads had fire-resistant roofs.

Other cantons soon followed suit, and Engel'gardt was able to report that areas that had switched to fire-resistant roofs saw a rapid reduction in the numbers of structures burned per fire. He offered the following cases as examples. First, in Shirokinsk Canton, 39 fires affecting 455 homeowners had required the payment of 88,000 rubles in zemstvo insurance funds in 1896–1898, before the roofs were changed. In 1899–1901, after the introduction of fire-resistant roofs, the number of fires remained roughly the same, at 37, but only 164 homeowners were affected, and the zemstvo had to pay out only 35,000 rubles. Second, in Viasovsk Canton, the number of fires in the first period was 32, and in the second period, 30. The number of owners affected, however, dropped from 143 to 48, and the insurance payments from 23,000 rubles to 5,000 rubles. And third, the settlement of Russkaia Norka experienced 17 fires in 1896–1898; they destroyed the property of 119 persons, who received 16,000 rubles from the zemstvo fund. In 1899–1901, by contrast, 11 fires burned the property of 71 persons, who received 6,000 rubles from the insurance fund.[37] Peasants who switched to fire-resistant roofs received payments from the zemstvo of 10–16 rubles after the work was finished. This grant was enough to cover the cost, but some peasants were unable to make the shift because they could not buy materials first and await the zemstvo's grant afterward.

In Samara Province, too, there was a high correlation between the introduction of clay and straw roofs and a reduction in the number of structures burned per fire. At the 1902 All-Russian Firefighters' Conference in Moscow, the Samara provincial zemstvo provided the figures shown in table 7.2. In presenting these results, the zemstvo representatives explained that they were all the more striking in Samara and Stavropol Districts, because the roofs had made such a difference in the face of the province's most crowded construction in its largest villages.[38]

Despite formidable financial obstacles, many zemstvos also encouraged the production and sale of tile and metal roofs. Again, Novgorod was one of the leaders, building tile factories through zemstvo subsidies and offering the tiles on favorable terms to peasant homeowners. Their accomplishments in this area were truly modest; by October 1902, only 869 tile roofs had been installed.[39] The Tauride, Khar'kov, Pskov, Ekaterinoslavl, Kursk, Tambov, and Moscow zemstvos also devoted funds to tile roofs, usually by issuing grants or loans for their purchase. In addition, sixteen zemstvos developed loan and grant programs for the purchase of roofing tin.[40]

Toward the century's end, zemstvos turned to fire-resistant construction below the roof. Having attacked straw, they now turned to wood as fire's second favorite fuel in Russia's villages. For those regions of European Russia outside Ukraine where wood had been the material for housing for centuries (Ukrainian

Table 7.2: Relationship between Frequency of Clay and Straw Roofs and Extent of Fires in Samara Province, 1891-1901

District	% Clay and Straw Roofs, 1901	Buildings per Fire, 1891	Buildings per Fire, 1900
Novouzensk	65	1.55	1.10
Samara	58	10.24	1.65
Stavropol	53	10.66	2.45
Buzuluk	50	12.34	3.81
Bogoruslan	33	5.93	1.65
Nikolaev	22	4.09	1.63
Bugulma	8	9.69	2.56

Source: Imperatorskoe Rossiiskoe pozharnoe obshchestvo 1903, 2: 193.

houses were mostly of adobe and stucco), the effort to convince peasants to shift to brick, stone, daub and wattle, or stucco was potentially the most radical of all. For here the zemstvos entered the most intimate spaces of peasant life. Whether one views the home as a spiritual location permeated with deeply held beliefs associated with the sacred icon or the familial stove, as well as prescribed positions for men and women in a clearly demarcated world, or more simply as a product of traditional construction practices and community mutual assistance, or finally as an expression through wooden walls and hearth fire of the deep union between the Russian peasantry and their forested past, the zemstvos were asking the peasants to abandon the familiar when they urged them to shift to new methods of housing construction.

One exchange in Smolensk Province in 1894 between a land captain and some local peasants captures the stakes involved. Following a major fire in April of that year in the village of Zamost'e, the land captain called the peasants to an assembly and convinced them that they must rebuild not simple wooden structures but stucco ones. With their approval secured, he approached the governor, who provided both a master builder to demonstrate the technique and subsidies to cover the additional costs of stucco construction. When these arrived and the master builder began to explain how to build the new houses, the peasants balked. En masse they refused to follow the builder's lead, declaring, "Our grandfathers did not live in dirt, and we won't either."[41] Resistance to "dirt" rather than wooden houses was not solely the product of fealty to tradition. Many early experiments with daub and wattle, stucco, and clay construction failed because these structures trapped moisture inside or sucked it up from the ground into the walls, leading to interior walls that wept or to exterior walls that crumbled. But zemstvo and other planners continued to search for alternatives to wooden houses.

Having recognized that direct observation of clay and straw roofs was the best proof for peasant builders, some zemstvos began to build model structures in their provinces. Entire model fire-resistant villages were built for the Nizhnii Novgorod Fair in 1896 and in the village of Porokhovshchikovo outside of Moscow in 1900. The model village erected by the Ministry of the Interior in Nizhnii Novgorod (and subsequently given to the Nizhnii Novgorod zemstvo) displayed several fire-resistant building techniques. It included ten buildings, both residential and nonresidential structures. When I. Gofshtetter inspected the village in 1899, he found some grounds for the peasants' skepticism. The house built as a model for northern Russia, for example, had walls constructed of clay with layers of small twigs applied running both horizontally and vertically. Gofshtetter described it as "a small izba with the most depressing appearance," with "traces of horrible dampness on everything." In addition, two large cracks ran from the doorway, and the exterior walls were crumbling. A shed with stuccoed lathing was somewhat more promising, especially because the roof extended far enough to protect the walls from rain. This overhang, Gofshtetter concluded, "was worthy of imitation" for stucco buildings in rainy climates. A daub and wattle schoolhouse was both dry and smooth, with no signs of cracks or settling. The builders had also experimented with different types of bricks made of various materials and plastered over with clay. But almost all of the brick, stucco, or daub and wattle structures had large cracks in the walls, caused by uneven settling or poor initial construction. The most successful building of all was a wooden izba, which had been plastered inside and out with clay, then roofed with an Adamov roof.[42]

Several zemstvos sent peasants to the Nizhnii Novgorod fair to examine these buildings in order to introduce their best elements into local construction practices. Some zemstvos, including that of Novgorod Province, built model structures throughout their provinces in order to provide visible proof of the structures' fire-resistant qualities. Between 1897 and 1902, they erected fifty-seven such structures as public buildings, orphanages, and so forth.[43] The Viatka zemstvo's experience suggests that given adequate proof of clay construction, peasants were more than willing to make the switch from wood. The zemstvo sent peasants to see both the Nizhnii Novgorod and Porokhovshchikovo model villages, and the delegates then built one adobe house with a clay and straw roof in each of the villages of Ukhtyma and Verkhosun'ia at the zemstvo's expense. The builders continued to receive salaries from the zemstvo as they built further structures at local peasants' request. The peasant clients, in turn, received loans from the zemstvo to support their projects. The demand was so high that the builders could not keep up with it, despite the fact that some questions remained about the suitability of adobe construction for Viatka's climate.[44]

In terms of financial assistance, the Viatka zemstvo led all others in its encouragement of fire-resistant construction. Between 1894 and 1903, its gave out 182,000 rubles in loans for the construction of brick buildings and 219,900 rubles for the construction of brick-making factories. The Novgorod zemstvo issued grants for the construction of 1,094 fire-resistant buildings between 1897 and 1904, and in 1904 it opened a school to teach fire-resistant building techniques. Beginning in the 1880s, several other zemstvos, including Riazan, Khar'kov, Kursk, Voronezh, Iaroslavl, Kazan, and Tambov, offered loans and grants on a smaller scale for construction projects.[45] The Saratov provincial zemstvo provided loans and grants between 1870 and 1900 for new construction conforming to village plans (3,347 rubles), construction of fire-resistant buildings and roofs generally (69,090 rubles), and the purchase of roofing tin (174,700 rubles).[46]

Zemstvos also supported construction projects to bring water to villages. In Vologda Province, for example, the provincial and district boards supported the construction of wells and ponds in villages where there were few or no such water reservoirs, beginning with a formal system for grant requests in 1898. In 1903–1905 alone, the zemstvo responded to more than two hundred requests for grants, loans, or matching funds for such projects. These requests, almost always submitted by individual peasants, offer stark evidence of the water problem in Russia's villages, even in the damp and forested north. The village of Voronovskaia had only one well and access to a stream 150 *sazhens* away. A village in Ust'sysol'skii District received support because it had not a single year-round water supply for its fifty-seven households, except for a stream one *verst* away. Sometimes grants enabled the construction of additional wells, as in one village of thirty-two houses with four wells among them. Grants were modest, usually from around ten to thirty rubles, and rarely covered the full cost of construction.[47] They represented the modest capital investments individuals and zemstvos needed to make to reduce fire's power in Russia's villages. The need for such projects at even this modest cost at the turn of the century serves as further testimony to the state's long record of failing to invest in its rural sector.

Stove Redesign and Child Care

Some zemstvos moved from the external construction of the peasants' residential and nonresidential spaces into their interiors in order to reduce the fire hazards of two central aspects of family life: the stove and child-care practices. Stove revision included such simple changes as replacing wooden chimneys with tile or brick ones, adding a turn to stovepipes to slow down the flight of sparks, putting a metal or tile collar around the stovepipe and chimney at the ceiling and roof, and insisting on the prescribed distances between stove and wooden walls. The most ambitious efforts aimed for total reconstruction of the stove according to a design developed by a Novgorod engineer named N. I. Kristalovich, which was both more efficient in producing and retaining heat and less prone to accidental fires. Some zemstvos also issued restrictions on the lighting of stoves as part of their fire safety regulations, usually limiting firings to once a day. In Khar'kov District, Khar'kov Province, peasants in several villages did not wait for instructions to come down from the zemstvo but made changes in their daily habits on their own. By village assembly votes, they decided that everyone should abstain from lighting fires on days when all the adults were out in the fields. Further, most households adjusted their cooking hours to the early morning—as early as three o'clock—in order to ensure that the stoves had died down before field work began.[48]

On the question of child care during the agricultural season, one can find evidence of peasant initiative as well. *The Firefighter* reported in August 1894 that in one village where unattended children had started several fires, the assembly had voted that one adult for each ten households would stay behind to watch the children during field work.[49] The reports of the Committees on the Needs of Agriculture, representing all of the provinces in European Russia, zemstvo and non-zemstvo alike, were nearly unanimous in calling for the establishment of infant and child care centers during the agricultural season as a fire prevention measure. A district police chief in Grodno Province, for example, called for a system like that devised by the peasants described in *The Firefighter*: one adult for every ten households to stay behind during field work to care for the small children.[50] The Khar'kov provincial zemstvo reported to the committees that nurseries had been opened in several villages during the previous three years, and that the peasants welcomed them.[51] Both the Poltava and Kursk provincial zemstvos established such centers during the agricultural season as well.[52]

One of the most ambitious programs took shape in Viatka Province, where a Dane, P. G. Hansen (in Russian, Ganzen), established fifteen village day-care centers across the province in 1899 through close cooperation with district zemstvo boards and doctors. Housed in village schools or other rented structures, the centers operated with hired caretakers and eventually attracted many children, despite early resistance by skeptical mothers, who feared everything from the Antichrist to the tsar himself as potential customers for their stolen children.[53] Like everything else in the campaign against fire in the villages of European Russia, Hansen's day-care program and the larger system of "work assistance" of which it was a part embodied progressive ideas based on the notion of enlightening the dark peasantry, for whom the approach to the nurseries' doors would run "through the thick undergrowth of prejudice and ignorance."[54]

Conclusion: Stuck in the Emergency Room

The zemstvo fire insurance and village planning programs were the imperial government's primary solution to the problem of fire in the countryside in thirty-four provinces of European Russia. In the history of the relationship between government and zemstvo, the fire program was an unusual development in terms of the expansion of responsibilities and powers imposed upon and granted to the zemstvo organizations by the government. On the one hand, the government's behavior in passing the problem and the budgetary burden for addressing it to the zemstvo was consistent with the government's effort to avoid additional direct financial burdens in the countryside and with the centuries of undergovernment across the wide expanses of the empire. Further, delegating to the zemstvos responsibility for fire prevention and for mitigating the economic losses incurred by peasant fire victims ran parallel to the government's imposition of public health obligations on the zemstvo organizations. On the other hand, despite the imperial government's willingness legally to define expanded powers for the zemstvos in their tutelary relationship with the peasantry, it was unwilling, up to the turn of the century, to allow the zemstvos to confer across provincial lines, thus building repetitive inefficiencies into individual zemstvo programs. Moreover, the government, through the decisions of the Governing Senate, denied the zemstvos an authority many of them coveted: the power to overrule the collective voice and the individual property rights of peasants in the name of rational planning.

The goals and challenges of the insurance and planning programs made the magnitude of European Russia's fire problem visible at the local, provincial, and capital levels of the empire. As N. V. Shirkov, a delegate to the Kursk Committee on the Needs of Agriculture, concluded in 1902: "Therefore it seems to me that we can discuss this question in connection with reconstructing the entire life of our village or not discuss it all."[55] From fundamental attitudes toward Providence and property to the shape of stovepipes, the zemstvo insurers and planners were trying to transform the peasantry's attitudes, behaviors, and physical environment. Because of fire's ubiquitous presence in the villages of European Russia, the campaign to contain it meant coming to know a broad array of daily practices and rituals and defining new norms for them—in sum, to transform a rich fire culture of long standing as well as the most basic traditions in housing and energy use. With the pressures of imperial decrees behind them; without any start-up funds to finance their operations; with no specialized knowledge to equip themselves for a charge as complicated as developing a solvent insurance program that could cover hundreds of thousands of rubles in losses each year; and faced with a daunting mix of population growth, deforestation leading to a preference for straw over wood, traditional building practices, and the peasants' unwillingness to move off their homestead land to other parcels, the zemstvos had been handed an impossible task. Furthermore, most zemstvo boards were imbued with progressive visions of a rational future, as well as a faith in statistical knowledge and solutions based on mathematically precise prescriptions that were almost certain to bring them into conflict with the peasants' alternative set of values and conceptions of space, time, and ability to control one's fate. The zemstvo representatives' frustrations were made explicit in sessions of the Committees on the Needs of Agriculture and the All-Russian Firefighters' Conference, both of which convened in 1902. As P. P. Kharnskii complained to the Skopin District committee in Riazan, after decades of zemstvo effort, "one has only to ride into any village you choose in order to see that it all exists on paper, while in reality—there is absolutely nothing."[56]

Of course this was not entirely true, as the decline in the numbers of structures burned per fire across European Russia testified. The gains made in Viatka and Samara Provinces were attracting particular attention, and the modest achievements in Novgorod offered hope that solutions could be found and peasants would be willing to participate in applying them if they received adequate exposure to the advantages of fire-resistant construction and subsidies to purchase the materials necessary to practice it. Zemstvos continued to push for village reconstruction, as sketches of successfully planned and rebuilt communities on the eve of World War I attest (fig. 7.2). Still, the opening line of the introduction to Hansen's account of his work assistance programs was, "No one doubts that our village is ill," and the fire crisis was known as the "fire epidemic." If we employ the metaphors of the era, the nearly fifty years

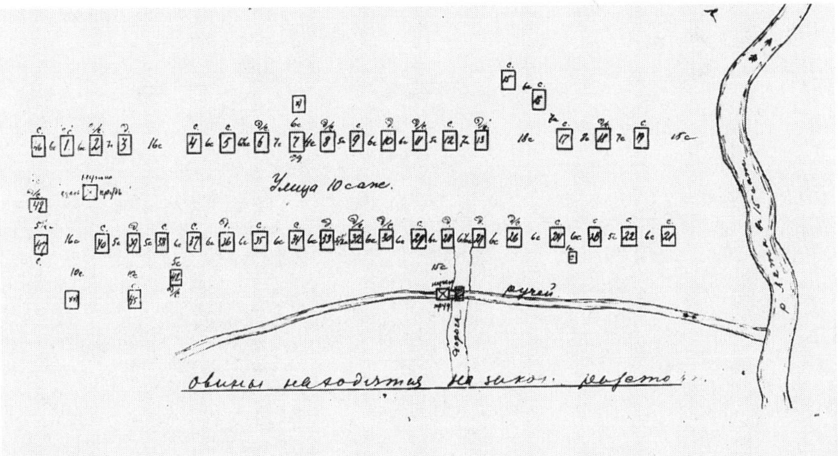

Fig. 7.2. *Village plan from Vologda Province, dated 1914. Source: GAVO, fond 34, opis' 5, delo 229, l. 7.*

following the legislation of a compulsory fire insurance program can justifiably be understood as a period of prolonged diagnosis and prescription, with widely scattered triage efforts. Data were gathered on the phenomenon, its etiology and morphology were delineated, and preferred treatments were identified. Without full government support, however, the zemstvos found themselves searching for partial, affordable solutions rather than optimal ones. Planning, roofing tiles or tin, and stucco or adobe construction (to say nothing of fired bricks) had to give way to roofs of clay and straw in villages that continued to be crowded and cluttered. So long as the imperial government continued to assume an essentially extractive approach to its rural population, the material conditions of rural life would continue to give birth to frequent, often ruinous fires.

In the face of that prospect, another cohort of fire activists concluded that they would fight fires once they began, rather than try to engage in the Sisyphean task of preventing them. Declaring the zemstvos' fire insurance and planning programs, as well as their fire regulations, nothing more than good intentions and wishful thinking, these men turned to the task of containing fire in Russia's villages through mutual assistance in volunteer firefighting brigades. In place of mathematical models of the future and prescribed fire practices, they placed their faith in civic virtue embodied in fraternal, rationally organized community units of men who would take on the wild element of fire and tame it.

8

Fire as the Internal Enemy: Peasants as Volunteer Firefighters

RUSSIA BEING A DESPOTIC GOVERNMENT DOES NOT ADMIT OF VOLUNTEER
FIREMEN, BUT "ELEVATES" THE DUTIES REQUIRED TO BE DISCHARGED BY
FIREMEN INTO A MILITARY PUNISHMENT. . . . IT IS TO BE HOPED THAT THE
SPIRIT OF PROGRESS MAY BE SUFFICIENTLY DEVELOPED IN THAT COUNTRY
TO LEAD TO THE ESTABLISHING OF AN EFFICIENT FIRE SYSTEM THROUGH-
OUT THE LAND, OF A CHARACTER AND ON A PLAN COMMENSURATE WITH
THE POSITION IT IS SO DESIROUS OF OCCUPYING AMONG NATIONS.
—Charles F. T. Young, *Fires, Fire Engines and Fire Brigades, 1866*

From the 1860s to the first decade of the twentieth century, in literary depictions
and eyewitness reports in newspapers, in government reports and responses to
ethnographic surveys, the scene of a rural fire contained stock features and char-
acters that added up to one overriding conclusion: it was complete and utter
chaos. From all corners of European Russia, observers noted common peasant
responses: disorder, hysteria, passivity, and inability to work together to fight the
blaze because of selfish individualism. In one of the earliest efforts to promote
better fire prevention and firefighting practices, P. Alabin explained to readers of
his 1869 pamphlet on village fires that "most often at village fires, anarchy and
disorder reign, made even more powerful by the complete absence of any instruments suitable to the task."[1] Twenty-five years later, contributors to one of the
major firefighting publications asserted that this was still the case. Reporting on
a big fire in the village of Ol'khi, Smolensk Province, in September 1894, one
correspondent stated: "It didn't occur to anyone to try to put out the burning
houses, since each person was trying only to pull his property out of his own
house."[2] Two weeks later, the lead editorial in *The Firefighter* called for greater
zemstvo support for volunteer firefighting as an antidote to the current scenario

at village fires, where "there is an uproar, shouting, absolute chaos, when often a few sensible instructions would be all that is needed to localize the fire and keep it from taking on large proportions."[3]

In reports to the Tenishev Ethnographic Bureau at the end of the century, such images appeared frequently in local observations. S. Mironov declared that fires gained their power in his neck of Saratov Province because of the panic that prevailed and because the peasants behaved "worse than children."[4] From Novgorod Province, N. Brukhanskii wrote: "I've frequently been at fires and witnessed the peasants' panic-stricken inability to join together in common effort to put out the blaze." From Smolensk Province, N. Kuznetsov explained that peasants so often showed up at fires empty-handed, without any kinds of buckets or other equipment, because they were panic stricken, screaming, crying, and wailing.[5] In almost identical terms, A. Vasil'ev reported from Novgorod Province that peasants were panic stricken during fires, when the air filled with "uproar, shouts, cries."[6] Reports of menstruating women being ordered to run around burning structures three times and of villagers throwing milk and eggs at lightning fires convinced Russia's reading public that peasants, as the sole local defenders against fire's voracious power, were at best helpless and at worst dangerously selfish, greedy, inept, and superstitious.[7]

Such depictions of peasant firefighting behaviors presumably rested on their authors' sincere convictions. But they also served several purposes for advocates of the alternative of organized volunteer firefighting. First, they highlighted the perils for Russia that resided in the countryside, encouraging alarmist visions of the desperate but futile struggle of peasants on their own against fire. Second, they mobilized activists to join in the battle against Russia's "historical evil." Third, they provided the opportunity to posit volunteer firefighters as Russia's rightful saviors, who would both guard over and teach the hapless peasants and defeat pernicious, capricious, mighty fire. Fourth, they stressed the virtues that peasants lacked and volunteer firefighting units would provide: mutual assistance through collective effort, organization, and cool-headed reason.

Behind the apparent chaos and selfishness that so offended educated observers, however, there was a system at work. This is only to be expected, for having been left to their own devices in putting out fires for as long as anyone could remember, peasants had developed their own strategy, which one finds time and again in the accounts of panic-stricken disorder. Before the Emancipation, by custom and by formal law, every peasant head of household was obligated to appear at the scene of a village fire with any firefighting equipment he had at his disposal. The village elder was responsible for maintaining a list of what each household had on hand that could be used to fight fires (buckets, ladders, axes, pitchforks, and so on).[8] Any firefighting equipment beyond these items, or further arrangements for fighting fires, rested with private serf owners or administrators of state and crown peasant villages. In the event of enormous runaway fires, military troops stationed in the region could be summoned to help put out the blaze.

Peasants clearly operated on the first principle that it was difficult to extinguish a fire once it started. All available evidence about the speed with which blazes spread confirmed this assumption. Goal number one, therefore, was to get everything they could out of the house, barn, and outbuildings before the straw or wooden roof collapsed. It was indeed "every man for himself" in the division of labor, as each household concentrated on salvaging its own goods. Women focused on the house; men focused on the barns if the animals were indoors. At every village fire, one could expect to find peasants rushing in and out of their homesteads, pulling possessions and livestock out onto the street. Until zemstvos began to insure movable as well as immovable property, this was a financially rational decision, for peasants could expect some compensation if they lost a structure, but none if they lost their animals and goods.

In some areas, there was a division of labor between men, on one hand, and women and children, on the other. The women and children focused on pulling possessions from the burning or threatened structures while the men tried to put the fire out.[9] To do this, they often climbed up to the roof, either to pull off the straw and throw it into the street or to pour water over the rooftops. Women ran to the nearest source of water to fill buckets and pass them up to the men; they also poured water around burning structures in an effort to slow the fire's spread. Women also sometimes plunged sheaves of straw in water, then laid them on the rooftops of houses near the fire.[10] As the people whose houses were already on fire struggled to pull what they could from the blaze, near and distant neighbors focused on extinguishing or containing the flames. This included both peasants from the same village whose houses were out of the fire's path or far from it and peasants from neighboring villages who immediately turned to extinguishing the blaze when they arrived at the scene.[11] Furthermore, once they succeeded in getting their goods out, those whose houses were on fire would turn to the task of destroying the houses in order to diminish the fire's power.[12]

One can well imagine how chaotic this must have seemed to outsiders who arrived at the scene. They would see peasants running in different directions, throwing clothes, mattresses, samovars, dishes, rakes, brooms, pots, and pans into piles in the middle of the street, while other peasants ran around or jumped over those piles lugging buckets of water, wet sheaves of straw, or pitchforks to pull straw from the roofs. Still others were dragging neighing horses, mooing cows, and bleating lambs from the barns or shooing frantic, squawking chickens and geese before them into the street—all in an atmosphere of screams and shouts as men reached down from rooftops to lift water buckets from their wives and daughters, and as children no doubt ran madly about in the excitement, eliciting shouted commands and reprimands from their parents. When fires broke out on holidays, there were usually also quite a few drunks who, like Chekhov's "Muzhiki," stumbled and bumbled in the midst of the mayhem. Reports to the Tenishev Bureau also stressed that peasants considered it essential for a priest to be present; he was to carry an icon aloft, praying as he circled the fire. His figure could only have reinforced the perception that reason itself had gone up in flames, especially when there were indeed peasant bystanders, both male and female, who went into hysteria or shock. In the face of this apparent chaos, zemstvos tried to improve firefighting by decree.

Zemstvo Prescriptions

After the Emancipation, zemstvo fire regulations superseded the specific articles in the Fire Code on firefighting procedures. The Novgorod zemstvo's regulations convey the level of detail that emerged in its efforts to encourage adequate firefighting resources in every village, first through regulations in the 1870s, then through revised prescriptions in 1901. In their effort to prescribe remedies, the regulations also reveal some of the problems observed in fire patterns and firefighting behaviors.

In the 1870s, the Novgorod zemstvo issued more than forty articles dealing with firefighting equipment, fire watches, and firefighting procedures. On equipment, it went beyond the Fire Code to prescribe the numbers of instruments required in each village and to call for the establishment of a storehouse of firefighting tools in each village, "to be kept in churches or other suitable locations." The number of instruments depended upon the size of the village. In 1879, the zemstvo stated that for every ten households in the village, there had to be the following items: one large hook, one oven fork, one three-*sazhen* (around 6.5-meter) ladder, one 20-*vedro* (around 53-gallon) barrel, and two mops to go with it. In addition, every village was to have on hand several hooks, pitchforks, and ladders, as well as a large barrel of water and a conveyance on which to carry it that was appropriate to the season. All these items were to be purchased by the commune at its own expense. The cantonal elder was to keep a list of the inhabi-

Table 8.1: Zemstvo-Required Firefighting Equipment in Novgorod Province, 1901

| Item | Minimum Number of Households in Village | | | | | |
	10	20	40	60	80	200
53-gal. barrels	1	2	3	3	4	4
Gig for summer	1	2	3	3	4	4
Sleigh for winter	1	2	3	3	4	4
12-gal. tubs	2	2	3	3	4	4
Buckets	5	7	10	12	15	20
Hooks	2	3	4	5	6	7
Crowbars	1	1	1	2	2	2
Oven forks	1	1	2	2	3	3
6.5-m ladders	1	1	2	2	2	2
Fire signal	1	1	1	1	1	1

Source: *Proekt ob'iazatel'nyia postanovleniia o merakh predostorozhnosti ot pozharov i o postroikakh v seleniiakh* 1901: 4.

tants of the village and the firefighting instruments they were to bring to a fire. In large villages or cantonal administrative centers, the inhabitants were also encouraged to purchase more sophisticated technologies. In its home, every household was to keep tubs of water, brooms, mops, and ladders in lofts, threshing barns, and other fire-prone locations. During the agricultural season, from June 1 to October 1, every other household was also to keep a large vat or rain barrel full of water on the street in front of its house on alternating weeks.

By 1901, firefighting knowledge had expanded, as had expectations of what was minimally necessary in the way of instruments and equipment. New regulations for Novgorod Province included the items listed in table 8.1. The inclusion of hooks and crowbars in these requirements pointed to their use during fires to destroy structures lying in the fire's path, to pull down beams and framing, and to haul buckets up from the street to rooftops (fig. 8.1).

The Novgorod zemstvo's fire regulations of the 1870s also went beyond the Fire Code in their detailed description of fire watches. Night watchmen were required during all seasons, as well as during the day at times of high need, such as on Sundays and holidays. The special reference to these occasions reflects the linkage between holiday carousing and village fires. Fire watches were a universal obligation for every resident of the village, regardless of estate or occupation. Villages were to be divided into fire districts no larger than 200 *sazhens* (around 425 meters) in length. Households were to contribute a watchman or woman through a system of rotation, to be approved by the cantonal authorities, with each watch consisting of one full night or one full day, and with those whose properties were most valuable serving most frequently. Once the members of the community had designated everyone's dates of service, they were to compile and sign the schedule and send one copy each to the village and cantonal elders, who then enforced it. During the watch, each watchman or woman was to walk around the assigned district, looking in particular for any "smoke at an odd time or in an inappropriate place, or any people moving about stealthily behind outbuildings or beyond them." The watcher was to inspect anything suspicious, and in the case of fire, to inform the residents of that homestead and raise the alarm in the village. Each watcher was to carry noisy rattles to shake in the event of a fire.[13] The 1901 regulations on watches were much more laconic—they were contained in one article that read simply, "In villages of ten homesteads or more, in order to protect them from fire, there must be night watches, and during the period of field work, day watches as well, either hired from communal funds or fulfilled according to a system decided by the communal assembly."[14]

Writing from his country estate in Smolensk Province in 1880, A. N. Engel'gardt derided the compulsory aspects of such night watches, but in doing so he revealed the community's compliance and the local police's ability to intrude and enforce zemstvo regulations.

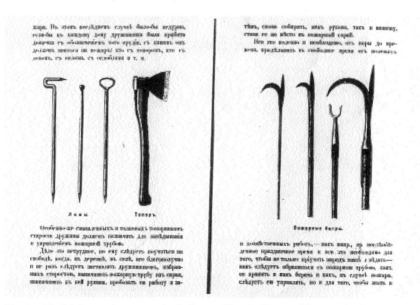

Fig. 8.1. *Firefighting equipment required of every village in Novgorod Province by the 1901 regulations.* Source: Pozharnoe delo 1902.

In one village the peasants told how a peasant woman had to be the night watchman in the winter; it was their household's turn and her husband was not there. So she . . . went back into the izba to breast-feed her child. . . . And to her misfortune, the police official turns up. "What's this? Where is the guard?" He shouted out, the noise filled the entire village, he gave the woman a five-ruble fine. Five rubles! . . . Five rubles! and her husband will beat her besides. The woman became afraid, she began to beg him to have mercy, she dragged on his feet, but he stood firm, with his arms akimbo, he laughed, he was cheerful![15]

The regulations issued by the Novgorod zemstvo in the 1870s on what village inhabitants had to do in the event of a fire were straightforward and hewed closely to those of the Fire Code. They called for every adult resident of a village in which fire broke out to go to the scene with his or her registered equipment, and for one adult from every homestead located within five *versts* of the village where the fire was to do the same. The only excuse was absence from the village at the time of the fire. Further, these regulations stated that local military regiments were to assist in extinguishing large blazes. In order to prevent confusion at the scene, sole command rested with either a police official or the village fire chief. Finally, the fire chief could seize "the first horse he saw" to pull the barrels of water to the fire. The 1901 revision made no important changes, except to state that residents were obligated to bring their horses with their tack and gear to the scene of the blaze.[16]

These regulations and others like them in other zemstvo provinces reveal the extent to which the imperial government continued to avoid financial and practical responsibility for the peasant population's defense against fire. Having left this duty to local serf owners and their serfs before Emancipation, it shifted the burden to the peasants themselves afterward, while placing the responsibility for developing and enforcing regulations on the zemstvos and local police. The result was that well into the 1890s, there was very little progress on the village front in the battle against fires once they broke out.

Noble Initiatives and Messianic Impulses

At the highest levels of Russia's privileged noble estate and among less prominent gentry and officials of the government and zemstvos, there were men who recognized the gap between the local resources available to the peasants and the government's limited largesse. They chose to step into the breach to marshal individuals from the local population in the campaign against fire. They founded volunteer firefighting brigades in the villages of European Russia as the latest form of firefighting in imperial Russia. The brigades lagged behind both state and volunteer systems in Russia's cities and towns by at least a century. In the imperial capital cities and in provincial capitals and towns, government firefighting units were attached to the local police under the Ministry of the Interior. Volunteer firefighting societies emerged in some provincial towns early in the century, but they were weak and often objects of ridicule. After the Emancipation, volunteer units in towns multiplied as a manifestation of the general activization of society during the reform era.

In Smolensk Province, for example, a volunteer firefighting society (*obshchestvo*) formed in 1874 in the capital city to engage local citizens in the battle against fire. The society's historian explained that the city needed a volunteer organization despite efforts by the central government to provide the city with a fire station and equipment, first in 1830 and again in 1860. Equipment alone was not enough, because "just as before, there was no proper, efficient battle against fire, there was no unity of action, there were no experienced leaders who could have shown exactly what to do and on exactly which section of the fire to apply one's efforts."[17] Within a year, 288 men had joined the society, donned uniforms, and were receiving training in their respective positions in the firefighting unit. By 1898, the society had fought more than 270 fires and grown to 517 dues-paying, firefighting members.[18]

In addition to such volunteer societies in provincial towns, there were also police units and units attached to factories in towns and rural factory communities. In the countryside, members of the gentry organized firefighting to meet factory owners' needs. Gentry dedication to service and the protection of property also led to the formation of some firefighting units. In 1892, in all of European Russia, there were around 215 volunteer firefighting units in cities and some 1,876 firefighting units in the countryside, 117 units attached to factories, and 12 private brigades.[19] They were scattered among almost 600,000 communities (or one for every 300). Organized firefighting was still "embryonic" at the end of the nineteenth century in imperial Russia.[20] By 1904, a contributor to *The Firefighter's Cause* estimated that there were around 100,000 firefighters serving Russia's population of roughly 140 million, or one firefighter for every 1,400 people.[21] Noble initiatives were central in these developments.

Scions of two of Russia's oldest families, Prince A. D. L'vov and Count A. D. Sheremetev, established, financially supported, and participated in firefighting brigades on their country estates, then spearheaded the formation of an empire-wide organization of volunteer firemen. Provincial and local zemstvo boards offered financial assistance to village units, and peasants joined as members of the brigades. Volunteer firefighting societies and brigades seemed to promise a kind of fraternity among Russian men from various estates that had previously existed only in the most idealized visions of military unity in the service of national defense. This was especially true of village brigades, although city brigades also provided opportunities for cross-class partnership. With Prince L'vov and Count Sheremetev the most visible figures at the center of the movement in the capital, volunteer firefighting at the village level held tremendous appeal for those seeking social harmony in a time of social differentiation, growing liberal activism, and urbanization.

The governments of both Alexander III and Nicholas II endorsed volunteer firefighting organizations for this reason. Minister of the Interior I. N. Durnovo chaired the first conference on firefighting in 1892, which Sheremetev and L'vov had organized with the government's approval.[22] Durnovo's opening speech stressed the importance of collaborative efforts and a spirit of cooperation in achieving success where government efforts and scattered individual initiatives had failed.[23] Under Sheremetev's leadership, the United Russian Firefighters' Society received its charter from the Ministry of the Interior on March 23, 1893, and quickly gathered into its membership thirteen existing volunteer firefighting societies from provincial towns. The grand opening of the society took place in May 1893 on Sheremetev's estate, Ul'ianka, near St. Petersburg, with Grand Duke Vladimir Aleksandrovich serving as honorary chair of the session.[24]

It was clearly important to the leaders of the society to cultivate relations with the tsar and his family. When conferences convened, they exchanged telegrams with the tsar. Upon the occasion of Alexander III's death, they established a fund in his name and received an audience with Nicholas II to describe its purpose. In honor of Nicholas II's coronation, Prince L'vov and others met with him again to present him with an icon of Christ in a pale blue velvet case faced with watercolor paintings of firefighting scenes. In these ways, they were able to represent their cause as both noble and sacred, appealing to Nicholas II's spiritual sentiments and his self-image as the protector of his land. When the society launched a traveling firefighting exhibit on a riverboat in 1897, several grand dukes and duchesses attended its inauguration in St. Petersburg. *The Firefighter's Cause* ran a series of portraits of members of the royal family and key ministers who served as patrons of the volunteer movement in 1901, devoting the front page of each issue to the portrait and often a short description of the individual's support as well. The imperial couple who could be considered the paternal and maternal patrons of the movement, Grand Duke Vladimir Aleksandrovich and Grand Duchess Maria Pavlovna, were featured in this way on the occasion of their twenty-fifth wedding anniversary (fig. 8.2). That each branch of the society outfitted its men in special uniforms reinforced the image of noble service to the nation by men of stature and loyalty to the Crown. On the five-year anniversary of the society's founding, Nicholas II granted it the title "Imperial" to replace the previous "United" Russian Firefighting Society.

These royal connections and rituals undoubtedly fed the nobility's need to fill a special role between tsar and people. Leading the rural firefighting movement granted them a tutelary position over the lower estates in a national cause. This restored some sense of the noble mission that the emancipation of the serfs and subsequent reforms and economic developments had eroded. Women in both Prince L'vov's and Count Sheremetev's families were simultaneously turning their energies to founding folk art workshops, where they were training peasant women to produce traditional art forms for the commercial market.[25] Volunteer fire brigades for the men and folk art workshops for the women offered noble men and women outlets for continuing to guide the peasants who lived near their estates.

Whether driven by emotional needs or pragmatic considerations, these efforts to nurture linkages with the court worked to the volunteer firefighters' advantage. Whereas zemstvos had been unable to extract permission for empire-wide conferences to discuss fire prevention and insurance programs, the volunteer firefighting societies were able to coordinate and consult in periodic conferences from 1892 forward and to send sizable numbers of delegates to international firefighting conferences in Paris, London, and Berlin.[26] In courting the royal family, volunteer firefighters may have taken their lead from the British, where one of London's most successful fire chiefs, Sir Eyre Massy Shaw, was able to recruit the Prince of Wales to serve in a London volunteer fire brigade and thus to attract larger numbers of educated men who sought fashionable associations with the Crown.[27]

Both L'vov and Sheremetev came to their national leadership roles through personal experience and experimentation on their estates. Sheremetev first established two firefighting teams in 1877 on his estate in the village of Voronovo in Podol'sk District of Moscow Province. When he sold the estate in 1883, he moved the teams to separate estates, one to Ul'ianka in Petersburg Province, the other to Vysokoe in Sychev District, Smolensk Province. Each team included thirty firefighters, seventeen horses, a fire wagon with two

Его Императорское Высочество Великій Князь
ВЛАДИМІРЪ АЛЕКСАНДРОВИЧЪ
Августѣйшій Предсѣдатель
Императорскаго Россійскаго Пожарнаго Общества.

Ея Императорское Высочество Великая Княгиня
МАРІЯ ПАВЛОВНА
Августѣйшая Покровительница
Всероссійской Передвижной Пожарной Выставки.

Fig. 8.2. *Portraits of firefighting patrons Grand Duke Vladimir Aleksandrovich and Grand Duchess Maria Pavlovna, featured in the magazine* The Firefighter's Cause *in 1901.*

pumps, sixteen barrels, five ladders, and hoses totaling 184 *sazhens* (around 400 meters) in length. Sheremetev also installed fire alarms, telegraph lines, and telephones, which eventually covered a population of almost fifty-five hundred people.[28] L'vov took the initiative in his community after several big fires in 1879–1880 demonstrated that the state-funded firefighting unit in Peterhof, seven *versts* distant from his estate, could take as long as two to three hours to arrive at a village fire. Before summer arrived in 1880, he purchased a fire hose; then a devastating runaway fire in the village of Izhorka in July convinced him that someone had to supply the local population with more technical assistance. He took it upon himself to buy a complete set of fire wagon, pump, and hose and to organize a firefighting brigade. He set up a fire station at one of the family's summer cottages and built a watchtower on the roof. By 1882, the brigade included eleven firefighters and the local zemstvo-funded physician's assistant. In order to solve the problem of communication between villages, L'vov sought Ministry of the Interior permission to install a telegraph system through all the most densely populated areas in the region, which he extended in 1887 to Sheremetev's estate in Ul'ianka. Sheremetev and L'vov also installed telephones on these lines. By 1892, there were twenty-seven men in L'vov's brigade, with fifteen horses. L'vov himself covered all of the expenses. In the first eleven years of its existence, the brigade fought 191 fires in the area.[29] Later, L'vov purchased an automobile in Paris, which he converted into a fire engine, and in 1904 he donated a half-acre plot of his land on the outskirts of St. Petersburg to the Imperial Russian Firefighters' Society for the construction of a firefighting training station.[30]

Prince L'vov and Count Sheremetev continued to feel a paternalistic responsibility for the inhabitants of the villages surrounding their estates, as well as an obligation to serve their country through the expenditure of their personal wealth and the exercise of their managerial abilities in the absence of adequate state provisions for firefighting. They were equally fascinated with new technologies and rational approaches to firefighting, that is, with the application of reason and science to cure this social and economic ill. Priscilla Roosevelt has described noble estates as "powerful cultural agents" and as islands scattered in an "archipelago" across the vastness of European Russia.[31] This is an apt metaphor for L'vov's and Sheremetev's estates as crucibles of the volunteer firefighting movement. Having come up with solutions in their small worlds, they gained the confidence to publicize and replicate them through a national network of volunteer organizations. They brought with them to the movement their mix of paternalism, dedication to service and the virtues of mutual assistance, search for reason, and faith in technology.

Religious overtones also characterized the noble leaders' definition of their cause. Sheremetev sounded this note in a speech he delivered in 1894. He was addressing a group of peasant officials (among others) who had approached him as a director of the United Russian Firefighters' Society to support their efforts to establish a volunteer brigade in Petersburg District, Petersburg Province. The supplicants feared that the town fire officials in Ul'ianka would block their charter. Sheremetev tried to reassure them by saying:

Our cause is pure and just, and God is on the side of the just. The path to salvation is narrow and full of thorns, while a wide and smooth path leads only to perdition. The very fact that we are encountering obstacles in our path serves as proof that our cause is sacred. We should regard all that has happened as only a test, sent down to us by Providence to fortify our faith. I firmly believe that the current state of affairs will not last long and that the brigade will open. Be courageous and pray, and He Who said, "Ask and you shall receive," will hear you and will send down consolation in your sorrow.[32]

At the other extreme from this prolix moralizing was L'vov's succinct statement in 1898 to the members of the United Russian Firefighters' Society on its fifth anniversary, and to Nicholas II and the archpriest V. I Pereterskii, who were present: "Russia is burning and she needs rational assistance."[33] Faithful messianism and clear-eyed rationalism combined to give noble birth to village firefighting in late imperial Russia.

For Sheremetev and many others who wrote on the volunteer firefighting movement in Russia's villages, there was indeed something sacred in what they were doing: individual sacrifice through mutual assistance in the service of the community, and trying to relieve, if not prevent, the suffering of the unfortunate. This conviction lent the movement its messianic quality. Even when he was addressing educated Russians, Sheremetev defined the firefighters' cause as a moral one, explaining that "as long as the world is unable to part with this powerful engine of human culture and progress [that is, fire], until then it is educated society's [*obshchestvo's*] absolute moral duty to apply the most zealous efforts to the salvation of those who are the unfortunate victims of fire."[34] Furthermore, the moral force of the movement found its expression in its mutuality, its *vzaimnost'*, whose wellspring was *sobornost'*, the reciprocity and gathering together that characterized Russian Orthodoxy as the national religion. Devoid of Sheremetev's references to God and Christ, a pamphlet by I. O. Fesenko on organizing village volunteer units pressed this point: "Man's victory over all that surrounds him depends completely on both the development of his mental forces and abilities, and on the fact that people, helping each other mutually, combine to form a great and invincible force. And truly, what one individual cannot do, people, if they can help each other, can do successfully!"[35]

That mutual assistance, however, required the application of "mental forces and abilities" to ensure success. The insistence on reason as the antonym of hysteria, and on order as the curative for chaos, provided the key elements of the pragmatism of the movement. As Fesenko continued: "Order in life, everywhere and in everything, is a great thing, and all the more so in the struggle with such a calamity as fire."[36]

Brigades: Brotherhoods in Action

Ultimately, the products of the volunteer firefighting movement were not sermons but conference proceedings, traveling exhibitions, pamphlets and brochures on firefighting directed at the peasant population, newspapers, and the volunteer fire brigades themselves with their fire stations and equipment. Just as in the zemstvo fire insurance program, the Russian tradition of mutual assistance and the sanctification of mutuality joined with the seemingly competing faith in reason, science, linear organization, and technology. Although the initial motivation may have been moral, even religious, the movement came to embrace several features of high modernism. Willy-nilly, engagement in the campaign against fire in European Russia's villages drew even the most idealistic and ethereal of proponents into the material reality of Russia's villages and toward the conviction that, however much they might accomplish in fighting individual fires and drawing peasants into collective and more orderly training, only the imperial government could genuinely solve the "fire question" through massive subsidies to undertake a wholesale reconstruction of European Russia's villages.

Volunteer firefighting in late imperial Russia involved more than a group of noblemen trying to carve out a sphere of activity for their interests and sense of place in Russian culture; it also encompassed town societies and village brigades (fig. 8.3). The number of village brigades increased substantially after 1897, when the state issued a new law that both made it possible for peasants to

Fig. 8.3. *Volunteer firefighting brigades in Vologda Province. Top, 1869–1870. Bottom, early twentieth century.*

initiate a volunteer firefighting unit and provided a standard form for the charters that would speed up the approval process. Before then, village units tended to be the products of noble initiative, as in the case of Sheremetev's activities around his Vysokoe estate. Within a year of its founding in 1893, there were 925 members on the force, of whom 18 were solely donors and 10 were honorary members. The remaining 897 were peasants, all active firefighters. The honorary members included the land captains and police chiefs over each division, as well as the governor. Sheremetev divided the region they served into thirteen separate divisions, then purchased a fully outfitted fire wagon for each division, with hooks, crowbars, ladders, and barrels of water, all to be pulled by one horse.[37]

Sheremetev and other local gentry joined with the peasants around his estate in Ul'ianka in 1894 to organize its volunteer fire brigade. In a characteristic nod to the royal family, the brigade named itself the Peter the Great brigade and sought the patronage of Empress Maria Fedorovna. Following a devastating fire in a village only twelve *versts* from St. Petersburg (roughly seven miles), which burned the entire village before the Ul'ianka town fire unit arrived, the local peasants and gentry concluded that "it is not enough to have a well organized fire unit nearby; it is necessary to have, in the village itself, a cadre of people who are experienced firefighters, capable of providing assistance immediately," as well as firefighting equipment. The Peter the Great brigade received its charter from the Ministry of the Interior in late February, 1894. By 1901, it had six hundred members, thirty fire hoses, one mechanical ladder, several scaling ladders, and a "complete set of rescue instruments."[38] The brigade's pride in its technological inventory is obvious in the staging of the photograph it submitted to *The Firefighter's Cause* in that year (fig. 8.4).

Information that Sheremetev received from local officials in 1892 in response to a survey he conducted on organized firefighting in the empire, as well as reports to firefighting publications, offer miniature portraits of firefighting units that crossed social boundaries. The brigades drew Russian men of peasant, merchant, clergy, and noble background into shoulder-to-shoulder and hand-over-hand cooperation with one another. According to Sheremetev's data, the provinces with the greatest numbers of village firefighting brigades were Voronezh (136), Nizhnii Novgorod (286), Penza (260), Pskov (100), Riazan (100), Saratov (426), Simbirsk (182), and Khar'kov (131). In Bogucharsk District, Voronezh Province, alone, there were 136 village brigades, often comprising large numbers of local residents, as in the case of the Berezov Canton, where 1,110 villagers participated in 10 separate brigades.[39] The Arzamass District in Nizhnii Novgorod Province similarly had 117 village brigades spread across 24

Пожарная Дружина имени Петра Великаго.

Fig. 8.4. *Sheremetev's Peter the Great fire brigade. Reproduced from* The Firefighter's Cause, *1901.*

cantons; in Sliznevsk Canton, 1,054 villagers served in 11 brigades.[40] Sheremetev did not specify whether these were volunteer brigades. He did identify the Dno village brigade in Pskov Province as a volunteer unit, manned by 104 rank-and-file firefighters plus 13 specialists. These 127 men served a region that included 909 households and 5,375 residents.[41] A volunteer unit of 272 men in the Pargolovo settlement of St. Petersburg Province was among the empire's most active, fighting 127 fires between its founding in 1876 and 1891, or more than 8 fires per year. Another St. Petersburg volunteer unit in the village of Lakhta boasted 127 men who served a community with 640 households and a population of 3,600.[42]

Whether as volunteers, village employees, or conscripts fighting fires as a form of "natural tax," the men in these village brigades joined the many fire activists who had taken up the challenge of fighting fire rather than submitting passively to it. They had become part of the struggle against futility and for futurity. After 1897, this opportunity was open to all citizens who wanted to found a volunteer village firefighting brigade. Following the publication of the model charter for volunteer brigades in that year, Fesenko explained in his firefighting manual, "anyone who wants to can be a member of a firefighting society: the poor and the rich, the strong and the weak—there is always work for everyone when a calamity such as fire strikes."[43]

The engagement of people from all levels of Russian society, from scions of ancient noble families to civil servants living in provincial towns and peasants living in villages, set the Russian volunteer firefighting movement apart from some of its European counterparts. In France, for example, the nineteenth century witnessed the decline of participation by members of the gentry and the professional classes and the expansion of workers and peasants in a process one historian has dubbed the "proletarianization" of firefighting.[44] Whereas members of the upper orders in France came to disdain participation in firefighting, which some perceived as "an indignity," in European Russia, members of the nobility saw themselves as mobilizers and patrons whose obligations and roles continued to include leading extragovernmental organizations and drawing peasants into active participation in them.

As the volunteer movement grew, it began to assume attributes of civil society at the same time it cultivated dynastic patrons. The naming of firefighting units in the 1890s reflected the distinctions being drawn between volunteer units and units attached to the police and military. In his 1892 survey, Sheremetev used the term *komanda*, which had military connotations, to refer to all units, and he broke them down further into the categories of urban, rural, military, private, and volunteer. By the mid-1890s, *komanda* was used in firefighting literature to refer only to police and military units whose members received regular salaries. Volunteer firefighting organizations in cities and towns, by contrast, were called societies (*obshchestva*), a term that made them microcosms of the larger phenomenon of society as distinct from the state, and of the vision of engaged citizens actively serving popular causes. Village units were called *druzhiny*, a term that has as its root the word for friend and harks back to the most ancient military associations in Russia's historical memory. This appellation had as much to do with the verb *druzhit'*, meaning to unite or to make friends, as it did with the historical reference to Kievan and Novgorodian princes' military forces. Summoning peasants to enter *druzhiny* thus meant calling them to unite with their friends and neighbors as popular soldiers in the campaign against fire.

After 1897, a group of prospective volunteers had only to follow the standard charter approved by the Ministry of the Interior on August 5, 1897, in order to receive permission to form and begin operating. Once the standard charter was in place, zemstvos began to support village brigades in earnest. Table 8.2 lists the financial contributions of various zemstvo boards to brigades in their provinces.

In Tver Province, the combination of a standard charter and the promise of zemstvo assistance had a noticeable effect on the establishment of volunteer brigades. Whereas there were only six volunteer brigades in the province when the standard charter went into effect, ten new brigades were formed in 1898, another eleven in 1899, and six more in 1900.[45] By 1903, the number of village brigades in zemstvo provinces had risen to 781, with Pskov, Smolensk, Tver, Novgorod, and Kaluga Provinces reporting the most extensive networks of village volunteer firefighters (table 8.3).

Brigades did not have to receive zemstvo funds in order to form, however. Instead, they had to submit a charter in its standard form, or one with a nearly identical set of requirements. The standard charter, however, was no simple instrument. On the contrary, its forty-nine articles provided standard guidelines to which any village brigade had to adhere, or to approximate very closely. Joining the volunteer firefighting movement through membership in a village brigade meant engagement not only with one's neighbors to serve the local community but also with the state through compliance with written regulations. Like the compulsory zemstvo insurance program, the cantonal court system, and the communal system of tax collection, volunteer firefighting drew peasants into a maze of prescribed procedures and activities.[46] These, in turn, defined the goals of any such volunteer brigade as those that served the state's interests by expanding the number of private citizens who assumed public responsibilities in the campaign against fire. In the model charter, following the first article's basic

Table 8.2: Zemstvo Financial Support for Volunteer Brigades after 1897

Province	Rubles
Iaroslavl	9,300 in 1903
Moscow	9,163 in 1903
Novgorod	11,850 in grants, 1,500 in loans in 1903
Penza	1,000 in 1903
Saratov	1,800 over 1898–1900 (9 brigades)
Smolensk	4,375 in 1903
Tver	50 each to 33 brigades in 1900
Viatka	900 over 1899–1903
Vladimir	100–500 per brigade in grants (1903: 6,000)
Voronezh	15,300 in 1903 (51 brigades)

Source: Veselovskii 1909: 622.

Table 8.3: Numbers of Village Volunteer Fire Brigades in Zemstvo Provinces in 1903

Village	No. Brigades	Village	No. Brigades
Bessarabia	3	Kursk	3
Poltava	1	Tauride	1
Chernigov	16	Moscow	41
Pskov	165	Tula	13
Ekaterinoslav	4	Nizhnii Novgorod	31
Riazan	10	Tver	58
Iaroslavl	19	Novgorod	52
St. Petersburg	22	Ufa	4
Kaluga	52	Olonets	20
Samara	4	Viatka	2
Kazan	3	Orel	32
Saratov	20	Vladimir	20
Khar'kov	1	Penza	3
Simbirsk	5	Voronezh	31
Kostroma	5	Perm	25
Smolensk	114		

Source: "Ocherk sovremennogo sostoianie pozharnogo dela v zemskikh guberniiakh Rossii," *Pozharnoe delo*, no. 35 (September 6, 1903): 565.

statement of the brigade's geographic location, the second article listed other duties beyond the broad definition of preventing and extinguishing fires. Among these was every volunteer's duty to enforce the particulars of the Building Code and the Fire Code by reporting to the police administration any infraction he observed in his community. By agreeing to these terms, every volunteer firefighter promised to become a volunteer building and fire inspector, as well. The charter also stated that anyone who failed to fulfill any duty assigned to him could be excluded through a vote by an assembly of the company's members.

Membership in the brigade offered not only technical training in fighting fires but also opportunities for administrative experience and local control, especially when direction of the brigade was in peasant hands, as it was in the Novo-Pokrovskaia brigade in Voronezh Province at the turn of the century.[47] Volunteer firefighters had numerous opportunities to develop organizational skills by participating in activities that became prerogatives of the brigades by grant of the charter—that is, making decisions on admission and exclusion of members, election of leadership, assignment of duties, the budget, granting of awards for exceptional service, length of tenure for any elected officers in the brigade, election of honorary members, purchase and sale of immovable property, setting salaries for any elected officials, and responding to complaints made against individual members or officers of the brigade. All of these matters were to be decided by the general assembly of the brigade's members (*obshchim skhodom*). Every brigade member over the age of twenty-one had the right to vote at the general assembly, with a simple majority of those present deciding most questions. A two-thirds majority was required for any changes in the company's charter, the election of an honorary patron and any honorary members, the premature removal of any elected official from his duties, the exclusion of any member, the purchase of property, and the decision to close the brigade down. The assembly was also to record each vote in a book specific to that purpose.

Members elected to the administration of the brigade (either as the fire chief or to the team of administrators) were responsible for bookkeeping, voting records, and communication of news to all members.[48] Just as the expansion of the zemstvo's powers in fire prevention and insurance programs departs from the accepted view of the zemstvo "counterreform" of 1890, so these detailed instructions in local democracy and organization are exceptions to Nicholas II's aversion to local activism and extrastate organs of control. Certainly these departures from the norm should not transform our understanding of the reactionary nature of the last two tsars. They do, however, underscore the prominence that rural fire and arson assumed in the state's vision and the power fire's threat had to force the state's hand open farther than was its wont.

The public face of volunteer firefighting in the countryside made the expansive gestures that much easier to make. The noble leadership of the Imperial Russian Firefighters' Society, in the persons of Prince L'vov, Count Sheremetev, and their peers, sent constantly reassuring signals to the tsar, his family, and his ministers. The reports of volunteer firefighting activities published in *The Firefighter* and *The Firefighter's Cause* offered equally inviting images of a village Nicholas II could embrace with pride as his own. The brigades' public celebrations, photographed portraits in uniform, and role as warriors against Russia's "historical evil" mirrored Nicholas's self-image as paternalistic benefactor and protector over his land and people.[49] Sheremetev's sincere, but also fortuitous, emphasis on the moral element in volunteer firefighting was sure to strike a sympathetic chord, as were any reports of overtly religious elements in the staging of volunteer firefighting displays.

An eyewitness account provided to *The Firefighter's Cause* in 1902 by an anonymous *druzhinnik* (volunteer firefighter) from Vladimir Province offered an especially appealing vision of what the movement generated in the countryside.[50] He reported on the festive launching of two new divisions of the Fominki settlement brigade, one in the village of Rebrov, the second in Sergievo-Gorsk. Both celebrations were community events that paid homage to tsar, church, and volunteers. On May 23, the full complement of fifty-six firefighters in the Rebrov brigade held a procession through the town, carrying icons and banners, accompanied by local clergymen and firefighters from the neighboring division from Ogryzkovsk. The procession halted at the location of the fire depot for a religious service, which concluded with a singing of the *mnogoletie* (a prayerful wish for a long life) for the tsar, his family, Grand Duke Vladimir Aleksandrovich as the royal patron of firefighters, and all firefighters in Russia. The procession continued to the church, where the firefighters returned the icons they had carried. The final event of the celebration was a fire drill, during which the brigade's "red fire engine" was driven through the village to the delight of the crowd of one thousand spectators.

The celebration in Sergievo-Gorsk, fifteen *versts* away, on June 9 followed much the same script. At three o'clock in the afternoon, the church bell began ringing, signaling a prayer service for the one hundred firefighters who had gathered. From there, they proceeded with icons and banners to their firehouse, where a prayer service began, with local officials in attendance. The guests included the land captain, a provincial zemstvo fire agent, representatives from other neighboring village brigades, honorary guests, and a large crowd of spectators. A local priest opened with a sermon stressing the need to provide assistance to one's brethren in time of need because of fire. As in Rebrov, the service concluded with the *mnogoletie* for the tsar, his family, and all fire activists. For its fire drill, the Sergievo-Gorsk brigade started two fires (one in the cantonal administrative offices and the other at a peasant's house), which they extinguished in model fashion. Their display was particularly striking because of the participation of several young priests from the local church, who rushed over from services, donned helmets, and fought the fire in their robes, side by side with their fellow members of the brigade. As the reporter opined, their presence provided another level of spiritual support for the brigade members as they strove "to realize along with us the idea of the firefighting cause and self-defense against fire disasters."

Icons, priests, church services, and prayers for tsar and royal family—these expressions of popular piety and fealty to the Crown within the familiar context of a village procession made volunteer firefighters ideal citizens in late imperial, autocratic, Orthodox Russia. But it is the image of the firefighter priests, those young men wearing black robes and fire helmets, that is most arresting. It offers a portrait in miniature of the peculiar mix of Orthodox morality and modernist technology that informed the volunteer firefighting movement in rural Russia. Not only Count Sheremetev, at the head of the movement, but also local organizers and the peasant volunteers themselves found in volunteer firefighting collective actions of united service as vivid fulfillment of biblical injunctions to be good Samaritans. Despite the self-conscious secularism and rejection of apocalyptic fatalism before God's punishment in the form of fire that Isaev had proclaimed in 1894 as editor of *The Firefighter's Cause*, and despite Prince L'vov's insistence on the need for "rational assistance" in 1898, Orthodox teachings and communal traditions of mutual aid made volunteer firefighting a natural phenomenon for European Russia. Spiritual and community values validated engagement in this new form of helping one's brothers and sisters. They made the countervailing values of science, technology, and reason less obvious, perhaps less threatening. Priests of the Orthodox church could serve directly as fire activists both in fighting fires and in counseling their parishioners. Among the pastoral duties for parish priests in the late nineteenth century were counseling peasants on fire prevention measures and participating in volunteer firefighting.[51] When the young priests of Sergievo Gorsk put fire helmets over their long hair, they saw no contradiction between service to God and fighting fire to protect their parishioners from fiery victimization.

Technology to the Rescue

The helmets were as important as the robes in defining the movement. Technology loomed large in the list of requirements for success against fire in rural Russia. The red fire engine that drove through Rebrov was every volunteer organizer's dream for his unit, but for few brigades was it easily available, because of its cost. More modest technologies were at hand, however, and they figured as prominently in annual reports and larger surveys as did the numbers of men who had joined the brigades. These technologies included such basic items as buckets, ladders, and crowbars, and more complex items such as fire hoses. Every issue of *The Firefighter* and *The Firefighter's Cause* published information in a "Technical Department" column on firefighting technologies and how to use them, as well as large advertisements from companies that sold them in the advertising back pages of each edition (fig. 8.5). For some fire activists, technology promised to vitalize the movement in nearly miraculous ways. One former zemstvo fire agent rhapsodized in 1902: "The acquisition of a new fire hose, especially if this hose turns out to be strong, will give birth to initiative among the peasants, firefighting enthusiasts will appear, often volunteer firefighting brigades will emerge, which, in turn, in the battle against the terrible enemy of the people's economic well-being-against fire, will produce from their midst daredevils and heroes."[52]

When Sheremetev surveyed localities' firefighting organizations, he included a question about each unit's inventory of equipment. For European Russia as a whole, including units funded by the state and private enterprises as well as volunteer societies and brigades, he received reports of the following items for 1892: 4,371 wagons, 146 steam engines, 8,985 fire hoses, 3,498 pumps, 33,600 barrels, 4,350 hooks, and 178 reels for hoses.[53] It is worth recalling that this equipment was at

Fig. 8.5. *An advertisement for firefighting equipment, typical of those published in* The Firefighter *and* The Firefighter's Cause.

the disposal of 600,000 communities and a population of roughly 140 million. The vast majority of village firefighters found themselves in the preindustrial era as the final decade of the nineteenth century began. In this, they were in much the same condition as rural communities in Britain, where mechanized firefighting devices also proved to be extremely rare beyond the borders of private estates.[54] In the United States, as well, firefighting materiel came late and in small quantities to rural communities. As late as the 1950s, one of Virginia's rural counties had only one fire engine.[55] A century earlier in Russia, provincial zemstvo boards and their fire agents joined the central leadership of the volunteer movement in recognizing that this was an area in which specific actions could lead to tangible results. The allure of technological solutions was that they seemed so controllable, in contrast to the attitudes, behaviors, and physical conditions of daily living that prevailed in Russia's villages.

When zemstvo boards allocated funds to enable local brigades to purchase firefighting equipment, they were behaving much as fire insurance companies had in Britain and the United States. They also assumed the leading role both in organizing firefighting and in equipping brigades in the eighteenth and nineteenth centuries. In Britain, insurance companies formed their own brigades to protect buildings they insured, while setting rates in ways to force policyholders to build in fire-resistant materials. In the United States as well, insurance companies were the earliest enthusiasts of steam engines, which they embraced along with paid firemen in a dual threat to the existing volunteer firefighting movement in cities.[56] In Russia, the existence of firefighting equipment producers and distributors testifies to a firefighting market as well.

Zemstvo financial support for firefighting technology came in three forms: outright gifts of equipment, loans to communities and brigades for the purchase of equipment, and grants for the purchase of equipment. Some zemstvos also tried to protect communities from full-scale commercial competition by establishing their own factories or equipment repair shops, hiring master repairmen, or arranging special pricing and financing terms with equipment distributors. Everywhere, the issues were money and the peasants' shallow economic resources. Because it was the local commune's, village's, or brigade's responsibility to pay for whatever equipment it hoped to acquire, access to technology was extremely limited. That access was usually expanded only as the local zemstvo fire insurance program began to accumulate enough of a reserve fund to direct rubles toward equipment.

The most generous of the zemstvos was the Viatka provincial zemstvo. In 1873, the board opened its own factory, and by 1903 it had spent 786,866 rubles on supplying the local population with equipment. Beginning in 1873 also, it hired a staff of circuit repairmen to maintain fire hoses in the province. The Khar'kov, Moscow, and Nizhnii Novgorod provincial zemstvos were also active and generous in this field. Khar'kov budgeted 10 percent of its insurance funds for equipment in 1874; beginning in 1875 it shifted to an annual allocation of 25,000 rubles, and in 1900, to an annual allocation of 45,000 rubles. In Moscow and Nizhnii Novgorod, zemstvo expenditures for equipment grew rapidly in the 1890s. The Moscow board supplied 84,728 rubles in loans and 47,624 rubles in grants from 1873 to 1889; in 1903 alone, it offered 20,917 rubles in grants. The Nizhnii Novgorod board operated a credit line for the purchase of equipment. Between 1898 and 1904, it issued 92,493 rubles through this system.[57] In Krasnoufimskii District, Perm Province, by 1903, the zemstvo's generosity had enabled village brigades to purchase 302 fire wagons with all requisite equipment and apparatus; 259 of these were described as *mashiny* (engines).[58] Not all of the equipment purchased through zemstvo assistance went to village communities, for town societies could also make use of the options for financial support. Still, zemstvo assistance was essential for villages and communes that maintained volunteer firefighting units and hoped to equip them with technologies beyond buckets, mops, axes, and ladders. Village assemblies also contributed to village brigades directly through collected donations. In zemstvo provinces alone, assemblies assigned 1.4 million rubles to firefighting units in 1900.[59]

The technologies available ranged from barrels to steam engines and, by the time Prince L'vov donated his purchase to his brigade, an automobile converted into a fire engine. These assisted any firefighter in achieving the steps necessary to limiting a fire's impact: denying the blaze its fuel in the form of oxygen and flammable materials, saving lives, saving property, and protecting the firefighter from injury. By the 1890s, the Russian market offered chimney caps to shut down the flow of oxygen into a burning house; hooks and ladders to enable firefighters to reach the roofs or upper stories of burning structures; manual fire pumps and fire hoses to draw water and direct it at flames; large barrels to be filled with water, along with carts or sleighs to convey them to the scene of the fire; crowbars and axes to break down wooden buildings in the fire's path; pitchforks to throw straw from thatched roofs; portable reels for fire hoses; steam pumps; specialty harnesses for the horses who had to pull the fire wagons; and fully equipped fire engines (fig. 8.6). For signaling, most communities continued to rely on the traditional methods of ringing the church bell or banging on

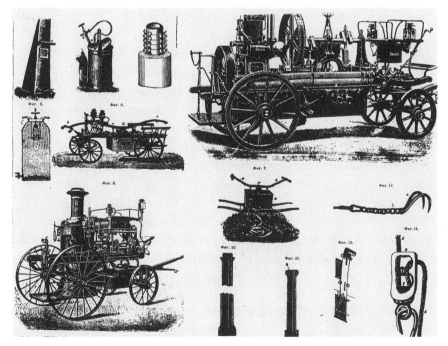

Fig. 8.6. *Firefighting equipment illustrated in* Entsiklopedicheskii slovarí, *1897.*

boards, but some enjoyed the good fortune of telegraph systems such as those installed by Sheremetev and L'vov.

The Russian firefighting movement was au courant about what was available worldwide. One of the first four effective, lightweight steam engines designed in England by Braithwaite and Ericsson was bought by Russia and was in use by 1833, along with identical models in Berlin, London, and France— fully two years before the Great Fire of 1835 in New York City inspired insurance companies there to order one.[60] The government ordered a new model from the English firm of Shand and Mason in 1858. In 1863, following the St. Petersburg fires, the Imperial Public Library there ordered a steam fire engine from T. W. Cowan of Greenwich, England, which offered the latest design and weighed in at four tons, to be drawn by three horses.[61] The challenges for those wishing to bring technology to the task of reducing fire damages in rural, rather than urban, Russia were the cost of equipping communities across a large territory and teaching people how to use and maintain it. As in almost every other aspect of rural Russia's development in these years, the state's fundamentally extractive approach toward the countryside meant that village communities had to purchase their own equipment. And, as in other areas of rural development, it fell to the zemstvos to educate local people about the options available and to figure out ways to encourage them to invest in them.

News of chemical fire extinguishers came to firefighters early in their development, but the more basic method of using water was, of course, more common. Some zemstvos realized in their fire prevention campaigns that villages in their provinces needed better access to water. Before expending scarce revenues on pumps and hoses, they had to contribute to the building of water reserves first. Between 1891 and 1900, zemstvo boards provided 115,259 rubles in loans and 64,509 rubles in grants to communities for building ponds, wells, and ramps to rivers and lakes, and to tree-planting campaigns. The top five zemstvos in this activity were the Kostroma provincial board (46,855 rubles in loans), Nizhnii Novgorod (21,766 rubles in loans and 7,186 rubles in grants), Iaroslavl (25,522 rubles in grants), Vladimir (10,167 rubles in loans and 523 rubles in grants), and Simbirsk (8,000 rubles in loans and 2,072 rubles in grants).[62] Requirements that households keep large barrels of water in front of their houses were also part of the effort to ensure that water would always be on hand when the need arose.

Much was made of the peasants' cavalier attitude toward equipment. They were faulted for failing to house the equipment properly and for thus leaving it exposed to the elements. The construction of a separate depot or firehouse was the ideal; as a stopgap measure, fire activists called on peasants to store their equipment in a church (perhaps following the English tradition of parish brigades) or in the cantonal offices.[63] Beyond storage, simple damage to equipment or wear and tear could spell the demise of a piece of equipment if no one in the village knew how to repair it. Anecdotal reports of peasants dragging split hoses to the scene of a fire only to have them spray water everywhere but on the fire itself illustrated the reality that getting equipment to volunteer brigades was not enough. Technical training had to accompany the equipment to the village. This realization led zemstvos to invest in master repairmen who served as both circuit or itinerant repairmen and as instructors for peasants who had purchased equipment for their communities.

The zemstvos tried to bring self-sufficiency to village communities by providing peasants not only with modern equipment but also with the knowledge to operate and care for it themselves after the zemstvo repairmen departed. Training took less appealing, less realistic forms when it came to the organization of firefighting itself.

Marshaling Volunteers

Men plus equipment equaled a volunteer brigade. This combination was evident in the photographs and sketches of village brigades that appeared in firefighting publications. But in order for assistance to be "rational," in Prince L'vov's words, it was essential that firefighting resources—human, animal, and technological— be organized at the scene of a fire. In the instructions offered to would-be organizers and participants in village firefighting, order, hierarchy, and regimentation appeared as the ingredients for an effective antidote against the anarchy and greed perceived to poison villages during fires. While the effort was part of civic activism, and the firemen were to be volunteers, the models at hand were military.

Both the language and content of training guides echoed the military. Because the firefighting movement had to compete for the attention and support of the autocracy, the use of military rhetoric may have been calculated to convince tsar and bureaucrats alike that fire and arson, as internal threats, were as important as external ones. Like flattery of the royal family, images of war and mobilization were more likely to appeal to the tsar than was an emphasis on the associative, activist-citizen-building aspects of volunteer firefighting. Fire was often identified as the internal enemy, as in V. Grigoriev's series of articles on training that appeared in *The Firefighter's Cause* in 1901 and 1902. In an early installment, he advocated fire drills as part of both military training and the schools' curriculum, which would enable the government "to prepare the masses for the battle against fire and found new, large reserves for an entire army against the domestic, dangerous enemy."[64] To counter the perceived chaos at village fires, training programs were to establish and prioritize objectives. Whereas anecdotal reports on peasant firefighting habits stressed the people's inclination to save goods, and only their own goods, training manuals repeatedly pressed the importance of saving people first. The simultaneous but secondary goals were to save property and extinguish the fire. The tertiary goal was to protect the property that firefighters were able to salvage. Reaching these goals required order and discipline, "as essential here, of course, as in the case of war."[65]

Order would result from a division of labor among task-specific units within the brigade. The strongest men were to save people and goods as the "ax men." Each member of this unit was to bring his assigned firefighting tools (axes, hatchets, crowbars, hooks) to the fire station or depot in the village when the alarm sounded, toss it into a wagon, and rush to the scene of the fire. He was also to hang a sign on his house listing the tool or tools he would provide to the unit. Arriving at the fire before the equipment wagon, ax men were, first, to rush into burning structures to save any people inside, and then return to pull out any movable property they could carry. They were also responsible for handling the fire hoses when they arrived, directing them at the blaze in an effort to extinguish the fire. Fesenko insisted that this task should be the exclusive task of only two men who would spell each other, rather than a task assumed by anyone who wanted to take the hose. Only after trying to extinguish the fire were the ax men to use their tools to destroy buildings that lay in the path of the fire and were likely to provide it with further fuel.[66]

The second team would comprise pump men, whose responsibilities included keeping the water reservoirs filled (barrels, buckets, and tanks on fire wagons), carrying the hoses from location to location, and being prepared to repair hoses on the spot. Because anecdotal reports had described lots of squabbling at the fire among men competing for the chance to handle the hoses while avoiding the mundane task of carrying buckets of water, Fesenko advised making the assignments absolutely clear and nontransferable ahead of time.

The third team would comprise guards drawn from the weakest or oldest members of the brigade. Their responsibility was to guard property and keep bystanders out of the way of the firefighters. Some organizers termed this group the column unit, because of their anticipation that the guards would form columns on the periphery of the fire scene. It was also common for the guards' unit to divide further into one team to pass property down a line beyond the fire and another to receive and stand guard over the property.[67] Finally, the principle of one-man command was to protect against confusion. All members of the brigade were to respond solely to the orders of their chief.

Beyond division of labor into regimented units, fire activists stressed preparedness. Volunteer firemen were to achieve this desideratum through physical training to develop agility and speed and through fire drills to learn their proper place and function during fires. In addition, ax men and pump men were to undergo technical training to ensure their ability to handle and repair all of the brigade's firefighting equipment. *The Firefighter's Cause* urged brigade leaders to bring calisthenics to the countryside as a way to improve volunteers' fighting capacity. In a lengthy series on training, V. Grigoriev devoted several articles in 1901 to specific exercises, ranging from neck rotations to complicated maneuvers on bars to develop balance, flexibility, and quick reactions in volunteers (fig. 8.7). The urge to eliminate anarchic movements around the scene of a fire trickled down to the urge to regulate the firemen's bodies, extending the reach of discipline and reason as deeply as possible into village culture. No more mad rushing about amid the shouts and cries of hysterical peasants. Instead, men with uniformly exercised limbs were to join in coordinated battle against the wild element of fire.

Instructions for fire drills were the apotheosis of the rational, modernist vision of the orderly assault on fire, and its most militarized expression. Grigoriev's coded diagrams for fire maneuvers prescribed a veritable strategic plan for battle, with equipment and men equally subject to categorization and assignment to specific location and movements according to astonishingly complicated schemes (fig. 8.8). Here one found the visual incarnation of the brigade

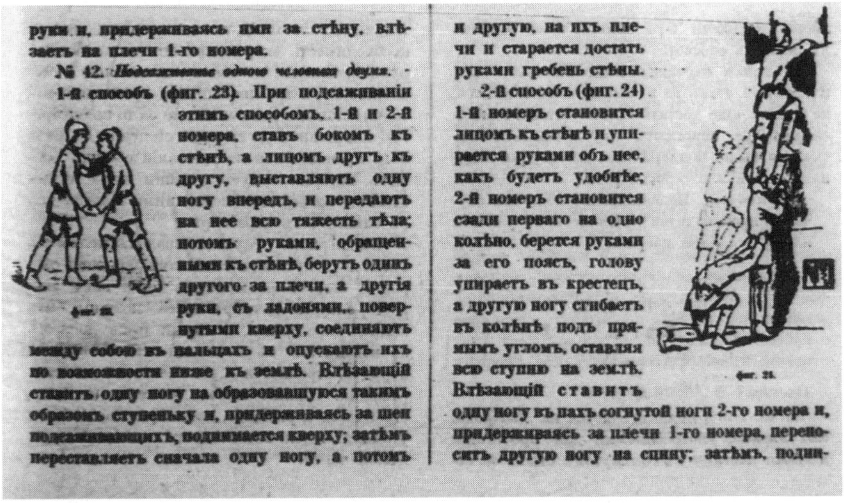
руки и, придерживаясь ими за стѣну, влѣзаетъ на плечи 1-го номера.

№ 42. *Подсаживаніе одного человѣка двумя.* 1-й способъ (фиг. 23). При подсаживаніи этимъ способомъ, 1-й и 2-й номера, ставъ бокомъ къ стѣнѣ, а лицомъ другъ къ другу, выставляютъ одну ногу впередъ, и передаютъ на нее всю тяжесть тѣла; потомъ руками, обращенными къ стѣнѣ, берутъ одинъ другого за плечи, а другія руки, съ ладонями, повернутыми кверху, соединяютъ между собою въ пальцахъ и опускаютъ ихъ по возможности ниже къ землѣ. Влѣзающій ставитъ одну ногу на образовавшуюся такимъ образомъ ступеньку и, придерживаясь за шеи подсаживающихъ, поднимается кверху; затѣмъ переставляетъ сначала одну ногу, а потомъ и другую, на ихъ плечи и старается достать руками гребень стѣны.

2-й способъ (фиг. 24) 1-й номеръ становится лицомъ къ стѣнѣ и упирается руками объ нее, какъ будетъ удобнѣе; 2-й номеръ становится сзади перваго на одно колѣно, берется руками за его поясъ, голову упираетъ въ крестецъ, а другую ногу сгибаетъ въ колѣнѣ подъ прямымъ угломъ, оставляя всю ступню на землѣ. Влѣзающій ставитъ одну ногу въ пахъ согнутой ноги 2-го номера и, придерживаясь за плечи 1-го номера, переноситъ другую ногу на спину; затѣмъ, подни-

Fig. 8.7. *Training exercises recommended for firefighters. Reproduced from* The Firefighter's Cause, *1901.*

units' division and specialization of labor, defined perfectly symmetrically in geometric space. Carts for barrels came to resemble cannons in these guides; volunteer firemen were placed like so many soldiers in ranks to execute the turns and steps to the shouted cries of their leaders, "March!" If fire activists' dreams could only come true, such elaborate coordination of strictly aligned peasant volunteers would take place in the open squares of equally geometric and carefully planned reconstructed villages.[68]

Disciplined order in the firefighting movement had the effect not only of marshaling male volunteers into a more rational assault on fire but also of removing women, those avatars of irrationality, carelessness, and impulsiveness

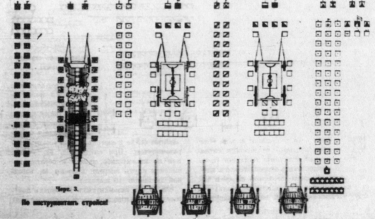

Fig. 8.8. *Coded schematics for drills by village fire brigades. Reproduced from* The Firefighter's Cause, *1901.*

in the fire narrative, from the scene of the battle. Amy Greenberg has recently presented urban volunteer firefighting in the United States in the nineteenth century as an aggressively masculine enterprise that shut women out of the fire station, deemed firemen who married lost to the movement, and made fire engines the fetishized feminine alternative to human objects of adoration and agents of emasculation.[69] The opportunities to say much the same about Russian volunteer firefighting in the countryside are considerable. Russia's fire narrative had presented peasant women as domestic fire mistresses, vengeful arsonists, ignorant mishandlers of fire, and hysterical or greedy bystanders at village conflagrations. At every point in the narrative, women held a special place associated with backwardness and harm to the society. Even as fire mistresses, their associations with fire had been attributed to "pagan" traditions. The analysis of fire as Russia's "historical evil" had identified women's carelessness as the characteristic expression of rural irrationality. In the reporting on arson, women's urge for vengeance had made them the representatives of uncontrolled passions in rural Russia. Descriptions of greedy old women rushing into burning buildings to retrieve miserly sums of money were the quintessence of selfish practices in peasant firefighting traditions.

By contrast, the volunteer fire brigade was to embody self-sacrifice, discipline, reason, science and technology, agility, strength, and technical know-how. It was an exclusively male organization, with the exception of the occasional grand duchess or princess who served as a patroness of the cause. Women who might have hoisted buckets before a volunteer brigade assigned the task to the pump men, or who might have stood watch over salvaged property before the formation of guards' units, now found themselves pushed from the scene to observe, perhaps to encourage, but not to participate in the battle against fire. When technology came to the village, it became the purview of only the strongest men, who were to pull carts, handle fire hoses, carry and climb ladders, wield crowbars and axes, press the levers on pumps, or manage the fire contained within steam engines. Tasks for the less physically able went to elderly men, not to healthy women. The conflation of women and fire in the national fire narrative made both of them objects of the urge to contain and defuse their power in the villages of European Russia.

Sharing the Vision of Rational Firefighting

The Imperial Russian Firefighters' Society (IRPO) strove to spread the word about the potential to defeat fire through volunteer firefighting in exhibitions and the press. These were additional strategies in the campaign against fire and for popular participation as a form of engagement in public life. These efforts brought news of technical and organizational developments, as well as demonstrations of firefighting skills, to urban and rural inhabitants across European Russia. Literate citizens could read about volunteer firefighting; illiterate citizens could see its models for themselves when demonstrations came to the community as part of traveling exhibitions or displays in local agricultural fairs.

Within three years of its founding, IRPO launched its first mobile exhibit. The All-Russian Traveling Firefighting Exhibition took the form of a steamboat, christened *First-Born*, that was launched in St. Petersburg on July 20, 1897, and then traveled as far as Iaroslavl over the next two summers. During those two seasons, 118,380 viewers visited the boat, of whom 106,272 were peasants. Members' contributions, government support through the Ministry of the Interior, and funds contributed by private insurance companies to city firefighting societies funded these IRPO activities. In 1899, the traveling exhibition switched venues to the railroad, moving to a ten-wagon train. The first eight cars were refitted freight cars containing exhibits of firefighting equipment and fire-resistant construction materials and methods. In addition to the exhibition directors, a fifteen-man demonstration firefighting unit took part in the journey, which began on May 19, 1899, and made seventy-eight stops before returning to St. Petersburg in September.[70] Through these exhibitions, the noble-led society used two of the most important symbols of a modern, industrial society—the steamboat and the railroad—to promote the dissemination of other technologies—firefighting equipment and fire-resistant construction materials and methods—beyond urban centers to peasants living in premodern villages. Through their displays and the firefighters' demonstrations, they were making visible the possibilities of volunteer firefighting and man's ability to fight and perhaps even conquer the "visitation of God" in the form of fire.

IRPO also contributed to local agricultural exhibitions, much like contemporary American state fairs, by setting up firefighting displays. In August 1903, for example, it built an extensive series of booths and activities at the Agricultural and Cottage Industry Exhibition in Tsarskoe selo, the suburban residence of the tsar outside St. Petersburg. The society constructed two extensive displays. Inside the exhibition hall, it presented fire prevention and firefighting technologies, including such construction items as tile roofs and brick walls and such equipment as fire carriages—on loan from several village brigades—and pumps, ladders, and hoses. Viewers were apparently quite taken with a harness designed to drop from the ceiling onto a horse as soon as the horse was put in position in front of a waiting fire wagon. The organizers also invited the major retailers of firefighting equipment to display their wares in booths in the hall. Finally, they offered all of their fire prevention and firefighting publications to visitors at the exhibition. Outdoors, they erected model fire-resistant buildings, including one built by the Novgorod zemstvo board to display its fire-resistant roofs and stucco walls. Representatives from several village brigades attended to serve as experts to answer visitors' questions. *The Firefighter's Cause* trumpeted the fact that many peasants visited these displays, and it called for other brigades to organize such exhibits for rural fairs in their regions.[71]

Literate firefighters could join a larger community beyond their locale by reading the publications *The Firefighter's Cause* and *The Firefighter*. There they found editorials describing issues in the movement, historical sketches of government fire regulations from the days of early Muscovy to the present, reports from local firefighting societies and brigades about their activities, eyewitness accounts of fires from all areas of European Russia, descriptions of the latest developments in firefighting technologies, and news of firefighting in Europe and the United States. It was in these pages, as well as at conferences, that fire activists debated the virtues of the various strategies against rural fires, ranging from zemstvo efforts to government subsidies for reconstruction, with volunteer firefighting in the middle. The broader political questions that were under discussion among educated Russians also surfaced obliquely in these newspapers. Contributors argued for greater centralization or decentralization in the governance of the movement and either praised or ridiculed the zemstvo programs and zemstvo activists. European achievements in firefighting were held up as models, and the tsar and his family were featured either prominently or not at all. Photographs of new societies and brigades, letters to the editor, news items from the provinces, and obituaries of fallen firefighters wove a web of personal identification with the movement by making the readers subjects and authors as well. Volunteer firefighters found in these publications portraits not only of royal patrons but also of themselves and their peers; obituaries not only of those patrons but also of valorous individual volunteers; and not only editorials written by the aristocratic leaders of the movement but also eyewitness reports and comments by their literate peers. Just as the press had contributed to the conceptualization of a Russia aflame, so it contributed to the construction of a mental map of European Russia dotted with ever-increasing fraternal brigades of volunteer firemen overlaid on the map of fire. A new kind of "imagined community" was available for those who joined the volunteer firefighting movement.

For hundreds of firefighters and other fire activists, that "imagined community" became flesh in 1902 when they gathered at the Moscow Conservatory for the All-Russian Firefighters' Conference. There they had days on end in which to socialize with each other and to attend sessions. Each session was dedicated to one aspect of fire activism and included several panels and papers per topic: fire prevention in cities, towns, and factories and on railroads; fire prevention in the countryside; firefighting technology; volunteer firefighting; urban firefighting, and fire insurance. Panelists ranged from peasant firefighters to noble leaders of the central organization. A wide-ranging discussion, with genuine differences of opinion and efforts to propose new ways to attack the stubborn problems still so evident in Russia's now forty-year-old "fire crisis," made for a genuinely lively conference.[72] One of the most ingenious and charming suggestions came in the technology discussions when one panelist, I. N. Livchak, shared his concept for "firefighting bombs." These were clay balls filled with sand, to be catapulted onto fires, where they would break open and suffocate the blaze. *The Firefighters' Cause* shortly labeled this invention "fantastic," and another suggestion that the zemstvos send peasants to Europe so they could see peasants there living in stone houses was termed "grandiose and original."[73] While this judgment may have been on the mark, both proposals suggest the continuing power of fire and arson in rural Russia to stimulate the popular imagination.

Conclusion

These male associations did cross class lines, did generate real as well as imagined communities, and did demonstrate some gains in Russia's campaign against her most dangerous "internal enemy, fire." Although the number of fires in European Russia did not decline in the 1890s and up to 1904, a time when volunteer firefighting brigades multiplied rapidly, the number of structures burned per fire did (table 8.4). This decrease in the average scale of fires was all the more impressive when compared with statistics gathered in the 1860s and 1870s, when the numbers ranged from 3.6 to 5.0 structures per fire. In some locales, the impact of volunteer firefighting was vivid. The Khrenovo village brigade in Voronezh Province, for example, was founded in 1899. In its first year, it fought 19 fires; in 1900, 21; in 1901 (a disastrously hot, dry summer in European Russia), 55; and in the first eight months of 1902, 40. Over those four years, the average number of homesteads burned per fire was 3.6, whereas in the period 1888–1898, it had been 7.5. Monetary losses similarly dropped from an average of 630 rubles per fire to 213 rubles per fire.[74]

Table 8.4: Numbers of Fires and Structures Burned
per Fire in Rural Russia, 1890-1904

Five-Year Period	Number of Fires	Structures Burned per Fire
1890–1894	223,394	3.5
1895–1899	249,050	2.8
1900–1904	285,044	2.8

Source: Tsentral'nyi statisticheskii komitet, Ministerstvo Vnutrennikh del 1912: xxx.

Successes such as these combined with the community events of firefighting drills and processions to generate popular enthusiasm for volunteer firefighting. In 1903, one enthusiast celebrated the public's embrace of the movement and explained the positive changes it had brought to the villages of European Russia:

Where they [volunteer firefighting brigades] appeared, there also appeared the reform of the organization of firefighting, and the tragicomic pre-Emancipation firefighting practices in villages immediately were transformed. Instead of feeble old men, there appeared splendid young men, each better than the rest, on the firefighting teams; instead of skinny and useless horses, there appeared strong, good horses; old firefighting tools and the fire wagons' apparatuses were replaced with new ones, and there, where a year ago you couldn't look at the fire wagon without revulsion, you now regard it with pleasure. The apathetic crowd, stupefied by terror, was replaced by people who were prepared for the task of extinguishing the fire, people who were ready to sacrifice a great deal for the social good. Such is the portrait, which I have drawn from nature, of villages where there are fire brigades.[75]

Despite the tenacity of fire itself as a threat to the villages of European Russia, volunteer fire brigades offered the promise of social and technological transformations. The evils of backwardness embodied in passive futility before fire or chaotic and ineffectual attempts to extinguish it, in unhealthy people and animals, and in decrepit tools and equipment could, through the agency of volunteer fire brigades, give way to the features of a modern society: activism, orderly training, service to society, good health, and new technologies. Though incapable of addressing the fundamental physical environment, rural poverty, and underinvestment that continued to make tinderboxes of late imperial

Russia's villages, the hundreds of brigades and thousands of peasant volunteers working with neighboring gentry, merchants, and priests testify to the potential for local solutions to local problems. They formed local partnerships willing to take up tasks the government had unloaded as legacies of serfdom a half-century before. They offer evidence that the visions of a fiery apocalypse in rural Russia had indeed begun to give way to rational, progressive responses at the beginning of what would prove to be Russia's tortured twentieth century.

9

Conclusion:
Fire as an Imperial Legacy,
Peasants as Partners in Progress

THE DISCUSSIONS WERE CARRIED ON CHIEFLY BY THE NOBLES, BUT ON
MORE THAN ONE OCCASION PEASANT MEMBERS ROSE TO SPEAK, AND
THEIR REMARKS, ALWAYS CLEAR, PRACTICAL AND TO THE POINT, WERE
INVARIABLY LISTENED TO WITH RESPECTFUL ATTENTION.

—Donald Mackenzie Wallace,
description of the Novgorod zemstvo in the early 1870s

In the autumn of 1901 and spring of 1902, peasant unrest gripped much of southern and southwestern Russia. The burning of gentry estates featured prominently in it. From Ekaterinoslavl Province, a local official reported that "a genuine arson epidemic has broken out in many, many villages." Characteristically, the peasants most frequently burned farm outbuildings and hayricks.[1] Upheaval and arson spread throughout March and April to Tambov, Poltava, Kiev, Saratov, Kherson, Voronezh, and Khar'kov Provinces.[2] Arson in these events could no longer be viewed as an individual action, because "whole villages, including their wealthiest members, participated. Units of up to 400 carts moved into action at a given signal, with a snowball effect spreading the revolt from village to village."[3]

These scenes registered critical new images for contemporary Russians and historians, who henceforth viewed peasant "masses as actors" whose association with fire was perceived almost exclusively as arson against gentry property in the context of social and political revolution.[4] Peasants plus fire have equaled class-conscious arsonists contributing to popular revolution. Peasants as such arsonists have, in turn, emerged as historical agents in crowd actions directed against the old regime in its most proximate forms—gentry landowners and government buildings. The arson fires of 1901–1902, the even more transformative events of 1905–1907, and the ultimate triumph of Bolshevik revolutionaries who commanded a historical enterprise devoted to documenting the inevitability and popular legitimacy of revolution generated visions of peasants and fire in rural Russia as nearly impenetrable as the black smoke billowing from a thatched wooden village on fire.

Before 1902, however, alternative associations between peasants and fire had existed, suggesting that there were more complex capacities for development within rural Russia than the limited capacity for destruction born of class hatred and resentment. Peasants, both women and men, were historical actors and agents in their local and national cultures, to be sure, but in a variety of roles beyond the frameworks employed by Soviet historians and many of their Western counterparts. Most generally, peasants were daily mistresses and masters of fire. They were adept manipulators of this powerful source of energy, illumination, fertilization, healing, and transformation. They were skilled fire technicians, however obscure their skills were to their more urbanized and educated fellow Russians. They were also active participants in the campaign against fire. As participants in that campaign, furthermore, they were willing to engage with their nonpeasant rural neighbors through the officially sanctioned institutions of the zemstvos, the courts, and volunteer firefighting brigades. Contrary to prevailing opinion in the national fire narrative, peasants were not trapped in passive futility before fire. The master roofer A. G. Adamov from Novgorod Province was the most famous and influential counterexample—an individual peasant innovator whose enterprising initiative captured the attention of local leaders in a position to broadcast his accomplishments across all of European Russia. But thousands of unnamed peasants were similarly active in moving to defuse fire's power in their communities. The peasants in Samara District who proposed a compulsory program in fire-resistant roofing in 1866, those in Khar'kov District who set their own rules about when they could fire up their stoves, others who established local systems of child care during field work or willingly sent their children to zemstvo-run child-care centers, the hundreds of peasant proprietors who built wells and ponds with zemstvo grants, and the thousands of homeowners who invested in fire-resistant roofing all made independent decisions to act rather than wait idly for fire to make its predictable entrance each spring, summer, and fall.

Peasants behaved like modern property owners and citizens in ways that belied their reputed captivity in premodern *kak nibud* (somehow or other) fatalism. Not only did thousands of them invest in fire-resistant roofs, but thousands more also invested in special appraisals and higher premiums beyond the mandatory minimums of the compulsory fire insurance program. Even those who economized on insurance displayed impressive accounting skills when they appealed for supplementary emergency assistance from the tsar: the detailed inventories of the movable and immovable property they lost in fires constituted quite precise appraisals and presentations. Property-owning peasants were also active litigants, willing and able to use laws and courts to defend their private interests against their neighbors or the pressures of zemstvo village reconstruction plans. Even the history of arson reveals examples of peasants who tried to pursue justice through law and the courts before turning to arson as a more immediate and trustworthy remedy.

Finally, peasants became active participants in rural civil society when they joined volunteer firefighting brigades. Through these units, especially in areas where peasant volunteers also served as the administrative officers, they had opportunities to engage in organization, management, and fiscal control. When they stepped forward to join a brigade, they were often stepping toward a member of the local gentry or old nobility who acted out of messianic paternalism.

Yet paternalism also yielded the urge to cooperate with the freed peasantry—to enter into communities of fraternal coordination and mutual assistance through the sponsorship of such peasant inventors as Novgorod's Adamov and through membership in volunteer fire brigades. This impulse toward voluntary association across class lines was as genuine as the impulse toward control. The village volunteer fire brigades are the consummate example of what Samuel Kassow has described as a search for "new identities," which "proceeded in intermediate places: the space between state and society, the moving ground between the ruling elites and the peasant masses."[5] The hope for connection and service impelled elites such as Sheremetev and L'vov to devote their energies, funds, and political connections to bringing rational firefighting organizations to the villages of Russia. Their brigades and the thousands who followed their example illustrate well Joseph Bradley's conclusion about such entities: "The myriad of societies and associations that sprang up in the last two generations before the Revolution offered an opportunity to correct the alleged spasms of public life, to introduce elements of equilibrium and steadiness, to provide outlets for the 'industrious and rational,' and to achieve national unity and reconciliation."[6]

All of these opportunities surfaced in the volunteer firefighting movement, in which promotion of the "industrious and rational" came to be expressed most fully in instructions for physical training and fire maneuvers. In those schemata, peasants were susceptible to being reduced to automata of bodily precision—geometric figures on strategic plans for efficient battle against "the internal enemy, fire." However these tendencies fit the urge identified by historiographers of modernism to order society and all the human bodies in it, we should not lose sight of the more conscious and passionate impulse toward "national unity and reconciliation" that these volunteer brigades realized.

The models at hand were military, and the leaders of the movement employed them. But they did so not so much to put the peasants back into their proper place as to develop proficient firefighting capacity. The focus here was on the wild element of fire, whose force they wished to tame. As for the peasants' own elemental strength, this they hoped to harness but not extinguish. The one measurable success in two generations of the effort to contain fire in late imperial Russia was the reduction in the average number of structures burned per fire across the European provinces. Perhaps the scattered clay-and-straw and tile roofs contributed to that decline. It is just as likely, however, that the enhanced ability to put out blazes once they began was an important factor. That was the fruit of paternalist collaboration and the "industrious and rational." As such, it makes the ultimate triumph of "high modernism's" coercive impulses in Soviet form seem all the more tragic and unnecessary, for it suggests that there were areas in which engaged and active peasants could meet engaged and messianic members of educated society to develop vibrant solutions to real problems. The Bolsheviks recognized the hazard the volunteer firefighting associations across European Russia posed to their model of a society driven by class conflict, as well as to their preference for centralized control: in April 1918, they placed all firefighting activities in city and countryside under a commissariat for insurance and firefighting[7]

If peasant and gentry activities in fire control in the countryside held so much promise, then why did fires continue to "dispossess Orthodox Rus'" so frequently into the twentieth century? The causes for the minimal scale of success against fire and arson as destructive elements in late imperial Russia lay in the poverty of physical conditions and judicial institutions in the countryside. There can be no doubt that the countryside in European Russia was in the thrall of competing economic developments in the late imperial era. Contradictory indicators have bedeviled historians trying to make judgment calls on whether the peasants were experiencing decline or prosperity, for each choice of variables and regions yields conclusions that are apparently mutually exclusive with other conclusions. How can we use the term "decline," Steven Hoch has astutely asked, to describe a population whose phenomenal growth could only indicate that more children were growing into adulthood and thus whose standard of living was clearly improving? Similarly, James Simms asked how increasing poverty could be an attribute of peasants who were buying more samovars, vodka, tea, matches, and other "luxury" items. Jeffrey Burds has gone so far as to call the villages of the central industrial region a "new consumer culture," and he points to new roofing patterns as one example of cash income's giving birth to a transformation of rural material culture.[8] As early as a century ago, A. N. Engel'gardt found evidence of a shift in rural Smolensk Province from subsistence to property acquisition and economic prosperity across entire villages.[9]

Each of these challenges to the conceptualization of a rural Russia in economic decline in the post-Emancipation period is apt. But economic progress was no more steady than putative decline. Instead, it was syncopated by periodic "shocks" in the form of natural disasters of the type Stephen Wheatcroft has analyzed and social catastrophes in the form that Eric L. Jones has termed "settlement fires."

These fires came to Russia's villages because there was so much fire in use there. They spread because, even in a period of increasing life expectancy and expanding consumption of commercial goods, European Russia's peasants did not have the financial wherewithal to invest in fire-resistant reconstruction of their homes and farming structures, or in enough firefighting technology to overcome the spread of conflagrations in wooden, thatched villages. Here, as in the case of fire insurance, the zemstvos tried to fill the gap by providing grants, loans, and subsidies to villages and individual peasants, and by going so far as to establish their own factories for fire-resistant building materials. But their programs were necessarily partial. What was needed, as they and their counterparts in the volunteer firefighting movement realized, was a fundamental reordering of the imperial government's budgeting priorities and attitude toward the rural sector of the economy. Investment in the material base was needed to complement extraction of the agricultural product. This no Russian, Soviet, or post-Soviet government since the time of Peter the Great has been willing to do. The value of the agricultural economy for military or display purposes has been inadequate to warrant a transformative reallocation of the national wealth. At the turn of the century, one price the imperial government paid for that tradition was fire as a perennial shock and impediment to capital accumulation and investment in rural Russia.

Of course, not only construction patterns and materials failed to change on a massive scale. Climatic factors did not either. Russia's fire season came and went, year in and year out, with the same regularity as heat, drought, and winds. This fundamental continuity appears in the fire statistics for the period 1905–1910. Although the revolutionary upheavals of 1905–1907 led to an

Table 9.1: Numbers of Fires per Season Outside Town Limits in European Russia

Year	Winter	Spring	Summer	Fall
1905	11,963	20,213	21,929	18,548
1906	10,495	19,320	23,450	20,953
1907	11,749	19,142	24,458	24,612
1908	11,217	18,532	22,722	21,838
1909	11,787	17,963	23,992	24,665
1910	11,324	18,520	21,158	21,338

Source: Tsentral'nyi statisticheskii komitet, Ministerstvo Vnutrennikh del 1912: 248.

increase in the number of fires that held through 1910, the seasonality of fires remained consistent with the patterns of the previous half-century. For the years from 1905 to 1910, the number of fires per season outside town limits (*v uez-dakh*) broke down as shown in table 9.1.

As deforestation proceeded apace in the service of industrial development and housing for the rapidly expanding population, water reservoirs and streams dried up and dusty villages became more exposed to seasonal desiccation. In a reversal of the historical interpretations found in Marxist analysis, the material conditions of life in Russia's villages lagged far behind the social transformations captured by historians such as Barbara Engel, Timothy Mixter, and Jeffrey Burds. No matter their new patterns of labor migration and consumer tastes, Russia's peasants were still captive to their natural and built physical environments, whose susceptibility to fire had the capacity to stun even the most prosperous household.

In the absence of extensive, penetrating, and effective institutions of the police and the judiciary, those prosperous households were among the most exposed to the risks of fire, because they were likely targets of arson attacks by their less prosperous, more envious peers. If wood and straw provided the fuel, then the arsonist's torch, cigarette, or match often provided the ignition. Here, too, the poverty of state institutions explains much of fire's power in rural Russia. The etiology of rural arson as revealed in district policemen's reports adds to our understanding of the social control peasants exercised over each other. Arson joins religious denunciation as a device of social control (recently explored by Jeffrey Burds) in the emerging historiography of peasants' oppression of fellow peasants in the reform and prerevolutionary eras. Arson's particular efficacy as a weapon of community control derived from the relative absence of legal constraints or consequences for those who practiced it. Despite gains in the peasants' use of the cantonal court system for civil disputes, arson continued to be an attractive alternative form of dispute resolution. This reality also blunted the peasants' willingness to invest heavily in housing reconstruction as a long-term financial strategy.

Finally, the history of Russia's "fire crisis" illuminates all the more brightly the negative portrayal of peasant women. Indeed, there is something breathtaking in the nearly universal chorus of voices decrying Russia's peasant women. Folktales depicted peasant women as lustful, venal, cunning, and stupid; contemporaneous accounts demonized peasant healers and seers as witches; even populist authors described peasant women as greedy, divisive, and dishonest. Tolstoy and Chekhov made them the incarnation of "the power of darkness."[10] Their excoriation as witless tenders of the hearth, greedy madwomen willing to rush into burning structures to save a few rubles or a counterpane, hysterical and useless bystanders at village fires, and vengeful arsonists setting ablaze familial structures and even their own children was true to form in late imperial Russia. Even as fire's victims, peasant women appeared in the national press as the most gruesome figures in Russia's fin-de-siècle inferno. As late as 1902, one former zemstvo fire agent used such a woman to embody his loss of faith in the ability of state or society to contain fire among rural Russians. Of his faith, he wrote:

It vanished from the moment that I first stood lost in thought and, with my blood turned icy with horror, looked at the blackened corpse of an incinerated woman. Even now, when many years have passed, I see it before me; I see the blackened face, the terrible bared teeth in bright, blood-red jawbones, the sockets out of which the eyes poured after they burst, the skin that had split open and the convulsively bent bones of the charred hands.[11]

This woman joined a long line of such negative images, marking the unholy, destructive relationship between women and fire. In the national fire narrative, as in the search for a modern national identity of which it was a part, women served as the repository of all the antirational, undisciplined, ignorant, and unclean attributes of Russia's infuriatingly premodern villages.

Their representation was a portent of worse to come. When Soviet visionaries in the late 1920s embarked on the most intensively extractive agricultural policy in Russia's history in the service of rapid industrialization, only to find that the peasants of European Russia were capable of resisting their own expropriation, all peasants became vulnerable to the dehumanizing categorization of their local communities as enemies of progress. Soviet allegations of their sins against the socialist state were as exaggerated and demonizing as had been the characterization of peasant women by their fin-de-siècle predecessors.

Russia's "fire crisis" and the national narrative it engendered sounded apocalyptic warnings of Russia's cultural conflagration. They also provided some evidence of the vengeance peasants would exact upon their more prosperous gentry and peasant neighbors. They composed an overture for the brutal Soviet cacophony that played between the *metis* of traditional practices in the countryside and the "high modernism" that would characterize Bolshevik visions and coercive plans. The victorious Soviet state strove to erase from the national score all record of collaborative paternalism, peasant mastery of the natural elements, peasants' and the state's defense of private property, and peasants' willing participation in the judicial system and nascent civil society. These, too, were part of Russia's national scene on the eve of the twentieth century. Perhaps their residues in the ashes of the Soviet visitation upon Orthodox Rus' may yet fertilize a more prosperous union of *metis*, popular engagement, and a modern state that reclaims the promise in its pre-Soviet past.

NOTES

Introduction

1. The rescript, or decree, was reprinted in *Pozharnyi*, no. 115–43, November 5, 1894: 949–950.

2. Hoch 1994; Kahan 1989: 108–144; Robbins 1975; Robinson 1949; Wheatcroft 1991.

3. See Anfimov 1984: 86–87; Wilbur 1991: 112, 119, 122–123; Worobec 1991: 18–19, 101, 103.

4. Dubrovskii 1956: 33–73; Edelman 1987: 86; Seregny 1991: 352, 368; Shanin 1986: 79–99.

5. This term is Geroid T. Robinson's (1949: 94ff.).

6. S. K-n, "Po povodu chastykh pozharov v Rossii (Pis'mo k redaktoru 'Golosa')." *Smolenskie gubernskie vedomosti* 36 (1865): 146–148.

7. In 1861, Tsar Alexander II issued the Edict of Emancipation, freeing all Russian serfs and abolishing serfdom.

8. Scott 1998: 4.

9. For another treatment of this tendency, see Frierson 1993a.

10. Maksimov 1896, 18: 210–211.

11. Bethea 1989.

12. Smiles was a prominent proponent of Classical liberalism and of individual responsibility as the source of moral and economic health.

13. The total absence of any discussion of fire is particularly striking in Wheatcroft 1991: 128–174.

14. In Novgorod, these files are found in Gosudarstvennyi arkhiv Novgorodskoi oblasti (hereafter GANO), *fond* (fund) 138, *opis'* (index) 1; they are the *dela* (files) on "Proisshestviiakh," which are organized around the year of reporting.

15. See note 4, this chapter. Also see Figes 1991: 381; Fitzpatrick 1994: 42, 66, 235, 304; Viola 1996.

16. Viola 1996: 124.

17. Burds 1998: 186–218.

18. The fire insurance program is an area of zemstvo activity that has not appeared in the Western literature on these locally elected public works councils. This book joins such previous studies of the zemstvo as Eklof 1986; Emmons and Vucinich 1982; Fallows 1981; Frieden 1981; and Porter 1991.

19. Bachelard 1964; Bayard 1973; Eliade 1978; Frazer 1930; Freud 1964; Goudsblom 1992; Lévi-Strauss 1990; Masson 1985; Pyne 1982.

20. References to Kuznets's work can be found in Jones's. See, for example, E. Jones 1987: 22, 24, 33–34, 39; Frost and Jones 1989.

21. Tenishev was a wealthy member of the nobility who hoped to undercut the appeal of Marxism and radical populism by learning about the material conditions and attitudes of rural and urban working people in Russia. He drafted and funded a major survey of rural life as the

foundation of a larger program of studying working people to prepare appropriate, nonradical responses to their interests and needs. He established a study center in St. Petersburg to receive and analyze responses to his survey; I refer to it in this book as the Tenishev Bureau.

22. The coincidence in the geographic distribution of arson during peasant protests in 1930 and the geographic distribution of arson across the period of this study is especially striking. Lynne Viola provided tables on the former in her *Peasant Rebels under Stalin* (1996: 105, 110).

23. Schulte 1994, first published in German in 1989.

24. Ibid.: 9.

25. Anderson 1983. See also Bassin 1991 for an elegant discussion of the historical construction within Russia of its identity as a European empire.

Chapter 1. Fire as Gentle Cookery and Paradise

1. Efimenko 1877: 30; Ivanitskii 1890: 14; Nikitinskii 1884; Staniukovich 1970: 73. The following dela in Russkii etnograficheskii muzei, fond 7, opis' 1 (hereafter Tenishev Fund), also describe these patterns of illumination in various regions of the empire: delo 1030 (Orel Province, Kromsk District), l. 55; delo 607 (Kostroma Province, Makar'ev District), l. 21; delo 1567 (Smolensk Province, Dorogobuzh District), l. 5; delo 1564 (Smolensk Province, Dorogobuzh District), l. 17; delo 432 (Viatka Province, Orlovskii District), l. 32; delo 252 (Vologda Province, Kadnikov District), l. 16; delo 102 (Vologda Province, Vel'skii District), ll. 18–19; delo 5 (Vladimir Province, Vladimir District), l. 27; delo 43 (Vladimir Province, Melenkov District), l. 9; delo 71 (Vladimir Province, Shuiskii district), l. 7.

2. See Tempest 1997: 1–14 for a similar treatment of the place of the stove in Russian peasant culture.

3. Quoted in Efimenko 1877: 15.

4. Efimenko 1877: 33, 41.

5. Vill'er de Lil'-Adam 1871: 246.

6. Chizhikova 1979.

7. See Levin 1993: 32–38.

8. Engel'gardt 1879: 133.

9. A. N. Afanas'ev (1986: 66) described this as an ancient ritual. See also Baiburin 1983: 106–107; Kharuzina 1906: 86, 154; Neustupov 1913: 245; Sokolov 1971: 164; Zvonkov 1889: 71. Christine Worobec (1991: 48) also accepts this interpretation.

10. Neustupov 1913: 246.

11. Afanas'ev 1969: 33.

12. Maksimov 1896, 18: 222–223.

13. Scott 1998: 6–7. Scott explains that this term comes "from Classical Greek and denotes the knowledge that can only come from practical experience" (1998: 6).

14. Mircea Eliade (1978: 57) described the furnace employed in metallurgy as a substitute for Mother Earth, "a new matrix, an artificial uterus where the ore completes its gestation." The hearth fire's femaleness had as much to do with its associations and shape as with its functions.

15. Baiburin 1983: 163–164.

16. Edelman 1993: 12–13; Matossian 1968: 5, 18. Vera Kharuzina (1906: 77) concluded that the "woman more than the man had the occasion to deal with fire, to study its properties, habits, and morals." See also Ivanitskii 1890: 14–15.

17. On the significance of food preparation in the development of civilization, see Lévi-Strauss 1990. Baiburin (1983: 162) also stressed this aspect of the stove's function of enabling the peasant to make the raw cooked and the unclean clean.

18. Rose Glickman (1991: 148–162) and Samuel Ramer (1991: 210) noted, as did nineteenth-century correspondents, that many village healers, if not most, were women.

19. Pokrovskii 1874: 106; Popov 1903: 21.

20. Kharuzina 1906: 137; Ramer 1991: 207.

21. Trunov 1869.

22. Popov 1903: 193.

23. Afanas'ev 1969: 31–32.

24. Arshinov 1889: 11; Min'ko 1974: 24–25. See also Bogaevskii 1889: 105; Vsevolozhkaia 1895: 28.

25. Balov 1896a: 262–264.

26. Verashchagin 1898: 130.

27. Gerasimov 1898: 165.

28. See Ransel 1991: 115–123.

29. Frazer 1930; see also Bachelard 1964; Bayard 1973; Eliade 1978; Freud 1964; Goudsblom 1992; Lévi-Strauss 1990; Masson 1985; Pyne 1982, 1991, 1997.

30. Popov 1903: 194.

31. Chicherov 1957: 30.

32. On the scarcity of formal medicine in the countryside, see Engel'gardt 1872: 174–177; Frieden 1981; Glickman 1991; Ramer 1991.

33. Popov 1903: 236–239.

34. Ibid.: 245.

35. Demidovich 1896: 133.

36. Ivanitskii 1890: 14; Kharuzina 1906: 133; Popov 1903: 192–193.

37. Maksimov 1896, 18: 219–220.

38. Ibid.: 220–221.

39. Tenishev Fund, delo 813 (Novgorod Province, Cherepovets District), l. 5.

40. Popov 1903: 255.

41. Balov, Derunov, and Il'inskii 1898: 74.

42. Efimenko 1877: 168–169. For other reports of "looking in the mirror," see Balov, Derunov, and Il'inskii 1898: 75; Vill'er de Lil'-Adam 1871: 313.

43. Efimenko 1877: 169.

44. Eleonskaia 1909.

45. Eliade 1978: 79–80.

46. Kharuzina 1906: 117.

47. Zvonkov 1889: 71.

48. Baiburin 1983: 128.

49. Ibid.: 158.

50. Ibid.: 162.

51. Masson 1985: 121ff.

52. See, for example, Chicherov 1957: 65.

53. Trubetskoi 1973: 17.

54. Ibid.: 18.

55. For a discussion of how to read icons, see Uspensky 1967. On the flames of the Holy Spirit, see Ouspensky and Lossky 1982: 207–208.

56. Sreznevskii 1895: 602.

57. See Uspensky 1967: 15.

58. Goudsblom 1992: 134–137.

59. Buslaev 1861: 144.

60. Ibid.: 134–136; Sreznevskii 1895: 602, 605.

61. Ivanitskii 1890: 119.

62. Kharuzina 1906: 122.

63. Tenishev Fund, delo 1115 (Orel Province, Orel District), l. 7.

64. Kharuzina 1906: 177.

65. Tenishev Fund, delo 857 (Novgorod Province, Cherepovets District), l. 1.

66. Many students of rural Russian belief systems have recognized the centrality of farming in determining the shape and meaning of calendrical celebrations and other rituals. For the most part, however, they have not taken the extra step beyond the veneration of the sun to go back into the forest from which peasant farming in central European Russia evolved. See Afanas'ev 1969: 12, 37, and elsewhere; Ivanits 1989: 11–12; Propp 1963: 14, 20–21, 56, 104, and elsewhere.

67. R. E. F. Smith 1977: 7, 113ff. Adam Olearius also noted the effects of such deforestation in the seventeenth century. See Baron 1967: 123.

68. Deal 1978: 222–224, 333.

69. Sreznevskii 1895: 603.

70. Engel'gardt 1881: 399; 1882: 356–358.

71. Maksimov 1896, 20: 99–101. Maksimov may have been drawing on the report of Adrianovskii (1884: 48), in which Andrianovskii described yields of forty to sixty seeds to one in Arkhangel'sk, Vologda, and Perm Provinces. Iurii M. Sokolov (1971: 161) also described deforestation in the countryside through the end of the century and the peasants' use of fire to smoke out wild bees in the forest. See also Blum 1971: 337; Portal 1969: 41–42; Zobnin 1894. This practice was described in *Nashi sel'skie pozhary* (1877: 89) as a frequent cause of forest fires.

72. Pallot and Shaw 1990: 113.

73. Kohl 1970: 474.

74. *Polnoe sobranie zakonov Rossiiskoi Imperii* [Laws of the Russian Empire] (hereafter PSZ), 25 (1850), 23807.

75. Tenishev Fund, delo 30 (Vladimir Province, Melenkov District), ll. 1–8; delo 3 (Vladimir Province, Vladimir District), l. 4; delo 1575 (Smolensk Province, Dorogobuzh District), l. 22; delo 597 (Kostroma Province, Galich District), ll. 9–10; delo 1087 (Orel Province, Orel District), ll. 1–2. See also Ivanitskii 1890: 196.

76. See Tenishev Fund, delo 30 (Vladimir Province, Melenkov District), ll. 8–9, and delo 3 (Vladimir Province, Vladimir District), l. 5. Peasants may have based this notion on their observations. Recent studies of lightning and agricultural production in the American Midwest have demonstrated that fields are more fertile following summers with a high incidence of thunderstorms.

77. Trunov 1869: 7. See also Tenishev Fund, delo 1670 (Smolensk Province, Smolensk District), l. 6.

78. Maksimov 1896, 18: 216; Sinozerskii 1896.

79. Neustupov 1902: 118.

80. See, for example, Efimenko 1877: 185; Kolchin 1899; Neustupov 1902: 118; Ushakov 1896; Zavoiko 1914: 118. Ushakov included reports of this belief from Tula, Riazan, Kaluga, and Vladimir Provinces. See also Tenishev Fund, delo 30 (Vladimir Province, Melenkov District), l. 7; delo 171 (Vologda Province, Vologda District), l. 26; delo 1568 (Smolensk Province, Dorogobuzh District), l. 26; delo 597 (Kostroma Province, Galich District), l. 9; delo 134 (Penza Province, Krasnoslobodo District), l. 44; delo 1087 (Orel Province, Orel District), l. 1. And see Ivanitskii 1890: 126.

81. Oleg Lyssenko, a research associate of the Russian Museum of Ethnography, suggested this interpretation to me during a conversation in December 1992.

82. Zvonkov 1889: 70.

83. Fires were most frequent in the summer. See, for example, "Statistika: Pozhary v Rossii," *Pozharnoe delo*, no. 3, September 1894, 61; and *Tsentral'nyi statisticheskii komitet, Ministerstva Vnutrennykh del* (hereafter TsSK, MVD) 1882: xxi. Between 1870 and 1874, for example, there were 3,428 reported fires during the summer months, compared with 2,093 during the winter, 2,282 during the spring, and 2,549 during the fall.

84. Between 1870 and 1875, for example, only 2.5 percent to 5.3 percent of all fires recorded in the empire were identified as lightning fires. TsSK, MVD 1882: xiv. See Ivanits 1989: 30.

85. GANO, fond 138, opis' 1, delo 3050, ll. 2–3, and delo 3334, l. 70.

86. Ivanits 1989: 34; Maksimov 1896, 18: 219.

87. Tenishev Fund, delo 1087 (Orel Province, Orel District), l. 1. See a similar report from Vologda in Ivanitskii 1896: 126. Here, Lord Savovich may have been a distortion of the name Svarogich, a pre-Christian celestial deity in Slavic belief systems.

88. Tenishev Fund, delo 1439 (Riazan Province, Zaraisk District), l. 8.

89. *Trudy kommissii po preobrazovaniiu volostnykh sudov* 1873, 4: 171–172.

90. Afanas'ev 1969: 322.

91. Propp 1963: 384–386. On Ivan Kupalo in Minsk, see also Byval'kevich 1891. Note that the spelling of Kupalo varies. I have chosen Ivan Kupalo rather than Ivan Kupala, although both are correct.

92. Bachelard 1964: 21–32; Jung 1976: 145–167.

93. See, for example, Afanas'ev 1969: 321–322; Ivanits 1989: 9–10; Propp 1963: 378–380.

94. Couples also leapt through bonfires following their wedding or on the morning after the wedding night as a way of enhancing their fertility (Kharuzina 1906: 13).

95. Frazer 1951: 745–753. One correspondent to *Zhivaia starina* also considered the Kupalo fires to be a reflection of sun worship. Balov (1896b) placed particular stress on the timing of the festival with the triumph of the sun and the climax of fertility.

96. Pyne 1982: 141.

97. See Simms 1977: 379–380. Wheatcroft (1991), Hoch (1994), and others have challenged Simms's conclusions about whether increased peasant tax payments on such items justify adjusting our view of the prosperity of Russian villages, but the evidence that some peasants were indeed buying these items is not in doubt. See also Engel 1994a: 49–54, in which she includes tea consumption as one of the indicators of peasants' relative prosperity in Kostroma Province. Most recently, see Burds 1998: 163.

98. TsSK, MVD 1882: lxxv.

99. *Trudy mestnykh komitetov o nuzhdakh sel'skokhoziaistvennoi promyshlennosti* (hereafter Trudy mestnykh komitetov) 1903, 11: 322. The state-sponsored Committees on the Needs of Agriculture gathered at the district, provincial, and capital levels in 1902 to discuss the condition of agriculture, with reports and recommendations forwarded to the relevant ministries. Participants included the full range of the local population, from peasants through zemstvo workers, landed gentry, and governors.

100. Goudsblom 1992 is the best recent study of fire cultures in the development of the West.

101. Bayard 1973: 10.

102. See Frierson 1993a: esp. chapter 8, "Baba: The Peasant Woman—Virago, Eve, or Victim?"

103. Pyne 1997: 58.

Chapter 2. Fire as Apocalypse or Pathology

1. There were fire scares in the 1830s and 1840s as well, as one of the first analyses of the post-Emancipation era stressed (Pogodin 1879: 8–114). See also Hudson 1997. In the 1840s, the government tracked and tried to reduce the incidence of village fires among state peasants (Druzhinin 1958: 270–273, 374–376). I discuss this further in chapter 6. Stephen Baehr (1998: esp. 233–34) has also considered fire as an apocalyptic metaphor in reference to the Moscow fire of 1812. Other examples of phenomena that predated the Emancipation but came to be associated with it were *samosud* (self-help or mob justice), family divisions, and alcoholism.

2. Pogodin 1879: 3.

3. Ibid.

4. For discussions of the psychological and cultural impact of these fires on specific individuals, see J. Frank 1986: 145–159; Gleason 1980: 166–170.

5. Baum 1924: 54–56.

6. "Pozhary," *Sankt Peterburgskie vedomosti*, no. 115 (May 31, 1862): 517.

7. *Moskovskie vedomosti*, no. 121 (June 6, 1862): 964.

8. For a description of the expansion of the public press and readership, see Leikina-Svirskaia 1971: 217. The number of newspapers alone leapt from 36 to 125 in this period.

9. McReynolds 1991: 283.

10. Dostoevsky 1973, 6: 124.

11. Chekhov 1948: 192.

12. S. K-n, "Po povodu chastykh pozharov v Rossii (Pis'mo k redaktoru 'Golosa')," *Smolenskie gubernskie vedomosti*, no. 36 (1865): 146–148.

13. Dostoevsky 1973: 377. This statement first appeared in *Vremia*, no. 7 (1862): 36.

14. Dostoevsky 1974, 10: 394.

15. Ibid.

16. Consistently across the period, urban fires (*v gorodakh*) accounted for only 8–10 percent of all reported fires.

17. These figures are calculated on the basis of tables in TsSK, MVD 1882, 1889, 1897, and 1912.

18. Bethea 1989: 30–31.

19. Ibid.: 34.

20. Ibid.: 37.

21. Ibid.: 26.

22. Paperno 1998: 305–332.

23. Bethea 1989: 22.

24. Maksimov 1896, 18: 210–211.

25. *Smolenskii vestnik*, no. 30 (September 10 [22], 1878): 3.

26. Louise McReynolds (1991: 59) discussed the tendency toward sensationalism in "boulevard newspapers" in St. Petersburg during this period, with the *St. Petersburg Sheet* the prime example.

27. Paperno 1998: 320–323.

28. "Borovichi," *Novgorodskii listok*, no. 38 (July 25, 1882): 7.

29. Tenishev Fund, delo 804 (Novgorod Province), l. 1.

30. Dostoevsky 1974, 10: 396.

31. See Frierson 1993a: esp. 164–171.

32. Saltykov-Shchedrin 1976: 119.

33. Ibid.: 125–126.

34. Peasants here displayed strategies similar to those explored by Andrew Verner (1995) for the period around the 1905 revolution.

35. *Rossiiskii gosudarstvennyi istoricheskii arkhiv*, fond 1287 (hereafter RGIA), opis' 10, delo 13, l. 27.

36. RGIA, opis' 10, delo 13, l. 126.

37. RGIA, opis' 10, delo 13, l. 271.

38. RGIA, opis' 9, delo 2171, ll. 2–3.

39. Tenishev Fund, delo 30 (Vladimir Province), ll. 1–8; delo 3 (Vladimir Province), l. 4; delo 1575 (Smolensk Province), l. 22; delo 597 (Kostroma Province), ll. 9–10; delo 1087 (Orel Province, Orel District), ll. 1–2. This behavior was also described by N. A. Ivanitskii (1890: 14). Chekhov employed these reports in his short story "An Encounter" (1968: 128), in which the church beggar, Yefrem, is collecting to rebuild his village's church. Yefrem explains that "Elijah the Prophet must have been wroth, the church was locked and the whole belfry was in flames."

40. Efimenko 1877: 185; Kolchin 1899: 3, 13; Neustupov 1902: 118; Ushakov 1896; Zavoiko 1914: 118. Ushakov included reports of this belief from Tula, Riazan, Kaluga, and Vladimir Provinces. See also Tenishev Fund, delo 171 (Vologda Province), l. 26; delo 30 (Vladimir Province), l. 7; delo 1568 (Smolensk Province), l. 26; delo 597 (Kostroma Province), l. 9; delo 134 (Penza Province), l. 44; delo 1087 (Orel Province), l. 1. In addition, see Ivanitskii 1890: 126.

41. *Pozharnyi*, no. 111-39 (October 8, 1894): 861.

42. See, for example, Tenishev Fund, delo 1554 (Smolensk Province), l. 10.

43. *Trudy mestnykh komitetov* 1903, 11: 321.

44. Alabin 1869: 1.

45. Pogodin 1879: 3.

46. *Smolenskii vestnik*, no. 98 (August 20, 1882), 1.

47. Sokolovich 1896: 5.

48. Report of A. I. Satin in *Trudy mestnykh komitetov* 1903, 11: 321.

49. *Trudy mestnykh komitetov* 1903, 25: 178.

50. Novgorodskaia gubernskaia zemskaia uprava 1892: 3–4.

51. For a survey of zemstvo fire insurance programs, see Gofshtetter 1902.

52. Isaev 1894: 10.

53. Fesenko 1899: 5.

54. Strukov 1903: 63.

55. Alabin 1869: 2.

56. Ibid.: 2–4.

57. Ibid.: 8.

58. Tenishev Fund, delo 1848 (no location provided), and delo 1103 (Orel Province), ll. 6–7.

59. Zinoviev 1877: 3.

60. See note 17, this chapter, for sources.

61. Esipov (1892) traced the history of Russian laws dealing with fire and arson.

62. This was so because, for all but the most miserable structures in the village, zemstvo fire insurance premiums typically covered only around one-third of the cost of rebuilding. RGIA, opis' 9, delo 2171, l. 26, and delo 467, ll. 60–123. See also Lunevskii 1912.

63. Isaev 1894: 11.

64. Strukov 1903: 2.

65. Ivanitskii 1890: 126.

66. Tenishev Fund, delo 804 (Novgorod Province), l. 8; delo 120 (Vologda Province), l. 5; delo 153 (Vologda Province), l. 16.

67. *Pozharnyi*, no. 110-38 (October 1, 1894), 826.

68. Tenishev Fund, delo 818 (Novgorod Province), l. 7.

69. Tenishev Fund, delo 729 (Novgorod Province), l. 6.

70. Tenishev Fund, delo 1757 (Iaroslavl Province), l. 12, and delo 151 (Vologda Province), l. 6; *Smolenskii vestnik*, no. 30 (September 10 [22], 1878): 3.

71. "Ustiuzhna," *Novgorodskii listok*, no. 42 (August 22, 1882): 5.

72. Tenishev Fund, delo 1695 (Smolensk Province), l. 17.

73. One exception to this rule came from an eyewitness account sent to the Tenishev Bureau. In it, the reporter said that women and children worked to save belongings while the men lost their heads. Tenishev Fund, delo 171 (Vologda Province), l. 24.

74. Tenishev Fund, delo 804 (Novgorod Province), l. 1.

75. Tenishev Fund, delo 333 (Vologda Province), l. 45.

76. De Sherbinin (1997); she cites also Axelrod 1991 and Pahomov 1992–1993.

77. Interestingly, Iu. K. Shcheglov (1986) does not explore these stories in his structuralist analysis of fire motifs in literature. Ronald LeBlanc first alerted me to this essay.

78. Chekhov 1955–1962, 4: 422.

79. De Sherbinin 1997: 64.

80. Chekhov 1955–1962, 4: 420.

81. Ibid.: 422.

82. Senderovich 1994: 256.

83. Chekhov 1955–1962, 8: 211.

84. Ibid.

85. Ibid.

86. Ibid.: 212.

87. Ibid.

88. Ibid.: 213.

89. Ibid.: 212.

90. Senderovich 1994: 257.

91. Comments by Stephen Baehr on a draft of this chapter when it was submitted as an article to *Canadian Slavonic Papers*.

92. Senderovich 1994: 258.

93. Chekhov 1955–1962, 8: 214.

94. De Sherbinin 1997: 42–43.

95. On Chekhov's experimentation with ethnographic style, see Popkin 1992: 36–51. Although Popkin argues that Chekhov failed at the task he undertook, his effort demonstrates his familiarity with the disciplinary requirements of the new field of ethnography and of the journals in which ethnographic explorations of fire in the countryside were published.

96. Frierson 1993a; McReynolds 1991.

97. Knight 1994.

98. Semenov 1902: 192.

99. On the peasants' relationship to the commune, see Bartlett 1990.

100. *Trudy mestnykh komitetov* 1903, 14: 212.

Chapter 3. Fire as Russia's Historical Evil

1. Stoliarov 1986: 26. I also want to note that this chapter, more than any other in this manuscript, reflects the influence of Stephen J. Pyne and his work, with his attention to the material reality of fire and its impact on the environment. Johan Goudsblom's *Fire and Civilization* (1992) also contributed to a comparative reading of Russia's fire condition at the end of the nineteenth century.

2. This was one of the forms of family division of extended peasant households that marked the post-Emancipation period. See Frierson 1987b.

3. Stoliarov 1986: 27.

4. Ibid.

5. RGIA, opis' 9, delo 3039 (1895), l. 10.

6. RGIA, opis' 10, delo 13, ll. 354–370.

7. RGIA, opis' 10, delo 13, l. 19.

8. RGIA, opis' 9, delo 2171, l. 2.

9. RGIA, opis' 9, delo 467, l. 1.

10. Tenishev Fund, delo 1449 (Riazan Province), l. 52.

11. Tenishev Fund, delo 1352 (Penza Province), ll. 64, 74.

12. *Trudy mestnykh komitetov* 1903, 7: 332–333.

13. Report of A. P. Engel'gardt, governor of Saratov, prepared for the minister of the interior and submitted also to the Provincial Committee on the Needs of Agriculture in 1902. *Trudy mestnykh komitetov* 1903, 27: 143–144.

14. RGIA, opis' 9, delo 3039, l. 170.

15. Illiustrov 1904: 317.

16. RGIA, opis' 10, delo 13, l. 157.

17. RGIA, opis' 10, delo 13, l. 159.

18. Tenishev Fund, delo 984 (Orel Province), l. 11.

19. Tenishev Fund, delo 805 (Novgorod Province), l. 8.

20. Tenishev Fund, delo 1454 (Riazan Province), ll. 9–11.

21. *Trudy mestnykh komitetov* 1903, 2: 32.

22. "O protivopozharnykh meropriiatiiakh Saratovskogo gubernskogo zemstva," in *Imperatorskoe rossiiskoe pozharnoe obshchestvo* 1903, 1: 305–306.

23. Gatti 1903.

24. See, for example, Anfimov 1984: 86–87; Wilbur 1991: 112, 119, 123; Worobec 1991: 18–19, 101, 103.

25. E. Jones 1987: 39.

26. Ibid.: 24, 33–34.

27. The quoted phrase is E. Jones's (1987: 22) for such disasters.

28. Ministerstvo Vnutrennikh del 1883: Article 89. This publication presents the articles of the Fire Code of 1857 as revised in 1876, 1879, 1881, and 1883.

29. *Tsentral'nyi gosudarstvennyi arkhiv literaturi i iskusstva*, fond 202 (N. N. Zlatovratskii), opis' 1, delo 34, l. 1.

30. Frierson 1993b: see esp. letter 8, pp. 185–198.

31. D. Jones 1982: 20–21.

32. Through maps of individual estates and analyses of systems of interaction, Roosevelt (1995) makes vivid how the serfs' world remained distant from the manor, often separated by fields or rivers that provided some insulation against daily, petty intrusion by nonpeasants.

33. TsSK, MVD 1893: 8; "Polozhenie o vzaimnom zemskom strakhovanii" 1869: 181–203.

34. The statistics published by the Central Statistical Committee enjoy certain advantages over those published in other sources. The primary advantage over statistics published in local newspapers and in zemstvo publications is their consistency in categorization and the regularity with which they were recorded. Zemstvo statistics most fully report fires damaging insured structures, whereas Central Statistical Committee statistics report all fires that came to the local officials' attention. One may turn to local newspapers and to zemstvo reports and statistical yearbooks for fuller descriptions of rural fires, but neither of these kinds of sources gathered or published statistics on fire, year in and year out, over these four decades

as the Central Statistical Committee did. In the following discussion I have relied on the latter to explore trends while drawing on local sources for the experiences of specific locations in specific years or periods.

35. Kahan 1989: 10.

36. Ibid.: 10–12.

37. Ibid.: 10.

38. Ibid.: 27.

39. *Trudy mestnykh komitetov* 1903, 24: 286.

40. Kahan 1989: 10.

41. Verkhovskoi 1910: 4.

42. *Novgorodskaia gubernskaia zemskaia uprava* 1902: 5–6.

43. E. Jones 1987: 22.

44. In Moscow, Kaluga, Nizhnii Novgorod, Kostroma, Tver, Iaroslavl, and Vladimir Provinces, most peasant houses did have chimneys by the turn of the century. In Pskov, Novgorod, Petersburg, Olonets, Penza, Orel, Tambov, Voronezh, Riazan, Kursk, and Tula Provinces, so-called "black" or chimneyless izbas were the norm. See Efimenko 1877: 22; Makovetskii 1962: 67–68; Semenov 1899: 101, 1900: 112, 1902: 176.

45. Belokonskii 1900: 20.

46. Ibid.: 33.

47. Ibid.: 33–34.

48. Ibid.: 37.

49. Articles 452 and 453, *Ustav stroitel'nyi* 1888: 179.

50. Ministerstvo Vnutrennikh del 1883: Article 32.

51. *Ustav stroitel'nyi* 1888: 184.

52. Ministerstvo Vnutrennikh del 1883: Article 34.

53. Efimenko 1877: 30; Ivanitskii 1890: 14; Nikitinskii 1884; Staniukovich 1970: 73. The following dela in the Tenishev Fund also describe these patterns of illumination in various regions of the empire: delo 1030 (Orel Province), l. 55; delo 607 (Kostroma Province), l. 21; delo 1567 (Smolensk Province), l. 5; delo 1564 (Smolensk Province), l. 17; delo 432 (Viatka Province), l. 32; delo 252 (Vologda Province), l. 16; delo 102 (Vologda Province), ll. 18–19; delo 5 (Vladimir Province), l. 27; delo 43 (Vladimir Province), l. 9; delo 71 (Vladimir Province), l. 7.

54. Ministerstvo Vnutrennikh del 1883: Article 36.

55. Dal' 1879, 2: 90.

56. *Ustav stroitel'nyi* 1888: 179.

57. Ministerstvo Vnutrennikh del 1883: Article 33.

58. Ibid.: Articles 135–148.

59. Tenishev Fund, delo 333, ll. 43–44.

60. Tenishev Fund, delo 1670 (Smolensk Province), l. 4, and delo 1559 (Smolensk Province), l. 22.

61. *Zemskii sbornik Chernigovskoi gubernii*, March 1870: 53; August 1870: 134; December 1870: 100; January 1871: 64; February 1871: 88; March 1871: 89; April 1871: 54; May 1871: 51; June 1871: 71; July 1871: 93; August 1871: 67; September 1871: 106; October 1871: 111; November 1871: 82; December 1871: 56.

62. Novgorodskaia gubernskaia zemskaia uprava 1902: 3.

63. *Trudy mestnykh komitetov* 1903, 19: 536, 30: 336; Zinoviev 1877: 3.

64. GANO, fond 138, delo 3049, l. 54.

65. Peasants of European Russia joined millions of other people around the globe in switching to matches in the late nineteenth century. See Goudsblom 1992: 170–171; Zinoviev 1877: 4. From the Tenishev Fund, the following files include references to children and fire:

delo 1103 (Orel Province), l. 7; delo 1568 (Smolensk Province), l. 24; delo 1670 (Smolensk Province, Smolensk District), l. 5; delo 171 (Vologda Province), l. 25; delo 656 (Nizhnii Novgorod Province), l. 6. In Trudy mestnykh komitetov, references to child's play as the cause of fire and statements on the need to establish nurseries may be found in the following volumes and pages: 21: 255–256 (Minsk Province); 5: 213 (Vitebsk Province); 47: 98 (Chernigov Province); 42: 69–71 (Tver Province); 11: 40 (Grodno Province); 28: 203 (Orel Province); 41: 29 (Tambov Province); 34: 31 (Riazan Province); 38: 130–132 (Simbirsk Province); 2: 34 (Astrakhan Province); 43: 326 (Tula Province); 30: 248 (Perm Province); 49: 6 (Iaroslavl Province). See also Buksgevden 1902: 103–110; Ransel 1994; Imperatorskoe rossiiskoe pozharnoe obshchestvo 1903, 2: 130–131; "Iz krestetskogo uezda," *Novgorodskii listok*, no. 41 (August 15, 1882): 4; "Ustiuzhna," *Novgorodskii listok*, no. 42 (August 22, 1882): 5. Also, GANO, fond 138, delo 3329, l. 54. One example from Samara Province may be found in *Samarskie gubernskie vedomosti*, no. 48 (June 20, 1870): 4.

66. RGIA, opis' 10, delo 13, l. 142.

67. *Trudy mestnykh komitetov* 1903, 19: 520.

68. Worobec 1990: 90.

69. Semenov 1902: 35–37.

70. Ibid.: 45–46.

71. TsSK, MVD 1889: 124–147.

72. TsSK, MVD 1897: 10–45.

73. Ibid.: 38.

74. *Trudy mestnykh komitetov* 1903, 37: 141.

75. Pyne 1997: 330–331.

76. Smirnov 1884: 4–5.

77. Semenov 1901: 53, 1902: 34–35.

78. Semenov 1899: 34.

79. Semenov 1901: 53.

80. Belokonskii 1900: 17.

81. Sofronov 1996: 231.

82. Isaev 1894: 10.

83. Pyne 1997: 6.

84. Ibid.: 50.

85. *Trudy mestnykh komitetov* 1903, 2: 32.

86. TsSK, MVD 1879–1884.

87. Gofshtetter 1902: 2–3.

88. *Novgorodskaia gubernskaia zemskaia uprava* 1902: 5.

89. GANO, fond 138, opis' 1, delo 3334, l. 58.

90. *Smolenskii vestnik*, no. 93 (August 8, 1882): 1.

91. *Trudy mestnykh komitetov* 1903, 12: 98.

92. Ibid., 38: 536.

93. Ibid., 47: 47. Similar statements were made before the Kursk committees (Ibid., 19: 402).

94. Ibid., 24: 289.

95. Nikitin 1903: 67.

96. E. Jones 1987: 33–34. Warsaw, for example, was already a brick and tile city by 1431. See also E. Jones 1968.

97. Frost and Jones 1989: 345.

98. See Frierson 1987b, 1990. For some of the numerous references made to this connection at the turn of the century, see statements made before the 1902 district and provincial committees in the following volumes: *Trudy mestnykh komitetov* 1903, 6: 67, 21: 59, 31: 963, 47: 48;

Zhurnaly uezdnykh komitetov Smolenskoi gubernii o nuzhdakh sel'sko-khoziaistvennoi promyshlennosti 1902 god 1903: 227. See also Tenishev Fund, delo 1454 (Riazan Province), l. 2.

99. *Trudy mestnykh komitetov* 1903, 31: 254.

100. Gofshtetter 1902: 92; *Kratkoe sel'sko-khoziaistvennoe opisanie po Malmyzhskomu uezdu, Viatskoi gubernii. Po dannym zemskoi statistiki* 1892: 1–2.

101. *Kratkoe opisanie orlovskogo uezda Viatskoi gubernii. Po dannym statistiki* 1892: 7.

102. RGIA, opis' 10, delo 13, l. 271.

103. RGIA, opis' 9, delo 2042, ll. 35–73.

104. RGIA, opis' 9, delo 2171, l. 2.

105. Lindenmeyr 1996: 51.

106. Tenishev Fund, delo 120 (Vologda Province), ll. 7–8; delo 1342 (Penza Province), l. 240; delo 173 (Vologdo Province), l. 56; delo 818 (Novgorod Province), l. 8; delo 977 (Orel Province), l. 12. See also Gromyko 1986: 38–50, 58–60, 1991: 73–74, 86–87.

107. Tenishev Fund, delo 1695 (Smolensk Province), l. 20.

108. RGIA, opis' 9, delo 467, ll. 3–4, 132–133.

109. RGIA, opis' 9, delo 3039, l. 170.

110. RGIA, opis' 9, delo 3039, l. 95.

111. Sazonov 1893: 437.

112. These decrees and laws appear in PSZ 6 (1831), 4538, no. 1, and 4845; 8 (1833), 6382; 14 (1839), 12859; 30 (1855), 29558; 35 (1860), 35534; 36 (1861), 36593, 37453, and 37585; 39 (1864), 40689 and 40849; 41 (1866), 42978, 43310, and 43618; 42 (1867), 44615.

113. PSZ 6 (1832), 4538, p. 312.

114. Ibid., 4808.

115. Ibid., 4845.

116. PSZ 12 (1838), 10367.

117. PSZ 41 (1866), 44615.

118. RGIA, opis' 9, delo 467.

119. Frierson 1993b: chapter 1. See also Frierson 1997a.

120. *Trudy mestnykh komitetov* 1903, 5: 213.

121. De Sherbinin 1997: 64.

122. Dostoevsky, *Devils*, 582.

123. Tenishev Fund, delo 1695 (Smolensk Province, Iukhnov District), L. 19.

124. *Ustav stroitel'nyi* 1888: 99.

PART TWO. LETTING LOOSE THE RED ROOSTER

1. In rural Russia, to threaten someone with the red rooster was to threaten to set his or her property on fire. One ethnographer (Maksimov 1890: 465) explained the red rooster image as both a borrowing from the German and an outgrowth of the ancient Slavic ritual of sacrificing roosters to the god of fire.

2. Tenishev Fund, delo 1292 (Penza Province, Gorodoshchensk District), ll. 77–79.

3. Hobsbawm and Rudé 1973.

4. Ibid.: 166.

5. Ivanov 1964: 662; Nifontov 1960: 280, 578–579, 791, 808, 813; Shapkarin 1959: 633, 634; Zaionchkovskii 1968: 111–112.

6. Arson is the most dramatic and prominent feature of the peasant rebellions of 1905–1907 in Shanin's account (1986: 79–99). See also Dubrovskii 1956: 33–73; Edelman 1987: 86.

7. Shanin 1986: 93.

8. Engel 1994b: 45.

9. S. Frank 1999: esp. 132–137; Frierson 1997b.
10. Figes 1991: 381.
11. Fitzpatrick 1994: 42.
12. Ibid.: chapter 9, "Malice," 233–261.
13. Viola 1996: 124.
14. D. Jones 1982: 33.
15. Ibid.: 51.
16. Thompson 1966: 63–65.
17. A. Smith 1985: 540.
18. Ibid.: 546.
19. Ibid.: 557. Also see Faulkner 1950: 3–25.
20. Archer 1990; Hussey and Swash 1994: 8. Hobsbawm and Rudé's conclusion (1973: 168) reads: "Moreover, the fires in the majority of counties where they occurred followed a pattern that links them more or less closely with the labourers' movement."
21. Zaionchkovskii 1964: 480–481.
22. Schulte 1994: 31.
23. Ibid.: 33.
24. Ibid.: 9.
25. Ibid.: 7.

Chapter 4. The Fiery Brand, Russian Style

1. Osterberg 1996: 41.
2. *Trudy mestnykh komitetov* 1903, 11: 349.
3. Ibid., 8: 111.
4. Ibid., 15: 1037.
5. Ministerstvo Iustitsii 1874: 36.
6. Ministerstvo Iustitsii 1885 [1880]: 30; [1881]: 30.
7. Ermolov 1910: 1.
8. Ibid.: 11.
9. *Kurskie gubernskie vedomosti*, nos. 41 (May 29, 1870): 3; 45 (June 15, 1870): 3; 50 (June 30, 1870): 3; 58 (July 28, 1870): 3.
10. Ministerstvo Iustitsii 1878: xlviii.
11. I think we might also want to consider arson within village communities as an antecedent to pogroms against Jewish villages.
12. For two examples of this, see Ermolov 1910 and Purishkevich 1909.
13. Thompson 1966: 63–65.
14. Hoch 1986: 57.
15. Frierson 1987b: 58–59, 1993a: 66.
16. Frierson 1987b: 59.
17. Frierson 1993b: 76–77. British colonial rulers encountered the same response on Cyprus when they tried to restrict access to forests in the early twentieth century. See Pyne 1997: 139.
18. Tenishev Fund, delo 1711 (Smolensk Province), l. 40; also delo 857 (Novgorod Province), l. 1.
19. Tenishev Fund, delo 1589 (Smolensk Province), l. 33.
20. *Trudy mestnykh komitetov* 1903, 34: 584–585.
21. *Smolenskii vestnik*, no. 119 (October 8, 1882): 8.
22. GANO, fond 138, opis' 1, delo 2380, ll. 10–11.

23. GANO, fond 138, opis' 1, delo 3050, ll. 1–2, 23.

24. They also appear in the chronologies of peasant actions in Zaionchkovskii 1968: 513 and Shapkarin 1959: 615, 641.

25. Uspenskii 1956: 376–377.

26. Ibid.: 383.

27. Tenishev Fund, delo 857 (Novgorod Province), l. 1.

28. *Smolenskii vestnik*, no. 115 (September 29, 1882): 2. For reports of similar fires, see *Smolenskii vestnik*, no. 24 (August 20, 1878): 2; no. 36 (October 1, 1878): 2; no. 41 (October 19, 1878): 2; no. 44 (October 29, 1878): 2; no. 97 (August 18, 1882): 1–2.

29. *Smolenskii vestnik*, no. 120 (October 10, 1882): 1. Similar incidents can be found in Ivanov 1964: 662; Nifontov 1960: 280, 578–579, 791, 808, 813; Shapkarin 1959: 633, 634; and Zaionchkovskii 1968: 111–112.

30. *Pozharnyi*, no. 106-34 (September 3, 1894): 738.

31. GANO, fond 138, opis' 1: delo 3049, ll. 44, 99, 103; delo 3050, l. 1, 23; delo 3069, l. 28; delo 3226, l. 12, 48, 82; delo 3468, l. 77.

32. Hobsbawm and Rudé 1973: 171.

33. D. Jones 1982: 47.

34. Hussey and Swash 1994: 1.

35. A. Smith 1985: 547.

36. *Trudy mestnykh komitetov* 1903, 15: 213, 34: 319.

37. "Proisshestviia," *Nizhegorodskii listok*, no. 58 (June 15, 1871): 3.

38. Gosudarstvennyi arkhiv Smolenskoi oblasti (hereafter GASO), fond 1, opis' 5, delo 82 (1884), ll. 1–2.

39. Gosudarstvennyi arkhiv Vologodskoi oblasti (hereafter GAVO), fond 179, opis' 3, delo 575 and delo 1927.

40. GANO, fond 138, opis' 1, delo 3050, l. 23.

41. Maslov 1923: 113.

42. See Fitzpatrick 1994; Viola 1996. Figes (1991) largely avoids this term, using instead "peasant farmers."

43. See Figes 1989: 192; Frierson 1993a: 139–160.

44. P. N. Miasoedov reported to the Roslavl District Committee in Smolensk Province in 1902 that this concern acted as a brake on programs for breaking up crowded village housing as a fire prevention measure, because peasants were afraid to be build homesteads isolated in the fields where they would be more vulnerable to arsonists. *Zhurnaly uezdnykh komitetov Smolenskoi gubernii o nuzhdakh sel'skokhoziaistvennoi promyshlennosti* 1902 god 1903: 227.

45. See also Shapkarin 1959: 641, where an incident in Poltava Province involving arson against the grain and outbuildings of a "kulak" is listed.

46. GANO, fond 138, opis' 1, delo 3226, l. 32.

47. GANO, fond 138, op. 1, delo 3329, l. 38.

48. GANO, fond 138, opis' 1, delo 3049, l. 129.

49. "Korrespondentsiia. Rybninsk," *Sudebnyi vestnik*, no. 76 (April 8, 1875): 4.

50. GAVO, fond 179, opis' 3, delo 1278, l. 2.

51. GAVO, fond 179, opis' 3, delo 1196, l. 3.

52. Shapkarin 1959: 641.

53. Tenishev Fund, delo 1393 (Penza Province), l. 31.

54. Uspenskii 1956: 378.

55. Ibid.: 380.

56. Ibid.

57. Hussey and Swash 1994: 14.

58. Mixter 1991: 297.
59. Lenin 1941: 49–99, 114.
60. Burds 1998: 143–185.
61. Frierson 1993b: 215.
62. Ibid.: 222.
63. Hoch 1986: 160.
64. Figes 1991; Shanin 1986.
65. Viola 1996.
66. Engel 1994b: 48.

Chapter 5. Arson as Impotent Spite or Potent Practice

1. Zenkovsky 1963: 58.
2. Pogodin 1879: 6–7.
3. "Sudebnaia khronika," no. 146 (July 6, 1867): 584.
4. Ibid.: 535.
5. See A. K. Afanas'ev 1994.
6. *Sudebnyi vestnik*, no. 146 (July 6, 1867): 585.
7. "Sudebnaia khronika," *Sudebnyi vestnik*, no. 273 (December 21, 1867): 1123–1125.
8. *Nizhegorodskii listok*, no. 114 (September 28, 1871): 2.
9. GAVO, fond 179, opis' 3, delo 529, l. 2
10. GAVO, fond 179, opis' 3, delo 1299, ll. 2, 6.
11. GAVO, fond 179, opis' 3, delo 1946, l. 2.
12. S. Frank 1996: 541.
13. Ibid.: 551–552.
14. Ibid.: 560.
15. These calculations are based on the relevant years of the Ministerstvo Iustitsii's (Ministry of Justice's) *Svod statisticheskikh svedenii po delam ugolovnym*, published in St. Petersburg from 1873 to 1907.
16. Foinitskii 1893: 132, 138–139.
17. TsSK, MVD 1912: 128–152; *Ministerstvo Iustitsii* 1899: Part 2, 101.
18. For Novgorod Province, for example, see GANO, fond 138, opis' 1, delo 3329, ll. 23, 61.
19. Regina Schulte (1994: 54–55) argued this position in analyzing arson in upper Bavaria. In her view, the association between women and the hearth fire explained the desire among excluded male hired hands, who became arsonists to destroy what they desired. She does not address this question in relation to female arsonists.
20. Foinitskii 1893: 123.
21. See Frierson 1993a: 164–168.
22. Foinitskii 1893: 135.
23. Hussey and Swash 1994: 14–16.
24. Tenishev Fund, delo 1115, ll. 3–7.
25. See also Tenishev Fund, delo 1490 (Saratov Province, Khvalinsk District), l. 8, and delo 656 (Nizhnii Novgorod Province, Vasil'-Sursk District), l. 8.
26. See Frierson 1987b: esp. 64–69.
27. Tenishev Fund, delo 1115 (Orel Province, Orel District), l. 6.
28. Ibid., ll. 6–7.
29. GASO, fond 1, opis' 5, delo 217, l. 2.
30. *Pozharnyi*, no. 105-33 (August 27, 1894): 715.
31. GANO, fond 138, opis' 1, delo 3049, l. 132.

32. *Pozharnyi*, no. 105-33 (August 27, 1894): 715.

33. Ibid., no. 108-36 (September 17, 1894): 793.

34. "Korespondentsiia. Rybninsk," *Sudebnyi vestnik*, no. 76 (April 8, 1975): 4.

35. *Trudy mestnykh komitetov* 1903, 9: 142, 16: 54.

36. Archer 1990: 9.

37. Rudé 1985: 119.

38. Neuberger 1993: 13.

39. Ibid.: 10–12.

40. Johnson and Monkkonen 1996: 7. See the same source for references to Elias's work.

41. Ibid.: 13.

42. Tenishev Fund, delo 805 (Novgorod Province), l. 12.

43. Tenishev Fund, delo 805 (Novgorod Province, Cherepovets District), l. 16. The nature
of this conflict between parish and priest was not unusual in rural Russia, where the under-
payment of parish priests remained a frustrating effect of the inadequate support of both
church and state for these religious servants. Tensions over fees characterized the relationship
in much of European Russia in the nineteenth century. See Freeze 1983: esp. chapters 7 and
8, and also his translation of I. S. Belliustin's *Opisanie sel'skogo dukhovenstva* (Belliustin 1985).

44. GANO, fond 138, opis' 1, delo 3559, l. 34.

45. Pogodin 1879: 66–67.

46. The percentage of landowners who were Polish in 1861 was 87 in Kiev Province, 89 in
Podolia Province, and 93 in Volynia Province (Hamm 1993: 56).

47. Ibid.: 57–59.

48. Whelan 1999.

49. Semenov 1901: 151.

50. These percentages are based on calculations from the respective years of the
Ministerstvo Iustitsii's *Svod statisticheskikh svedenii po delam ugolovnym* (1873–1907).

51. Figes 1980: 24–26.

52. Hobsbawm and Rudé 1973: 37.

53. For a good discussion of informal courts of peasant justice, see Czap 1967.

54. *Pozharny*i, no. 103-31 (August 13, 1894): 668.

55. Pallot and Shaw 1990: 118–119.

56. Mixter 1991: 295.

57. Ibid.: 313.

58. Archer 1990: 24.

59. D. Jones 1982: 33.

60. On these two peasant disturbances, see Field 1976.

61. See Worobec 1992, 1995.

62. See Burbank 1988, 1997: 82–106; Frierson 1997b; Popkins 1996, 1999, 2000. On the
justice of the peace, see Neuberger 1994: 231–246.

63. Farnsworth 1986.

64. See Frierson 1997b for a discussion of the scene at cantonal court sessions.

65. Eklof 1986: 422.

66. Ibid.: 430.

67. Ibid.

68. Goody 1986: 142.

69. Ibid.: 143–144.

70. Ibid.: 153.

71. See, for example, GANO, fond 359, opis' 1, delo 8 (1894–1895); fond 359, opis' 1, delo
12 (1894); fond 364, opis' 1, delo 6 (1894).

72. D. Jones 1982: 61.

73. Schulte 1994: 56.

74. This pattern was consistent in Novgorod district police reports from the 1860s through 1904.

75. Schulte 1994: 57.

76. See note 9, chapter 4, for sources on Kursk. For Novgorod, see, for example, GANO, fond 138, opis' 1, delo 3049, ll. 10, 59, 79; delo 3050, ll. 2, 17; delo 3069, ll. 30, 46, 56; delo 3329, ll. 23, 61, 65, 78; delo 3559, ll. 3, 25, 34. For Smolensk, see as examples *Smolenskii vestnik*, no. 41 (19 October 1878): 2; no. 44 (29 October 1878): 2; no. 48 (12 November 1878): 2; no. 73 (23 June 1882): 2; no. 77 (June 2, 1882): 3; no. 123 (17 October 1882): 2; and GASO, opis' 4, delo 316, l. 1.

77. For a discussion of the importance of these criteria in the peasants' appraisal of deeds in the community, see Frierson 1987a.

78. *Pozharnyi*, no. 103-31 (August 13, 1894): 668–669.

79. Several local respondents to the Tenishev Ethnographic Survey in 1897–1898 reported this pattern of evaluating the seriousness of arson among the peasants in their area. See Tenishev Fund, delo 1466 (Riazan Province), l. 36; delo 1475 (St. Petersburg Province), l. 11; delo 656 (Nizhnii Novgorod Province), l. 7; delo 1115 (Orel Province), ll. 2–3.

80. Tenishev Fund, delo 1475 (St. Petersburg Province), l. 11.

81. Thompson 1966: 63.

82. Schulte 1994: 56.

83. GANO, fond 138, opis' 1, delo 3468, ll. 57, 76.

84. *Pozharnyi*, no. 108-36 (September 17, 1894): 788.

85. Sergeevskii 1882: 108.

86. The following discussion comes from Article 40774, PSZ 39 (1867): 333–339.

87. Miachin 1904.

88. Gofshtetter 1902.

89. Ibid.: 92.

90. Zemstvo fire statistics diverged from the statistics submitted to the Ministry of the Interior because they focused only on fires involving insured structures and because they listed only three possible causes: arson, carelessness, and "other."

91. Gofshtetter 1902: 93.

92. Ibid.: 93–94.

93. TsSK, MVD 1897: 67.

94. TsSK, MVD 1912: 132.

95. Gofshtetter 1902: 29.

96. Ibid.: 28.

97. Ibid.: 31.

98. TsSK, MVD 1897: 69.

99. Besedkin 1885: 67; Kaiser 1980: 65–66.

100. Daniel Kaiser (1980: 66–67) hesitated to accept the translation of "potok" as exile, preferring to leave it undefined rather than reaching beyond contextual or linguistic evidence to conclude that it meant exile.

101. Besedkin 1885: 75–98.

102. Ibid.: 105.

103. Ermolov 1910: 39.

104. The following discussion is based on *Svod zakonov ugolovnykh* 1885: 333–336.

105. Esipov 1892.

106. Hay et al. 1975: 17–63.

107. Gradovskii 1884: 9.

108. *Trudy mestnykh komitetov* 1903, 21: 60.

109. Tarnovskii 1897.

110. These percentages are calculated on the basis of the annual volumes of the Ministerstvo Iustitsii's *Svod statisticheskikh svedenii po delam ugolovnym* (1873–1907).

111. *Imperatorskoe Rossiiskoe pozharnoe obshchestvo* 1903, 2: 202–203.

112. For example, *Trudy mestnykh komitetov* 1903, 46: 20.

113. *Trudy mestnykh komitetov* 1903, 27: 766.

114. This was a perennial problem in the cantonal court system, too, where peasants equally avoided serving as witnesses. See Frierson 1997b.

115. *Trudy mestnykh komitetov* 1903, 21: 60, 28: 760–764.

116. Ibid., 9: 142, 16: 54.

117. *Pozharnyi*, no. 105-33 (August 27, 1894): 715. See also *Smolenskie gubernskie vedomosti*, no. 21 (1862): 157.

118. D. Jones 1982: 21.

119. Frierson 1993b: 185.

120. Ibid.

121. Zaionchkovskii 1964: 67.

122. Yaney 1973: 250, 334–335; Zaionchkovskii 1964: 67–68.

123. *Trudy mestnykh komitetov* 1903, 16: 54.

124. Ibid., 43: 490.

125. For example, GANO, fond 138, opis' 1, delo 3050, l. 33.

126. *Trudy mestnykh komitetov* 1903, 16: 44.

127. Yaney makes this point (1973: 232).

128. Kahan 1989: 108–143; Wheatcroft 1991.

129. Kahan 1989: 111, 140.

130. Wheatcroft 1991: 166.

131. Such levels of damages would come to approximately two rubles per arson fire. If that were true, then it would testify all the more to arson's function within village communities as a warning and not to the more common image of blazing manor houses.

132. C. White 1987: 215.

133. Ibid.: 213.

134. Ibid.: 97.

135. *Trudy mestnykh komitetov* 1903, 11: 349.

136. See Frierson 1993a: esp. chapter 5.

137. *Pozharnoe delo*, vol. 11, no. 1 (January 3, 1904): 5.

Part Three. Mobilizing to Make Russia Modern

1. Fallows 1982: 178, 196.

2. I have chosen to discuss only the zemstvo compulsory insurance program and not the governors' program that was instituted simultaneously in non-zemstvo provinces, because the zemstvo program became part of the larger story of society's mobilization against fire, whereas the gubernatorial programs were state affairs.

3. These peasant players in the zemstvo fire insurance program illustrate the potential of peasants in local governance, as discussed by Atkinson (1982: 115–121).

Chapter 6. Fire as Insurance Hazard

1. Ewald 1991: 207.

2. Clark 1993; Ferrara 1993; Tracy 1966; Welsh 1963.

3. Macey 1987: 18–19.

4. Starr 1972: 303.

5. Defert 1991; Zelizer 1979: 53.

6. Druzhinin 1958: 273.

7. Ibid.: 274.

8. PSZ 32 (1858), 33877.

9. PSZ 36 (1861), 36593.

10. PSZ 36 (1861), 37585.

11. The peace mediator was an official introduced by the Emancipation primarily to help negotiate and register land settlements between peasants and their former lords.

12. PSZ 42 (1867), 44615.

13. Ibid.

14. PSZ 39 (1864), 40457.

15. PSZ 41 (1866), 42978 and 43310.

16. Veselovskii 1909: 453.

17. PSZ 39 (1864), 40774.

18. Ibid.

19. Ibid.

20. Frieden 1981: 93, 96.

21. Veselovskii 1909: 451.

22. Defert 1991: 223.

23. E. Jones 1968: 145.

24. Defert 1991: 219.

25. The following discussion comes from Veselovskii 1909: 459–537.

26. Ibid.: 492.

27. Ibid.: 502.

28. Senate decisions of July 28, 1900 (no. 9237), and July 26, 1871 (no. 31313), in Kuznetsov 1902: 569–572.

29. TsSK, MVD 1893: 9.

30. Novgorodskaia gubernskaia zemskaia uprava 1902: 3.

31. Veselovskii 1909: 603–607.

32. Ibid.: 607–608.

33. GAVO, fond 34, opis' 5, delo 68, ll. 1–8.

34. Veselovskii 1909: 454.

35. "Zapiska Zemskago Strakhogo Agenta Charushina po voprosu o sodeistvii meram k umen'sheniiu pozharov, razvitiiu proizvodstva i rasprostraneniiu ogneupornykh materialov," *Trudy mestnykh komitetov* 1903, 10: 157.

36. TsSK, MVD 1879–1884: 404–405.

37. RGIA, opis' 9, delo 467, ll. 60–105.

38. RGIA, opis' 9, delo 2171, ll. 6–26.

39. RGIA, opis' 10, delo 13, l. 142.

40. GAVO, fond 18, opis' 1, delo 2803, ll. 13–17.

41. RGIA, opis' 10, delo 13, l. 186.

42. *Trudy mestnykh komitetov* 1903, 37: 143.

43. "Zapiska Zemskago Strakhovogo Agenta Charushina," *Trudy mestnykh komitetov* 1903, 10: 157.

44. PSZ 19 (1899), 17286.

45. Veselovskii 1909: 599, 1914: 456–502.

46. PSZ 48 (1873), 52396.
47. PSZ 54 (1879–1880), 59513.
48. PSZ 10 (1890), 6927.
49. Senate decision of March 9, 1902, published in Kuznetsov 1903: 269.
50. McKenzie 1982: 36–37.
51. PSZ 48 (1873), 52396.
52. Senate decision of May 31, 1891 (no. 6799), in Kuznetsov 1902: 574.

Chapter 7. Fire Contained in the Planned Village

1. GANO, fond 195, opis' 1, delo 7, ll. 1–16.
2. Ibid., l. 36.
3. The quoted description is from Alabin 1869: 8.
4. Mysh 1901: 34–35.
5. Gofshtetter 1902: 4.
6. PSZ 48 (1873), 52396.
7. See, for example, Viatskoe gubernskoe zemstvo 1883; Olonetskoe gubernskoe zemstvo 1910; Pskovskaia gubernskaia zemskaia uprava 1899.
8. *Proekt ob'iazatel'nyia postanovleniia o merakh predostorozhnosti ot pozharov i o postroikakh v seleniiakh* 1901.
9. Frierson 1993b: 169.
10. Purishkevich 1909: 204–205.
11. This pattern is also evident in the state's approach to poor relief (Lindenmeyr 1996: esp. chapters 2–4).
12. See Brumfield and Ruble 1993.
13. These features conform to the definition of modernism in Scott 1998.
14. *Proekt ob'iazatel'nyia postanovleniia* 1901: 11–16.
15. Ibid.: 24–26.
16. Veselovskii 1909: 612–614.
17. Gofshtetter 1902: 28–36.
18. Ibid.: 211–234.
19. Senate decision no. 10865 (October 19, 1899), in Kuznetsov 1902: 577–578.
20. Senate decision no. 2293 (March 13, 1903), in Kuznetsov 1903: 259–260.
21. PSZ 36 (1861), 36662, Articles 110, 149.
22. Gofshtetter 1902: 112–113.
23. Ibid.: 289.
24. Decision of October 7, 1885, published in *Resheniia obshchago sobraniia pervago i kassatsionnykh departamentov i kassatsionnykh departamentov Pravitel'stvuiiushchago senata 1885 g.* (1886): 65.
25. *Pozharnyi*, no. 109-37 (September 17, 1894): 802–803.
26. *Trudy mestnykh komitetov* 1903, 11: 315, 533, 19: 11, 41: 64–66, 47: 8.
27. Gofshtetter 1902: 289.
28. See, for example, "Zapiska krest'ianina A. Ermakova," *Trudy mestnykh komitetov* 1903, 24: 220.
29. *Trudy mestnykh komitetov* 1903, 37: 145.
30. See, as one example, "Zapiska Zemskago Strakhovogo Agenta Charushina," *Trudy mestnykh komitetov* 1903, 10: 157.
31. *Pozharnyi*, no. 102-30 (August 6, 1894): 641.
32. Prokofiev 1903: 11.

33. The twenty-three provinces were Moscow, Viatka, Pskov, Simbirsk, Chernigov, Kostroma, Kaluga, Kursk, Tula, Smolensk, Orel, Nizhnii Novgorod, Riazan, Penza, Poltava, St. Petersburg, Vladimir, Voronezh, Olonets, Khar'kov, Kherson, Iaroslavl, and Kazan (Veselovskii 1909: 616).

34. For example, *Trudy mestnykh komitetov* 1903, 1: 313, 5: 464, 28: 536–537, 34: 238.

35. Imperatorskoe Rossiiskoe pozharnoe obshchestvo 1903, 2: 193.

36. *Pozharnyi*, no. 106–34 (September 3, 1894): 734.

37. *Trudy mestnykh komitetov* 1903, 37: 146–147.

38. Imperatorskoe Rossiiskoe pozharnoe obshchestvo 1903, 2: 200–201.

39. Novgorodskaia gubernskaia zemskaia uprava 1902: 6.

40. These were the zemstvos of Moscow, Simbirsk, Poltava, Orel, Ufa, Kazan, Samara, Saratov, Kostroma, Iaroslavl, Tambov, Penza, Voronezh, Kaluga, Kursk, and Tula Provinces (Veselovskii 1909: 616–618).

41. *Pozharnyi*, no. 103–31 (August 13, 1894): 668.

42. Gofshtetter 1909: 298–299.

43. Novgorodskaia gubernskaia zemskaia uprava 1902: 6.

44. *Trudy mestnykh komitetov* 1903, 10: 239.

45. Veselovskii 1909: 618–619.

46. Imperatorskoe Rossiiskoe pozharnoe obshchestvo 1903, 2: 318–319.

47. GAVO, opis' 5, delo 179, ll. 1, 5, 7, 9, 15, 58, 64, 127, 286, 341.

48. *Pozharnyi*, no. 102–30 (August 6, 1894): 648.

49. Ibid.

50. *Trudy mestnykh komitetov* 1903, 11: 373.

51. *Trudy mestnykh komitetov* 1903, 45: 127.

52. Imperatorskoe Rossiiskoe pozharnoe obshchestvo 1903, 1: 105.

53. Ganzen 1902: ESP. 22–113.

54. Ibid.: 27.

55. *Trudy mestnykh komitetov* 1903, 19: 410.

56. *Trudy mestnykh komitetov* 1903, 34: 639.

Chapter 8. Fire as the Internal Enemy

1. Alabin 1869: 13.

2. *Pozharnyi*, no. 108–36 (September 17, 1894): 788.

3. *Pozharnyi*, no. 110–38 (October 1, 1894): 826.

4. Tenishev Fund, delo 1499 (Saratov Province), l. 51.

5. Tenishev Fund, delo 729 (Novgovod Province); l. 6; delo 1695 (Smolensk Province), ll. 17–18.

6. Tenishev Fund, delo 818 (Novgorod Province), l. 7.

7. See discussion of the reporting on these practices in chapter 2.

8. Ministerstvo Vnutrennikh del 1883: Article 74.

9. Tenishev fund, delo 151 (Vologda Province), l. 6.

10. Tenishev fund, delo 333 (Vologda Province), ll. 43–45; delo 1103 (Orel Province), ll. 5–6; delo 996 (Orel Province), l. 6.

11. Tenishev fund, delo 120 (Vologda Province), l. 2; delo 1388 (Penza Province), l. 4; delo 1490 (Saratov Province), l. 8; delo 1103 (Orel Province), l. 5; delo 151 (Vologda Province), l. 6; delo 1454 (Riazan Province), l. 4; delo 1554 (Smolensk Province), l. 10.

12. Tenishev Fund, delo 1454 (Riazan Province), l. 3.

13. *Proekt ob'iazatel'nyia postanovleniia* 1901: 4–8.

14. Ibid.

15. Frierson 1993b: 192–193.

16. *Proekt ob'iazatel'nyia postanovleniia* 1901: 9–10.

17. Grachev 1899: 6.

18. Ibid.: 26–41.

19. Sheremetev 1892: 233–238.

20. Ibid.: xvii.

21. "Nabroski sedeiushchago pozharnogo," *Pozharnoe delo*, no. 4 (January 24, 1904): 57.

22. The proceedings of the conference were published as *Trudy pervago obshchago s'ezda sostoiashchago pod Avgusteishim Pochetnym predsedatel'stvom Ego Imperatorskogo vysochestva Velikogo Kniaza Vladimira Aleksandrovicha soedenennogo Rossiiskogo Pozharnogo obshchestva u osobogo pri nem pozharno-strakhovogo otdela 1897.*

23. Strukov 1903: 6.

24. Ibid.: 14.

25. Salmond 1996: esp. 191–211.

26. See, for example, *Trudy pervago obshchago . . . 1897.*

27. Green-Hughes 1979: 50.

28. *Pozharnyi*, no. 73-1 (January 8, 1895): 10–11.

29. *Obzor deiatel'nosti Strel'ninskoi chastnoi pozharnoi komandy Kn. A. D. L'vova s 1881–1892* (1912): 3–21.

30. *Pozharnoe delo*, no. 5 (January 31, 1904): 74.

31. Roosevelt 1995: xii.

32. *Pozharnyi*, no. 73-1 (January 8, 1895): 9.

33. Strukov 1903: 63.

34. Sheremetev 1892: xv.

35. Fesenko 1899: 5.

36. Ibid.: 7.

37. *Otchet Obshchago sobraniia chlenov Vysokovskoi pozharnoi druzhiny, 1893–1894. God pervyi 1895.*

38. Sheremetev 1901: 3–5.

39. Sheremetev 1892: 26, 232–238.

40. Ibid.: 81.

41. Ibid.: 114.

42. Ibid.: 126–127.

43. Fesenko 1899: 13.

44. Lussier 1987: 71–75.

45. Iordan 1901.

46. On the cantonal court system, see Frierson 1997b. On state efforts to co-opt peasant officials into state service through tax-collecting functions, see Burds 1998: esp. chapter 2.

47. *Pozharnoe delo*, no. 49 (December 14, 1902): 769.

48. Fesenko (1899: 53ff.) included in his manual a copy of the model charter approved by the Ministry of the Interior on August 5, 1897. One finds the annual reports of volunteer brigades in publications such as *Otchet Aleksandrovskoi dobrovol'noi sel'skoi pozharnoi druzhiny* (Vladimir, 1908) and *Otchet Besvodninskoi sel'skoi pozharnoi druzhiny Nizhegorodskago uezda za 1908 god* (Nizhnii Novgorod, 1909).

49. On Nicholas II's images of his duties as tsar, see Mark Steinberg's introductory essay in Steinberg and Khrustalev 1995: esp. 16–21.

50. "Korrespondentsia," *Pozharnoe delo*, no. 47 (November 30, 1902): 749–750.

51. G. Young 1997; see also Pisiotis 2000.

52. Miachin 1902b: 634.

53. Sheremetev 1892: 239.

54. Green-Hughes 1979: 58–60.

55. Perkins 1987: 345.

56. Greenberg 1995: 306.

57. Veselovskii 1909: 619–621.

58. "Nemnogo statistiki (Krasnoufimskii uezd Permskoi gubernii). O sostoianii pozharnykh obozov v seleniiakh," *Pozharnoe delo*, no. 41 (October 18, 1903): 665.

59. Purishkevich 1903: 689.

60. Ditzel 1969: 17; Green-Hughes 1979: 35–36; J. White 1973: 167.

61. C. Young 1866: 147, 161.

62. "Ocherk sovremennago sostoianiia pozharnogo dela v zemskikh guberniiakh Rossii," *Pozharnoe delo*, no. 39 (October 4, 1903): 626.

63. On parish brigades in England, see Green-Hughes 1979: 49.

64. Grigor'ev 1901 (3): 50.

65. Ibid.: 51.

66. Fesenko 1899: 21–25.

67. Ibid.: 25–32.

68. Grigor'ev 1901.

69. Greenberg 1995.

70. Strukov 1903: 49–52, 71–73.

71. "Pozharno-stroitel'nyi otdel Imperatorskogo Rossiiskogo Pozharnogo Obshchestva na sel'sko-khoziastvennoi i kustarno-promyshlennoi Vystavke v Tsarskom sele," *Pozharnoe delo*, no. 35 (September 6, 1903): 559–560, and no. 36 (September 13, 1903): 574–576.

72. Imperatorskoe Rossiiskoe pozharnoe obshchestvo 1903.

73. *Pozharnoe delo*, no. 28 (July 20, 1902): 434–435.

74. "Zamechatel'noe v pozharnom otnoshenie selo," *Pozharnoe delo*, no. 35 (September 7, 1902): 551–552.

75. Khelmovskii 1903: 809.

Chapter 9. Conclusion

1. Maslov 1923: 113.

2. Veselovskii 1905: 21.

3. Shanin 1986: 10.

4. The quoted phrase is from Shanin 1986: 7.

5. Kassow 1991: 370.

6. Bradley 1991: 147.

7. *Pozharnoe delo*, no. 5 (May 1918): 50–53.

8. Hoch 1994; Simms 1977; Burds 1998: 160–161.

9. Frierson 1993b: letters 11 and 12.

10. See Frierson 1993a: chapter 8; Worobec 1992, 1995.

11. Miachin 1902a: 475.

REFERENCES

Archives

Arkhiv Tsentra Protivopozharnoi propagandy i obshchestvennykh sviaz (St. Petersburg)
Gosudarstvennyi arkhiv Novgorodskoi oblasti (GANO)
Gosudarstvennyi arkhiv Smolenskoi oblasti (GASO)
Gosudarstvennyi arkhiv Vologodskoi oblasti (GAVO)
Rossiiskii gosudarstvennyi istoricheskii arkhiv (RGIA)
Russkii muzei etnografii, fond 7, opis' 1 (Tenishev Fund)

Newspapers and Journals

Etnograficheskoe obozrenie
Iuridicheskii vestnik
Izvestiia imperatorskogo obshchestva liubitelei estestvoznaniia, antropologii, i etnografii
Kurskie gubernskie vedomosti
Moskovskie vedomosti
Novgorodskii listok
Pozharnoe delo
Pozharnyi
Samarskie gubernskie vedomosti
Sankt Peterburgskie vedomosti
Smolenskie gubernskie vedomosti
Smolenskii vestnik
Sudebnyi vestnik
Zapiski imperatorskogo russkogo geograficheskogo obshchestva po otdeleniiu etnografii
Zemskii sbornik Chernigovskoi gubernii
Zhivaia starina

Published Sources

Adrianovskii, A. "Ob"iasnenie kollektsii po udobreniiu." *Izvestiia imperatorskogo obshchestva liubitelei estestvoznaniia, antropologii i etnografii* 44, no. 2 (1884): 47–50.

Afanas'ev, Alexander K. "Jurors and Jury Trials in Imperial Russia, 1866–1885." In *Russia's Great Reforms 1855–1881*, edited by Ben Eklof, John Bushnell, and Larissa Zakharova, pp. 214–230. Bloomington: Indiana University Press, 1994.

Afanas'ev, A. N. *Poeticheskie vozzreniia slavian na prirodu*, vol. 2. Moscow: Izdanie K. Sladatenkova. Reprint. The Hague: Mouton, 1969.

———. *Narod-khudozhnik. Mif fol'klor. Literatura.* Moscow: Sovetskaia Rossiia, 1986.

Alabin, P. "Kakie mery predpriniat' dlia preduprezhdeniia i oslableniia pozharov v selakh i derevniakh." St. Petersburg: tip. N. M. Sokovnina, 1869.

Anderson, Benedict. *Imagined Communities: Reflections on the Origin and Spread of Nationalism.* London: Verso, 1983.

Anfimov, A. M. *Ekonomicheskoe polozhenie i klassovaia bor'ba krest'ian Evropeiskoi Rossii.* Moscow: Nauka, 1984.

Archer, John. *By a Flash and a Scare: Incendiarism, Animal Maiming, and Poaching in East Anglia, 1815–1870.* Oxford: Clarendon Press, 1990.

Arshinov, V. N. "O narodnom lechenii v Kazanskom uezde." *Trudy etnograficheskogo otdela imperatorskogo obshchestva liubitelei estestvoznaniia, antropologii i etnografii*, vol. 9, no. 1: *Sbornik svedenii dlia izucheniia byta krest'ianskogo naseleniia Rossii.* Moscow (1889): 10–12.

Atkinson, Dorothy. "The Zemstvo and the Peasantry." In *The Zemstvo in Russia: An Experiment in Local Self-Government*, edited by Terence Emmons and Wayne Vucinich, pp. 79–132. Cambridge: Cambridge University Press, 1982.

Axelrod, Willa. "Russian Orthodoxy in the Life and Fiction of A. P. Chekhov." Ph.D. dissertation, Yale University, 1991.

Bachelard, Gaston. *The Psychoanalysis of Fire.* Translated by Alan C. M. Rose. Boston: Beacon Press, 1964.

Baehr, Stephen. "Is Moscow Burning? Fire in Griboedov's *Woe from Wit*." In *Russian Subjects: Empire, Nation, and the Culture of the Golden Age*, edited by Monika Greenleaf and Stephen Moeller-Sally, pp. 229–242. Evanston, Ill.: Northwestern University Press, 1998.

Baiburin, A. K. *Zhilishche v obriadakh i predstavleniiakh vostochnykh slavian.* Leningrad: Nauka, 1983.

Balov, A. "Svechi i ladon v narodnykh pover'iakh." *Zhivaia starina*, Series 2, Part 5 (1896a): 262–264.

———. "K voprosu o kharaktere i znachenii drevnikh kupal'skikh obriadov i igrishch." *Zhivaia starina* 1 (1896b): 133–142.

Balov, A., S. Ia. Derunov, and Ia. Il'inskii. "Ocherki Poshekhon'ia." *Etnograficheskoe obozrenie*, no. 4 (1898): 69–92.

Baron, Samuel H., trans and ed. *The Travels of Olearius in Seventeenth-Century Russia.* Stanford, Calif.: Stanford University Press, 1967.

Bartlett, Roger, ed. *Land Commune and Peasant Community in Russia: Communal Forms in Imperial and Early Soviet Society.* London: Macmillan, 1990.

Bassin, Mark. "Russia between Europe and Asia: The Ideological Construction of Geography." *Slavic Review* 50, no. 1 (Spring 1991): 1–17.

Baum, K. "Opisanie naibolee interesnykh pozharov, proisshedshikh v S. Peterburge–Petrograde s 1703–1922 gg." Part 1. Manuscript completed in 1924 by this former fire chief for St. Petersburg–Petrograd (1897–1916). The manuscript is in the Arkhiv Tsentra protivopozharnoi propagandy i obshchestvennykh sviaz. Upravlenie gosudarstvennoi protivopozharnoi sluzhby in St. Petersburg.

Bayard, Jean-Pierre. *La Symbolique du feu.* Paris: G. Tredaniel, 1973.

Belliustin, I. S. *Opisanie sel'skogo dukhovenstva.* Paris, 1858. Published in English as *Description of the Clergy in Rural Russia: The Memoir of a Nineteenth-Century Parish Priest,* translated and edited by Gregory L. Freeze. Ithaca, N.Y.: Cornell University Press, 1985.

Belokonskii, I. P. *Derevenskiia vpechatleniia (iz zapisok zemskogo statistika).* St. Petersburg: T. P. M. Stasliuvich, 1900.

Besedkin, P. V. *Istoricheskii ocherk prestupleniia podzhoga po rimskomu, germanskomu i russkomu pravu.* Iaroslavl: tip. G. Fal'k, 1885.

Bethea, David M. *The Shape of Apocalypse in Modern Russian Fiction.* Princeton, N.J.: Princeton University Press, 1989.

Blum, Jerome. *Lord and Peasant in Russia from the Ninth to the Nineteenth Century.* Princeton, N.J.: Princeton University Press, 1971.

Bogaevskii, Petr. "Zametki o narodnoi meditsine." *Etnograficheskoe obozrenie* 1 (1889): 101–105.

Bradley, Joseph. "Voluntary Associations, Civic Culture, and Obshchestvennost' in Moscow." In *Between Tsar and People: Educated Society and the Quest for Public Identity in Late Imperial Russia,* edited by Edith W. Clowes, Samuel D. Kassow, and James L. West, pp. 131–148. Princeton, N.J.: Princeton University Press, 1991.

Brumfield, William Craft, and Blair A. Ruble, eds. *Russian Housing in the Modern Age: Design and Social History.* Cambridge and New York: Cambridge University Press and Woodrow Wilson Center Press, 1993.

Burbank, Jane. "Law without the State? Peasant Ideas of Justice in Revolutionary Russia." Paper presented at the national convention of the American Association for the Advancement of Slavic Studies, Honolulu, November 1988.

———. "Legal Culture, Citizenship, and Peasant Jurisprudence: Perspectives from the Early Twentieth Century." In *Judicial Reform in Russia, 1864–1994,* edited by Peter Solomon, pp. 82–106. White Plains, N.Y.: M. E. Sharpe, 1997.

Burds, Jeffrey. *Peasant Dreams and Market Politics: Labor Migration and the Russian Village, 1861–1905.* Pittsburgh: University of Pittsburgh Press, 1998.

Buslaev, F. I. *Drevne-russkaia narodnaia literatura i iskusstvo,* vol. 2. St. Petersburg, 1861.

Byval'kevich, P. "Ivan Kupala." *Etnograficheskoe obozrenie,* no. 4 (1891): 190–192.

Chekhov, A. P. *Polnoe sobranie sochinenii i pisem,* vol. 13: *Pis'ma 1875–1887.* Moscow, 1948.

———. *Sobranie sochinenii.* 6 vols. Moscow: Molodaia gvardia, 1955–1962.

———. "An Encounter." In *The Portable Chekhov,* edited by Avrahm Yarmolinsky, pp. 125–140. New York: Viking, 1968.

Chicherov, V. I. *Zimnii period russkogo zemledel'cheskogo kalendaria xvi–xix vekov (Ocherki po istorii narodnykh verovanii).* Moscow: Akademiia nauk SSSR, 1957.

Chizhikova, L. N. "Zhilishche." In *Etnografiia vostochnykh slavian,* edited by K. V. Chistov, pp. 238–239. Moscow: Nauka, 1979.

Clark, Geoffrey W. "Betting on Lives: Life Insurance in English Society and Culture, 1695–1775." Ph.D. dissertation, Princeton University, 1993.

Clowes, Edith W., Samuel D. Kassow, and James L. West, editors. *Between Tsar and People: Educated Society and the Quest for Public Identity in Late Imperial Russia.* Princeton, N.J.: Princeton University Press, 1991.

Czap, Peter, Jr. "Peasant-Class Courts and Customary Justice in Russia, 1861–1912." *Journal of Social History* 1 (1967): 149–179.

Dal', Vladimir. *Poslovitsy russkogo naroda*, vol. II. 2nd ed. St. Petersburg, 1879.

Deal, Zack Jeremiah III. "Serf and State Peasant Agriculture: Kharkov Province 1842–1861." Ph.D. dissertation, Vanderbilt University, 1978.

Defert, Daniel. "Popular Life and Insurance Technology." In *The Foucault Effect: Studies in Governmentality*, edited by Graham Burchell, Colin Gordon, and Peter Miller, pp. 218–223. Chicago: University of Chicago Press, 1991.

Demidovich, P. "Iz oblasti verovannii i skazanii belorussov, II–IV." *Etnograficheskoe obozrenie*, nos. 2–3 (1896): 90–120.

de Sherbinin, Julie. *Chekhov and Russian Religious Culture: The Poetics of the Marian Paradigm*. Evanston, Ill.: Northwestern University Press, 1997.

Ditzel, Paul C. *Firefighting: A New Look in the Old Firehouse*. New York: Van Nostrand Reinhold, 1969.

Dostoevsky, F. M. *Polnoe sobranie sochinenii v tridtsati tomakh*. 30 vols. Leningrad: Nauka, 1973.

——. *Devils*. Translated by Michael R. Katz. Oxford: Oxford University Press, 1992.

Druzhinin, N. M. *Gosudarstvennye krest'iane i reforma P. D. Kiseleva*, vol. 2: *Realizatsiia i posledstviia reformy*. Moscow: Izdatel'stvo Akademii nauka SSSR, 1958.

Dubrovskii, S. M. *Krest'ianskoe dvizhenie v revoliutsii 1905–07 gg*. Moscow: Izdatel'stvo Akademii nauk, 1956.

Edelman, Robert. *Proletarian Peasants: The Revolution of 1905 in Russia's Southwest*. Ithaca, N.Y.: Cornell University Press, 1987.

——. " 'Everybody's Got to Be Someplace!' Organizing Space in the Russian Peasant House, 1880–1930." In *Russian Housing in the Modern Age: Design and Social History*, edited by William Craft Brumfield and Blair A. Ruble. Cambridge and New York: Cambridge University Press and Woodrow Wilson Center Press, 1993.

Efimenko, P. S. *Materialy po etnografii russkogo naseleniia Arkhangel'skoi gubernii*, vol. 1: *Opisanie vneshnego i vnutrennego byta*. Moscow: tip. F. B. Miller, 1877.

Eklof, Ben. *Russian Peasant Schools: Officialdom, Village Culture, and Popular Pedagogy 1861–1914*. Berkeley: University of California Press, 1986.

Eleonskaia, Elena. "Gadan'e pod Novyi God v Kozel'skom uezde." *Etnograficheskoe obozrenie* 81–82, nos. 2–3 (1909): 174–175.

Eliade, Mircea. *The Forge and the Crucible: The Origins and Structures of Alchemy*. 2d ed. Edited by Stephen Corrin. Chicago: University of Chicago Press, 1978.

Emmons, Terence, and Wayne Vucinich, eds. *The Zemstvo in Russia: An Experiment in Local Self-Government*. Cambridge: Cambridge University Press, 1982.

Engel, Barbara Alpern. *Between the Fields and the City: Women, Work, and Family in Russia, 1861–1914*. Cambridge: Cambridge University Press, 1994a.

——. "Women, Men, and the Languages of Peasant Resistance, 1870–1907." In *Cultures in Flux: Lower-Class Values, Practices, and Resistance in Late Imperial Russia*, edited by Stephen P. Frank and Mark D. Steinberg, pp. 34–53. Princeton, N.J.: Princeton University Press, 1994b.

Engel'gardt, A. N. "Iz derevni, II." *Otechestvennye zapiski* 202, no. 6 (June 1872): 161–182.

——. "Iz derevni, VII." *Otechestvennye zapiski* 242, no. 1 (January 1879): 101–142.

Ermolov, A. S. *Sovremennaia pozharnaia epidemiia v Rossii*. St. Petersburg, 1910.

Esipov, V. V. *Povrezhdenie imushchestva ognem po russkomu pravu*. St. Petersburg: Marksa, 1892.

Ewald, Francois. "Insurance and Risk." In *The Foucault Effect: Studies in Governmentality*, edited by Graham Burchell, Colin Gordon, and Peter Miller, pp. 197–211. Chicago: University of Chicago Press, 1991.

Fallows, Thomas Stuart. "Forging the Zemstvo Movement: Liberalism and Radicalism on the Volga, 1890–1905." Ph.D. dissertation, Harvard University, 1981.

———. "The Zemstvo and the Bureaucracy, 1890–1904." In *The Zemstvo in Russia: An Experiment in Local Self-Government*, edited by Terence Emmons and Wayne S. Vucinich, pp. 177–241. Cambridge: Cambridge University Press, 1982.

Farnsworth, Beatrice Brodsky. "The Litigious Daughter-in-Law: Family Relations in the Second Half of the Nineteenth Century." *Slavic Review* 45, no. 1 (Spring 1986): 49–64.

Faulkner, William. "Barn Burning." *Collected Stories of William Faulkner*. New York: Random House, 1950.

Ferrara, Peter J. "Social Security and Taxes." In *The Amish and the State*, edited by Donald B. Kraybill, pp. 125–143. Baltimore: Johns Hopkins University Press, 1993.

Fesenko, I. O. *Kak ustroit' sel'skuiu pozharnuiu druzhinu. Sovety, ukazaniia, i rukovodstvo k uchrezhdeniiu sel'skikh pozharnykh druzhin*. St. Petersburg, 1899.

Field, Daniel. *Rebels in the Name of the Tsar*. Boston: Houghton Mifflin, 1976.

Figes, Orlando. *Peasant Russia, Civil War: The Volga Countryside in Revolution* (1917–1921). Oxford: Oxford University Press, 1989.

———. "Peasant Farmers and the Minority Groups of Rural Society: Peasant Egalitarianism and Village Social Relations during the Russian Revolution (1917–1921)." In *Peasant Economy, Culture, and Politics of European Russia, 1800–1921*, edited by Esther Kingston-Mann and Timothy Mixter, pp. 378–401. Princeton, N.J.: Princeton University Press, 1991.

Fitzpatrick, Sheila. *Stalin's Peasants: Resistance and Survival in the Russian Village after Collectivization*. New York: Oxford University Press, 1994.

Foinitskii, I. Ia. "Zhenshchina-prestupnika." *Severnyi vestnik*, no. 2 (1893): 123–144.

Frank, Joseph. *Dostoevsky: The Stir of Liberation, 1860–1865*. Princeton, N.J.: Princeton University Press, 1986.

Frank, Stephen P. "Confronting the Domestic Other: Rural Popular Culture and Its Enemies in Fin-de-Siécle Russia." In *Cultures in Flux: Lower-Class Values, Practices, and Resistance in Late Imperial Russia*, edited by Stephen P. Frank and Mark D. Steinberg, pp. 74–107. Princeton, N.J.: Princeton University Press, 1994.

———. "Narratives within Numbers: Women, Crime and Judicial Statistics in Imperial Russia, 1834–1913." *Russian Review* 55, no. 4 (October 1996): 541–566.

———. *Crime, Cultural Conflict, and Justice in Rural Russia, 1856–1914*. Berkeley: University of California Press, 1999.

Frazer, Sir James George. *Myths of the Origin of Fire*. London: Macmillan, 1930.

———. *The Golden Bough: A Study in Magic and Religion*, vol. 1 of abridged edition. New York: Macmillan, 1951.

Freeze, Gregory L. *The Parish Clergy in Nineteenth-Century Russia: Crisis, Reform, Counter-Reform*. Princeton, N.J.: Princeton University Press, 1983.

Freud, Sigmund. "The Acquisition and Control of Fire." In *The Standard Edition of the Complete Psychological Works of Sigmund Freud*, translated by James Strachey, pp. 185–193. London: Hogarth Press, 1964.

Frieden, Nancy Mandelker. *Russian Physicians in an Era of Reform and Revolution, 1856–1905*. Princeton, N.J.: Princeton University Press, 1981.

Frierson, Cathy A. "Crime and Punishment in the Russian Village: Rural Concepts of Criminality at the End of the Nineteenth Century." *Slavic Review* 46, no. 1 (1987a): 58–59.

———. "Razdel: The Peasant Family Divided." *Russian Review* 46 (1987b): 35–52.

———. "Peasant Family Divisions and the Commune." In *Land Commune and Peasant Community in Russia: Communal Forms in Imperial and Early Soviet Society*, edited by Roger Bartlett, pp. 303–320. London: Macmillan, 1990.

———. *Peasant Icons: Representations of Rural People in Late-Nineteenth-Century Russia.* New York: Oxford University Press, 1993a.

———, ed. and trans. *A. N. Engel'gardt's Letters from the Country, 1872–1887.* New York: Oxford University Press, 1993b.

———. "Forced Hunger and Rational Restraint in the Peasant Diet: One Populist's Vision." In *Food in Russian History and Culture*, edited by Musya Glants and Joyce Toomre, pp. 49–66. Bloomington: Indiana University Press, 1997a.

———. " 'I must always answer to the law . . .': Rules and Responses at the Reformed Volost' Court." *Slavonic and East European Review* (April 1997b): 308–334.

Frost, L. E., and E. L. Jones. "The Fire Gap and the Greater Durability of Nineteenth-Century Cities." *Planning Perspectives* 4 (1989): 333–347.

Ganzen [Hansen], P. G. *Opyt' ozdorovleniia derevni.* St. Petersburg: tip. A. F. Marks, 1902.

Gatti, I. A. "O pomoshchi pogorel'tsam-lesom." *Trudy vserossiiskogo pozharnogo s'ezda 1902 g. v Moskve* (Imperatorskoe Rossiiskoe pozharnoe obshchestvo), vol. 1, pp. 212–213. St. Petersburg, 1903.

Gerasimov, M. K. "Materialy po narodnoi meditsine i akusherstvu v Cherepovetskom uezde, Novgorodskoi gubernii." *Zhivaia starina*, no. 2 (1898): 165.

Gleason, Abbott. *Young Russia: The Genesis of Russian Radicalism in the 1860s.* New York: Viking Press, 1980.

Glickman, Rose. "The Peasant Woman as Healer." In *Russia's Women: Accommodation, Resistance, Transformation*, edited by Barbara Evans Clements, Barbara Alpern Engel, and Christine D. Worobec, pp. 148–162. Berkeley: University of California Press, 1991.

Gofshtetter, I. *Pozharno-strakhovoe delo v zemskikh guberniiakh (Novgorodskoi, Kazanskoi, Viatskoi, Permskoi i Nizhegorodskoi), istoriia ego razvitiia i sovremennaia postanovka.* St. Petersburg: tip. Uchilischa glukhonemykh, 1902.

Goody, Jack. *The Logic of Writing and the Organization of Society.* Cambridge: Cambridge University Press, 1986.

Goudsblom, Johan. *Fire and Civilization.* London: Allen Lane, 1992.

Grachev, V. I. *Kratkii istoricheskii ocherk dvadtsatipiatiletnago suschchestvovaniia Smolenskogo Vol'nogo Pozharnogo Obshchestva (s 1874–1899).* Smolensk, 1899.

Gradovskii, G. "Na sude." *Sudebnaia gazeta* 16 (April 15, 1884): 9.

Greenberg, Amy Sophia. "Cause for Alarm: The Volunteer Fire Department in the Nineteenth-Century City." Ph.D. dissertation, Harvard University, 1995.

Green-Hughes, Evan. *A History of Firefighting.* Ashbourne, Derbyshire: Moorland Publishing, 1979.

Greenleaf, Monika, and Stephen Moeller-Sally, eds. *Russian Subjects: Empire, Nation, and the Culture of the Golden Age.* Evanston, Ill.: Northwestern University Press, 1998.

Grigor'ev, V. "Obuchenie pozharnykh. Prakticheskoe rukovodstvo pozharnogo dela." *Pozharnoe delo* 3 (January 29, 1901): 50–52, and subsequent articles in this series.

Gromyko, M. M. *Traditsionnye normy povedeniia i formy obshcheniia russkikh krest'ian xix v.* Moscow: Nauka, 1986.

———. *Mir russkoi derevni.* Moscow: Molodaia gvardiia, 1991.

Hamm, Michael F. *Kiev: A Portrait, 1800–1917.* Princeton, N.J.: Princeton University Press, 1993.

Hay, Douglas, Peter Linebaugh, John G. Rule, E. P. Thompson, and Cal Winslow. *Albion's Fatal Tree: Crime and Society in Eighteenth-Century England.* New York: Allen Lane, 1975.

Hobsbawm, E. J., and George Rudé. *Captain Swing.* Harmondsworth, UK: Penguin, 1973.

Hoch, Steven L. *Serfdom and Social Control in Russia: Petrovskoe, a Village in Tambov.* Chicago: University of Chicago Press, 1986.

———. "On Good Numbers and Bad: Malthus, Population Trends and Peasant Standard of Living in Late Imperial Russia." *Slavic Review* 53, no. 1 (Spring 1994): 42–75.

Hudson, Hugh. "Fire, the Second Coming, and Peasant Freedom: The Arson Panic of 1839." Paper presented at the national convention of the American Association for the Advancement of Slavic Studies, Boston, November 1997.

Hussey, Stephen, and Laura Swash. "'Horrid Lights': Nineteenth-Century Incendiarism in Essex." Essex, UK: *Studies in Essex History* 5, 1994.

Illiustrov, I. I. *Sbornik rossiiskikh poslovits i pogovorok.* Kiev, 1904.

Imperatorskoe Rossiiskoe pozharnoe obshchestvo. *Trudy vserossiiskogo pozharnogo s"ezda 1902 g. v Moskve,* vols. 1 and 2. St. Petersburg, 1903.

Iordan, K. "Sel'skie pozharnye druzhiny Tverskoi gubernii v 1900 godu." *Pozharnoe delo* 1 (January 6, 1901): 8–10.

Isaev, M. K. "Neskol'ko slov po povodu 700-letnei godovshchiny velikogo novgorodskogo pozhara (1194–1894)." *Pozharnoe delo,* no. 1 (July 1894): 10–13.

Ivanits, Linda J. *Russian Folk Belief.* Armonk, N.Y.: M. E. Sharpe, 1989.

Ivanitskii, N. A. *Materialy po etnografii Vologodskoi gubernii. Sbornik svedenii dlia izucheniia byta krest'ianskogo naseleniia Rossii.* Series 2. Moscow, 1890.

Ivanov, L. M., ed. *Krest'ianskoe dvizhenie v Rossii v 1861–1869 gg. Sbornik dokumentov.* Moscow: Mysl', 1964.

Johnson, Eric A., and Eric H. Monkkonen. "Introduction." In *The Civilization of Crime: Violence in Town and Country since the Middle Ages,* edited by Eric A. Johnson and Eric H. Monkkonen, pp. 1–13. Urbana: University of Illinois Press, 1996.

Jones, David. *Crime, Protest, Community and Police in Nineteenth-Century Britain.* London: Routledge and Kegan Paul, 1982.

Jones, Eric L. "The Reduction of Fire Damage in Southern England, 1650–1850." *Post-Medieval Archeology* 2 (1968): 140–149.

———. *The European Miracle: Environments, Economies and Geopolitics in the History of Europe and Asia.* 2d ed. Cambridge: Cambridge University Press, 1987.

Jung, C. G. *Symbols of Transformation: An Analysis of the Prelude to a Case of Schizophrenia.* 2d ed. Translated by R. F. C. Hull. Princeton, N.J.: Princeton University Press, 1976.

Kahan, Arcadius. *Russian Economic History: The Nineteenth Century.* Edited by Roger Weiss. Chicago: University of Chicago Press, 1989.

Kaiser, Daniel H. *The Growth of the Law in Medieval Russia.* Princeton, N.J.: Princeton University Press, 1980.

Kassow, Samuel D. "Russia's Unrealized Civil Society." In *Between Tsar and People: Educated Society and the Quest for Public Identity in Late Imperial Russia,* edited by Edith W. Clowes, Samuel D. Kassow, and James L. West, pp. 367–371. Princeton, N.J.: Princeton University Press, 1991.

Kharuzina, Vera. "K voprosu o pochitanii ognia." *Etnograficheskoe obozrenie* 70–71, nos. 3–4 (1906): 68–205.

Khelmovskii, A. "Nuzhny-li sel'skie pozharnye druzhiny?" *Pozharnoe delo* 50 (December 20, 1903): 808–809.

Knight, Nathaniel. "Constructing the Science of Nationality: Ethnography in Mid-Nineteenth Century Russia." Ph.D. dissertation, Columbia University, 1994.

Kohl, J. G. *Russia: St. Petersburg, Moscow, Kharkoff, Riga, Odessa, the German Provinces on the Baltic, the Steppes, the Crimea, and the Interior of the Empire.* New York: Arno Press, 1970.

Kolchin, A. "Verovaniia krest'ian Tul'skoi gubernii." *Etnograficheskoe obozrenie*, no. 3 (1899): 1–60.

Kratkoe opisanie orlovskogo uezda Viatskoi gubernii. Po dannym statistiki. Viatka, 1892.

Kratkoe sel'sko-khoziaistvennoe opisanie po Malmyzhskomu uezdu, Viatskoi gubernii. Po dannym zemskoi statistiki. Viatka, 1892.

Kuznetsov, N. I. *Sistematicheskii svod ukazov Pravitelstvuiushchago Senata, posledovavshikh po zemskim delam. 1866–1900.* St. Petersburg: tip. A. E. Kolpinskago, 1902.

——. *Sistematicheskii svod ukazov Pravitel'stvuiushchago Senata, posledovavshikh po zemskim delam,* vol. 2: 1899–1903 gg. Voronezh: tip. S.P. Iakovleva, 1903.

Leikina-Svirskaia, V. R. *Intelligentsiia v Rossii vo vtoroi polovine xix veka.* Moscow: Mysl', 1971.

Lenin, V. I. *Sochineniia,* vol. 3: *Razvitie kapitalizma v Rossii.* Moscow, 1941.

Levin, Eve. "Dvoeverie and Popular Religion." In *Seeking God: The Recovery of Religious Identity in Orthodox Russia, Ukraine, and Georgia,* edited by Stephen K. Batalden, pp. 32–38. Dekalb: Northern Illinois University Press, 1993.

Lévi-Strauss, Claude. *The Raw and the Cooked.* Translated by John and Doreen Weightman. Chicago: University of Chicago Press, 1990.

Lindenmeyr, Adele. *Poverty Is Not a Vice: Charity, Society, and the State in Imperial Russia.* Princeton, N.J.: Princeton University Press, 1996.

Lunevskii, S. P. *Strakhovanie ot ognia.* St. Petersburg, 1912.

Lussier, Hubert. *Les Sapeurs-Pompiers au XIXe siécle: Associations volontaires en milieu populaire.* Paris, 1987.

Macey, David A. J. *Government and Peasant in Russia, 1861–1906: The Prehistory of the Stolypin Reforms.* Dekalb: Northern Illinois University Press, 1987.

Makovetskii, I. V. *Arkhitektura russkogo narodnogo zhilishcha. Sever i verkhnee povolzh'e.* Moscow: Akademiia nauk SSSR, 1962.

Maksimov, S. V. *Krylatyia slova.* St. Petersburg: Prosveshchenie, 1890.

——. *Sobranie sochinenii,* vols. 18 and 20. St. Petersburg: Prosveshchenie, 1896.

Maslov, P. *Krest'ianskoe dvizhenie v Rossii,* part 1. Moscow, 1923.

Masson, Denise. *L'eau, le feu, la lumiére d'apres la Bible, le Coran et les traditions monotheistes.* Paris: Desclee de Brouwer, 1985.

Matossian, Mary. "The Peasant Way of Life." In *The Peasant in Nineteenth-Century Russia,* edited by Wayne S. Vucinich, pp. 1–40. Stanford, Calif.: Stanford University Press, 1968.

McKenzie, Kermit E. "The Zemstvo and the Administration." In *The Zemstvo in Russia: An Experiment in Local Self-Government,* edited by Terence Emmons and Wayne S. Vucinich, pp. 31–78. Cambridge: Cambridge University Press, 1982.

McReynolds, Louise. *The News under Russia's Old Regime: The Development of a Mass-Circulation Press.* Princeton, N.J.: Princeton University Press, 1991.

Miachin, N. "Iz zapisok zemskogo strakhovogo agenta." *Pozharnoe delo* 30 (July 27, 1902a): 475–476.

——. "Iz zapisok zemskogo strakhovogo agenta." *Pozharnoe delo* 40 (October 12, 1902b): 633–634.

——. "Staroe i novoe." *Pozharnoe delo* 26 (June 1904): 392.

Ministerstvo Iustitsii. *Svod statisticheskikh svedenii po delam ugolovnym, proisvodivshimsia v 1873 gody v sudebnykh uchrezhdeniiakh, deistvuiushchikh na osnovanii ustavov 20 noiabria 1864 g.* St. Petersburg, 1874.

———. *Svod statisticheskikh svedenii po delam i ugolovnym proizvodivshimsia v 1876 godu v sudebnykh uchrezhdeniiakh, deistvuiushchikh na osnovanii ustavov 20 noiabria 1864 g.* St. Petersburg, 1878.

———. *Svod statisticheskikh svedenii po delam ugolovnym delam poisvodivshimsia v 1880–1881 godakh.* St. Petersburg, 1885.

———. *Svod statisticheskikh svedenii po delam ugolovnym proizvodivshimsia v 1895 godu.* Part 2. St. Petersburg, 1899.

Ministerstvo Vnutrennikh del. *Ustav pozharnyi. Svod ustavov pozharnykh.* St. Petersburg, 1883.

Min'ko, L. I. "Magical Curing (Its Sources and Character, and the Causes of Its Prevalence)," Part 1a. *Soviet Anthropology and Archaeology* 12 (1974): 3–33.

Mixter, Timothy. "The Hiring Market as Workers' Turf: Migrant Agricultural Laborers and the Mobilization of Collective Action in the Steppe Grainbelt of European Russia, 1853–1913." In *Peasant Economy, Culture, and Politics of European Russia, 1800–1921,* edited by Esther Kingston-Mann and Timothy Mixter, pp. 294–340. Princeton, N.J.: Princeton University Press, 1991.

Mysh, M. "Zakliuchenie konsul'tatsii prisiazhnykh poverennykh po voprosu obiazatel'nykh pravil o merakh predostorozhnosti protiv pozharov, sostavlennomu Novgorodskoi gubernskoi zemskoi upravoi." In *Proekt ob'iazatel'nyia postanovleniia o merakh predostorozhnosti ot pozharov i o postroikakh v seleniiakh.* Novgorod, 1901.

Nashi sel'skie pozhary. Nastavlenie volostnym starshinam, sel'skim starostam i vsem gramotnym krest'ianam: kak oberegat'sia ot pozharov v seleniiakh, lesakh, stepakh i torfianinakh i kak ikh tushit'. St. Petersburg, 1877.

Neuberger, Joan. *Hooliganism, Crime, Culture, and Power in St. Petersburg, 1900–1914.* Berkeley: University of California Press, 1993.

———. "Popular Legal Cultures." In *Russia's Great Reforms, 1855–1881,* edited by Ben Eklof, John Bushnell, and Larissa Zakharov, pp. 231–246. Bloomington: Indiana University Press, 1994.

Neustupov, A. D. "Verovaniia krest'ian Shapinskoi volosti, Kadnikovskogo uezda." *Etnograficheskoe obozrenie* 55, no. 4 (1902): 118–120.

———. "Sledy pochitaniia ognia v Kadnikovskom uezde." *Etnograficheskoe obozrenie* 96–97, nos. 1–2 (1913): 245–247.

Nifontov, A. S., ed. *Krest'ianskoe dvizhenie v Rossii v 1881–1889 gg. Sbornik dokumentov.* Moscow: Sotsial'no- Ekonomicheskaia literatura, 1960.

Nikitin, A. K. "O nesgoraemykh postroikakh i o dostupnykh sredstvakh umen'sheniia derevenskikh pozharakh." *Trudy vserossiiskogo pozharnogo s"ezda 1902 g. v Moskve* (Imperatorskoe Rossiiskoe pozharnoe obshchestvo), vol. 1, pp. 67–92. St. Petersburg, 1903.

Nikitinskii, Ia. Ia. "O gorenii." *Izvestiia imperatorskogo obshchestva liubitelei estestvoznanii, antropologii, i etnografii* 44, no. 3 (1884): 81–83.

Novgorodskaia gubernskaia zemskaia uprava. *Opisanie sel'skogo pozhara. O prinatii mer protiv pozharov. Sklad zemledel'cheskikh orudii gubernskogo zemstva v g. Novgorode.* Novgorod, 1892.

———. *Ocherednomu gubernskomu zemskomu sobraniiu sessii 1902 g. Doklady po dobrovol'nomu i obiazatel'nomu strakhovaniiu i o merakh protiv pozharov.* Novgorod, 1902.

Obzor deiatel'nosti Strel'ninskoi chastnoi pozharnoi komandy Kn. A. D. L'vova s 1881–1892.
St. Petersburg, 1912.

"Ocherk sovremennogo sostoianiia pozharnogo dela v zemskikh guberniiakh Rossii."
Pozharnoe delo 35 (September 6, 1903): 565, and 39 (October 4, 1903): 626.

Olonetskoe gubernskoe zemstvo. *Obiazatelnye postanovleniia o merakh predostorozhnosti ot
pozharov i o tushenii ikh vne gorodskikh poselenii, v otmenu obiazatelnykh postanovlenii.
Proekt, Obiazatel'nyia postanovlenii izdanykh 3 avgusta 1899 goda.* Petrozavodsk, 1910.

Onasch, Konrad. *Icons.* South Brunswick and New York: A. S. Barnes and Co., 1969.

"O protivopozharnykh meropriiatiiakh Saratovskogo gubernskogo zemstva." *Trudy vserossiiskogo s'ezda 1902 g. v Moskve* (Imperatorskoe Rossiiskoe pozharnoe obshchestvo), vol. 1,
pp. 305–306. Moscow, 1903.

Osterberg, Eva. "Criminality, Social Control, and the Early Modern State: Evidence and
Interpretations in Scandinavian Historiography." In *The Civilization of Crime: Violence
in Town and Country since the Middle Ages,* edited by Eric A. Johnson and Eric H.
Monkkonen. Urbana: University of Illinois Press, 1996.

Otchet Aleksandrovskoi dobrovol'noi sel'skoi pozharnoi druzhiny. Vladimir, 1908.

Otchet Besvodninskoi sel'skoi pozharnoi druzhiny Nizhegorodskago uezda za 1908 god.
Nizhnii Novgorod, 1909.

Otchet Obshchago sobraniia chlenov Vysokovskoi pozharnoi druzhiny, 1893–1894. God pevyi.
Smolensk, 1895.

Ouspensky, Leonid, and Vladimir Lossky. *The Meaning of Icons.* Crestwood, N.Y.: St.
Vladimir's Seminary Press, 1982.

Pahomov, George. "Religious Motifs in Chekhov's 'Muzhiki.' " *Zapiski russkoi akademich-
eskoi gruppy v SSHA 25* (1992–1993): 111–119.

Pallot, Judith, and Denis J. B. Shaw. *Landscape and Settlement in Romanov Russia.* Oxford:
Clarendon Press, 1990.

Paperno, Irina. "Constructing the Meaning of Suicide: The Russian Press in the Age of the
Great Reforms." In *Imperial Russia: New Histories for the Empire,* edited by Jane Burbank
and David L. Ransel, pp. 305–332. Bloomington: Indiana University Press, 1998.

Perkins, Kenneth B. "Volunteer Fire Departments: Community Integration, Autonomy, and
Survival." *Human Organization* 46, no. 4 (Winter 1984): 342–348.

Pisiotis, Argyrios K. "Between Intelligentsia and Narod: Clerical and Lay Political Dissidents
in Rural Russia, 1905–1914." Paper presented at the 32d annual convention of the
American Association for the Advancement of Slavic Studies, Denver, November 2000.

Pogodin, D. M. *Pozhary i podzhogi v provintsii (Iz otryvochnykh vospominanii).* 2d ed.
Moscow, 1879.

Pokrovskii, N. A. "Iz istorii narodnogo dvoeveriia." *Izvestiia imperatorskogo obshchestva liubitelei estestvoznaniia, antropologii, i etnografii,* vol. 13, no. 1: Trudy etnograficheskogo
otdela, vol. 3, no. 1 (Moscow, 1874).

Polnoe sobranie zakonov Rossiiskoi Imperii (PSZ) [Laws of the Russian Empire]. Sobraniia
pervoe i vtoroe. Published annually. St. Petersburg.

"Polozhenie o vzaimnom zemskom strakhovanii." *Zemskii sbornik Chernigovskoi gubernii na
1869 god.* Chernigov, 1869.

Popkin, Cathy. "Chekhov as Ethnographer." *Slavic Review* 51, no. 1 (Spring 1992): 36–51.

Popkins, Gareth. "The Russian Peasant Volost' Court and Customary Law, 1861–1917."
Ph.D. dissertation, Oxford University, 1996.

———. "Popular Development of Procedure in a Dual Legal System: 'Protective Litigation'
in Russia's Peasant Courts, 1889–1912." *Journal of Legal Pluralism* 43 (1999): 57–87.

———. "Peasant Experiences of the Late Tsarist State: District Congresses of Land Captains, Provincial Boards and the Legal Appeals Process, 1891–1917." *Slavonic and East European Review* 78, no. 1 (January 2000): 90–114.

Popov, T. *Russkaia narodno-bytovaia meditsina po materialam etnograficheskogo biuro V.N. Tenisheva.* St. Petersburg: A. S. Suvorin, 1903.

Portal, Roger. *The Slavs: A Cultural and Historical Survey of the Slavonic Peoples.* Translated by Patrick Evan. New York: Harper and Row, 1969.

Porter, Thomas Earl. *The Zemstvo and the Emergence of Civil Society in Late Imperial Russia, 1864–1917.* San Francisco: Mellen Research University Press, 1991.

Proekt ob'iazatel'nyia postanovleniia o merakh predostorozhnosti ot pozharov i o postroikakh v seleniiakh. Novgorod, 1901.

Prokofiev, M. A. "Meropriiatiia Novgorodskogo gubernskogo zemstva protiv pozharov." *Trudy vserossiiskogo pozharnago s'ezda 1902 g. v Moskve* (Imperatorskoe Rossiiskoe pozhar-noe obshchestvo), vol. 1, pp. 3–41. St. Petersburg, 1903.

Propp, V. Ia. *Russkie agrarnye prazdniki (opyt istoriko-etnograficheskogo issledovaniia).* Leningrad: Izdatel'stvo Leningradskogo universiteta, 1963.

Pskovskaia gubernskaia zemskaia uprava. *Proekt obiazatelnykh postanovlenii o rasplanirovanii selenii, o vozvedenii postroek i o merakh predostorozhnosti ot pozharov v Pskovskoi gubernii.* Pskov, 1899.

Purishkevich, V. M. "Ocherk sovremennogo sostoianiia pozharnogo dela v zemskikh guberniiakh rossii." *Pozharnoe delo* 43 (November 1, 1903): 688–689.

———. *Natsional'noe bedstvie Rossii.* St. Petersburg: Russkii narodnyi soiuz imeni Mikhaila Arkhangela, 1909.

Pyne, Stephen J. *Fire in America: A Cultural History of Wildland Fire.* Princeton, N.J.: Princeton University Press, 1982.

———. *Burning Bush: A Fire History of Australia.* New York: Holt, 1991.

———. *Vestal Fire: An Environmental History, Told through Fire, of Europe and Europe's Encounter with the World.* Seattle: University of Washington Press, 1997.

Raeff, Marc. *Origins of the Russian Intelligentsia: The Eighteenth-Century Nobility.* New York: Harcourt, Brace and World, 1966.

Ramer, Samuel C. "Traditional Healers and Peasant Culture in Russia, 1861–1917." In *Peasant Economy, Culture, and Politics of European Russia, 1800–1921,* edited by Esther Kingston-Mann and Timothy Mixter, pp. 307–232. Princeton, N.J.: Princeton University Press, 1991.

Ransel, David. "Infant-Care Cultures in the Russian Empire." In *Russia's Women: Accommodation, Resistance, Transformation,* edited by Barbara Evans Clements, Barbara Alpern Engel, and Christine D. Worobec, pp. 113–134. Berkeley: University of California Press, 1991.

———. "Bringing Modern Mothering to the People: The Bolshevik 'Civilizing' Mission." Paper presented at the national convention of the American Historical Association, San Francisco, January 1994.

Resheniia obshchago sobraniia pervago i kassatsionnykh departamentov Pravitel'stvuiiushchago senata 1885 g. St. Petersburg, 1886.

Robbins, Richard G., Jr. *Famine in Russia, 1891–1892: The Imperial Government Responds to a Crisis.* New York: Columbia University Press, 1975.

Robinson, Geroid T. *Rural Russia under the Old Regime: A History of the Landlord-Peasant World and a Prologue to the Peasant Revolution of 1917.* New York: Macmillan, 1949.

Roosevelt, Priscilla. *Life on the Russian Country Estate: A Social and Cultural History*. New Haven, Conn.: Yale University Press, 1995.

Rudé, George. *Criminal and Victim: Crime and Society in Early Nineteenth-Century England*. Oxford: Oxford University Press, 1985.

Salmond, Wendy R. *Arts and Crafts in Late Imperial Russia: Reviving the Kustar Art Industries, 1870–1917*. Cambridge: Cambridge University Press, 1996.

Saltykov-Shchedrin, M. E. "A Village Fire." In *Fables*, translated by Vera Volkhovsky. London: Chatto and Windus, 1931. Reprint. Westport, Conn.: Greenwood Press, 1976.

Sazonov, G. P. *Obzor deiatel'nosti zemstv po narodnomu prodovol'stviiu (1865–1892)*, vol. II. St. Petersburg, 1893.

Schulte, Regina. *The Village in Court: Arson, Infanticide, and Poaching in the Court Records of Upper Bavaria, 1848–1910*. Translated by Barrie Selman. Cambridge: Cambridge University Press, 1994.

Scott, James C. *Seeing Like a State: How Certain Schemes to Improve the Human Condition Have Failed*. New Haven, Conn.: Yale University Press, 1998.

Semenov, V. P., ed. *Rossii: Polnoe geograficheskoe opisanie nashego otechestva*, vol. 1, *Moskovskaia promyshlennaia oblast i Verkhnee Povolzh'e*. St. Petersburg: A. F. Devrien, 1899.

———. *Rossii: Polnoe geograficheskoe opisanie nashego otechestva*, vol. 3, *Ozernaia oblast'*. St. Petersburg: A. F. Devrien, 1900.

———. *Rossiia: Polnoe geograficheskoe opisanie nashego obshchestva*, vol. 6, *Srednee i nizhnee povolzh'e i zavolzh'e*. St. Petersburg: A. F. Devrien, 1901.

———. *Rossiia: Polnoe geograficheskoe opisanie nashego otechestva*, vol. 2, *Srednerusskaia chernozemnaia oblast'*. St. Petersburg: A. F. Devrien, 1902.

Sementkovskii, P. I. "Chem bol'na nasha derevniia?" Essay in the introduction to *Opyt' ozdorovleniia derevni*, by P. G. Ganzen [Hansen]. St. Petersburg: tip. A. F. Marks, 1902.

Senderovich, Savelii. *Chekhov—s glazu na glaz. Istoriia odnoi oderzhimosti A. P. Chekhova*. St. Petersburg, 1994.

Seregny, Scott J. "Peasants and Politics: Peasant Unions during the 1905 Revolution." In *Peasant Economy, Culture, and Politics of European Russia, 1800–1921*, edited by Esther Kingston-Mann and Timothy Mixter, pp. 341–377. Princeton, N.J.: Princeton University Press, 1991.

Sergeevskii, N. D. *Kazuistika. Sbornik sudebnykh sluchaev dlia prakticheskikh zaniatii po ugolovnomu pravu*. Iaroslavl: Tip. G. Fal'k, 1882.

Shanin, Teodor. *Russia, 1905–1907: Revolution as a Moment of Truth*, vol. 2, *The Roots of Otherness: Russia's Turn of Century*. New Haven, Conn.: Yale University Press, 1986.

Shapkarin, A. V., ed. *Krest'ianskoe dvizhenie v Rossii v 1890–1900 gg. Sbornik dokumentov*. Moscow: Sotsial'no- Ekonomicheskaia literatura, 1959.

Shcheglov, Iu. K. "O goriachikh tochkakh literaturnogo siuzheta (motivy pozhara i ognia u Bulgakova i drugikh)." In *Mir avtora i struktura teksta. Stat'i o russkoi literature*, edited by A. K. Zholkovskii and Iu. K. Shcheglov, pp. 118–150. Tenafly, N.J.: Ermitazh, 1986.

Sheremetev, Aleksander Dmitrievich. *Kratkii statisticheskii obzor pozharnykh komand Rossiiskoi imperii*. St. Petersburg: tip. R. Golike, 1892.

———, compiler. *Pozharnaia tekhnika. Rukovodstvo dlia pozharnykh komand obshchestv i druzhin*. Petersburg: "Slovo," 1901.

Simms, James. "The Crisis in Russian Agriculture at the End of the Nineteenth Century: A Different View." *Slavic Review* 36, no. 3 (September 1977): 377–398.

Sinozerskii, M. "Otchego porazhennye grozoi sviatye?" *Zhivaia starina*, year 6, no. 2 (1896): 537–538.

Skripitsyn, V. A., compiler. *Pozhar.* One of the series *Vysochaishe uchrezhdennoe osoboe soveshchanie o nuzhdakh sel'skokhoziaistvennoi promyshlennosti, Svod trudov mestnykh komitetov po 49 guberniiam Evropeiskoi Rossii.* St. Petersburg, 1904.

Smirnov, N. *Ekonomicheskii byt' krest'ian Saratovskogo i Kuznetskogo uezdov Saratovskoi gubernii. Opyt' issledovaniia fizicheskikh, ekonomicheskikh i tekhnicheskikh uslovii.* Moscow, 1884.

Smith, Albert C. " 'Southern Violence' Reconsidered: Arson as Protest in Black-Belt Georgia, 1865–1910." *Journal of Southern History* 51, no. 4 (November 1985): 527–564.

Smith, R. E. F. *Peasant Farming in Muscovy.* Cambridge: Cambridge University Press, 1977.

Sofronov, M. A. "Pyrological Zoning." In *Fire in Ecosystems of Boreal Eurasia,* edited by Johann Georg Goldammer and Valentin V. Furyaev. Dordrecht, Netherlands: Kluwer, 1996.

Sokolov, Iurii M. *Russian Folklore.* Translated by Catherine Ruth Smith. Detroit, Mich.: Folklore Associates, 1971.

Sokolovich, Martinian. *O krasnom petukhe i kak ot nego uberech'sia. Samopomoshch' v bor'be s pozharami v seleniiakh, Izdaniia dlia naroda.* St. Petersburg, 1896.

Sreznevskii, I. I. *Materialy dlia slovaria drevne-russkago iazyka po pis'mennym pamiatnikam.* St. Petersburg: Tip. Imperatorskoi Akademii Nauk, 1895.

Staniukovich, T. V. "Vnutrenniaia planirovka, otdelka i meblirovka russkogo krest'ianskogo zhilishcha." In *Russkie. Istoriko-etnograficheskii atlas. Iz istorii russkogo narodnogo zhilishcha i kostiuma (ukrashenie krest'ianskikh domov i odezhdy) seredina xix-nachalo xx v,* edited by V. A. Aleksandrov. Moscow: Nauka, 1970.

Starr, S. Frederick. *Decentralization and Self-Government in Russia, 1830–1870.* Princeton, N.J.: Princeton Univerity Press, 1972.

Steinberg, Mark D., and Vladimir M. Khrustalev. *The Fall of the Romanovs: Political Dreams and Personal Struggles in a Time of Revolution.* New Haven, Conn.: Yale University Press, 1995.

Stoliarov, Ivan. *Zapiski russkogo krest'ianina (Recit d'un paysan russe).* Paris: Institut d'Etudes Slaves, 1986.

Strukov, D. L. *Desiatiletie Imperatorskogo Rossiiskogo Pozharnogo Obshchestva. Istoricheskii ocherk. 1893–1903.* St. Petersburg, 1903.

Svod zakonov ugolovnykh. Chast' pervaia. Ulozhenie o nakazaniiakh ugolovnykh i ispravitel'nykh. St. Petersburg, 1885.

Tarnovskii, E. N. "Otnoshenie chisla opravdannykh k chislu podsudimykh v evropeiskoi Rossii za 1889–1893 gg. (Sravnitel'no-statisticheskii ocherk)." *Zhurnal ministerstva iustitsii* 9 (November 1897): 180.

Tempest, Snejana. "Stovelore in Russian Folklife." In *Food in Russian History and Culture,* edited by Musya Glants and Joyce Toomre, pp. 1–14. Bloomington: Indiana University Press, 1997.

Thompson, E. P. *The Making of the English Working Class.* New York: Vintage Books, 1966.

Tracy, Myles A. "Insurance and Theology: The Background and the Issues." *Journal of Risk and Insurance,* March 1966: 85–93.

Troinitskii, N. A. *Naselennyia mesta Rossiiskoi imperii v 500 i bolee zhitelei s ukazaniem vsego nalichnago v nikh naseleniia i chisla zhitelei preobladaiushchikh veroispovedanii, po dannym pervoi vseobshchei perepisi naseleniia 1897 g.,* vol. 8. St. Petersburg, 1905.

Trubetskoi, Eugene N. *Icons: Theology in Color.* Translated by Gertrude Vakar. Scarsdale, N.Y.: St. Vladimir's Seminary Press, 1973.

Trudy kommissii po preobrazovaniiu volostnykh sudov. 7 vols. St. Petersburg, 1873.

Trudy mestnykh komitetov o nuzhdakh sel'skokhoziaistvennoi promyshlennosti, vols. 1–49. St. Petersburg, 1903.

Trudy pervago obshchago s'ezda sostoiashchago pod Avgusteishim Pochetnym predsedatel'stvom Ego Imperatorskogo vysochestva, Velikogo Kniaza Vladimira Aleksandrovicha soedenennogo Rossiiskogo pozharnogo obshchestva u osobogo pri nem pozharno-strakhovogo otdela. St. Petersburg, 1897.

Trunov, A. N. "Poniatiia krest'ian Orlovskoi gubernii o prirode fizicheskoi i dukhovnoi." *Zapiski Imperatorskogo russkogo geograficheskogo obshchestva po otdeleniiu etnografii* 2 (1869): 14.

Tsentral'nyi statisticheskii komitet, Ministerstvo Vnutrennikh del (TsSK, MVD). *Vzaimnoe zemskoe strakhovanie 1866–1876.* St. Petersburg, 1879–1884.

———. *Statisticheskii vremennik Rossiiskoi imperii,* series 2, vol. 19. St. Petersburg, 1882.

———. *Vremennik tsentral'nago statisticheskago komiteta Ministerstva vnutrennikh del,* series 2, no. 13: *Pozhary v Rossiiskoi imperii v 1883–1887 god i svod dannykh za 28 let.* St. Petersburg, 1889.

———. *Vremennik tsentral'nogo statisticheskogo komiteta Ministerstva Vnutrennikh del,* no. 27: *Vzaimnoe strakhovanie ot ognia gubernskoe, zemskoe i gorodskoe 1889–1892.* St. Petersburg, 1893.

———. *Vremennik tsentral'nago statisticheskago komiteta Ministerstva vnutrennikh del,* series 2, no. 44: *Pozhary v Rossiiskoi imperii v 1888–1894 godakh.* St. Petersburg, 1897.

———. *Statistika Rossiiskoi imperii,* vol. 76: *Statistika pozharov v rossiiskoi imperii za 1895–1910 gody.* St. Petersburg, 1912.

Ushakov, D. "Materialy po narodnym verovaniiam velikorussov." *Etnograficheskoe obozrenie,* nos. 2–3 (1896).

Uspenskii, G. I. "Svoi sredstva." *Sobranie sochinenii v deviati tomakh* 5 (Moscow, 1956): 376–384.

Uspensky, Boris. *The Semiotics of the Russian Icon.* Edited by Stephen Rudy. Lisse, Netherlands: Peter de Ridden Press, 1967.

Ustav stroitel'nyi (sv. zak., T. XII, Ch. 1, izd. 1857 g.) izmenennyi i dopolnennyi po Prodolzheniiam 1886 goda (svodnomu) i 1887 goda (ocherednomu). Khar'kov: Izdanie knizhnago magazina V. i A. Biriukovykh, 1888.

Verashchagin, Gr. "0 narodnykh sredstvakh vrachevaniia v sviazi s pover'iami." *Etnograficheskoe obozrenie,* no. 3 (1898): 113–152.

Verkhovskoi, V. "0 bedstviiakh, prichiniaemykh krest'ianstvu sel'skimi pozharam i o sredstvakh k ikh oslableniiu." St. Petersburg, 1910.

Verner, Andrew. "Discursive Strategies in the 1905 Revolution: Peasant Petitions from Vladimir Province." *Russian Review* 54 (January 1995): 65–90.

Veselovskii, B. B. *Krest'ianskie bunty.* St. Petersburg: Izdatel'stvo O. M. Popovoi, 1905.

———. *Istoriia zemstva za sorok let,* vol. 2. St. Petersburg: tip. O. N. Popov, 1909.

———. *Istoricheskii ocherk deiatel'nosti zemskikh uchrezhdenii tverskoi gubernii 1864–1913.* Tver: Tverskoe gubernskoe zemstro, 1914.

Viatskoe gubernskoe zemstvo. *Pravila o merakh predostorozhnosti ot pozharov v uezdakh Viatskoi gubernii (vne gorodskikh poselenii), v zhilykh mestakh, tak v lesnykh i napolnykh sostavlennye na osnovanii zakona 16 iunia 1873 goda.* 3d ed. Viatka, 1883.

Vill'er de Lil'-Adam, Vladimir. "Derevnia Kniazhnaia gora i ee okrestnosti. Etnograficheskii ocherk." *Zapiski imperatorskogo russkogo geograficheskogo obshchestva po otdeleniiu etnografii* 4 (St. Petersburg, 1871): 235–266.

Viola, Lynne. *Peasant Rebels under Stalin: Collectivization and the Culture of Peasant Resistance.* New York: Oxford University Press, 1996.

Vsevolozhkaia, Evgeniia. "Ocherki krest'ianskogo byta Samarskogo uezda." *Etnograficheskoe obozrenie*, no. 1 (1895): 1–34.

Vucinich, Wayne, ed. *The Peasant in Nineteenth-Century Russia*. Stanford, Calif.: Stanford University Press, 1968.

Welsh, Andrew. "The Religion of Insurance." *Christian Century*, December 11, 1963: 1541–1543.

Wheatcroft, Stephen G. "Crises and the Condition of the Peasantry in Late Imperial Russia." In *Peasant Economy, Culture, and Politics of European Russia, 1800–1921*, edited by Esther Kingston-Mann and Timothy Mixter, pp. 128–172. Princeton, N.J.: Princeton University Press, 1991.

Whelan, Heide W. *Adapting to Modernity: Family, Caste and Capitalism among the Baltic German Nobility*. Koln, Germany: Bohlau, 1999.

White, Colin. *Russia and America: The Roots of Economic Divergence*. London: Croom Helm, 1987.

White, John H., Jr. "The Cover Design: Origins of the Steam Fire Engine." *Technology and Culture* 14, no. 2, part 1 (April 1973): 166–169.

Wilbur, Elvira M. "Peasant Poverty in Theory and Practice: A View From Russia's Impoverished Center at the End of the Nineteenth Century." In *Peasant Economy, Culture, and Politics of European Russia, 1800–1821*, edited by Esther Kingston-Mann and Timothy Mixter, pp. 112–123. Princeton, N.J.: Princeton University Press, 1991.

Worobec, Christine D. "The Post-Emancipation Russian Peasant Commune in Orel Province, 1861–90." In *Land Commune and Peasant Community in Russia: Communal Forms in Imperial and Early Soviet Society*, edited by Roger Bartlett, pp. 86–105. London: Macmillan, 1990.

———. *Peasant Russia: Family and Community in the Post-Emancipation Period*. Princeton, N.J.: Princeton University Press, 1991.

———. "Witchcraft and Hysteria in the Late-Nineteenth-Century Russian Village." Paper presented at a conference on the peasantry of Eastern Europe, Ukrainian Research Institute, Harvard University, April 1992.

———. "Witchcraft Beliefs and Practices in Prerevolutionary Russian and Ukrainian Villages." *Russian Review* 54, no. 2 (April 1995): 165–187.

Yaney, George L. *The Systematization of Russian Government: Social Evolution in the Domestic Administration of Imperial Russia, 1711–1905*. Urbana: University of Illinois Press, 1973.

Young, Charles F. T. *Fires, Fire Engines and Fire Brigades*. London, 1866.

Young, Glennys. *Power and the Sacred in Revolutionary Russia: Religious Activists in the Village*. University Park: Pennsylvania State University Press, 1997.

Zaionchkovskii, P. A. *Krizis samoderzhaviia na rubezhe 1870–1880-x godov*. Moscow: Izdatel'stvo Moskovskogo Universiteta, 1964.

———, ed. *Krest'ianskoe dvizhenie v Rossii v 1870–1880 gg. Sbornik dokumentov*. Moscow: Nauka, 1968.

Zavoiko, G. K. "Verovaniia, obriady i obychai velikorussov Vladimirskoi gubernii." *Etnograficheskoe obozrenie* 103–104, nos. 3–4 (1914): 81–178.

Zelizer, Viviana A. Rotman. *Morals and Markets: The Development of Life Insurance in the United States*. New York: Cambridge University Press, 1979.

Zenkovsky, Serge A., trans. and ed. *Medieval Russia's Epics, Chronicles, and Tales*. New York: Dutton, 1963.

Zhurnaly uezdnykh komitetov Smolenskoi gubernii o nuzhdakh sel'skokhoziaistvennoi promyshlennosti 1902 god. Smolensk, 1903.

Zinoviev, P. V. *Nashi sel'skie pozhary. Nastavlenie volostnym starshinam, sel'skim starostam i vsem gramotnym krest'ianam: kak oberegat'sia ot pozharov v seleniiakh, lesakh, stepiakh i tor-*

INDEX

241, 252–57; financing of, 248, 254–55; government expectations around, 237; hoses, 252–53, 258; as messianic cause, 242–43; military model for organization of, 257–58, 270; nobility role in, 237–43; peasant practices, 56, 178, 231–34; preparedness, 259; public opinion on, 265; rationality in, 261–64, 266; rituals, 251; sexism in, 260–61; technology's role in, 241, 252–57, 262; tools, 234–36; training for, 257, 259; volunteer brigades, 176, 230; zemstvo regulations, 234–37

Fire hazards: agricultural practices, 84–85; and childcare practices, 19; and climate, 38; and labor patterns, 60, 121; matches and, 36; samovars, 36, 83; stoves, 79–80; tobacco, 36, 83; in the United States, 56; village architecture, 87, 88–91

Fire insurance programs: agents, 197–98, 202; anticipation as governing principle, 181–82; in England, 192; establishment by zemstvos of, 97, 153–54, 181, 185–87, 191–92; financing of, 183; inspections, 179–81; Interior Ministry mandate for development of, 70; payments to victims, 96, 190; peasants and, 183; property appraisal, 154–57, 188–91, 193; risk classifications, 192–96; self-arson as issue in, 187; for state peasants, 183–84; success and failure in, 196–201; underinsurance and, 198–200

Fire prevention, 191, 201–3, 206–12, 271
Fire watches, 235–37
Fire zone, 74
Fitzpatrick, Sheila, 105
Foinitskii, I. Ia., 133–34
Folk art, 240
Forests, 117–19
Foucault, Michel, 138
France, 192, 247
Frank, Stephen P., 104, 133
Frazer, James, 9, 22, 35
Frederiks, Vice Governor, 96
Frost, L. E., 91

Gentry, 117–21, 267–68
Germany, 11, 27, 107, 149
Gofshtetter, I., 88, 157, 213, 224
Goody, Jack, 147, 162, 165
Goudsblom, Johan, 9, 27
Gradovskii, G., 162
Grain, 98, 119–21, 123
Greenberg, Amy, 261
Grigoriev, V., 257, 259
Grigorovich, D. V., 42
Grodno Province, 110, 115, 227

Hansen, P. G., 227–28
Hay, Douglas, 11, 162

Hell, 27–28
High modernism, 4, 44, 244, 274
Hobsbawm, Eric, 11, 103, 107, 142
Hoch, Steven, 126, 270
Hussey, Stephen, 106, 120
Hysteria, 57, 59, 145, 231, 243

Iaroslavl Province, 170
Icons, 25–28, 151
Ignition risk, 87
Imperial Russian Firefighters' Society (IRPO), 240, 242, 250, 261–62. See also United Russian Firefighters' Society.
Imperial Russian Geographic Society, 10
Individualism, 6–7, 231
Insects, 80–81
Interior Ministry. See Ministry of the Interior
Irrationality, 53–56
Ivan IV (the Terrible), 208
Ivanitskii, N. A., 28, 56
Ivanov, P. A., 17

John the Baptist, 31, 34–36
Johnson, Eric A., 139
Jones, David, 11, 105, 120, 145, 148, 165
Jones, Eric L., 9, 68, 78–79, 87, 88, 91, 171, 192, 271
Judicial Herald, 10
Judicial Reform (1864), 159, 167
Justice Ministry. See Ministry of Justice

Kahan, Arcadius, 73, 168
Kassow, Samuel, 269
Kazan Province, 141, 157, 168, 187, 213
Kerosene lamps, 36, 82
Khar'kov Province, 29, 34, 199, 226
Kharuzina, Vera, 24
Kiev Great Fire of 1811, 141
Kiev Province, 115, 129, 137
Kiselev, P. D., 209
Kohl, J. G., 30
Komanda, 247
Korsakov, P. A., 200
Kostromo Province, 49, 56, 95
Kotov, S. A., 51
Kristalovich, N. I., 226
Krugovaia poruka, 196
Kulaks, 105, 121–26, 171–72
Kupalo, Ivan (John the Baptist), 31, 34–36
Kupalo fires, 34–35
Kursk Province, 86, 115, 222
Kursk Provincial News, 111
Kuznets, Simon, 9, 68
Kuznetsov, N., 232

Lampada, 16, 25
Lamps, kerosene, 36, 82

Land captains, 167
Land shortages, 143–44
Laws. *See* Regulations
Lebedev, A., 123
Lenin, V. I., 121, 126
Lentovskii, Z., 66
Lévi-Strauss, Claude, 9
Lifland Province, 169
Lightning, 31–33
Literacy, 146–48
Literary representations of fire, 10
Livchak, I. N., 264
Lopott, V. P., 162–63
Luchina, 82
L'vov, Prince A. D., 238–43, 250, 252, 255–57,269

Macey, David, 182
Magical fire, 23–25
Maksimov, S. V., 4, 19, 23, 46
Malice, 135–38
Manor homes, 128
Maria Federovna, Empress, 245
Massy Shaw, Sir Eyre, 240
Matches, 36–37
Matriarchal fire, 25–26
McReynolds, Louise, 42, 61
Media, 42–44
Medicinal fire, 20–23
Migrant agricultural workers, 144–45
Mikhailov, P. P., 89
Miller, P. A., 167
Ministry of the Interior: arson statistics, 108–10,
142; Central Statistical Committee, 3, 43, 61,
69, 71, 78; chartering of firefighting units,
245, 47; Economic Department, 48, 97, 171;
economic losses from fires, 170; emergency
relief requests, 65–66, 78, 95, 222; fire insur-
ance program mandate, 70
Ministry of Justice: arson statistics, 108–11, 142,
156; concern with fire, 171; and women arson-
ists, 133
Ministry of State Domains, 183, 186
Minsk Province, 115
Mixter, Timothy, 126, 272
Modernization, 3–5, 205–6, 209–10, 229
Monkkonen, Eric H., 139
Moral economy, 117
Moscow News, 41–42
Moscow Province, 67
Murder, 140–41
Mutual responsibility, 196, 243, 252
"Muzhiki" (Chekhov), 57–60, 62, 99, 234

Narod, 178
Natural taxes, 246
Nestor's Chronicle, 27

Neuberger, Joan, 138
Neustupov, A. D., 32
New York Great Fire of 1835, 256
Nicholas II, 177, 239, 243, 250–51
Nikitin, A. K., 90
Nizhnii Novgorod Sheet, 132
Nobles, 237–43
Notes of the Fatherland, 118, 165–66
Novgorod, 206–12, 219–21, 235–37
Novgorod Province, 23, 30, 49, 52, 56, 67, 75,
83, 88, 97, 118–19, 140, 152, 204; deforestation
of, 208
Novgorod Sheet, 46
Nurseries, 227

Objectivity, 61
Obshchestvo, 137, 238, 243, 247
Olga, Saint, 129
Olonets Province, 115
Order, 243, 257–58
Orel Province, 21, 28, 67, 83, 85, 135
Orenburg Province, 30
Orthodox church, 25–29, 243
Osterberg, Eva, 109
Outsiders, 139–45

Paganism, 18–19, 38
Pallot, Judith, 143
Passivity, 53–56
Pavlovna, Grand Duchess Maria, 240
Peasant Land Bank, 126
Peasants: arson as protest by, 79, 103–5; as cause of
backwardness, 171–72; as culprits, 28; daily life
of, 15–16; disaster relief appeals by, 48–49,
65–66, 78, 95, 222; Emancipation (*1861*),
62–63; ethnographic reports on, 61; fire insurance and, 182–84; firefighting equipment and,
256–57; firefighting practices, 56, 178, 231–32;
gentry vs., 117–21, 267; mastery of fire by,
37–38, 268; mistrust of courts by, 163–65; passivity and irrationality in, 53–56; peasants vs.,
121–26; poaching by, 117–19; post-Emancipation images of, 38; pre-Emancipation, 126;
as property owners, 125–26; rebellion by, 79; in
the Soviet era, 273–74; state, 183–84; state loans
and grants to, 96–97; state as protector of
rights of, 209, 216–17
Penza Province, 66, 123, 198, 245
Pereterskii, V. I., 243
Perm Province, 30, 213–14, 254
Perun, 32
Peter the Great, 45, 158, 208, 271
Peterov, L. K., 67
Poaching, 117–19
Pochitanie ognia, 19
Podolia Province, 115